The Principal in Metropolitan Schools

Carolyn S. Swallow

THE NATIONAL SOCIETY
FOR THE STUDY OF EDUCATION

Series on Contemporary Educational Issues
Kenneth J. Rehage, Series Editor

The 1979 Titles

The Principal in Metropolitan Schools, Donald A. Erickson and
Theodore L. Reller, Editors
Educational Environments and Effects: Evaluation, Policy, and Productivity, Herbert J. Walberg, Editor
Research on Teaching: Concepts, Findings, and Implications,
Penelope L. Peterson and Herbert J. Walberg, Editors

The National Society for the Study of Education also publishes Yearbooks which are distributed by the University of Chicago Press. Inquiries regarding all publications of the Society, as well as inquiries about membership in the Society, may be addressed to the Secretary-Treasurer, 5835 Kimbark Avenue, Chicago, IL 60637. Membership in the Society is open to any who are interested in promoting the investigation and discussion of educational questions.

The Principal in Metropolitan Schools

Edited by

Donald A. Erickson
University of San Francisco

and

Theodore L. Reller
University of California, Berkeley

Sponsored by
The University Council for
Educational Administration

McCutchan Publishing Corporation
2526 Grove Street
Berkeley, California 94704

© by McCutchan Publishing Corporation
All rights reserved

Library of Congress Catalog Card Number 78-62641
ISBN 0-8211-0417-9

Printed in the United States of America

Cover illustration and design by Terry Down, Griffin Graphics

To the Memory
of
Robert J. Coughlan

Foreword

Late in the 1960's the University Council for Educational Administration (UCEA) sponsored nine regional planning meetings in different parts of the United States. The meetings were attended by approximately three hundred professors and graduate students of educational administration, who expressed concern about the way urban school leaders, especially school principals, should be prepared to fill their positions. The participants certainly questioned whether programs then in use were adequate in helping principals meet the challenge of effective education for students of markedly heterogeneous backgrounds.

The teaching and administrative experience of most of the people who attended the meetings was almost totally in rural and suburban school districts rather than in urban ones. In addition, most of the teaching materials available to them had been aimed more at suburban and rural environments than at urban ones. Cases, simulated situations, other kinds of practice materials, and even textbooks reflected this orientation. Problems encountered in urban environments received little attention. It was in response to the needs identified in the planning meetings that the UCEA decided to develop new materials to train people who expected to assume positions of leadership in urban schools — materials based on the reality of urban administration — by simulating an urban school system and a number of positions in it.

The school system used for the simulation was among the twenty largest urban districts in the United States, and it possessed, in varying degrees, most of the major problems confronting urban school leaders. A team of fifty professors from more than twenty universities was assembled initially to gather data on the actual urban area, which was assigned the pseudonym "Monroe City." Leaders in the Monroe City school system provided data on teachers, students, educational administrators, the school board, curricula, decision making, organization, and other aspects of the system. Information was assembled on the demographic characteristics and the power structure of the community, on community organizations and the demands they make on the schools, on the economic and political environment of the school system, and on the mass media and their effects on education. The information was organized and presented in sixteen "Background Booklets." A filmstrip was made to depict important features of the school system and the community, and a film was produced to communicate the "spirit" of the city. Booklets, filmstrip, and film were all designed to emphasize problems encountered in an urban environment.

Soon after the project began, it was decided that the first position to be simulated was that of school principal. One principal was to be from a senior high school, one from a junior high school, and one from an elementary school.

The senior high school, called "Wilson," was located in an area where both residential and business properties were rapidly deteriorating and residents, predominantly white, were leaving in substantial numbers. Families displaced by urban renewal in the center of Monroe City, predominantly black, were moving into the Wilson High School area. The school was termed "transitional." What had been a predominantly white student body soon became 40 percent black, and the proportion of blacks, according to Monroe City leaders, would probably continue to increase.

The junior high school was called "Janus." Bordered on two sides by freeways and on another by North Columbia State University, it served an area four miles long and two miles wide near the core of Monroe City. Some sections of the area were blighted and were plagued by social problems, while other smaller sections housed middle- and upper-middle-class families. This school was also "transitional" because the student population was shifting from predominantly white to predominantly black. Approximately 70 to 80 percent of the land was occupied by residences; the remainder was about equally divided between industrial and retail buildings. Two low socioeconomic neighborhoods, one primarily white and the other primarily black, were located in the Janus attendance area, and Janus Junior High School fed into Wilson Senior High School.

In the third situation the school was called "Abraham Lincoln Elementary School." It was located in the inner city in a building constructed in 1902 and designed for approximately 780 pupils. There were, however, more than 1,000 students enrolled. Administrators judged this to be a "typical" inner-city ghetto school. The student body had recently undergone the transition from being largely white to being largely black. The white teachers remaining at the school tended to be older, while the black teachers tended to be younger. The attendance area was characterized by single- and multiple-family dwellings. The families were almost totally lower middle or lower class, from a socioeconomic perspective. There had been considerable redevelopment in the area, which meant that there had been movement in and out of the community.

The information gathered on Wilson, Janus, and Abraham Lincoln Schools and on the attendance areas served by them was organized and presented in films, filmstrips, and various written materials intended to convey some understanding of the positions to prospective trainees. It was then possible to introduce a wide range of problems — in the form of in-basket communications, audiotaped messages, or conflict situations highlighted on film — typical of those faced by principals in the schools and requiring that trainees make decisions. A letter in the in-basket, for example, might contain an irate comment from a parent concerning school busing; a tape recording might inform the principal that a student had been stabbed; a film might depict a neighborhood group demanding that the principal fire a fourth-grade teacher.

In the early 1970's the simulated materials for principals were made available to institutions of higher education and to school districts for use in training situations. Another half-dozen simulations were developed within the Monroe City context, and the number of professors involved in the project increased to 180. This meant that a wide range of materials on urban educational administration was available, and the UCEA institutes on "New Instructional Materials and Methods" became the principal mechanisms for bringing materials to the profession. From 1971 to 1975, the materials were demonstrated in more than seventy institutes in different parts of the United States and Canada. The institutes were most frequently sponsored by institutions of higher education, sometimes in cooperation with local school systems, or by local school systems in cooperation with neighboring institutions.

Those who attended the institutes were professors of educational administration interested in the potential use of the materials and educational administrators interested in participating in simulation workshops. At the institutes leaders explained the simulations, demonstrated their components, and gave participants opportunities to make decisions about simulated problems. Participants could explore the instructional purposes of the various simulations and weigh the relevance of those purposes in terms of their own teaching or learning interests.

At the end of each institute, participants were asked to evaluate the simulations by answering questions that centered largely upon three criteria: instructional potential, technical quality, and credibility. The data obtained indicated that both professors and practitioners valued the simulations. More than three-quarters of the professors rated the materials "high" or "very high," and an even greater proportion of administrators assigned the materials to one of these two categories. During discussions of the institutes themselves, however, it became evident that supplementary tools were needed so two more types of material were planned as additions to the reality-oriented simulations.

The first type, termed "interpretive content," took the form of essays in which ideas or modes of analysis were applied to specific decisional problems or to the larger context in which the problems were embedded. Concepts of conflict resolution, for example, were applied to decisional problems depicted in films. Various strategies for dealing with the demands that community organizations were making on the schools in Monroe City provided the basis for another essay. Still another essay set forth ideal ways urban planning could take place within Monroe City and similar contexts.

This book responds to the need for a second type of supplementary material, termed "conceptual." The chapters represent an attempt to draw together ideas and research findings and organize them in ways that logically related to the problems of Monroe City and its school system or to important variables bearing upon the problems. Titles and content were influenced by the topics covered in the sixteen original "Background Booklets."

It is hoped, then, that this book will prove especially helpful to those using the simulated principalship provided through the UCEA. Certainly the volume should serve as general background reading for those who participate in the simulation workshops or in practicums at universities where the simulations are used. And, apart from instructional situations involving the Wilson, Janus, or Abraham Lincoln simulations, the research findings and generalizations included here can serve a variety of instructional purposes external to simulations, for they are now available to practicing principals interested in learning more about challenges or variables inherent in or impinging upon urban educational leadership and to administrators participating in courses, workshops, seminars, or other instructional settings. The fact that this book fills both special and general needs makes it a valuable contribution in the field of educational administration. Donald Erickson and Theodore Reller deserve special recognition for their planning and editorial work, as do the other scholars who have contributed to this volume.

Jack A. Culbertson, Executive Director
University Council for Educational Administration

Preface

This book was originally envisioned as a part of a set of materials developed by the University Council for Educational Administration (UCEA), which would illuminate UCEA's "Monroe City" simulation of the urban school principalship. But it became increasingly obvious that the discussions in the book, though certainly pertinent to "Monroe City," were of far broader applicability. We now believe that the chapters which follow are as useful to readers unacquainted with UCEA's simulations as to anyone else.

The chapters were not assembled in the usual way—either by looking for outstanding work already published or by asking favorite authors to prepare discussions on topics on which they were known to be experts. Rather, the book began with an extended three-man conference in which the two of us and Jack Culbertson of UCEA discussed the major challenges that must be confronted by any principal in a major metropolis. The conference eventuated in extended descriptions of the analyses that would be needed to prepare administrators to meet those challenges. Then outstanding scholars were commissioned to write the analyses along the lines described.

As seems typical of multiauthored books, this one took much longer to complete than we originally thought. Several authors were prevented from completing their work. This book is dedicated to the memory of one of them, Robert J. Coughlan, whose untimely death robbed the field of a researcher of extraordinary promise. Despite changes in authorship, however, the book retains much of its original emphasis. We must acknowledge two gaps. We have been unable to produce sufficiently compelling chapters on the planning, modification, and utilization of school facilities, or on the prevention and handling of particularly disruptive student behavior (next edition, perhaps?).

To say that the original thrust of the book was largely retained is not to suggest, however, that our authors merely followed our blueprints. They exercised much freedom in determining what to emphasize and deemphasize, and in many cases included ideas that had not occurred to us at all. Authors sometimes venture into the same issues, and occasionally disagree. The overlap and disagreement helps, in our opinion, to provide a more balanced discussion than might otherwise have been possible.

Beginning with Bridges' illuminating analysis, the book is designed, in the main, to proceed from the general to the specific. The early chapters assess the broader challenges of the metropolitan school principalship. Later chapters focus specifically on various aspects of the topic.

Particular thanks are due to Gertrude H. McPherson, who came to our rescue with an exceedingly provocative chapter at a time when we had almost abandoned our quest for an outstanding discussion of what every principal should know about teachers.

We are grateful to Jack Culbertson and the UCEA for sponsoring this venture and for their continuing advice and encouragement. We are indebted to all the chapter authors and to the universities that supported our efforts. We think these materials represent an important addition to the literature on the school principalship.

San Francisco and Berkeley, California   *Donald A. Erickson*
May 1978   *Theodore L. Reller*

Contributors

Baehr, Melany E., Senior Research Psychologist, Industrial Relations Center, University of Chicago

Bridges, Edwin M., Professor of Education, Stanford University

Caldwell, William E., Associate Professor of Education, Pennsylvania State University

Cibulka, James G., Associate Professor, Department of Administrative Leadership, University of Wisconsin, Milwaukee

Cooper, Bruce S., Assistant Professor of Education, Dartmouth College

Culbertson, Jack A., Executive Director, University Council for Educational Administration

Erickson, Donald A., Director, Center for Research on Private Education, University of San Francisco

Levine, Daniel U., Director, Center for the Study of Metropolitan Problems in Education, University of Missouri at Kansas City

Lutz, Frank W., Professor of Education, Pennsylvania State University

McPherson, R. Bruce, Director, University of Chicago Laboratory Schools

McPherson, Gertrude H., Professor of Sociology, University of Saskatchewan

Manley-Casimir, Michael E., Associate Professor of Education, Simon Fraser University

Meskin, Joan D., Doctoral Candidate in Educational Administration, University of Chicago

Pedersen, K. George, Vice-President (Academic), University of Victoria

Reed, Rodney J., Associate Professor in Educational Administration, University of California at Berkeley

Reller, Theodore L., Professor Emeritus, University of California, Berkeley

Salley, Columbus, Senior Research Associate, Industrial Relations Center, University of Chicago

Schrag, Francis, Associate Professor, Departments of Educational Policy Studies and Philosophy, University of Wisconsin, Madison

Watson, Bernard C., Vice-President for Academic Administration, Temple University

Wayson, W. W., Professor of Educational Development, Ohio State University

Webster, Staten W., Professor of Education, University of California, Berkeley

Contents

xvii

Chapter One

Edwin M. Bridges

The Principalship as a Career

This chapter does not contain an account of the origins and development of the urban principalship. Important as that topic is, it has been treated elsewhere.[1] Nor does the chapter provide a definitive answer to the urban principal's most current pressing problem — the ambiguity of this position in the educational community.[2] It would be presumptuous of one individual, a relative newcomer at that, to deliver a pronouncement on an issue that demands the sustained attention and discussion of the entire profession. What the chapter does is examine, in a limited way, several facets of the urban principalship — how a person is chosen for this position, the kind of person who is chosen, and the dilemmas and satisfactions that a person might experience while filling the role. Discussion of these topics may at times reflect more uncertainty than certainty because the knowledge base for the urban principalship appears to be in the larval stage, and the role of principal manifests the same lack of permanence that most other aspects of urban life exhibit. Stability, like the fabled phoenix, must yet rise from the ashes.

SELECTION: A QUESTIONABLE PROCESS

During the twentieth century large urban systems have tended to select their principals through an agency called a board of examiners. The general public and professional educators have assumed that the selection processes were fair and effective. As more has become known about the selection processes, however, the views of both citizens and

1

educators have changed markedly. There is mounting evidence[3] that the procedures used for selecting principals can be unfair; they may also be completely unrelated to the merit of individual candidates. Perhaps the procedures followed by the New York City Board of Examiners will provide some understanding of why selection procedures have become suspect.

Before 1971, the New York Board of Examiners[4] ascertained the merit and fitness of prospective principals by written and oral examination. The written test was more important as it counted for more than one-half of the total grade on the examination. This written test included from 175 to 200 short-answer questions covering English usage, vocabulary, grammar, social studies, literature, music, and art. The questions that follow are typical of those asked on a fairly recent elementary school principals' test:[5]

47. Of the following novels, the one NOT witten in the nineteenth century is:
    (1) Clarissa Marlowe
    (2) The Heart of Midlothian
    (3) Mill on the Floss
    (4) Vanity Fair
48. A recently published book entitled "To a Young Actress" consists of a series of letters written by George Bernard Shaw to:
    (1) Mellie Tompkins
    (2) Sarah Bernhardt
    (3) Mrs. Patrick Campbell
    (4) Ellen Terry
49. These lines of Ben Jonson's, "Soul of the age, The applause, delight, and wonder of our stage," were written to honor which one of the following:
    (1) Christopher Marlowe
    (2) William Shakespeare
    (3) Francis Beumont
    (4) Francis Bacon

There also were essay questions that concentrated on the principles and problems of school organization, administration, and supervision. This test was constructed by "examination assistants," that is, a group of teachers and supervisors chosen by the board from within the system. These individuals had neither experience nor formal training in test construction.

A personal interview, the second most important component of the New York City principal's examination, counted for approximately 25 percent of the total grade, and the interviews were conducted by the same group of untrained "examination assistants." The interview was intended to establish the candidate's ability to discuss problems relating to the major subject of interest, the teaching of that subject, or the position being sought. The remainder of the oral examination covered the candidate's training, experience, and health.

Neither the written nor the oral examination was supported by evidence of validity. The Board of Examiners had never conducted a study to determine if performance on these two types of tests was significantly related to on-the-job performance, even though two types of studies were feasible. One, a predictive validity study, would have involved administering tests to applicants, hiring them without regard to their scores, and relating assessments of their subsequent job performance to their test scores. The other, a concurrent validity study, would have involved administering tests to those serving as principals in order to assess each principal's performance and relating the assessments to the test scores. Despite the fact that the examination was never validated in either way, only the names of candidates who passed it appeared on the eligibility list, and individuals were assigned to principalships in the order of their rank on the examination.

Given the well-documented cultural unfairness of written and oral tests for nonwhites, it is not surprising that such practices have had an adverse impact on opportunities for the career advancement of minorities in New York City. As can be seen in Table 1-1, 55.3 percent of the student body and 9.8 percent of the teaching staff in 1968-69 were either black or Puerto Rican, yet only 1.4 percent of the principals were from those racial groups. Similar, though less pronounced, patterns were evident at the same time in Los Angeles, Chicago, Detroit, and Philadelphia.[6]

TABLE 1-1. Ethnic distribution of the school population in New York City (percent)

School population	Black	Puerto Rican	White	Other
Principals	1.3	0.1	98.4	0.2
Teachers	9.2	0.6	89.6	0.6
Students	31.7	23.6	43.4	1.3

Source: Facts and Figures, 1968-69 (New York: Board of Education, 1969).

In light of these findings — the use of an invalid test and a higher rejection rate for nonwhites than whites — a United States District Court judge has ruled that the New York board's examination violated the equal protection clause of the Fourteenth Amendment to the United States Constitution. The judge issued an injunction restraining the

Board of Examiners from giving tests for any supervisory post and from preparing eligibility lists based on existing test results. The board is now seeking to develop a more defensible means of selecting school principals.

Other urban areas, sensing the vulnerability of the procedures used to select principals, have modified their practices substantially. Chicago, for example, has switched from a written test, similar in form and character to that of New York City, to one that gives equal emphasis to each of four areas: communications skills and human relations, principles of learning and child development, public school supervision, and public school administration. A unique feature of this new test is the addition of a maximum of ten points to the test score total for certain kinds of experience, for example, five points for six or more months of "excellent" or "superior" service as an assistant principal in the system, ten points for two or more months of "excellent" or "superior" service as an acting principal, and five points for two years of "excellent" or "superior" teaching in a Title I ESEA school.[7] These points for experience are especially significant because an absolute cutoff score of eighty is used. The Chicago Public School System has retained its oral examination, with just minor modifications, as the second stage of their selection procedures. Although the new arrangements have proved to be racially nondiscriminatory, there is no evidence that the tests either select the most promising blacks and whites for the principalship or screen out the least promising.

In fairness to examining boards, the challenge of developing valid personnel tests is a formidable one. There is growing recognition of the necessity to match certain types of individuals with particular kinds of situations to ensure successful performance.[8] The measurement tools needed to effect this match are not, however, currently available; nor is there agreement as to what constitutes successful performance in the principalship.[9] Until these technical and philosophical problems are solved, boards are likely to exhibit much less concern about administering tests that are valid than ones that are nondiscriminatory because the courts insist on evidence of validity only when there is unconstitutional discrimination.

CHARACTERISTICS OF URBAN PRINCIPALS

Those who survive such questionable selection processes share certain characteristics divided here, for purposes of discussion, into those that are personal and those that are professional.[10] Personal characteristics are those attributes that are innate and ordinarily not subject to environmental influence — for example, sex, race, and age. Professional characteristics, on the other hand, are those acquired through affiliation with an institution or a formal organization. Experience as a teacher, degree held, and field of graduate work are examples.

Personal

Historically, urban principals have been male and white. Although they come almost exclusively from the teaching ranks, where there are more females than males, the percentage of principals who are female remains relatively low. According to national studies of the principalship conducted between 1965 and 1968, 63.4 percent of the urban elementary school principals,[11] 97 percent of the junior high school principals,[12] and 84 percent of the senior high school principals[13] were male. Prior to 1970, more than 90 percent of the principals in Chicago, Detroit, Los Angeles, New York, and Philadelphia were also white. By 1977, there was some evidence of a change in the ethnic and sex distribution of individuals in the urban principalship. Although white males continued to be the dominant group, their numerical supremacy was declining. For example, in the 1976-77 school year white males constituted 46 percent of the principals in Chicago and 60 percent of the principals in New York City.

Age is a third personal characteristic that has substantial relevance when selecting an urban principal.[14] Individuals are most likely to be appointed to their first elementary principalship before they are thirty-five years old. After they reach the age of fifty, the probability that they will be selected for a principal's post at this level declines sharply (less than 15 percent of the elementary principals are appointed from the over-fifty age group, and the older appointees are more likely to be female than male). The pattern for senior high school principals is similar. Most are appointed before the age of thirty-nine; a few are appointed after age forty-five. Data are not currently available on junior high school principals.

Professional

Graduate work leading to an advanced degree is essential for those who aspire to be urban principals.[15] More than 90 percent of the elementary, junior high, and senior high school principals in urban school systems have at least a master's degree, and the trend is toward higher levels of formal education. Only 16 percent of the elementary principals had a master's degree in 1928, but that figure climbed to 67 percent in the following twenty years, to 82 percent by 1958, and to more than 90 percent by 1968.

Graduate work is most likely to be in the field of educational administration and supervision. More than three-fourths of all urban principals choose this area as their major field of interest, while less than 5 percent major in a more traditional academic discipline.

In addition to possessing an advanced degree with work concentrated in educational administration and supervision, the urban principal is likely to have taught at either the elementary or the secondary level. The average elementary principal has six years of classroom teaching experience, and the average junior or senior high school principal in an urban school has taught from ten to twelve years. Women, however, have three times as much experience prior to their appointment as their male counterparts.

Profile of the Urban Principal for the Future

By 1980 the urban principal is apt to manifest a different set of personal and professional characteristics. For one thing, formal graduate preparation in educational administration as a precondition for appointment is likely to change. For the greater part of the twentieth century advanced education has served as a "test"[16] for employment. Individuals have not been considered for appointment as a principal unless they possessed an administrative certificate, a credential typically acquired by doing graduate work in educational administration and by accumulating credits in other areas within a department of education.

If it can be demonstrated that there are proportionately fewer females or members of minority groups in the principalship because they lack the administrative credential, a school district, if challenged in court, must show that the certification requirement is a valid one. Previous research provides a weak base on which to rest claims that formal graduate preparation is a valid criterion.

Most studies show no relationship between educational training and subsequent success in the principalship as judged by superiors and subordinates. Three different measures of educational preparation — number of years spent in college,[17] number of years devoted to graduate study,[18] and number of hours in graduate education courses[19] — are apparently unrelated to judged effectiveness. A fourth measure — the total number of courses in educational administration — is related to the exercise of executive professional leadership, but the relationship is negative.[20] Principals with less extensive formal preparation in the field of educational administration exhibit greater professional leadership.

Measures of technical and professional knowledge gained through formal course work in educational administration show a somewhat similar pattern. William Schutz[21] found that the mastery of the content of educational administration, namely, school law, finance, personnel, and school facilities, was unrelated to success as a principal. A study by John Hemphill and his colleagues,[22] on the other hand, showed a positive relationship between the professional knowledge of elementary principals and ratings by superiors. The relationship was, however, a moderate one.

When results of behavior, rather than ratings, are used to indicate effectiveness, the case for formal administrative preparation is further weakened. There appears to be a negative relationship between the instructional flexibility of elementary schools and the extent of the principal's preparation in educational administration.[23] Schools that are managed by principals with little formal preparation in school administration apparently make a greater effort to vary the curriculum, materials, and methods according to the needs of the pupils being served.

Direct assessments of administrative preparation programs by principals at all levels also point to the lack of fit between academic training and the role demands of the urban principalship. Elementary principals attribute their success to two types of practical experience: experience as a classroom teacher, and on-the-job experience as a principal.[24] Few principals (less than 2 percent) single out college preparation as an important determinant of their success in the role. Junior high school principals are no less critical of their preparation. When asked to rate six subjects ordinarily required for certification, most principals felt that none was absolutely essential for the beginner.[25] The situation for senior high school principals is not much different. When asked to rate the value of twenty-five graduate courses in education and administration, the majority identified only one course (supervision of instruction) as being absolutely essential for the beginning high school principal.[26] Similarly, a great majority (72 percent) reported that they have not found a single textbook on the school principalship that was of any practical value in guiding their day-to-day behavior on the job.

Based on the research reported in the preceding paragraphs, a reasonable argument can be made that formal graduate preparation constitutes an inappropriate "test" for appointment to the principalship. Legal precedent already exists for a court decision of this kind when there is evidence of discrimination. A United States District Court in Mississippi recently prohibited the Starksville Public Schools from requiring a master's degree as a precondition to employment.[27] Although the case focused on teaching rather than on administrative positions, the court's rationale is clearly applicable to administrative posts. If formal administrative preparation is challenged in the courts and they rule as we have forecast that they will, professional requirements of future urban principals will be altered substantially.

Changes in two personal characteristics, sex and race, are already discernible, as has already been suggested. Mounting pressure from civil rights groups, coupled with decentralized appointment procedures, are affecting the racial and sexual composition of the urban principalship in significant ways. Long denied black leadership for their schools, black communites are exhibiting a clear preference for principals of their own race. In one large area of the Chicago Public School System, a black person was selected in every school where the majority of the students were black and a new principal was needed, just as schools where the majority of the students were white consistently chose white males as principals.

If this trend continues, the burden of integration will fall most heavily on white females. In Berkeley, California, the number of white female administrators has dwindled in recent years; this group has, moreover, been relegated to the bottom of the administrative pyramid.[28] Within the Chicago School System, white females who passed the principal's examination in 1970 have, for the most part, remained unchosen. Only legal action by the advocates of equal employment opportunities for females is apt to reverse this trend.

PERSISTENT DILEMMAS FOR URBAN PRINCIPALS

Urban principals, regardless of their personal and professional characteristics, face fundamental role tasks, that is, problematic issues with which each executive must deal in seeking to make productive use of himself and his organizational position.[29] These dilemmas are inherent in the role itself, and neither the employing organization nor previous educational experience prepares an individual to cope with them. How a principal deals with role tasks is a major determinant of managerial style and, ultimately, of a principal's fate.

Success as a Principal

The individual who searches for evidence that performance as a principal is or is not successful[30] confronts conditions that impede the quest for reliable information. These conditions are prevalent in educational organizations and are aggravated by certain features of training programs in educational administration.

Few school systems in this country evaluate the performance of principals on a regular, continuing basis, which means that relatively few principals routinely receive organizationally prescribed feedback on their progress that they might use to reach realistic judgments about the extent of their success or failure. Even when principals are targets of evaluation, the information is more likely to be reported to the board of education than to the principal.

There is another factor that contributes to the psychological darkness in which most principals enact their organizational roles. It seems that executives are inclined to manage by guilt. Having been socialized in middle-class ways, executives are conditioned to believe that anger is an inappropriate sentiment. When they experience angry feelings, they feel guilty. These sentiments, which shape the executive's behavior without his knowledge, result in the denial of feedback to subordinates. Significant indicators of management by guilt are "disappointment in the man; failure to confront him realistically about his job behavior; procrastination in reaching a decision about him; cover-up to ease the guilt of managerial anger; transfer to another position; finally, discharge."[31] Such a pattern also deprives principals of dependable, reliable data about their own performance, and principals quickly, though painfully, recognize this disquieting fact of organizational life. Gauging personal success is, again, problematic for the principal.

Formal administrative preparation further skews any attempts a principal might make to evaluate performance, for scholars are predisposed to treat success in neutral terms and to stress objectivity when they discuss it. Principals, through education and training, are sensitized to the difference between intermediate and ultimate criteria of success and are exposed to the functions and limitations of the two types of criteria. The trainee who happens to ask, "But what type of principal is best?" will be told that he has posed the wrong question. The proper form is, "When a given type of principal is placed in a given type of situation, on what types of dimensions is he likely to demonstrate certain strengths and weaknesses, as judged by a given set of raters?" Several studies will be cited to illustrate the point, limitations will be noted, and the caveat will be issued: More research must be undertaken before we can confidently conclude what leads to successful performance in the principalship in particular types of situations. Educational experiences such as these, as well as inadequate knowledge of results from the school system, force principals to find other ways to reduce the uncertainty about their performance.

The yardsticks principals actually use to measure success and failure are as diverse as the line and staff roles pictured on the most elaborate organizational chart. Some principals judge the extent of their success by the speed with which they ascend the district's hierarchical pyramid. This type of principal engages in GASing (Getting the Attention of Superiors) behavior[32] and is supersensitive to the muted criteria that superiors seem to use in judging effectiveness. The GASer invests heavily in high payoff activities and slights other responsibilities.

Other principals use the opinions of subordinates as a way of measuring success. Success in these terms requires the satisfaction of those who work in the school, and the principal attaches great importance to their opinions. Unlike GASers, such persons support the members of their staff and do not hesitate to confront superiors if the welfare of the staff appears to be at stake. They are sensitive to the goals of subordinates and anxious to please them.

Then there are principals who judge their success by how smoothly the school runs. These individuals pride themselves on having a predictable, well-organized, and synchronized environment. They carefully attend to details and derive personal satisfaction from bureaucratizing the organization's operations. They develop rules, systematize procedures, and elaborate policies. They experience a strong sense of accomplishment when people know what is expected of them and when events happen as planned and scheduled. These three examples by no means exhaust the many yardsticks that principals may use to measure their success.

Role Conflict

Principals are highly vulnerable to the conflict that exists when individuals or groups hold incompatible expectations for a person's performance in the role. Simultaneous demands for mutually exclusive or contradictory role behavior are major sources of organizational stress for urban principals, especially secondary school principals.[33]

One common role conflict that urban principals face is in the area of supervision. Teachers, though not yet accorded full-fledged professional status within society, view themselves as professionals and have internalized a norm of professional autonomy. Consequently, "they claim the right to know what their clients' interests are and what best serves these interests, without direction or interference from fellow practitioners or, if they are employed by an organization, from subordinates."[34] At the same time principals are expected to safeguard the interests of the organization by acting to upgrade the quality of their staff's performance. As the bureaucracy's agent of quality control in instructional matters, the principal is expected to observe, evaluate, and improve the instructional performance of teachers. In short, the organization's expectation conflicts with the teachers' norm of professional autonomy. As the principal's background, competence, and experience diverge more and more from that of the teacher to be supervised and as the bureaucratic pressure to supervise intensifies, the dilemma grows. A principal is, quite understandably, reluctant to supervise a more experienced teacher who is likely to be hostile toward supervision even if it emanates from a fellow professional.

Role conflict can also develop in matters relating to student discipline. Teachers expect the principal to back them up even if they have mishandled or mistreated students. If a parent challenges the authority of a teacher or complains about the actions of a teacher, the principal is expected to do whatever is necessary to uphold the authority of the teacher, even to the point of lying.[35] Parents, on the other hand, expect the principal to be fair and to reach decisions that protect their children from arbitrary, punishing actions by teachers. If the principal fails to support the teacher, there may be serious problems with the staff. If, on the other hand, a parent's grievance is ignored, the principal may incur the wrath of the parents or deprive a child of the right to justice.

A third type of role conflict, ever present in the life of the principal, arises from contradictory expectations about how to administer a school. Teachers, according to a study by Robert Moser,[36] want their principals to keep things on an even keel, to cater to the individual needs of staff members, to advocate the staff's point of view with top management, and to seek suggestions from teachers before decisions are made. The superintendents of these same principals expect them to be forceful in their relationships with subordinates, to initiate action, to emphasize the achievement of organizational goals, and to show greater concern for the institution than for the individual. As a member of the middle-management group, the principal must deal with both superiors and subordinates. Taking these two frequently conflicting forces into account is no minor role task.

Finally, there is continuous role conflict for principals who are expected to devote themselves to meeting the needs of family members while simultaneously exhibiting near-total commitment to their jobs. Principals are expected to spend long hours at their work, and most fulfill their organizational obligations. One-half of the elementary school principals, two-thirds of the junior high school principals, and three-fourths of the nation's senior high school principals spend more than fifty hours per week on school-related activities.[37] Balancing family and organizational responsibilities is a source of constant tension for the married principal.

Constraints on Leadership

Throughout a program of preparation for the principalship, the trainee is bombarded with an ideology that emphasizes the leadership functions of the position. As head of the school, the principal is portrayed as initiating action for others. In all facets of the school's operations, the principal is viewed as guiding and influencing what others in the organization are thinking, feeling, valuing, believing, and doing. The principal is the one who has a special sense of where the school is heading. It is the vision of the principal that presumably gives people something to work for and something to be proud of when it is achieved. The principal is to elicit the requisite energies and commitments of others and to bind their wills in the service of the organization and its mission.

The organizational reality that the principal actually confronts is scarcely conducive to the exercise of such bold, far-reaching leadership, however. There are numerous restrictions, formal and informal, that limit the urban principal's freedom of action.[38] Most have no voice in selecting their teaching staffs; teachers are assigned by the central office, and the principal rarely has the opportunity to reject a candidate recommended by that office. Nor does the urban principal play a decisive role in preparing the school's budget. More than 40 percent report no involvement in constructing the budget, which is prepared by the central office without consultation. Of the 40 percent that acknowledge limited involvement, most report in writing on the general needs of their schools, with the central office still making the final decisions.

Even when the principal has the formal power to act, discretionary power is curbed substantially. If a principal rates the efficiency of a temporarily certified teacher as unsatisfactory, there must be a conference with the department of personnel, the teacher must be informed as to why the rating is unsatisfactory, and the teacher must receive constructive feedback. Teachers who, in the judgment of the principal, continue to perform unsatisfactorily are transferred to another school as they cannot be terminated unless rated unsatisfactory by at least two principals. The barriers to dismissal of regularly certified teachers are even more formidable.

Union contracts that regulate student discipline, class size, scheduling, and salaries and provide for an elaborate grievance procedure also limit the discretionary power of a principal. Teachers are entitled to press formal complaints when they are dissatisfied with some aspect of their work situation, when there is deviation from or misapplication of established practices and policies, or when any provision of the union contract is violated. If the validity of a teacher's grievance is denied by the principal, the teacher has the right to appeal the decision — first to higher-level administrators and then to the board of education. The teacher can ultimately demand binding arbitration from the American Arbitration Association if necessary.

These formal limits and curbs on discretionary power mean that the urban principal is constantly wrestling with the problem of leadership. The struggle is to become the influential person one is expected to be, or would like to be, or that others expect. Becoming the person "in charge" is not an inevitable consequence of becoming the principal; rather, the role task is performed in an organizational context that is resistant, if not hostile, to forceful leadership.

Role-Related Activities

The urban principal spends the day countering the initiatives of others.[39] Upon entering the schoolhouse door, the principal confronts a steady flow of problem situations. Regardless of the school's socioeconomic setting, the urban principal is apt to encounter roughly one hundred problems daily. If the school is in a lower-class section of the city, however, more than 60 percent of those problems are appellate in nature, that is, they are occasions for decision generated by teachers, parents, or pupils. Even the principal with a high socioeconomic clientele will discover that half of the problems encountered on any given day are defined by someone else. An operating work environment riddled with so many occasions for making decisions can interfere with the ability to make long-range plans, afflicting the urban principal with institutional myopia.

The way the school system sees the principal generally aggravates this dilemma, for there is no indication of relative importance or possible interconnection in the long list of responsibilities a principal is expected to take. This role diffuseness, combined with the burdensome flow of daily problems, can divert the principal's attention from the intermediate and long-range planning activities that lend continuity to administrative behavior. If the principal has a short time-span capacity[40] and is unable to sustain performance without somewhat immediate feedback, this role task will be even more difficult to perform.

The Design of a Productive School

Evidence mounts that parents of school-age children are more concerned about a school's ability to foster academic achievement than about the school's openness and willingness to include parents in decision making. Urban schools, especially those for blacks and Mexican-Americans, have dismal performance records on standardized reading and arithmetic tests, and the performance gap between whites and these two groups widens the longer the children remain in school. Where this gap persists, parents continue to question the school's legitimacy as a social institution, and efforts to redistribute power by granting parents a substantial role in decision making have failed to restore the community's confidence in the schools.[41]

In part the antagonism of the community stems from the conviction that school personnel are able, but unwilling, to teach lower-class minority children how to read, write, and compute. Parents believe that their children do not progress because teachers harbor negative attitudes about their children's capacity to learn. These parents reason that the attribution of inferior intellectual ability results in an uncaring, indifferent performance on the part of teachers which, in turn, depresses the child's growth in traditional academic subjects. If one were to follow this line of reasoning, the reign of error would be ended by employing teachers who possess a positive conception of the child's motives and learning capacity.

Constructive, favorable teacher attitudes are, however, insufficient, though necessary, conditions for student growth. Bruce McPherson,[42] in his case study of two inner-city elementary schools exhibiting dissimilar teacher turnover patterns during the same five-year period, discovered the failure of a dedicated, optimistic school staff to reverse the achievement trends of poverty-ridden black students. The principal and teachers of the low turnover school were bound together by a common mission; they desired to create an intellectual oasis in the inner city—a school where lower-class black children would succeed academically. After five years and despite inspired service rooted in a conviction that these students would achieve if taught by dedicated, experienced teachers, the academic performance of the students was no different than that of other students in inner-city schools. Most of the students who had spent their first four years in this school were reading below grade level, and a number of them had actually regressed.

An essential, missing ingredient in the school was the lack of an adequate scientific base for the staff's actions. At this point in time the educational community does not understand how to structure a productive learning environment for inner-city youngsters. Nor is there a strong research and development tradition in schools that would foster a systematic search for the materials, the methods, and the modes of organization that are most effective.[43] In spite of these barriers to productivity, the principal must create an effective school if it is to achieve legitimacy as an educational institution. None of his role tasks equals this one in difficulty.

CAREER SATISFACTIONS

As is evident from the preceding section, urban principals make substantial organizational contributions. Besides exhibiting a willingness to tackle major role tasks, they contribute ideas, services, and time. In return for these contributions, the organization offers the principal economic rewards, status, and opportunities for self-fulfillment. It is the balance between inducements and contributions that determines the level of job satisfaction,[44] and that is a major factor in retarding the development and growth of work-connected stress. Medical researchers have linked occupational stress to a range of physical and mental disorders.[45] It appears, then, that a favorable balance between inducements and contributions promotes the physical and mental health of the principal, while a serious imbalance leads to unwanted and undesirable physical disorders.

Perhaps the clearest indication of whether a satisfactory balance exists for the urban principal is an assessment of choice of career. Principals throughout the nation were asked: "If you had your life to live over, would you choose educational administration as a career?" In response, 65 percent of the nation's urban senior high school principals responded affirmatively; another 20 percent were undecided; the remaining 15 percent opted for a different career.[46] Urban junior high school principals also evaluated their career choices,[47] and, for both groups, the inducements-contributions balance was significantly more favorable for urban than for rural principals. This urban-rural difference did not emerge among elementary principals, where nearly 60 percent of the country's elementary principals indicated that they probably would choose the same career again. The evidence indicates that most urban principals and principals at every level in the educational system have achieved a satisfactory balance between inducements and contributions.

With this generally positive view of the inducement-contribution ratio in mind, the next logical step is to examine the nature and extent of inducements that urban principals receive for enacting their roles. Four types — financial rewards, professional status and recognition, satisfactions from performing specific role-related activities, and opportunities for personal fulfillment — are examined, and wherever known differences exist between the inducements of principals and teachers or between those of urban and rural principals, the discrepancies are noted.

Economic Rewards

Principals earn considerably higher incomes for performing their roles than teachers do. Although salary schedules for urban principals are typically independent of teachers' salaries, the salary differentials have remained somewhat constant over time. For the past decade elementary principals have earned about 36 percent more than teachers with comparable experience and training, while the salaries for junior and senior high school principals have exceeded those of teachers by 44 and 54 percent, respectively.[48] Promotion from classroom teaching to the principalship substantially improves a person's economic standing, and time-series data suggest that this economic advantage will continue.

Professional Status and Recognition

Prestige, status, and recognition are among the psychic, intangible gratifications valued by employees of formal organizations. As professionals functioning within a bureaucratic setting, principals are especially sensitive to these rewards. Self-esteem is inextricably bound with role-esteem, and stature of office in part determines standing as an individual. In light of this interdependence, the status deprivation apparently experienced by some urban principals constitutes a significant problem. Although most senior high school principals report that their position has considerable or very much prestige in the community where their school is located, they feel that their professional prestige is unequal to their education, training, and work responsibilities. More than half of the urban secondary principals believe that the National Association of Secondary School Principals should take steps to increase the prestige and status of its membership.[49] Whether the status deprivation experienced by senior high school principals exceeds, matches, or fails to equal that of classroom teachers and principals at other levels is not yet clear.

Intrinsic Satisfactions

Urban principals evidently enjoy performing role-related activities. Despite the unfavorable conditions under which they often work, most urban principals report high levels of satisfaction with the quite varied aspects of their job. In a study assessing the degree of enjoyment experienced in twenty separate work activities, male elementary, junior high, and senior high school principals expressed highly favorable attitudes toward their work responsibilities.[50] More than half of the principals who participated in this national study indicated that they derived a great deal of enjoyment from performing their organizationally prescribed duties, and 80 percent or more of the principals derived considerable enjoyment from working with exceptionally able teachers, supervising the instructional program, working with guidance personnel, talking with parents about a problem concerning their child, and talking with a group of parents about a school problem. There was no work activity toward which a majority of the principals expressed negative sentiments.

Self-Fulfillment

According to Maslow, the ultimate in human needs is "to become more and more what one is, to become everything that one is capable of becoming."[51] Achieving one's maximum potential is the psychological state to which individuals aspire when their basic needs for safety, love, and esteem have been satisfied.[52] Urban principals, like other organizational participants, bring this self-actualization need to their role. The available evidence suggests that urban principals achieve more self-actualization in their roles than their rural counterparts.[53] Of the junior high school principals, 70 percent and, of the senior high school principals, 58 percent in urban areas feel that their roles offer them either considerable or very much opportunity to use their unique capabilities and to realize their potential. Since the possibilities for self-fulfillment increase as one ascends the organizational hierarchy,[54] the level of self-actualization experienced by principals presumably surpasses that of teachers. A definitive test of this hypothesis remains to be made, however.

To this point the discussion of the balance between inducements and contributions, with the exception of status rewards, paints a generally favorable picture for the urban principal. Imbalance does, nevertheless, occur for some principals. When they raise questions about their job and career satisfaction, principals focus on relationships with their superiors and subordinates.[55] Particularly crucial in the relationship between principals and their superiors are the amount of autonomy; the number of constructive suggestions, the degree of professional encouragement, and the extent of emotional support the principal receives from his superior; the importance a superior attaches to the work of the principal; the degree of role clarity present; and the effectiveness of decision making at higher levels. With respect to the relationships a principal has with the staff, four factors seem to affect the level of work satisfaction: the amount of personal loyalty and support coming from the staff, the level of staff interest in innovation and change, the commitment of staff members to their organizational obligations, and the quality of the staff's performance.

INDETERMINATE PROSPECTS

The outlook for urban principals is by no means a cheerful one, for the future will be shaped in some measure by three of the conditions highlighted in this chapter. If communities continue to be dissatisfied with the performance of their schools, if urban systems persist in selecting principals without a studied regard for their merits, and if institutions of higher education maintain their current indifference toward the major role tasks of the urban principal, the principalship will become an increasingly hazardous occupation. On the other hand, if the profession seizes the initiative, confronts the challenges that clearly lie before it, and succeeds in these undertakings, the principalship will offer even greater inducements to those who choose and are chosen to become urban principals. Which will it be?

NOTES

1. Paul Revere Pierce, *The Origin and Development of the Public School Principalship* (Chicago: University of Chicago Press, 1935).

2. Gerald Becker *et al.*, *Elementary Principals and Their Schools* (Eugene: University of Oregon Press, 1971).

3. Edwin M. Bridges and Melany E. Baehr, "The Future of Administrator Selection Procedures," *Administrator's Notebook,* 19 (January 1971).

4. "Discriminatory Merit Systems: A Case Study of the Supervisory Examinations Administered by the New York Board of Examiners," *Columbia Journal of Law and Social Problems,* 6 (September 1970), 374-410.

5. *Ibid.*

6. *Ibid.*

7. *Agreement between the Board of Education of the City of Chicago and the Chicago Teachers Union* (Local No. 1, American Federation of Teachers, AFL-CIO, January 1, 1971, to December 31, 1972).

8. William C. Schutz, *Procedures for Identifying Persons with Potential for Public School Administrative Positions* (Berkeley: University of California, Cooperative Research Project No. 1076, 1966).

9. Donald A. Erickson, "The School Administrator," *Review of Educational Research,* 37 (October 1967), 417-431.

10. Roald F. Campbell *et al., Introduction to Educational Administration,* 4th ed. (Boston: Allyn and Bacon, 1971), 374.

11. Department of Elementary School Principals, *The Elementary School Principalship in 1968* (Washington, D.C.: Department of Elementary School Principals, National Education Association, 1968).

12. Donald A. Rock and John K. Hemphill, *Report of the Junior High School Principalship* (Washington, D.C.: National Association of Secondary School Principals, 1966).

13. John K. Hemphill, James M. Richards, and Richard E. Peterson, *Report of the Senior High School Principalship* (Washington, D.C.: National Association of Secondary School Principals, 1965).

14. See Department of Elementary School Principals, *School Principalship in 1968;* Hemphill, Richards, and Peterson, *Senior High School Principalship.*

15. *Ibid.*

16. According to the EEOC guidelines, the term "test" is defined "as any paper-and-pencil or performance measure used as a basis for any employment decision . . . . This definition includes, but is not restricted to, measure of general intelligence; mental ability and learning ability; specific intellectual abilities; mechanical, clerical, and other aptitudes; dexterity and coordination; knowledge and proficiency; occupations and other interests; and attitudes, personality and temperament. The term 'test' includes all formal, scored, quantified or standardized techniques of assessing job suitability including, in addition to the above, specific qualifying or disqualifying personal history or background requirements, specific educational or work history requirements, scored interviews, biographical information blanks, interviewers' rating scales, scored application forms, etc." See "Guidelines on Employee Selection Procedures," *Federal Register,* 35 (August 1, 1970).

17. John K. Hemphill, Daniel E. Griffiths, and Norman Frederiksen, *Administrative Performance and Personality* (New York: Teachers College, Columbia University, 1962).

18. James M. Lipham, "Personal Variables of Effective Administrators," *Administrator's Notebook,* 9 (September 1960).

19. Neal Gross and Robert E. Herriott, *Staff Leadership in Public Schools: A Sociological Inquiry* (New York: John Wiley and Sons, 1965).

20. *Ibid.*

21. Schutz, *Procedures for Identifying Persons with Potential.*

22. Hemphill, Griffiths, and Frederiksen, *Administrative Performance and Personality.*

23. Donald A. Erickson, R. Jean Hills, and Norman Robinson, *Educational Flexibility in an Urban School District* (Vancouver: Educational Research Institute of British Columbia, 1970).

24. Department of Elementary School Principals, *School Principalship in 1968.*

25. Rock and Hemphill, *Junior High School Principalship.*

26. Hemphill, Richards, and Peterson, *Senior High School Principalship.*

27. *Bernice Armstead et al.* v. *Starksville Municipal Separate School District et al.,* United States District Court for the Northern District of Mississippi, Eastern Division, No. EC 70-51-S.

28. Stephen B. Lawton, "Social, Economic, and Organizational Factors Affecting the Promotion Rate of Administrators" (Ontario: Institute for Studies in Education, n.d., mimeo).

29. Richard C. Hodgson, Daniel J. Levinson, and Abraham Zaleznik, *The Executive Role Constellation* (Boston: Harvard University, Division of Research, Graduate School of Business Administration, 1965).

30. For a more detailed discussion of this dilemma, see Edwin M. Bridges, "Personal Success as a Determinant of Principals' Managerial Style," in *The Principalship in the 1970's,* ed. Kenneth E. McIntyre (Austin: University of Texas Press, 1971), 13-24.

31. Harry Levinson, *Emotional Health in the World of Work* (New York: Harper and Row, 1964), 267-291.

32. Daniel E. Griffiths *et al.,* "Teacher Mobility in New York City," *Educational Administration Quarterly,* 1 (No. 1, 1965), 15-31.

33. For a thorough review of the role conflict studies, see Jacob W. Getzels, James M. Lipham, and Roald F. Campbell, *Educational Administration as a Social Process* (New York: Harper and Row, 1968).

34. Anne E. Trask, "Principals, Teachers and Supervision: Dilemmas and Solutions," *Administrator's Notebook,* 13 (December 1964).

35. Howard S. Becker, "Social-Class Variations in the Teacher-Pupil Relationship," *Journal of Educational Sociology,* 25 (April 1952), 451-465.

36. Robert P. Moser, "A Study of the Effects of Superintendent-Principal Interaction and Principal-Teacher Interaction in Selected Middle-Sized School Systems," unpub. diss., University of Chicago, 1954.

37. See Department of Elementary School Principals, *School Principalship in 1968;* Rock and Hemphill, *Junior High School Principalship;* Hemphill, Richards, and Peterson, *Senior High School Principalship.*

38. Seymour B. Sarason, *The Culture of the School and the Problem of Change* (Boston: Allyn and Bacon, 1971).

39. Ray Cross, "The Principal as a Counterpuncher," *National Elementary Principal,* 51 (October 1971), 26-29.

40. This concept is treated at length in Elliott Jacques, *Measurement of Responsibility* (Cambridge, Mass.: Harvard University Press, 1956).

41. Harriet Spivak, "School Legitimacy Study," *Working Paper No. 1* (New York: Center for Urban Education, May 1972).

42. R. Bruce McPherson, "A Study of Teacher Turnover in Two Inner-City Elementary Schools," unpub. diss., University of Chicago, 1970.

43. For an interesting statement of this problem, see Robert J. Schaefer, *The School as a Center of Inquiry* (New York: Harper and Row, 1967).

44. James G. March and Herbert A. Simon, *Organizations* (New York: John Wiley and Sons, 1958), 84-111.

45. For example, see Stephen M. Sales, "Organizational Role as a Risk in Coronary Disease," *Administrative Science Quarterly*, 14 (September 1969), 325-337; and Robert L. Kahn, Donald M. Wolfe, Robert P. Quinn, and J. Diedrock Snoek, *Organizational Stress* (New York: John Wiley and Sons, 1964).

46. Hemphill, Richards, and Peterson, *Senior High School Principalship*.

47. Rock and Hemphill, *Junior High School Principalship*.

48. See *Maximum Salaries Scheduled for School Administrators, 1971-72* (Washington, D.C.: Research Division, National Education Association, 1972).

49. Hemphill, Richards, and Peterson, *Senior High School Principalship*.

50. Neal Gross and David A. Napior, *The Job and Career Satisfaction of Men School Principals* (Cambridge, Mass.: Harvard University, Graduate School of Education, Cooperative Research Project No. 2536, 1967).

51. A. H. Maslow, "A Theory of Human Motivation," in *Readings in Managerial Psychology*, ed. Harold J. Leavitt and Louis R. Pondy (Chicago: University of Chicago Press, 1964), 16.

52. Since Maslow postulates that the basic human needs are arranged in a hierarchy of prepotency and that self-actualization is a higher order need than self-esteem, there appears to be contradiction in the data. Urban principals report more gratification of their self-actualization needs than their esteem needs. Maslow's discussion does not preclude this possibility, however, as he acknowledges that reversals within the average order of the hierarchy are sometimes observed.

53. Rock and Hemphill, *Junior High School Principalship*; Hemphill, Richards, and Peterson, *Senior High School Principalship*.

54. Chris Argyris, *Personality and Organization* (New York: Harper and Row, 1957).

55. Gross and Napior, *Job and Career Satisfaction of Men School Principals*.

Chapter Two

Columbus Salley
R. Bruce McPherson
Melany E. Baehr

What Principals Do:
A Preliminary Occupational Analysis

The principalship continues to be one of the most durable and critical positions in the administration of American schools. Although there are variations in the size and location of schools and school systems, differences in the personalities and experiential backgrounds of principals, and variations in the socioeconomic circumstances of children, youth, and parents served, the building principal remains the administrator most closely associated with the daily operation of the school, with the implementation of its curriculum, and with its association with the community.

Yet, in spite of this crucial role, little is known about the job dimensions of the principalship and of their interactions with the variety of circumstances under which principals perform their tasks. To be certain, much research has been conducted and a multitude of articles, monographs, dissertations, and textbooks has been written in an attempt to describe the work and responsibilities of the principal. But these rarely have had a broad or substantial empirical base demonstrating the interrelatedness of job function and a variety of contextual circumstances. Furthermore, it often has been assumed that the work of the principal is constant from school to school, from system to system, and from community to community, though even the casual observer of schools in, say, affluent Scarsdale and low-income Harlem can witness striking distinctions in daily behavior of principals in those

Reprinted, with permission of the authors, from *Consortium Currents*, 2 (Fall 1975), 1-10.

school settings. However, there are a few studies which speak to the important interface between the work of the principal and the social-system variables that differentially affect his or her concept of priorities for performance. Among these are two books, Seymour Sarason's *The Culture of the School and the Problem of Change* and James Lipham and James Hoeh's *The Principalship: Foundations and Functions.*[1]

BACKGROUND OF THE STUDY

The present inquiry is one step in a long-range research program intended to help bridge the gap in our knowledge about the principalship. The research program had its origin in the amended Civil Rights Act of 1972, which for the first time brought state and local governments, their agencies, and public and private schools under the provisions of Title VII of the 1964 Civil Rights Act. The major objective of Congress in the enactment of Title VII was to achieve equality of employment opportunities for all Americans and to remove any obstacles or barriers that in the past favored white employees over minorities. Occupations in these institutions thus became subject to the requirements of the EEOC *Guidelines* regarding employee selection, promotion, and testing procedures.[2]

Griggs v. *Duke Power Company* was the first test case of these guidelines to receive national attention.[3] It was a class action by black employees against the Duke Power Company's Dan River Power Generation Facility in Draper, North Carolina, and challenged the imposition of educational requirements and testing as a condition for employee selection and promotion under Title VII. The Supreme Court ruled against the use of such requirements and tests in this situation. (See *Armstead* v. *Starkville Municipal Separate School District, Allen* v. *City of Mobile,* and *Davis.* v. *Washington* for other cases challenging educational requirements and tests.[4] It should be noted that in the last two cases the courts upheld the use of those particular tests.)

Of particular significance for our research, selection procedures for school principals were newly coming under fire, as evidenced by a suit brought by the NAACP in a federal court to block the use of tests in the hiring of principals for the New York City elementary schools.[5] The plaintiff claimed that the tests discriminated against black and Puerto Rican candidates and that the written part of these tests was not "job related." School systems as defendants in such suits are vulnerable for three major reasons:

1. prima facie underrepresentation of blacks and other minorities in supervisory positions in most school systems;

2. the lack of empirical evidence for the validity of the selection devices whose use has led to this underrepresentation; and

3. research findings reported in the literature generally attesting to the lack of "fit" between academic preparation and on-the-job performance as a school principal.

As a result of the litigation cited above, employers now must be able to prove that the standards they use for selection and advancement are fair to every applicant and employee, that is, that these standards are job related or valid. Demonstrating validity involves making a precise analysis of the job in question and of the abilities required to perform it, and then proving a relationship between scores on certain tests or measures of these abilities and actual performance on the job.

These issues provided the impetus for the research program on the principalship, which has six major goals:

1. to describe the basic functions of the principal's job;

2. to describe the varying conditions under which principals work;

3. to develop training programs to help principals work more effectively under these varying conditions;

4. to develop job-clarification programs to help principals reach agreement with supervisors and colleagues on what functions are most important in a particular school setting;

5. to establish validated procedures for the selection of school principals; and

6. to design improved methods for the evaluation of principals' job performance.

It was to these goals that the Consortium for Educational Leadership [CEL] turned its attention in early 1974.[7] Working in collaboration with Melany E. Baehr of the Industrial Relations Center at the University of Chicago, and building on earlier work of faculty members of the Midwest Administration Center in the university's Department of Education, CEL planned and completed the "National Occupational Analysis of the School Principalship."[8] That study involved the creation of a new instrument, administration of the instrument to over 700 principals nationwide, analysis of the subsequent data, and publication of the results of this first stage of the research program.

INSTRUMENT CONSTRUCTION

During the design stage of the research, it became evident that the development of measures of principals' performance would be a considerable challenge, the first challenge being merely to describe the functions of a principal. In industrial organizations such job descriptions — and their related programs of job clarification — are common-place. However, these descriptions and programs are comparatively rare in educational institutions. Of necessity, fundamental approaches to job description were employed.

A pilot study was developed jointly by the Industrial Relations Center and the Midwest Administration Center. The usual procedures for occupational analysis were used. These included library research into the content of the principal's job and the effects on this job of environmental constraints, such as type and size of school, student-teacher ratio, geographic location, and ethnic composition of student body and staff. Also utilized were interviews with persons familiar with the principal's responsibilities, such as the principals themselves, teachers, and superintendents. In the course of these interviews a limited amount of observation of on-the-job behavior was possible. However, a major effort was directed toward the development of a standardized and quantified instrument for describing the key dimensions of the principal's job and determining their relative importance for job performance.

The pilot study produced the following results:

1. a rationale for developing the quantified instrument, based on two assumptions: that generic items could be written to describe the behavior underlying the day-to-day activities of principals and that the functions performed by principals would be generally similar but would vary in their importance from school to school according to operational variables;
2. a data bank of items describing a wide variety of activities;
3. a technique for rating the importance of these activities, based on a forced-normal-distribution card sort;
4. an instrument incorporating selected items from the data bank and utilizing the card sort technique;
5. data from administration of this instrument to over two hundred principals, mainly in the Chicago public schools;
6. a factor analysis of responses from this group of principals, revealing an underlying structure of nineteen dimensions of principals' performance that were interpreted and defined in cooperation with school administrators; and
7. a multivariate analysis of variance, revealing that the instrument was sensitive enough both to differentiate between the demands of the principal's job under different conditions of

operation and to reveal differing descriptions of the job held by individual principals.

These results were considered encouraging, with potential for a variety of practical applications in educational settings. Nevertheless, the study could be regarded only as a pilot since its findings and the conclusions based on them were largely limited to operating conditions in the Chicago public schools.

At this juncture CEL entered the study. The first step in the new stage of the project was a substantial revision of the pilot instrument into the present Job Functions Inventory [JFI] for School Principals.[9] This work covered all three of the essential elements of the quantified procedure for job description:

1. the JFI item content;
2. the measurement technique used by respondents to express their judgments; and
3. the separate Data Summary Sheet for principals.

Forty-six items from the original JFI were deleted, thirty-one revised, and forty-six new items added, resulting in a total of 180 items. Three new dimensions of behavior were postulated and represented among the revised or new items—dealing with gangs, staffing, and fiscal control.

In the pilot study a forced-normal distribution was chosen as the means by which principals would respond to the JFI items. This technique minimized the conscious and unconscious distortions and the constant errors of judgment which beset the use of rating scales. It was implemented with a deck of IBM cards (with one item printed on each card) that was hand sorted by each respondent. Because such a procedure involved mechanical and some statistical difficulties, a single-use paper-and-pencil form of the JFI was developed, retaining the advantages of the forced-distribution sort. The distribution here, however, was rectangular with items distributed equally over the six intervals that represented the assessed degree of importance of each item.

The Data Summary Sheet was designed to provide significant and comprehensive information about the principal and the characteristics of his or her school that could be used to classify responses to the JFI for purposes of statistical analysis. It was essentially similar to the form used in the pilot study, but included information such as the principal's educational background, the number of administrative levels in his or her school and school district, and the percentage of paraprofessionals and noncertified staff—information not dealt with in the original JFI.

DATA COLLECTION

Each of the seven member universities and the central office of CEL participated in all phases of the data collection and coordinating activities. One objective was to generate a purposive sample by taking measures to ensure adequate representation of types of principalships that might be excluded by reliance on random sampling techniques. Thus, specific types of principals representing various segments of the total population were intentionally sought out for inclusion, for example, blacks, females, principals of both small schools and those with heterogeneous student populations. Representation of these groups of principals in the final sample would make possible comparisons of responses that would enhance the significance of the findings. In addition, it was felt that the geographic locations and metropolitan areas of the participating universities would provide sufficinet diversity for a meaningful sample.

Data collection procedures yielded a return of 719 Job Functions Inventories. Of these, one hundred were discarded because of incomplete responses, failure to adhere closely enough to the rectangular distribution, and other miscellaneous reasons. The balance of 619 correctly completed inventories constituted the sample used for statistical analysis in this project. Table 2-1 shows the distribution of total inventories returned by geographic location.

TABLE 2-1. Description of sample by type of school and geographic location

Type of school, by state	Total inventories returned
Public	
California	258
Georgia	92
Illinois	35
Massachusetts[a]	54
New York	72
Ohio	22
Pennsylvania	151
Parochial	
Florida	8
Illinois	7
New York	9
Pennsylvania	11
Total	719

[a] Includes Connecticut, North Carolina, and Virginia

FACTOR ANALYSIS

While useful information can be obtained by analyzing responses to individual items, a more parsimonious and ultimately more meaningful procedure is to analyze associated groups or clusters of items that represent interpretable dimensions of principals' performance. Such underlying dimensions were identified by determining the strength of associations between each pair of the 180 items on the JFI with statistical procedures including product-moment correlation coefficients and principal-axis factor analysis. Twenty factors were produced and then rotated through an orthogonal equamax to an oblique promax structure.[10] The latter structure allows the axes or dimensions of principals' performance to be correlated and constitutes the simplest way in which these dimensions can be identified or defined by the items in the JFI.

Seventeen factors emerged, with each factor defined by a particular cluster of items and showing a distinctive profile of validity according to the groupings on the classification variables. By and large the validity patterns conform to expectations. The final factor structure included 108 of the original 180 items on the JFI, with the numbering and logical grouping of factors made possible in part by a second-order factor analysis. The factors are listed as job dimensions in Figure 2-1.

MULTIVARIATE ANALYSIS OF VARIANCE

One of the premises of the research was that the definition of the job (the principal's description of the important functions in his work) would vary with differing conditions of operation (environmental constraints) and probably also with the ethnic composition of the staff and student body and with the personal background and experience of the principal. Responses to the Data Summary Sheet provided information on all these classification variables. Study of the distribution of responses in each classification variable indicated the logical or numerically feasible breakdowns or subcategories under each to be used for purposes of analysis.

The comparison of JFI responses between or among the subcategories of the total sample of principals was implemented through a multivariate analysis of variance (MANOVA). Results are given in Figure 2-1. The columns of this figure are headed by twenty-one classification variables. The first seven of these deal with characteristics of the principal. Following are ten which cover information about the school (school district in the case of "Administrative levels up"), the

FIGURE 2-1. Analysis of variance across JFI dimensions

Job dimensions		Sex of principal	Age of principal	Race of principal	Number of years as principal	Years as principal here	Number of prior principalships	Prior principalships at different levels	Administrative levels up	Administrative levels down	Grade range of school	Number of students	Number of teachers	Student-teacher ratio	Percentage of paraprofessional teaching staff	Percentage of student turnover	Percentage of teacher turnover	Percentage of paraprofessional turnover	Dominant race of students	Dominant race of teachers	Dominant race of para professionals	School socioeconomic status
Relations with people and groups																						
Personal handling of student adjustment problems	1	⊗														X	X	X				
Organizations and extracurricular activities	2	X								X	X	X	X	X		X	X		X	X		X
Individualized student development	3												X		X							
Utilization of specialized staff	4	⊗								X	X	X	X		X							
Evaluation of teacher performance	5														X							
Collegial contacts	6								X			X	X			X		X	X	X	X	X
Racial and ethnic group problems	7											X	X						X	X	X	X
Trouble shooting and problem solving	8										X	X										
Community involvement and support	9						X				⊗	X										
Dealing with gangs	10									X	X	X	X			X		X	X	X	X	X
Curriculum																						
Curriculum development	11								X				X									X
Instructional materials	12	⊗			X						X	X	X			X		X	X	X	X	X
Personnel administration																						
Staffing	13	X		X					X	X	X	X	X							X	X	
Working with unions	14								X			X	X									
General administration																						
Working with central office	15			X					X	X	X	X	X							X	X	X
Safety regulation	16							X		X	X	X	X					X				
Fiscal control	17																					

X Significant at .001 level of confidence or better   ⊗ Insignificant with size of school covaried students, and the teaching staff. The final four columns relate to the ethnic composition of the student body and teaching staff and the socioeconomic status of the school. Rows in the table are the final identified factors or major functional dimensions of principals' performance. An "X" (circled or uncircled) in any square indicates that there are significant differences between or among the subcategories of that variable on the corresponding factor. The criterion used for significance was a stringent .001 level of significance.

FINDINGS

The three major findings of the research are these:

1. Variables relating to type and size of school accounted for the greatest number of differentiations in the way principals described their jobs, although socioeconomic status and ethnic composition of student body and teaching staff made a sizable contribution.

2. Personal characteristics of the principal produced the fewest differentiations. However, there were some differentiations based on race and sex that should not be overlooked.

3. The age of the principal and years in present position yielded no significant differentiations.

Only two identified job dimensions, "evaluation of teacher performance" (Number 5) and "fiscal control" (Number 17), failed to reveal significant differentiation for any classification variable. All others showed at least two significant differentiations. The job dimension making the most differentiations was a new one to appear in this study—"dealing with gangs" (Number 10). Following this in number of differentiations were "organizations and extracurricular activities" (Number 2), "racial and ethnic group problems" (Number 7), and "personal handling of student adjustment problems" (Number 1).

The most pervasive influences on the principal's job were exerted by the size of the school (as represented either by number of teachers or by number of students) and by grade range. Widest differences occurred on such important aspects of the job as "personal handling of student adjustment problems" (Number 1), "organizations and extracurricular activities" (Number 2), "utilization of specialized staff" (Number 4), "dealing with gangs" (Number 10), "instructional materials" (Number 12), "staffing" (Number 13), and "safety regulation" (Number 16).

It is not surprising that significant differences associated with the ethnic composition of the student body should occur for dimensions such as "racial and ethnic group problems" (Number 7). Principals of racially mixed schools placed strongest emphasis on this dimension, followed by principals of predominantly white schools. Principals of racially mixed and predominantly minority group schools also placed greater emphasis on "dealing with gangs" (Number 10), whereas principals of predominantly white schools emphasized "curriculum development" (Number 11), "organizations and extracurricular activities" (Number 2), and "collegial contacts" (Number 6).

Two classification variables, both dealing with characteristics of the principal, yielded no significant differences between or among the subcategories. These were the principal's age and the number of years as a principal in the present school.

It was considered possible that even the small number of significant differentiations associated with the personal characteristics variables might not be main effects of these variables but rather might be a result of their relationships with other variables exercising more powerful effects. For example, it could be hypothesized that females or, perhaps, minority group members are more often principals of elementary schools. Grade range of school is, in turn, related to school size, which (as represented either by number of students or by number of teachers) seemed to exert the strongest influence of any of the variables. This particular hypothesis was tested by rerunning the MANOVA's for the principal's sex and race and for grade range and student-teacher ratio with the effects of school size removed. Circled "X's" in Figure 2-1 represent a situation where the significance level drops below (one in one thousand) when size of school is covaried.

If we concentrate now on the uncircled X's, only two significant differences remain in the importance which male and female principals ascribed to the various job functions: "organizations and extracurricular activities" (Number 2) and a personnel administration factor called "staffing" (Number 13). As in the pilot study, male principals ascribed greater importance to both of these dimensions than did female principals.

A second-order factor analysis was also performed on the matrix of intercorrelations obtained from the oblique first-order rotation. The correlation matrix was not modified on the basis of visual rotation and, therefore, yielded only rough results. Both six- and four-factor solutions were obtained and examined, using the same factor analysis programs as before.

The second-order factors yielded may represent different leadership styles or approaches of principals to the complexity of their work:

Factor A pictures the principal who places high priority on the *involvement and support of groups*—community groups, such as parents, local agencies, and religious organizations, or groups within the educational administrative structure, such as the central office.

Factor B depicts the principal who emphasizes the evaluation and improvement of *student academic performance* through the use of internally developed or standardized evaluation tests, effective utilization of instructional materials, and efficient deployment of specialized staff.

Factor C represents the principal who stresses the *development of qualified teaching staff* through personal involvement in hiring them, coaching them on their handling of student problems, evaluating their performance, and, if necessary on the basis of this evaluation, firing those who perform unsatisfactorily.

Factor D portrays the principal who stresses *a managerial approach,* involving tight fiscal control and close working relationships with the central office.

A more holistic interpretation of the results portrays the principals of smaller schools as more involved with the students themselves — their personal adjustment problems and safety and the associated utilization of specialized staff. Principals of larger schools more closely resemble managers in other institutions in dealing with staffing and union issues and, at policy levels, with personnel issues, in their case with the complex of factors relating to a racially mixed student body. It seems axiomatic that principals who perform successfully in these different types of principalship will have different interests, skills, and leadership styles.

Results obtained in this national study largely corroborate those from the pilot study. The pilot study identified a fairly sound underlying structure of job dimensions, which was more sharply defined on the basis of the larger sample. Furthermore, in the present study, the three new hypothesized dimensions of performance, covered by new items in the revised JFI, appeared as clear additional factors. The Job Functions Inventory for School Principals derived from this study is based on a sizable and diverse sample drawn from a number of geographic locations. We consider it both stable and reliable enough for practical use in school systems.

We will consider next some specific applications of this study for principals, central office administrators, university training programs, and for those involved in the selection and evaluation of principals.

APPLICATIONS OF THE STUDY

Expectations for the Principal

Currently, narrative characteristic profiles, which will pinpoint the behavior of principals working within a variety of environmental conditions, are being developed. Such profiles begin to articulate an answer to the question: "What reasonable expectations can be held for building principals?"

Preservice and In-Service Training

Characteristic profiles can be used as reality-based descriptions for the improvement of education programs for principals. The profiles might be applied to university training programs to assess fit between program components and competencies being taught, on the one hand, and the demands of the position in its varying forms, on the other. Further, the profiles can suggest priority areas for consideration in the creation of staff development programs for principals already at work in schools and school districts.

Programs of Job Clarification

Principals must adapt their activities not only to the circumstances of their jobs but also to the expectations and needs of supervisors, colleagues, and members of the community served by the school. The JFI offers an objective means for clarifying these needs and expectations. An individual principal's concept of his job can be compared with the concept of it held by the superintendent, the board of education, other principals, teachers, parents, and students. Obvious discrepancies can then be discussed and possibly reconciled.

Validation of Selection Procedures for Predicting Job Performance

The JFI can be used in many ways to develop the "criterion" and "predictor" variables needed to carry out a validation study. "Criterion" variables are measures of performance on the job — data in any form that indicate the principal's overall worth to his particular school and system. "Predictor" variables are measures of the objective and subjective qualifications that the principal brings to the job — the education, experience, skills, and personality characteristics that help or hinder him in doing his job. Some of these are matters of record. Others can be determined by psychological tests chosen to assess the aptitudes and traits needed to perform well on the dimensions identified in the job analysis. Statistical techniques determine the relationship between the predictors and the criteria. All qualifications and measures incorporated in the final recommended selection procedure would reflect and predict performance in the principal's job.

Another use of the JFI is to allow an applicant for a position to indicate the extent to which he or she would prefer to work in certain ways or, for applicants who have held prior principalships, how well he or she feels certain activities would be performed. This profile can be compared with an established importance profile that represents the demands of the particular principalship. Study of any differences on the dimensions between the two profiles could suggest the need for specialized training or selective placement.

Reliable Indexes of Principals' Performance

When the demands of the job and of all interested parties are clear, the matter of competence remains. The measurement technique employed in the JFI can be used to rate the proficiency of the principal's work. Research may demonstrate that it is possible to match proficiency profiles against importance profiles to generate a single reliable index of principals' performance.

IMPLICATIONS

This study has established statistically significant interactions among seventeen job dimensions, or clusters of principals' performance, and twenty-one variables in the work environment of the principal. Such interaction does not establish causality. The research is descriptive, and, while we believe it presents a more coherent picture than has been available before of the complexity of the principalship, we are not dealing with cause and effect. It should also be observed that this is a picture of the job functions of many principals, and for any one principal that picture may be different. However, our data base provides an effective means for comparing the situation of any one principal with that of a broad population of principals. In addition, because the study is descriptive and hypothesis generating, both its findings and implications are susceptible to further inquiry.

Our data analysis suggests that, to a certain extent, principals are captives of their environments. This is not to intimate that some individual principals will not overcome organizational obstacles in performing their work and changing their particular school environment. What we do suggest is that the commonly expressed idea that principals are or should be change agents may be subject to considerable revision.[11]

We are not the first to question the viability of the principal as change agent. Sarason comments, "I have yet to see any proposal for system change that did not assume the presence of a principal in a school. I have yet to see in any of these proposals the slightest recognition of the possibility that the principal, by virtue of role, preparation, and tradition, may not be a good implementer of change."[12] The present study influences us to believe that, unless some environmental characteristics, particularly those related to the organization of the school and school system, are changed, the principal rarely will be a change agent and his or her work will be routinely predictable. In such circumstances the work of the principal will tend to perpetuate and reinforce the status quo, or what Sarason calls the "programmatic and behavioral regularities" of educational settings.

More specifically, the size of the school system, size of the school, and number of grade levels in the school are organizational variables that influence the principal's definition of his or her work and militate against his or her emerging as an innovator. We argue that the organizational constraints on the principal must be changed before the general role of the principal can change. Such a view does not diminish the importance of principals as individual human beings. We agree with Sarason's view that, for the principal, "The ultimate fate of ideas and values depends on the principal's conception of himself in relation to the system."[13] That is, personality can become an important factor after organizational constraints are understood, and it seems likely that increased relief from organizational constraints will permit the individual personality of the principal to have greater effects in the school setting.

Occasionally, in recent years, organizational changes have been permitted in what are called alternative schools. In many of those situations principals have been able to define their work differently and to bring about varying instructional and administrative patterns. Unfortunately, alternative schools rarely have an impact on system regularity. In the main, they are organizational aberrations, and their effects are ephemeral.

The analysis of our data also indicates that ethnic and socio-economic characteristics play a significant part in defining the work of the principal. We have observed that racial and ethnic group problems and dealing with gangs become important job priorities for the principal of racially mixed and minority group schools. By contrast, principals of predominantly white schools emphasize the development of school organizations and extracurricular activities; the strengthening of contacts between the principal and colleagues outside that particular school and development of curricula, with particular emphasis on interaction with parents, residents, and organizations in the community.

It was suggested earlier that changing the organizational circumstances is a major part of the solution to permitting the principal to emerge as a force for change. None of our findings should give countenance to the notion that we consider personal characteristics or personality totally unimportant. Neither do we want to give comfort to those who claim a false dichotomy between organizational factors and personal factors when one is considering change in a complex social system. Personality is indeed important in how a principal defines her or his relationship with a school. The success of the principal in developing ideas for the school and maintaining values as an educator is closely related to how the individual human being organizes his or her inordinately demanding and complicated work. Some principals view themselves as servants of the system and become mere administrators. They learn to accept the values of the system, and they generate few new ideas in interaction with participants in the school. Others recognize the reality of a job that is too unwieldy and develop different approaches to their work and values, as our second-order factor analysis hints. Still others, albeit few in number, tend to disregard school and school system constraints at every opportunity and march to their own drummers.

However, our data analysis presents a bleak picture with regard to the importance of those personal characteristics examined as determinants of the work of the principal. Several of the time-honored myths related to principals as school administrators seem to be without foundation: The reasons for excluding women, particularly from secondary school principalships, have no substance. The idea that the particular race or sex of a principal would be an essential attribute for saving a school in trouble appears to be unsupportable. The idea that the older principal is wiser than his younger counterpart and, as a result, works differently receives no substantiation from this inquiry. But even more stunning is the fact that experience is not a differentiating factor in the principal's description of his or her job. If both experienced and inexperienced principals describe their work almost identically, then it appears that those with more experience in the principalship are not performing any crucial additional or different functions. The justification for graduated salary schedules and differential reimbursement based on time in position, it seems, would have to rest on the improved quality of performance of these tasks. Unlike most industrial organizations, educational institutions ordinarily do not implement performance appraisal to determine salary adjustments or merit increases. We believe that the cost to American taxpayers for increasing remuneration to principals solely on the basis of experience, which involves hundreds of millions of dollars each year, is open to serious scrutiny.

Thus far our implications have emanated rather directly from the data analysis of this study. At this point we would like to move to some more personal observations and conjectures about the principalship. We know that there are some principals who, in spite of the system, are making a significant and human difference in their schools (note, in this regard, Chapter 3). We know that such principals have a clear view of their own personal and professional values and a strong commitment to the position that it is their job to generate new ideas and to bring creative tension to the school organization. They are leaders rather than simply administrators. Why are they so few, and why do they appear to be so underrepresented in a study such as this one (see Chapter 4).

In our judgment there has been change in American education, but it has only been to solidify the bureaucratization and mechanization of American schools and school systems. Professional educators, as well as many adult clients of the schools, appear to be more obsessed with management than with education. Thus, the job of a principal is increasingly defined in terms of administrative rather than instructional functions. We doubt, perhaps cynically, that this pattern will be altered. If anything, the federal government, state departments of education, foundations, universities, local boards of education, and citizens-at-large are tending to increase the pressure on the principal to become a production manager. If this is so, we only ask that the principal be given a set of unambiguous expectations by these groups. In short, we may want to take the principal off the hooks marked "change agent" and "instructional leader."

We are concerned about the growing tendency to see the principal as scapegoat, as an organizational messiah whose ultimate fate is professional crucifixion. In looking at the complexity of the job dimensions of the principalship under varying environmental conditions, we are convinced that the principal ought to be relieved of the misery and agony of being a panacea to so many of the problems imposed by American education and the society at large. After all, they shoot horses, don't they?

NOTES

1. Seymour B. Sarason, *The Culture of the School and the Problem of Change* (Boston: Allyn and Bacon, 1971); James M. Lipham and James Hoeh, Jr., *The Principalship: Foundations and Functions* (New York: Harper and Row, 1974).

2. Equal Employment Opportunity Commission, *Guidelines on Employment Testing Procedures* (Washington, D.C.: the Commission, August 24, 1966; July 21, 1970).

3. *Griggs* v. *Duke Power Company*, 401 U.S. 424, 91 S. Ct. 849, 28 L.Ed. 2d (1971), 158.

4. *Armstead* v. *Starkville Municipal Separate School District*, 325 F. Supp. 560 (N.D. Miss. 1971); *Allen* v. *City of Mobile*, 466 F. 2d 122 (5th Cir. 1973); *Davis* v. *Washington*, 348 F. Supp. 15 (D.D.C. 1972).

5. *Chance* v. *Board of Examiners*, in *Employment Practices Decisions*, Number 71 (Chicago: Commerce Clearing House, Inc., 1971), 148-164; "Discriminatory Merit Systems: A Case Study of the Supervisory Examinations Administered by the New York Board of Examiners," *Columbia Journal of Law and Social Problems*, 6 (September 1970), 374-410.

6. Donald A. Erickson, R. Jean Hills, and Norman Robinson, *Educational Flexibility in an Urban School District* (Vancouver: Educational Research Institute of British Columbia, 1970); Neal Gross and Robert E. Herriott, *Staff Leadership in Public Schools: A Sociological Inquiry* (New York: John Wiley and Sons, 1965); John K. Hemphill, Daniel E. Griffiths, and Norman Frederiksen, *Administrative Performance and Personality* (New York: Teachers College, Columbia University, 1962); James M. Lipham, "Personal Variables of Effective Administrators," *Administrator's Notebook*, 9 (September 1960); Kenneth J. Preble, Jr., "Success in Administration: The Judges and the Judged," unpub. diss., University of Chicago, 1962; William C. Schutz, *Procedures for Identifying Persons with Potential for Public School Positions* (Berkeley: University of California, Cooperative Research Project No. 1076, 1966).

7. The study was conducted under the auspices of the Consortium for Educational Leadership, a program sponsored jointly by seven universities interested in improving preparation programs for educational administrators through collaboration. The Consortium, funded by the Ford Foundation, terminated its activities in 1977.

8. Melany E. Baehr, "A National Occupational Analysis of the School Principal-

ship," Final Report (Chicago: Manpower Research and Development Division, Industrial Relations Center, University of Chicago, May 1975).

9. *Job Functions Inventory for School Principals,* developed by Melany E. Baehr, Frances M. Burns, R. Bruce McPherson, and Columbus Salley (Chicago: Industrial Relations Center, University of Chicago, 1974).

10. David R. Saunders, "Factor Analysis of UFO-Related Attitudes," in *Perceptual and Motor Skills,* Monograph Supplement 5-V27, Multivariate Studies of UFO's (1968), 1207-1218.

11. See Maurice F. Seay, "Administrative Acts and Their Consequences," in *Urban Schooling,* ed. Herbert C. Rudman and Richard L. Featherstone (New York: Harcourt, Brace, and World, 1968), 117-133; and Donald Mitchell, *Leadership in Public Education Study: A Look at the Overlooked* (Washington, D.C.: Academy for Educational Development, Inc., 1972), for views supporting the idea of principals as change agents.

12. Sarason, *Culture of the School and the Problem of Change,* 111.

13. *Ibid.,* 148.

Chapter Three

Bernard C. Watson

The Principal against the System

The popular picture of the urban school principal is that of the man in the middle, caught up in a storm of angry and frequently contradictory demands. Besieged by noisy delegations of students, parents, teachers, or community residents, he finds himself simultaneously to blame for poor facilities, too much homework, insufficient time for faculty planning, and students' misconduct on the way to school. When he is finally able to close his office door, he is confronted by a desk full of forms to be filled out and telephone calls to be returned to the district superintendent, the curriculum office, and the personnel department. Should he ever venture from the comparative safety of his building, he is likely to run into representatives of the press or the local television station who are eager to record his views on the latest crisis for those watching the evening news. Once he might have been the dignified scholar-statesman, presiding over serene classrooms of dutiful pupils. Today he often resembles the unfortunate victim of a pack of avenging furies.

THE PRINCIPAL'S ROLE

The basic organizational pattern of most urban school systems has not changed greatly in recent years, despite the publicity given to some scattered experiments with decentralization or community control. There is still a superintendent of schools, who has the overall responsibility for the smooth functioning of the educational system. With him at the central office is a complete hierarchy of administrators who may

40

have staff or line functions. In the field there may be intermediate line officials, district or area superintendents, who supervise the several subdistricts and who, in turn, have their own staff to monitor and advise on specific aspects of the local educational program. The individual student or parent may view a principal as master of all he surveys; the principal is more likely to see himself as the bottom man on a large and imposing totem pole.

Formal constraints are imposed on the prerogatives of the administrative offices by state statutes and the rules of the state department of education, which deal with such matters as the basic curriculum, qualifications of teachers, length of the school day and year, and so on. Closer to home, the size of the local operating budget and the various contracts with employees' organizations circumscribe all too clearly the area within which the systems' administrators may exercise their judgment in the allocation of funds. While the individual principal's degree of freedom may vary from one system to another, he is generally empowered to modify or add courses, assign personnel within the limits of student enrollment and interest, select books, materials, and equipment from approved lists, expend varying sums of discretionary monies according to his own priorities, and seek the involvement of parents and other community residents. No doubt the philosophy of his general and district superintendents and the city board of education (whether or not expressed in specific goals and objectives for the system as a whole) will constitute an influence on the principal's decision-making process, as will issues of current concern, such as the need for expansion of ethnic studies, the institution of innovative approaches to teaching science, or the interest of local businesses in creating a work-study program.

When all these real and possible constraints are taken into account, however, the fact remains that most large school systems define the formal limits of the principal's authority in only the most general way. Such definitions usually take the form of memorandums from the central office that are far from specific, except as they relate to the law and to regulations and policies of the local board of education. It would not be inaccurate to say that they are intended to avoid controversy or to prevent a recurrence of actions that have led to past controversy, in other words, to protect the board and central administration from embarrassment. Why, then, has the notion of the beleaguered principal — beset, so to speak, behind and before — taken hold of the popular and even professional imagination?

THE PRINCIPAL'S TRAINING

Part of the explanation may be found in the literature on educational administration, which has all too often defined the principal's
role in a simplistic way. In the early part of this century, Frederick
Taylor and the other exponents of administrative efficiency depicted
the principal as a business manager who needed only to learn and apply the newfound principles of scientific management in order to
assure his success.[1] Luther Gulick and Lyndall Urwick, in their formulation of organizational principles, devised POSDCORB (planning,
organizing, staffing, directing, coordinating, reporting, and budgeting) as an exhaustive description of an executive's responsibilities.[2]
The so-called "human relations movement" in administration, brilliantly exemplified by Mary Parker Follett, added important new insights from psychology and sociology,[3] but, in lesser hands, these often
served merely to soften the cold, calculating approach of the business
manager by the addition of some humane and rather paternalistic
techniques. The search for generalizations was far from over, but the
field was, perhaps, too narrow. It remained for Talcott Parsons, Herbert Simon, Jacob Getzels, and others to invent a wider lens, focusing
on entire organizations in their social context.[4] Then it was possible to
engage in systematic research and analysis, model building, and theoretical work on a base sufficiently broad to take into account the rapidly changing and complex realities of various administrative roles.

It has now become apparent that leaders are not simply born with
the ability to lead, but neither are they engineers who can apply a
tried and true remedy to each specific problem. They must learn to be
conceptualizers, mastering theory in order to use it in understanding
the day-to-day demands, while simultaneously modifying their
theories with pragmatic experience. It should not be inferred, however, that theories of social organization, political processes, or group
dynamics are sufficiently sophisticated to explain why and how human
beings act as they do. The social sciences are — and may always be —
far from exact. And it is unfortunate that not all prospective principals have been exposed, in their educational administration courses,
to even the available interdisciplinary insights that might help prepare
them to deal with their multifaceted role in a complex organization.

If an urban principal's background is limited to the more traditional knowledge, he is likely to be ill prepared to handle the new demands and expectations pressing in upon him. Teachers' militancy,
agitation for civil rights, pressure from the community for involve-

ment or control, rebellion by students—all these movements have been creating issues and problems that are scarcely touched on in the conventional wisdom of the schools and do not yield to a cookbook approach to management. Compounding the error, some departments of educational administration have not only restricted their students' thinking to a POSDCORB type of framework, but they have also led them to believe that a principal's "bag of tricks" is as useful in one setting as in another. They have failed, in other words, to take into consideration, or to convey to those who are candidates for principalships, that very different skills, competencies, and understandings may be needed in one setting from those appropriate for another.

It is small wonder, then, that many principals feel ill prepared, ill used, or both, when confronted by the apparently endless crises racking urban schools. A common complaint among them is that they are blamed for situations that they did not create and that they have no power to ameliorate. The angry parent who goes to the school office to request that a poor teacher be admonished or transferred is not interested in being told of the threat of union intervention. The teacher who is in need of aides or supplies or a bus for a trip does not want to hear the principal repeat that the budget or personnel or order department is holding things up. As far as parents, teachers, and students are concerned, the buck stops on the principal's desk. And yet, one harassed school administrator has said: "A few years ago, when there were only 100 employees in the central office, it took four weeks to get the crayons we ordered. Now they have 1000 people working down there, and we can't even get the requisitions for crayons. I wish I could just go out and buy the damn crayons myself!"

DECENTRALIZATION

It is ironic that the moves toward administrative decentralization, conceived as a way of restoring to field administrators authority and resources commensurate with their responsibilities, have in many instances simply increased the pressures upon them. While the need for massive training and development for both central and field personnel has been recognized, there has seldom been sufficient time between crises—and never enough money—to carry out even minimal decentralization in an orderly way that is calculated to maximize goodwill and acceptance. (It is significant, however, that in at least one system contemplating extensive reorganization, principals were not even represented in the initial planning sessions.) When actual steps are finally taken to decentralize, such as transferring resource personnel from the central office to district offices or school clusters or installing a PPBS system, many principals view these steps as, at best, bureaucratic juggling with little relevance to their own pressing needs or, at worst, the imposition of new tasks that they are poorly equipped to handle. Indeed, that such management innovations as PPBS might comprise more of a threat than a promise was made explicit in such statements as "It would be a serious error to conclude that PPBS allows greater freedom. On the contrary . . . ."[5] All the accompanying speeches about creating an atmosphere of mutual trust, in which honest failure is to be encouraged rather than penalized, can hardly erase the resulting climate of fear and emergent hostility. The old caveat against pouring new wine into old wineskins was never more pertinent, and yet all of the sincere efforts to revive and renew the wineskins seem uncannily to run afoul of political and financial realities that make impossible the provision of the critical time and funds for careful transition. Even where substantial decentralization has occurred, the effect has been largely to push down to the second and third levels of administration the agonizing problems of stretching pitifully limited resources over ever-increasing needs.

COMMUNITY CONTROL

While some urban systems attempted, with varying degrees of frustration or success, to make running the schools more manageable through organizational shifts, others chose — or were forced into — the even more hazardous paths of achieving decentralized management through participation by the community in school operations. The underlying rationale is similar: moving the decision-making process closer to the interface between teacher and pupil is an admirable attempt to remove schools from their bureaucratic lethargy and make them the responsive and dynamic institutions they ought to be. But the history of some of these experiments (too well known or too complex to be recounted here) is hardly calculated to persuade the fearful or cautious of their worth. In many circles, the mention of Ocean Hill-Brownsville, Adams-Morgan, or Woodlawn strikes terror or contempt into educators' hearts.

Community control is a topic that has disturbed teachers and principals all over the country, largely because of the widely publicized controversy in New York City several years ago. The argument, however, should be put in its proper context: that of the American tendency toward doublethink. When whites demand community control, it is regarded as logical, normal, and appropriate. Indeed, they seldom need to "demand" it because they have generally been in control of their schools from the start. But once poor people or minority groups begin to talk about control, blood pressures skyrocket, eyes bulge, and people begin to see some dark and devious plot being concocted by militants and revolutionaries. Derrick Bell of Harvard University Law School has put the issue in perspective: "The essence of community control is the sense of parents that they can and do influence policy-making in their children's school in ways beneficial to their children. Parents in highly regarded suburban school communities have this sense, and, in varying degrees, teachers and administrators in those schools convey an understanding that their job success depends on satisfying not the board or union but the parents whose children are enrolled in the school.[6] Or, as John Smith of Howard University said more succinctly, "White schools are not 'better' because whites are more superior, but because those responsible are required to act responsibly."[7]

Initially, parents' groups in a number of cities, aware of the depressing failures of the schools to educate their children, asked only how they could help to improve the situation. But "community involvement," as Peter Schrag bitterly commented, turned out in all too many instances to be a farce. It means, he wrote in 1967, "at best, that the locals are invited to meetings where they can express their view; usually it only means that, in return for cookies and a glass of punch, they have the privilege of being told what they are doing wrong at home and how they should instill proper attitudes in their children."[8] Driven to desperation by the bland assurance, meaningless committee work, and subtle (or not so subtle) put-downs, while the evidence accumulated of systematic favoritism for certain schools and planned inferiority for others, parents and concerned citizens began to talk of taking over the schools. And yet, even when state legislatures and the courts have taken up their cause, their victories have been hollow. Marilyn Gittell, one of the country's major analysts of educational politics, summed up the problem by saying that "mere election of local boards is not a guarantee of a redistribution of power." She noted that professionals have seen to it that boundaries and election procedures were such as to assure continued control by the old forces; that, in any case, organized groups — even those such as parochial school parents with no direct interest in the public schools — are favored; and that local boards are limited to dealing with "at best minor housekeeping arrangements."[9] Barbara Sizemore's analysis of the Woodlawn School in Chicago leads to similar conclusions: "there the community board was simply an advisory group, recommending policies, not controlling much of anything."[10] And, in Philadelphia, the Board of Education's two-year efforts to devise (in conjunction with professional and community groups from all over the city) a rational approach to shared decision making resulted in a report recommending three options for community groups: informal participation; advisory participation, and shared authority and responsibility.[11] To date, however, not one of these options has been picked up, no visible change has occurred, and none is expected. Community control may or may not be a current issue for many principals, but parents' involvement is here to stay. In those places where schools have begun to recognize the constructive potential in strong home-school-community relationships, the payoff in terms of improved student attitudes, behavior, and achievement has been measurable. Continuing to miseducate children while ignoring or patronizing their parents is no longer possible. The explosive mixture of parental frustration, anger, and despair threatens to burst into a raging fire that may well destroy public education as it is known today.

NEGATIVE REACTIONS

The setting in which most urban principals must operate may seem — and perhaps is — sufficiently forbidding to authenticate the description given earlier. Caught in the squeeze between mounting pressure from their clients on one side and the central administration on the other, many principals have sought to keep peace at any price, including the sacrifice of their professional integrity. Do the students demand academic credit for frivolous experiments? Fine, we must be relevant, you know. Does the community demand a voice in determining the curriculum? Of course, invite the militants in: we can always snow them with pedagogical jargon; blame downtown for not cooperating; or play the martyr. Is the system attempting serious renewal or reform? Quick, learn the new game, mouth the current rhetoric, and proceed up the ladder of career advancement on a newly acquired reputation of insight into contemporary problems. However he decides to play the game, the school for which a principal of this sort has charge will continue to deteriorate. In one school, educational, moral, and behavioral standards dissolve altogether in the name of students' rights, freedom, or sentimentality. In another, a power struggle between school administrators and self-appointed community spokesmen exhausts all the participants, and students are forgotten altogether. In still another, a flurry of activity, touted as change, earns approving nods, and before anyone catches on to the superficiality and gimmickry, the principal has moved on to a more lucrative position.

Some principals and field administrators have found that the best way to cope with the new realities is to develop a power base among their constituents: students, parents, community activists. They have discovered that, especially in "disadvantaged areas," the advocacy role has served them well in dealing with the central office and board of education, both of which wish to avoid confrontation as much as possible. Still others have insulated themselves from criticism and punitive sanctions by using special programs to demonstrate some improvement in the education of students. With the ready assistance of the news media, they have acquired a regional or even national reputation as "innovators" and can thus defy even the best-intentioned attempts of the local system to monitor or change the program.

For those principals whose political and public relations skills are not so well honed, still another response is possible: organization. Unable to deal with the new realities, smarting from the real or apparent slurs on their ability—which they perceive in each new effort by the central office to train, sensitize, or make them accountable—some principals have sought the safety of numbers in unions or professional associations (see Chapter 13). This organizational activity is attributable in no small part to the growing urgency of demands from hitherto excluded groups now seeking admittance to administrative and supervisory ranks in education. Affirmative action plans (usually labeled reverse discrimination or favoritism by those who oppose them), or the increased participation of parent and community activists in the process of selecting principals, are correctly interpreted as frontal assaults on the carefully established "rights" of an entrenched and privileged group. This has led to a series of cases that have cast the professional associations in the not altogether admirable role of opposing in practice what they presumably preach to their students: equality of opportunity for all Americans. In Newark, for instance, the proposal to appoint nonwhite administrators until some semblance of racial parity had been achieved was legally challenged by the principals' association. The New Jersey Pleas Court upheld the local board's position. In New York, where there was not one black high school principal, a

temporary expedient was found through appointing acting high
school principals. Both the teachers' union and the administrative and
supervisory association opposed it. Late in 1972, the New York Board
of Examiners was prevented from adding oral and written tests to the
basic credentials required for positions as administrators in the system—and their chagrin at their defeat was not ameliorated by the
chancellor's public opposition to their stand.

Still another form of reaction to the new realities has been the politicizing of many principals. Educational administrators, like their colleagues on the bench, have never been quite so apolitical as American
mythology would indicate. But educational ideology has promoted,
and the public has subscribed to, the notions of autonomy and insula-
tion for school administrators in the name of localism, unique service,
and professional expertise. More recently, however, the threats to
their prestige and to their jobs have motivated some principals to engage in overt political behavior, such as cultivating city councilmen or
other political leaders who support their point of view. Ethnic and
racial organizations—Italian, Jewish, and black, for example—have
been established by educators to provide a power base and a protection from the incursions of competing groups. The politicizing of educators has its corollary in the invasion of the supposedly sacrosanct
school system by politicians seeking to use it as a source of patronage
and power. Given the size of urban school payrolls, construction programs, and budget for supplies and equipment, this should hardly be
surprising. Rather than reacting with shock and horror to these developments, however, educators might well encourage the demythologiz-
ing of their profession and eagerly support the renewed recognition
that education is a matter of gravest political significance and concern. The great classic treatises on the state, beginning with Aristotle's
Politics or Plato's *Republic,* devote many pages to education. In recent times, the work of such eminent scholars as Karl Mannheim,
Emile Durkheim, and Max Weber, to name but a few, clearly indicates the integral relationship between education and the social
milieu. The notion that politics and education could be separated,
that schools should and could somehow exist "uncontaminated" by
politics, is a relatively recent aberration. The developments that are
currently forcing eductional matters into the political arena may succeed only in making the schools pawns in endless power plays. But
there is a chance that the questions revolving around the education of
future citizens may, as a result of the charges and countercharges of

competing interests, recover their rightful importance on the public agenda.

POSITIVE REACTIONS

There is another approach to the principal's job. Instead of reacting to the indubitable difficulties with resentment, panic, or attempts to be all things to all men, some individuals have viewed them as exciting challenges. Using their relative autonomy and what Charles Bidwell called the "structural looseness" of the school system,[12] they have learned to operate in ways that may at first seem to have little to do with the traditional role of the principal or the formal definition of his job as prescribed by the system. While their colleagues are still earnestly seeking the correct policy, the safe approach, and the guaranteed technique, these principals devote their energies and time to seeing that their teachers are teaching and their students learning. Their context may be the same school system, and their problems may be identical to those faced by all urban principals. But, if they must, they will act in spite of the system; they accept problems, not as unusual or undeserved phenomena but as an integral part of their job. These people are human, not superhuman; they, too, suffer from exhaustion and failure and weakness. But instead of focusing on their limited resources and abilities, or searching for other people to blame for the deplorable conditions under which they work, these people seem almost to thrive on impossible situations. Some have been identified and honored for their work; others continue to plug away in relative obscurity. But here and there across the nation, word continues to filter out that, amid the confusion and complexity of the urban principalship, creative and flexible people are redefining the role of the principal in a way that commands respect and replication. What are the characteristics, so far as they can be gleaned from the sparse and scattered accounts, of successful urban principals? If these principals were to compile a list of operating instructions, it resembles the following.

First, the principal has to take stock of his situation. To indicate that he must know where he is before he can determine where to go may seem painfully obvious. But, like other commonsense propositions, it is more often honored in the breech than in the observance. Analyzing strengths and weaknesses and identifying resources and needs, is the essential first step. "Taking stock" is, of course, a term borrowed from the business world: it means counting the inventory, making a list of what is on hand and what is missing. One of the most widely publicized innovative ventures in the country, the Parkway School, was born in just such a moment of taking stock. The director of development for the school system in Philadelphia was reviewing a familiar dilemma: more space was needed for high schools and yet money was limited and land was hard to find. As it happened, his office looked out on several of the city's major cultural institutions—the Art Museum, the Franklin (science) Institute, the public library. "Why could those grand facilities not be put to use during the school day, when few people are free to visit them?" he thought to himself, and not many months later the Parkway School was a reality. Few principals' offices are across the street from art museums; nor will their pressing needs be met in such an unusual moment of illumination. But the lesson to be drawn from the Parkway story underlines the importance of initial and continuing assessment of current needs *and* possible resources, even unlikely or untried resources.

Second, the urban principal must determine to deal with the school's most pressing problem, whether or not it appears to be an "educational" one. The late Marcus Foster, whose success in changing both the image and the reality of a high school whose faculty and students had given up, won him the prestigious Philadelphia Award. It is understandable that he had little patience with educators who bemoan the failure of others to ameliorate the conditions of their students' lives. Whatever problems prevent students from learning—whether they concern health, nutrition, housing, or clothing—*are* educational problems, and they must, therefore, be regarded as educators' problems. To think otherwise, said Foster, "not only removes from the teacher (and the principal) the blame for our educational failures . . . it also robs the educator of the initiative for getting things moving."[13] After all, the "experts" in other fields may never solve the problems, or new ones may materialize overnight. Certainly other professional individuals and agencies have a responsibility for seeing to the health and welfare of the young, but the principal cannot afford to wait until "they" do the job. He must be prepared and willing to bargain, beg, or borrow what his youngsters or his school requires to enable the teaching-learning process to go forward. Perhaps curricular reform or some other project dear to the principal's heart may have to be delayed while the ingenuity and energy of his staff are turned to more urgent needs.

There are many ramifications of the common, though often inchoate, view of education as something restricted to cognitive devel-

opment, the filling of empty heads with facts, or a job done in an arti-
ficial, not a "real life," setting called school. The same narrow mental-
ity attempts to divorce education from politics, insulate the school
from the community, and remove controversy from the classroom. It
is curious that the constricted definition belongs not only to "traditional" educators, but colors the thinking of even the most devastating
critics of public education.

The principal who is not concerned about and willing to take on the
crises outside his classrooms may be the most fatally irrelevant item in
the school inventory. Foster's program will not fit all school administrators; it was not intended to serve as a prescription, simply a description. But his philosophy — that principals should find out what is hurt-
ing most and fix that first — is a healthy antidote to the poisonous effects of defining educational responsibilities too narrowly.

A theme that appears again and again in stories of successful school
administration is that of willingness to consider the conventional wisdom and, if necessary, discard it. This is not to be confused with pe-
remptory dismissal of all that has been done in the past — a naive and
misleading attitude that has gained a certain radical chic appeal
among some younger members of the educational professions. On the
contrary, there is much to learn from careful study of the problems
faced and the solutions attempted by an earlier generation. (One
thinks, for instance, of the classic treatise on the art of teaching, Willard Waller's *Sociology of Teaching,* written more than forty years
ago.[14]) But one must be careful not to mistake the merely conventional ("We have always done it that way.") for truly timeless insights.

One principal of a middle school in Philadelphia, well-known for
the variety of interesting programs in her school, explained her strategy this way: "Most administrators go to someone higher up to get
permission to do something new. The guy up the line knows that if he
approves the program and it doesn't work, he will be blamed for the
failure — so as likely as not he'll play it safe and say no. But in this
school, we try something out quietly. If it flops, we scrap it. But if it
seems to be going well, and we want to expand it, then I march down
to my area superintendent and announce that we have a successful
program going and we want him to know about it. Of course, I come
back with official approval — what else can the superintendent do?" In
another school, it became obvious that more time was needed for
teachers' planning and staff development to work out the details of a
recently installed innovative approach. After much discussion, the

principal was able to convince the school authorities that the loss of class time that resulted from dismissing the students early several times a month would be more than repaid by the higher quality of teachers' preparation for the time spent with pupils. In still another school, attended largely by boys already labeled as misfits and delinquents, a new principal quickly became aware of the students' painfully limited exposure to art and music. A fresh supply of books, records, and pictures was helpful, but, convinced that these were not sufficient to catch the imagination of her boys, she decided to purchase season tickets to the Friday afternoon concert series of the renowned local orchestra. Staff members and colleagues were horrified at the idea of mixing a busload of unruly younsters with the staid, white-haired matrons who comprised the concert audience. But she persisted, and the boys' pride, enthusiasm, and excellent behavior confounded the doubting souls who had envisioned riots in the aisles.

These few examples — and many more are possible — should serve to illustrate the point that principals can and do function creatively in spite of the constraints and limited resources imposed by the larger system. This imaginative type of administrator recognizes that his chief, perhaps his only, job is to design and implement programs that will improve the learning of the children and that will respond realistically to the aspirations and desires of their parents and the community. He tends to be convinced that rules and regulations are useful only when they are relevant to the social context in which he operates. With refreshing candor, he is likely to admit that the "system" so feared or hated by many lower-echelon administrators is largely a myth. When it is challenged by those with common sense and a sense of humor, its threatening powers tend to dissolve, like the Wizard of Oz, to fairly ordinary and manageable proportions. Freed from illusions about the oppressive nature of the educational hierarchy, and having shaken off the restrictive traditional definitions of his role, the principal is able to undertake the critical task of assessment and to marshal school and community forces to deal with the real needs of his student body. The particulars of each situation — students' performance, teachers' abilities, neighborhood resources — will determine his agenda. But while programs may differ, accountability for the product is a universal.

Richard Saxe has stated that "none of the theories and certainly none of the principles based upon experience in other institutions is adequate to explain all the phenomena of the principalship. All of the previous theoretical and experimental data combined are not sufficient for this purpose."[15] But, far from being discouraged, Saxe suggests that there is much available in the literature to aid principals. It is the principal's task to determine the relevance of the data supplied.

Today's urban school presents a unique challenge to an administrator's ingenuity, energy, and patience. He must wear many hats, draw on many sources for wisdom and inspiration. He must be analyst, strategist, and diplomat. But with commitment to his task of making and maintaining an environment in which teaching and learning can flourish, he may discover that the system can be made to work.

NOTES

1. See Bertram H. Gross, "The Scientific Approach to Administration," in *Behavioral Science and Educational Administration,* ed. Daniel E. Griffiths, Sixty-third Yearbook of the National Society for the Study of Education, Part II (Chicago: University of Chicago Press, 1964), chap. 2.

2. Luther H. Gulick, "Notes on the Theory of Organization," in *Papers on the Science of Administration,* ed. *id.* and L. Urwick (New York: Institute of Public Administration, 1937).

3. Henry C. Metcalf and L. Urwick, eds., *Dynamic Administration: The Collected Papers of Mary Parker Follett* (New York: Harper and Row, 1942).

4. See, for example, Talcott Parsons and Edward A. Shils, *Toward a General Theory of Action* (Cambridge, Mass.: Harvard University Press, 1951); James G. March and Herbert A. Simon, *Organizations* (New York: John Wiley and Sons, 1958); Jacob W. Getzels, "Theory and Practice in Educational Administration," in *Administrative Theory as a Guide to Action,* ed. Roald F. Campbell and James M. Lipham (Chicago: Midwest Administration Center, University of Chicago, 1960), chap. 3.

5. See, for example, Barbara Sizemore's statement to the Mondale Committee, July 27, 1971, Pt. 13, "Quality and Control of Urban Schools," *Hearings before the Select Committee on Equal Educational Opportunity* (Washington, D.C.: Government Printing Office, 1971); Marilyn Gittell's statement to the Mondale Committee, July 14, 1971, Pt. 12, "Quality and Control of Urban Schools," *ibid.;* Bernard C. Watson, *Crusades and the Educational Crisis* (Boston: Massachusetts State Board of Education, n.d.); and the report on decentralization of the Philadelphia schools prepared by the Greenfield Commission in 1970.

6. Derrick A. Bell, Jr., "Integration— Is It a No-Win Education Policy for Blacks?" unpub. paper prepared for the National Policy Conference on Education for Blacks in 1972 (p. 18; summarized in *Proceedings,* National Policy Conference on Education for Blacks, ed. Bernard C. Watson [Washington, D.C.: Congressional Black Caucus,1972]).

7. John W. Smith, "Some Afterthoughts Concerning the National Policy Conference on Education for Blacks," unpub. paper.

8. Peter Schrag, *Village School Downtown* (Boston: Beacon Press, 1967), 178.

9. Gittell, statement to the Mondale Committee.

10. Sizemore, statement to the Mondale Committee.

11. See report of the Greenfield Commission on decentralization of the Philadelphia schools.

12. Charles Bidwell, "The School as a Formal Organization," in *Handbook of Organizations*, ed. James G. March (Chicago: Rand McNally and Company, 1965), 927-1022.

13. See discussion of how Dr. Marcus Foster carried out his role as a high school principal in *Making Schools Work* (Philadelphia: Westminster Press, 1971).

14. Willard W. Waller, *Sociology of Teaching* (New York: John Wiley and Sons, 1932).

15. Richard W. Saxe, ed., *Perspectives on the Changing Role of the Principal* (Springfield, Ill.: Charles C. Thomas, 1968).

Chapter Four

William W. Wayson

A View of the Leadership Shortage
in School Buildings

Probably no people in the United States are exhorted to be leaders as much as school principals. Probably no group has been excoriated so much for lacking the qualities of leadership.

Some observers deny that principals can ever be leaders:

> The position, not only the person, largely dictates the principal's status as a functionary. . . . A defining characteristic of the functionary is that almost all significant decisions concerning his role are made for him. . . . Various forces operate to keep the principal at the functioning level . . . . 1) societal factors that constrain the principal's actions; 2) organizational factors, such as the bureaucratic structure of schools and the growing power of teacher organizations; and 3) sociological and psychological factors concerning the nature of schooling and learning.[1]

Self-conscious about such charges, principals frequently report that they have no opportunities for leadership. They cite all sorts of constraints against their leading. The most pressing influences this year seem to be negotiated teacher contracts and state-imposed evaluation procedures. Of course there are perennial favorite restrictions — lack of opportunity to pick faculty members or to eliminate poor ones, paperwork for the central office, monitoring systems, irate or pushy parents, curriculum requirements, lack of time and communication problems. The excuses for lack of leadership appear endless. As these are repeated, reported, and analyzed, they prove the *Man of La Mancha*'s observation that "Facts are the enemies of Truth." They simply hide the real situation.

None of those constraints explain lack of leadership because leadership aims to overcome or circumvent barriers. There would be no need for leadership if there were not apparent restrictions upon persons or groups; consequently, constraints against the principal are manifestations of the opportunity, and the need, for leadership in the position.

Lack of leadership is currently a problem throughout American society. Government, religion, industry, labor, education — all lack verve and all seem to be foundering upon great problems. Crises in energy, in environmental conditions, in the Middle East, in teacher-administration relationships, in family life, in public confidence — all defy resolution because of a leadership crisis that became evident in the middle 1960's. John Gardner spoke of an "Antileadership Vaccine" in his Annual Report to the Carnegie Corporation in 1965:

The sad truth is that a great many of our organizations are badly managed or badly led. And because of that, people within those organizations are frustrated. They are not helped when they could be helped. They are not given the opportunities to fulfill themselves that are clearly possible.

Another observer wrote in 1969:

There is unleashed in this society a kind of relentless, self-proliferating, all consuming institutional process — institutional life, really — that assaults, dispirits, defeats and destroys human life. It does this even among, *primarily among,* those men in positions of institutional leadership. They are left with titles but without authority, with the condiments of power but without control over the institutions they head. They are in nominal command but bereft of dominion. These same principalities threaten, defy and enslave human beings of other status in multiple ways, but the most poignant victim of this form of totalitarianism is the so-called leader.[2]

Often the call for leadership is a yearning for some superhuman on a white horse to rescue the nation or the group or the person from some fate that seems beyond individual control. Too often the lack of prominent leader-figures prompts hasty and regrettable reliance upon liberators who use rhetoric and slogans to lead frightened and uncertain constituencies against imagined or manufactured enemies. Tendencies toward dependence, manipulability, and lack of leadership are inherent in our social institutions, no less in our educational system. No one has depicted the process so succinctly as Carl Jung. His comments seem worthy of extensive quotation because they are particularly relevant for school principals:

Judged scientifically, the individual is nothing but a unit which repeats itself ad infinitum and could just as well be designated with a letter of the alphabet. For understanding, on the other hand, it is just the unique individual human being who, when stripped of all those conformities and regularities so dear to the heart of the scientist, is the supreme and only real object of investigation. . . .[3]

Scientific education is based in the main on statistical truths and abstract knowledge and therefore imparts an unrealistic, rational picture of the world, in which the individual, as a merely marginal phenomenon, plays no role . . . .[4]

Under the influence of scientific assumptions, not only the psyche but the individual man, and indeed, all individual events whatsoever suffer a leveling down and a process of blurring that distorts the picture of reality into a conceptual average . . . . it displaces the individual in favor of anonymous units that pile up into mass formations.

The moral responsibility of the individual is then inevitably replaced by the policy of the State. . . . The rulers, in their turn, are just as much social units as the ruled and are distinguished only by the fact that they are specialized mouthpieces of the State doctrine . . . .[5]

The State in particular is turned into a quasi-animate personality from whom everything is expected. In reality it is only a camouflage for those individuals who know how to manipulate it. . . . In so far as society itself is composed of de-individualized persons, it is completely at the mercy of ruthless individualists. . . . A million zeros joined together do not, unfortunately, add up to one. Ultimately everything depends on the quality of the individual . . . .[6]

The suffocating power of the masses is paraded before our eyes in one form or another every day . . . , and the insignificance of the individual is rubbed into him so thoroughly that he loses all hope of making himself heard. . . . Resistance to the organized mass can be effected only by the [person] who is as well organized in his individuality as the mass itself.[7]

Lack of leadership is an unanticipated, though inherent, outcome of events that dominated educational administration from 1955 to 1965.[8] During that decade professors turned to social science and to some vaguely conveyed "theories" as the basis for preparing educational administrators. It was not a misguided move; educational administration had for some years operated on the basis of successful practice and armchair retrospect (although the extent to which that was true has been exaggerated by proponents of the new approaches). The move to greater conceptual elegance was a logical and productive one for the field. Salaries and status improved for administrators, and graduate departments of administration gained power within colleges of education. The financial and political management of school systems was markedly improved. Managers in the superintendency gained somewhat higher respect from businessmen and politicians. However, their new knowledge hastened—or did nothing to retard— their becoming bureaucratic zeros, the specialized mouthpieces that Jung described.

The principalship suffered ill effects that were not recognized at the time, though some observers sensed the probability that the principalship was not keeping pace with the field.[9] Deleterious effects sprang from two weaknesses in the movement. First, professors accorded the principalship very low esteem and devoted themselves to preparing professors or superintendent or to soliciting funds to do "research" to raise their own status in the university. Second, no one effectively accounted for or counteracted the deficiencies of so-called "scientific" approaches that neglect the elements that give education peculiar power and character—values, perceptions, virtually unlimited versatility and uniqueness, and unceasing dynamism.[10] Those deficiencies are exacerbated by the limited definitions and doctrinaire procedures imposed upon scientific inquiry within most universities today.

None of the above is intended to denigrate the contributions that science has made to human existence. We must place science in proper perspective in the world, and we must accord it its proper place in our schools. Otherwise, we will continue to ignore significant aspects of existence. Educational decision making has been blinded for several decades, perhaps for the last century,[11] and the lack of individual initiative (leadership) from principals is one price we are paying.

The traditions of the principalship also stifle leadership. The job was conceived as a clerical, managerial position to relieve superintendents of unwanted tasks.[12] Of course, it is too easy to generalize about this matter, and to ignore that outstanding schools probably always had outstanding principals (or some outstanding teacher or parent) who provided unusually effective stimulation and guidance for staff and students. We should always be wary of glib generalizations about what things were like in the past. However, myths govern human behavior even more readily than reality, and the traditions of the principalship—if they are believed and acted upon—govern what principals do more surely than any call to reality. Therefore, it is useful to examine some of the traditions that retard principals from using their power.

During the 1940's, 1950's and 1960's school systems did not want principals to be leaders. Principals still on the job (indeed principals appointed in 1977) can recall numerous incidents during their training and their early experience when people tried to force them into a job description whose chief tenets are:

1. following the rules, doing what you are told, seeing that centralized decisions are carried out;

2. not rocking the boat, not thinking of better ways to do things;
3. keeping conflict down; keeping students, teachers, and parents calm;
4. disciplining (controlling) students and staff;
5. protecting teachers from the consequences of their own actions;
6. backing up the system regardless its questionability; and
7. getting records in on time. [13]

One principal trained to fulfill that job description responded to a challenge that principals had taken no lead to provide equal educational opportunities for disadvantaged children by shouting, "You can't blame us for what happened to kids; we always did what the school board told us to!" In many respects principals are being blamed for doing well those things they were selected, trained, and assigned to do: teaching people to be followers; to accept orders; to keep a leaky boat steady; to move mindlessly and uncritically into subordinate, dull, dehumanizing occupations; to become a piece of machinery and to accept one's proper place as others thought it should be. There is some evidence that many people still want a school system like that. For example, in 1973 a member of the Ohio State Board of Education reminded a public hearing that "most of us around this table are employers and we want schools that will produce employees who will do what employers want." No one objected, although all major educators' organizations were represented in the audience.

However, such goals are out of tune with what the nation (including its businesses) needs. Historic practices that reinforce low-level functioning are wholly unsatisfactory for times that demand initiative and problem solving. There is a growing need for educators who can help other people to find within themselves the strength and will to create educational programs based upon faith in individual integrity, responsibility, and ability. Such programs cannot spring from, or be controlled by, centralized hierarchies in which officials have been selected because they were unlikely to try to change the system.

A study of the federal programs created under the Elementary and Secondary Education Act of 1965 suggested that the school building and the classroom are the places where successful educational reforms must take place:

More specifically, high morale of teachers at a school, the active support of principals *who appear to be the "gate-keepers" of change,* and the teacher's willingness to expend extra effort on the project all increased the chances of teacher change and perceived success [italics added]. [14]

Findings such as those, coming from many sources,[15] indicate that principals currently are in a key position for helping American education meet new demands. The question is: "Will more principals capitalize upon the position or will other persons fill the vacuum?"[16] Of course, leadership is not something reserved solely for principals; stimulation and guidance could come from students, teachers, and parents as well.

Experience with schools, industries, churches, and universities indicates that failure to exercise leadership arises from three sources: a common feeling among administrators that they are *not supposed to* do what leadership demands or that they are supposed to do things that militate against leadership; a lack of specific definition for leadership although the term is bandied about as if it were universally understood; and a lack of knowledge about *how to perform* in ways that would be commensurate with leadership.[17] Help principals see that they are not limited by expectations, give them some way of seeing what leadership is in real situations, help them know and practice skills for effective leadership, and there would be more educational leadership. In the remaining pages we will attempt to do some of all three.

FREEING PRINCIPALS OF CONSTRAINTS

What people can achieve is determined more by *what they believe they can achieve* than by any other force. Faith in oneself is shaped by attitudes perceived in other persons whose opinions are relevant and important. If a starving child believes that nothing edible is available, he will starve while sitting on top of a crate of apples. If his mentors tell him that he cannot get food or that his condition dictates that he must starve, he probably will starve though a banquet is served in the next building.

If the principal holds narrow views of what is possible, or if "relevant others" communicate limited views of what can be achieved, few leadership behaviors will be forthcoming. Many principals hold limited views of what is possible within the principalship. Training programs and colleagues often communicate limited views. Narrow views arise from inaccurate perceptions of what the world is; nevertheless, if unchallenged or unchanged they determine and limit what the principal does. Principals will not exercise leadership unless they acquire more accurate pictures of what a principal can or cannot, should or should not, do and clearer sense about who exerts the strongest influence over what is done.

Teachers and principals have helped me develop a way of examining the role of principal (or teacher) that has been useful for uncovering formerly unseen possibilities in their work. The process proceeds through three steps: defining the stereotyped role, differentiating expectations, and owning the role. Those three steps can help principals discover their potential for leading.

Defining the Stereotyped Role

Ask an educator why he or she does not do a certain thing, and the reply reveals a belief that the individual can do nothing to change what has to be done every day. Teachers or principals often say, "I am in a box." That box is the position, the formal role, to which the person is assigned. Ask principals to diagram it, and they frequently draw a square with hard, rigid, well-defined sides. It is perceived as immutable.

It is reasonable for a principal to assume that somewhere there is a definition of what principals do, thinking all the while that he or she is the only person who really does not understand what all those other people who come into the office or call on the phone or write memos know. There are books on the principalship, and courses devoted to it, and certificates granted for being able to do it—whatever it is. The idea that the role is well carved out is depicted in the organization chart and backed up by a "job description" and a title. Students, parents, teachers, the central office staff and college professors all talk about the principalship, and each assumes that everyone else *understands* what it is. It is natural that persons filling the office should feel guilty if they do not know.

Research reports also reinforce the concept that principals must conform to explicit limitations.[18] When investigators interview large numbers of people to determine what they expect of principals, the findings are reduced to a few categories that obscure original responses. Reports emphasize those categories that contain responses from the largest numbers of respondents. Even though the number of responses in each may be less than a majority, the emphasis can lead one to believe that they are universally expected. The variability, the essence, and the individuality of responses are lost when results are reduced to brief labels in a numerical table; yet the table appears to be *objective*. Even if original investigators report their findings fully, principals receive only abbreviated summaries in articles or speeches. From beginning to end, currently accepted research processes involve intellectual leaps that distort rather than illuminate the principal's role. Such research reports are the substance of college work; hence, training also reinforces principals' believing that the role is well defined. Though role theories have played a large part in preparatory programs during the past two decades,[19] instruction has not emphasized the transactional nature of roles. Often professors convey more about the expectations to which principals presumably must conform than about processes by which a principal may influence both those expectations and his or her own behavior. Even new preparatory programs are based upon surveys of what principals do, or what principals think they do, rather than what could be done if all potentialities were exploited. Consequently, the principal is trained to know more about what cannot be done than what can, more about what the law will not permit than what it will, more about what teachers will not do than what they can do, more about what resistances might be encountered than about what support can be marshaled. Professors often ask aspiring principals to identify constraints in a given situation or to list the disadvantages of various courses of actions; so, the feeling that leadership is dangerous and that desired goals cannot be reached is reinforced. Aspirants could as easily be required to identify the possibilities for leadership, to develop the creative potentialities in any situation, or to transform perceived constraints into advantages.

So it is that many seemingly legitimate and knowledgable forces conspire to convince principals that the principalship is a box within which the individual has little control. Nevertheless, it is difficult to describe the box. Few people in any organizational position have really tried to specify what their role is, though they talk about it in abbreviated descriptions or judgments.

Principals have little difficulty answering the questions: Who holds expectations for what a principal does? What do they expect a principal to do? They can name groups who expect things, and they can list expectations. They almost universally accept that *all* people expect *all* principals to fulfill the expectations. They describe an organizational box that it is held in place and given its shape by monolithic and powerful forces named "they": *They* don't want sex education. *They* don't want anyone to rock the boat. *They* won't let us abolish marks. *They* want me to get the reports done. *They* expect you to discipline kids. The ephemeral "they" controls behavior and will not tolerate deviance. Principals typically list a standard set of "they's": *the* parents, *the* students, *the* teachers, *the* central office (often called *the* board), and a few other groups. *The* board is backed up by THE LAW, by POLICY, or by REGULATIONS, which are perceived as perfectly conceived, precisely defined, and irresistibly enforced.

At this level of examination the principal's functioning is thought to be totally circumscribed by what outside forces want. The role is conceived as depicted in Figure 4-1. So, principals tend to see their role as a box surrounded by groups whose opinions and expectations are stereotyped into monolithic, unified, and unchangeable expectations for what a principal should be doing. Those stereotyped expectations frequently define the role in research reports as well as in common parlance.

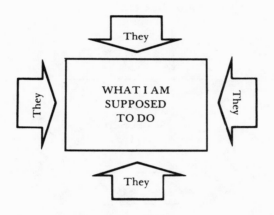

FIGURE 4-1. The stereotyped view of the role

Differentiating Expectations

To become a leader, the principal must break the monolithic stereotype and differentiate the expectations directed toward him or her. As principals discuss the box they can see that teachers' expectations often are incompatible with what the central office wants, and both are inconsistent with what parents want. Yet, a principal often feels that he or she must satisfy all of the demands. Trying to satisfy incompatible or inconsistent demands leaves the principal feeling like a slice of bread being pecked by sparrows with everyone taking away little pieces. Decisions yield no satisfaction because they either bring or threaten to bring further demands from other quarters.

Principals can get a clearer view of the box by estimating the *percentage* of each demanding group that expects certain behaviors. Not *all* parents expect educators to discipline their child or to hover over the child's safety as a mother hen; so, what percentage does? Not *all* officials at the board office expect clerical reports to supersede other activities; so, what percentage does? Not *all* teachers expect to be protected from parents; so, what percentage does? And so on. As these estimates are made and debated, it should become apparent that there are very few universal expectations. Few demands are supported by *all* persons in any of the groups. In reality there is no unified or monolithic "they" out there.[20] Rather *thirty* people in the central office, *thirty-five* teachers, *three hundred* parents, and *six hundred* students each hold differing opinions about what a principal should do. No two of them agree totally about all of what should be done. Realizing that, we can redraw the box to look like Figure 4-2.

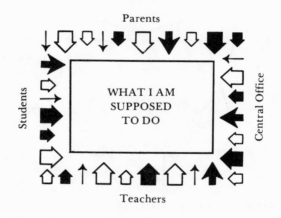

FIGURE 4-2. The differentiated view of the role

Knowledgeable people readily see that the expectations perceived during the stereotyped stage are stated in vague terms that cannot be translated into practice without much interpretation and translation. For example, "backing teachers" or "disciplining students" or "being loyal" all mean different things to different people. Furthermore, there is more inconsistency among the people in a group than there is between groups. Parents who want the principal to "be fair" will disagree among themselves about whether that means to treat all children alike or to give some preferential treatment to their child or some other child. To one parent or teacher, "disciplining children" means to swat their behinds; to another, it means to treat children as equal members of the school. One central office functionary defines "filling out reports" as meticulously computing the last two digits while another means "get any damned figure on the form and get it in." No principal can satisfy both a teacher who expects to be "backed" even if the principal must lie and a teacher who expects to be treated as a professional and an adult. No principal can achieve goals of the Title I program that cannot be achieved unless staff members gain respect and acceptance from teachers they are supposed to help and at the same time honor a rule from the central office that prohibits Title I teachers from taking lunch duty or from lending any of their materials.

Owning the Role

Having differentiated expectations, principals may readily see that they cannot possibly please everyone all the time. The principal with such insight is freer than was ever imagined. There is no box shaped by outside forces and pressures. Rather, the role looks like Figure 4-3, and, in significant ways, it is different for every individual principal.

FIGURE 4-3. The responsible view of the role

Outside expectations are really there — at least most of them are; there should be no foolish attempt to deny that. Furthermore, pressures will always be there, and it seems a waste of energy to try to remove them all or to refrain from leadership until they are gone. Neither expectations nor the people who hold them are totally beyond the principal's influence. By taking appropriate actions to win credibility, to define terms, to gain respect, to demonstrate that he or she shares in their purposes, the principal shapes many outside forces in the same manner that they try to shape him or her. Pressures are not all manufactured in a principal's mind, but the power they have is primarily in the mind; therefore, the principal can develop responses that are compatible with what he or she has decided the role should be.

Leadership expresses itself in actions that break through limits that many others see as impenetrable. We often frighten principals by indicating that leadership requires a lot of risk taking. It is another matter altogether; leadership is not undertaken by people who perceive themselves as taking greater risks than others are willing to take. Rather, leadership is undertaken when a person perceives less risk than others do.

The power that the incumbent has over a role becomes evident as one answers these questions about Figure 4-3: Who determines the shape of the role I play? Who do I typically permit to influence my behavior and why? What do I do to shape my role in the face of incompatible pressures from outside? Those questions permit principals to examine their behavior, to take responsibility for their interpretations and responses, and to choose to take leading rather than reactive actions. Regardless of the expectations, whatever a principal does is actually a personal decision and within personal control — at least to a far greater degree than is typically admitted. As the three questions are answered, it is undeniable that the role is not determined by "what *they* want," which places the principal's work outside his command; it is shaped by "what *I* permit to control my actions." Just as a professional basketball player knows that he and not chance controls what the ball does, so the professional educator must find greater confidence in his or her control over the role.

Principals will never lead their schools to new levels of effectiveness unless individuals take personal responsibility for the role they play. Exercising leadership depends more upon overcoming one's own perceptions than upon removing constraints from elsewhere.[21] Once freed from our self-imposed boxes, we are free to do whatever it is that leaders do.

UNDERSTANDING WHAT LEADERSHIP MEANS

Educators commonly misconstrue that an abstract term derived and supported by statistical averages has concrete and/or behavioral meaning. In fact, words may have no meaning at all because of the progressive abstraction of the term and the artificiality of the averaging process. Many people have not the vaguest idea what leadership would look like in a specific instance involving individual people; small wonder that school principals have difficulty translating leadership into action.

Leadership occurs when an individual's actions combine, through the mediation of various situational forces, with the willingness and ability of a group to attain some desired purpose. Though leadership seems to result from individual efforts, those efforts must coincide with what other members will do and with situational factors; so, it cannot be approached solely through any given individual. Leadership must be translated into action by the people who consent to be led. A principal who wants to lead must learn how to facilitate a staff's collectively learning how to express leadership.

The most that a school district can do to make a principal or any other person a leader is to bestow upon him or her some of the symbols that members of the school faculty and community have come to respect. However, those symbols are only a part of the power needed to lead.[22] They answer only the question, "Does this person have the formal status to serve my needs when I have need of such help?" They do not answer two other questions that are in the minds of personnel when they decide to accept leadership: Is this person *capable* of serving my needs when I need help? *Will* this person serve my needs when I need help? Answers to those two questions are highly personal and subjective judgments made by followers who vote decisively by their actions.

Of course, the vote is influenced strongly by principals who act in ways that will cause others to identify the essential character of a situation, to determine their most constructive role in it, to carry out that role directly, and to sustain it as long as necessary. Such skills are learned, not commanded, and the school must be organized in ways that enable every person there to practice them. Creating such an organization is one form of leadership, and the principal currently is in a key position for doing so.

From this perspective, the *principal* does not have to define goals, initiate action, follow up, or evaluate and revise. Rather, *someone* in the school building must do those things when they are needed and must do them effectively. That someone does not have to be the same person at all times. The principal should create conditions that will elicit leadership behaviors from everyone in the building in circumstances and at times that their contribution is essential for achieving the school's purposes. That is quite a different matter from the principal's having to do everything. And yet, many principals seem to feel that being a leader requires them to do everything.[23]

Leadership is any *act that helps a group or organization achieve its*

purposes, including both its public and its private purposes. No leadership is possible without a sense of what the world is all about, how
the school contributes to that world, and how one's personal actions
will affect that contribution. A person who cannot link actions with
larger purposes (or who refuses to listen closely to people who can) will
never provide educational leadership. Lawrence Cremin has stated the
need very well:

> I think we need to raise up a new kind of educational leader in this country if the great
> questions of educational purpose are to receive intelligent discussion by teachers and
> the lay public . . . . He [she] will need fundamental preparation . . . that will enable
> him [her] to develop a clear and compelling vision of education and of its relation to
> American life . . . Only as educators begin to think deeply about the ends of learning
> will the politics of popular education . . . become . . . a constant reaching for the good
> society.[24]

Principals deprived of practice in relating means to ends have great
difficulty leading. They tend to make three common errors about
goals. Perhaps knowing what those errors are can facilitate more
effective leadership.

First, they assume that people know what the school's purposes are
when, in fact, few people either inside or outside the school have given
the matter much thought. Schools are now old enough in American
culture that they are taken for granted. Few people in this generation
have had to defend the schools' existence or to persuade powerful op-
ponents of unhappy consequences if schools do not exist; so, few people have had to piece together a logical or persuasive philosophy.
What passes for educational philosophy is academic and lifeless mem-
orization or review of literature with seemingly little relevance for
modern life.

Second, principals fail to see that no single group has exclusive interest in educational outcomes. Often assuming that one group's goals
(or their perceived goals) are good for everyone, principals defend actions solely with tradition, expediency, or hierarchical authority
rather than examining educational consequences for the many groups
who have an interest in the educational enterprise. Persons within the
system often substitute their own convenience for original purposes;
persons from without often demand actions that are detrimental for
others. Principals alone cannot define purposes, but they can assist
others to think more soundly, and they can create circumstances in
which differences can be clarified and accommodated.

Third, principals often focus only upon one or two types of goals and neglect other goals that any school must achieve. Trained chiefly to carry on maintenance functions required by the school system, they have few skills for working effectively with the interpersonal and inter-group dynamics that govern life in the school building, for producing whatever the school is expected to produce, for securing necessary re-sources, for integrating goals expressed by diverse sources, or for adapting to changing conditions in the outside world.[25] Yet, every school staff must meet all of those goals if it is to function effectively over time. Someone must attend to each.

Principals sometimes feel that their management duties prevent them from being leaders. They are sometimes denounced for being "mere managers." The dichotomy between leadership and manage-ment, which dominates much discussion about the principalship, is misleading and false. It is arguable only so long as both parties agree to the proposition that management and leadership are mutually ex-clusive. They are not. Leaders tend to use management prerogatives to stimulate leadership and educational progress in their buildings.[26] Furthermore, principals do not spend as much time on unproductive detail as they think they do.[27]

Management is a tool that can be put to effective use as frequently as it is abused. Management destroys leadership if it attempts to con-trol all action, if it delimits choices, if it uses procedures that prohibit creative adaptation to circumstances, if it lulls people into thinking that someone else is watching out for exigencies, or if it prevents per-sonnel from accepting responsibility. However, management can be different from that. It can establish processes that require participa-tion from all personnel. It can facilitate problem solving throughout the organization. It can develop channels to carry communications in all directions, and procedures to assure their getting careful attention. In complex organizations management carries major responsibility for creating structure-in-action—an activity that has been found essential for effective leadership.[28] Stated in barest terms, the leader's responsi-bility is to set up ways in which other people can get things done. The major difference between leaders and nonleaders is that the former set up ways that get things done the best way under fluid conditions while the latter try to get things done the way the organization (or tradition) dictates, no matter what the conditions. The latter kind of manage-ment brings severe criticism upon principals. It is a corruption of management. Effective management practices behaviors that foster and express leadership.

LEARNING TO DO WHAT LEADERS DO

Principals whose perceptions are freed and whose understanding of leadership has substance will find more opportunities for leadership than they can use. Uncommon views of the commonplace uncover possibilities that never before seemed to exist.

Leaders have the ability to see leadership possibilities in most situations. Principals have reported that negotiated contracts have deprived them of power when, in fact, the contracts afford several opportunities to lead. The inanities of state-mandated evaluation systems do seem to increase meaningless details with no predictable gain, but the pressures of the accountability movement can be used to effect educational gains for students and improvements in teacher status and satisfaction as well. The intricacies of budgeting give principals new control over some significant educational matters. Faculty meetings, lunch periods, PTA meetings, room assignments, scheduling — all afford tremendous leadership potentials, and the principal controls them more than any other individual. Each has its routine and unrewarding aspects, of course, but they become bearable if educational gains are realized.

Educational literature uses ill-defined terms like "discipline" or "community relations" to describe what principals do. Such terms provide no guidance for a principal who wishes to be a leader. There is need to accompany the semantics of leadership with illustrations that empower principals to know what the concept looks like in practice. For example, the principal is often said to be "powerless" because "the principal controls virtually no rewards."[29] However, principals do not lose leadership because they control no rewards but, rather, because they think only of salary, other money, or promotions as rewards. Principals fail to lead because *they fail to perceive the many other things over which they have some control that are rewarding to teachers.* They may also fail to understand that rewards are highly idiosyncratic; one person's reward can be another's punishment.

Armed with a new understanding of what rewards are, a principal can utilize and benefit from formerly unused opportunities to lead. In average schools with no more than normal resources principals control and distribute many rewards as they

assign rooms, space, and time;
make small but highly desired changes in facilities;
meet teachers' needs to feel competent;
give others credit for problems solved in the school;

interpret policy in ways that facilitate staff actions;

free teachers from things they think limit their ability to produce;

help teachers discover talents they never recognize or use;

help teachers prove they can make a difference in the school;

enable teachers to work with children whom they find rewarding;

enable teachers to do the things they find rewarding;

get teachers' names and pictures in local news media; and

promote teachers' personal contact with school and community leaders.

Every term used to describe the principal's functioning should be given meaning that helps each person see the possibilities it contains.

So, principals should ask each person who exhorts them to be leaders to state explicitly what behavior is expected. Many would have some idea, and some of those would be very useful. However, the greatest thing to be learned from the question is that people are caught up with labels, slogans, and abstractions and can name few specific behaviors. Principals could point out the uselessness of the replies; however, intelligent principals can look beyond the momentary advantage to determine just what concerns the critic. They will learn quickly that the critic is concerned about whether certain goals are being achieved in the school and expects the principal to take specific action to enhance their achievement. If the critic can be persuaded that the goal is being attained or that another better one is being pursued, he or she will be more confident that leadership is occurring. If the goal is being neglected or poorly addressed, any action that is directed to it will be interpreted as leadership.

Educators do not have to be superhuman to behave as leaders. They have only to make small adjustments in school practice that will promote better education, greater staff morale, and stronger community support. Many such adjustments have been listed elsewhere,[30] but anyone can develop a comprehensive list after applying four precepts that seem to guide educational leaders.

Precept 1: *Look at all standardized practices and see if there are other, more educational options.* If there are, change the existing practice. All other things being equal, it is both educationally and administratively more productive to have choices and options open to personnel. The more ways children have to behave, the less likely they are to become discipline problems. The more ways parents have to voice concerns and seek some response, the less likely they are to become a chronic thorn in the school's side or to lead a dissident group.

The more ways teachers have to teach children or to get things done in the school, the more productive and the more satisfied they will be. Schools are filled with standardized practices that militate against productiveness, problem solving, and satisfaction. Use the following questions to identify some.

Is it necessary that all classes and teachers have recess at the same time?

Is it educationally sound to have all children reading from the same textbooks?

Is it necessary or educationally sound to have all children attending school on the same calendar or daily schedule?

What problems would be solved if teachers' arrival and leaving times were varied according to educational needs?

Is it useful to have class periods all the same length?

Are educational purposes served by having all parents at the same parent meeting?

What problems are caused by ringing bells to mark the changes in classes, recess periods, or other events in the school?

How much harm is caused if a city-wide standardized report card is the major communication between schools and homes?

How much more education would occur if we used every opportunity to have children of different ages interacting with one another?

Precept 2: *Look at the school as a community rather than an institution and use every opportunity to utilize the forces of community to enhance educational purposes.* Many problems that are blamed upon the size of schools or upon poor organization are really caused by over-organizing rather than giving rein to the educative forces of community.[31] If schools operate more like a small town and less like prisons or armies, they generally experience fewer discipline problems, less criticism of "management," more responsible actions from teachers and students, and better education. The principal can help to create a community by:

involving each person in a small enough group (a team) to give personal support and assistance when needed;

giving each small group a great deal of autonomy to solve its problems and to work out its relationship with the rest of the school;

creating and using communication channels that maintain interdependence among the small groups;

establishing practices that demonstrate that every person belongs in the school and is a vital and necessary part of life there;

making sure that strangers (both adult and child) are taught how to get things done in the community, how to perform their particular functions, and how to redress grievances against other members;

making sure that practices in the school are more like family and community life than like prisons or armies (the cafeteria is a good place to start here); and

redirecting problems to groups or persons nearer the situation.

Precept 3: *Continuously ask yourself and others why things are done the way they are done.* If the only answer is that it has always been done that way, drop it. If there are good reasons, make sure that the people who are doing the things know the reasons and are not merely parroting tradition. Perhaps young educators have not read *The Sabre-Tooth Curriculum,* [32] but its tongue-in-cheek descriptions of curriculum point out commonplace absurdities in many educational practices. Practices that were sound for a particular time, place, and group often are immortalized in policy or tradition and are followed without question even though original purposes have been lost, commonplaceness has destroyed their usefulness, or they no longer meet any need. The question, "Why?" should be directed to any activity that is occurring; however, the following questions illustrate the value of the procedure.

How many teachers can state educational reasons for putting children in circles for reading instruction?

Why do people raise their hands when they want to speak in class?

What children are harmed when their parents have to sign a permission slip before they can go on a field trip?

What educational values could be gained if children carried their lunch money and paid at the lunchroom?

When do people in real-life situations go to the "potty?"

Why do we feel that teachers are more productive when they have a class of children all day long?

Why does the lunch count come to the principal or even the principal's office?

Why does a child have to "do problems" he can already do?

Why do people on the phone take precedence over people in the office?

Why does a classroom have to be the teacher's office?

Why does an "open house" have to be so ritualized?

Why does the principal have to know about [whatever]?

Why are central office personnel more important than teachers or students?

Why do we give more status to people who are supposed to be helping the teacher than to teachers themselves?

Why should people not ask, "Why?" before they do something?

Precept 4: *Always consult original sources about decisions that limit you.* If someone says that policy prohibits some action that is desired, insist upon reading the policy. If necessary, go to the people who formulated the policy to determine if the interpretation that is being made is an accurate one. In most instances, no policy exists; no one has read it for a long time; or the interpretation is far afield from what was originally intended. Third-party interpretations of any decision are much more likely to be stringent and limiting than the originator ever intended. Even if the intent is as limiting as has been stated, it is wise to inform the decision maker of its impact. Your information may be sufficient to bring about a modification. Without that information, decision makers can hardly be faulted for making poor decisions. In any event, it is a wise dictum never to accept another person's interpretation of what policy is. In all cases, it is a mark of leadership to recognize that you have as much intelligence to interpret a policy as anyone else; therefore, your interpretations are as likely to be legitimate as any. A few examples may show what can be gained from practicing this precept:

A teacher, told by her principal that the fire marshall would not permit the use of the hallway as a learning place, went to the state fire marshall and was told that "What is permitted is determined by what the principal will defend educationally."

A principal who wondered why everyone was plagued with lunch counts and money instituted a plan to make the lunch line as much like a restaurant as possible, eliminated counting money in classrooms, and reduced the lunch count time to less than a minute.

A principal who questioned submitting requisitions through a complicated series of offices triggered an overhaul of the supply system that saved the district money and reduced the amount of time between ordering and delivery to one-third the former time.

Teachers who protested a rule against children playing with snow were able to design a new playground structure and a new set of rules that reduced the number of discipline problems on snowy days to a negligible figure.

Applying the four precepts will not relieve the principal of drudgery, frustration, or criticism. However, daily efforts to use them should increase the sense that many things are possible, the exhilaration of taking control of ones own destiny, and feelings of accomplishing something important. Those are the things of which leadership is made.

POSTSCRIPT

The fate of the principalship rests in the performance of principals. By their daily operations, those executives will either enhance the principalship or diminish it. People carve out roles from the reality they see. Much has been done in the past two decades to develop a corps of educators more able to describe what *is* than to see what *ought* to be, or what is possible in education. Minds trained to examine what *is* are blinded to the importance of relatively intangible forces and difficult-to-measure interrelationships that make it possible to understand learning processes. Such minds can be obsessed with the purely mechanical, the easily measurable, the lifeless elements of life and learning. They can easily believe that what currently exists *ought to be* or has to be. Such blindness is pseudoscience, of course, but it passes for wisdom when the trappings of science are substituted for insights and intuitions that are possible only when scientists recognize and account for their own limitations. Paul Torrance once compared creativity with intelligence by saying that an intelligent person challenged to improve the whale oil lamp would improve the design of the lamp, improve the efficiency with which the lamp consumed oil, and brighten the light from the wick; the creative person would invent the electric light. We need educators who see potential for electric lights in what appears to be an oily and sooty problem.

The major barriers to leadership come from within; consequently, the major way to help anyone become a leader is to enable him or her to discover and to practice ways of expressing latent potentials. To the degree that training, selection, and assignment procedures open new perspectives, promote problem solving, and encourage initiative, those procedures will facilitate leadership. Too many principals and too many of their tutors are damning "reality" when they should be actively engaged in improving the view.

NOTES

1. Donald A. Myers, "The Chautauqua Papers: A Dissent," *National Elementary Principal,* 54 (September-October 1974), 19.

2. William Stringfellow, "The Demonic in American Society," *Christianity and Crisis*, 29 (September 29, 1969), 247.

3. Carl G. Jung, *The Undiscovered Self* (New York: Mentor Books, New American Library, 1959), 19-20.

4. *Ibid.*, 20.

5. *Ibid.*, 21-22.

6. *Ibid.*, 26.

7. *Ibid.*, 72.

8. See Luvern L. Cunningham, Walter G. Hack, and Raphael O. Nystrand, eds., *Educational Administration: The Developing Decades* (Berkeley, Calif.: McCutchan Publishing Corporation, 1977).

9. William W. Wayson, "Will the Elementary Principalship Be Part of the New Administration?" *National Elementary Principal*, 44 (April 1965), 10-15.

10. Nicholas Murray Butler, "What Knowledge Is of Most Worth?" in *The Meaning of Education and Other Essays and Addresses* (New York: Macmillan, 1898). See also Andrew Halpin, "The Development of Theory in Educational Administration," in *Administrative Theory in Education*, ed. *id.* (Chicago: Midwest Administration Center, University of Chicago, 1958), 9-16; *id.* "Ways of Knowing," in *Administrative Theory as a Guide to Action*, ed. Roald F. Campbell and James M. Lipham (Chicago: Midwest Administration Center, University of Chicago, 1960), 3-20. See also Jung, *Undiscovered Self.*

11. Lawrence A. Cremin, *The Transformation of the School* (New York: Vintage Books, 1964), chap. 2. See also Raymond Callahan, *Education and the Cult of Efficiency* (Chicago: University of Chicago Press, 1962).

12. See Samuel Goldman, *The School Principal* (New York: Center for Applied Research in Education, 1966).

13. Joseph Cronin, "School Board and Principals—Before and After Negotiations," *Phi Delta Kappan*, 49 (November 1967), 124. See also Jesse B. Sears, *City School Administrative Controls* (New York: McGraw-Hill Book Company, 1938), 47, 117-120.

14. Paul Berman and Milbrey McLaughlin, *Federal Programs Supporting Educational Change*. Volume IV, *The Findings in Review* (Santa Monica, Calif.: Rand Corporation, April 1975), 20.

15. Ford Foundation, *A Foundation Goes to School: The Ford Foundation Comprehensive School Improvement Program, 1960-70* (New York: the foundation, November 1972). See also Chapters 1 and 3 in this book; Gerald Becker *et al.*, *Elementary Principals and Their Schools* (Eugene, Ore.: Center for the Advanced Study of Educational Administration, University of Oregon, 1971); William Wayson, "The New Principal," *National Elementary Principal*, 51 (February 1971), 8-19.

16. Harold McNally, "Summing Up," *National Elementary Principal*, 54 (September-October 1974), 6-15.

17. William Wayson, "Misconceptions about Leadership," *National Elementary Principal*, 55 (November-December 1975), 12-17.

18. Jacob Getzels, James Lipham, and Roald Campbell, eds., *Educational Administration as a Social Process* (New York: Harper and Row, 1968), reviews many studies. See also Neal Gross and Robert E. Herriott, *Staff Leadership in Public Schools* (New York: John Wiley and Sons, 1965).

19. Getzels, Lipham, and Campbell, *Educational Administration as a Social Process*. For an excellent analysis of training programs and their impact upon leadership, see Edwin M. Bridges, "The Nature of Leadership: 1954-1974," *Educational Administration*, ed. Cunningham, Hack, and Nystrand.

20. Gross and Herriott, *Staff Leadership in the Public Schools*. If these studies are read carefully, they support the variability cited in the text.

21. George T. Land, *Grow or Die: A Unifying Principle of Transformation* (New York: Random House, 1973); Milton Cudney, *Eliminating Self-Defeating Behaviors* (Kalamazoo, Mich.: Life Giving Enterprises, Inc., 1975).

22. Egon Guba, "Research in Internal Administration — What Do We Know?" in *Administrative Theory*, ed. Campbell and Lipham, 113-130.

23. This discussion is expanded in William Wayson, "Six Ideas That Keep Principals from Leading," *National Elementary Principal*, 55 (November 1975).

24. Lawrence Cremin, *The Genius of American Education* (New York: Vintage Books, 1965), 112.

25. Discussed more thoroughly in Wayson, "Six Ideas That Keep Principals from Leading."

26. Roland Barth, "Is There a Way Out?" *National Elementary Principal*, 54 (March-April 1974), 12-18. See also Becker *et al., Elementary Principals and Their Schools;* Wayson, "New Principal"; and *id.,* "Organizing Urban Schools for Responsible Education," *Phi Delta Kappan*, 52 (February 1971), 344-347.

27. Samuel M. Goldman, *The Principal's Leadership Role: Practice vs. Preference* (Rockville, Md.: Department of Research of the Montgomery County Public Schools, 1976), presents a detailed analysis of principals' activities that incorporates a large number of activities in a category labeled "management," but the breakdown supports the point being made here.

28. Andrew Halpin, "The Leader Behavior and Leadership Ideology of Educational Administrators and Aircraft Commanders," *Harvard Educational Review*, 25 (Winter 1955), 18-32.

29. Myers, "The Chautauqua Papers," 20.

30. For example, see the Chautauqua Series of the *National Elementary Principal*, 53 and 54 (March-April through September-October 1974). See also Wayson, "Organizing Urban Schools for Responsbile Education"; and *id.,* "Education for Renewal in Urban Communities," *National Elementary Principal*, 52 (April 1972), 6-18.

31. The idea is discussed in more detail in William Wayson, "A Proposal to Remake the Principalship," *ibid.,* 54 (September-October 1974), 33-34.

32. J. A. Peddiwell, *The Sabre-Tooth Curriculum* (New York: McGraw-Hill Book Company, 1939).

Chapter Five

James G. Cibulka

Creating a New Era for
Schools and Communities

Of the many social forces that have reshaped the role of urban school principals, the community revolution, as it is sometimes called, has been one of the most important. Emphasis on the community dimensions of the urban principal's role assumed a sudden importance at the height of the social ferment of the 1960's. Numerous journal and magazine articles, in-service sessions, and convention speeches were devoted to urging prinicipals to involve themselves with their neighborhood communities.[1] Such messages reached the platitudinous stage, a sure sign that principals stopped really listening.

More recently, as social unrest has subsided, and as communities no longer threaten the job security of as many principals, the relationship between school and community has returned to its earlier place as one of the least emphasized aspects of the urban principal's role.

This declining emphasis on school-community relations by many (but by no means all) school principals is unfortunate, for the development of effective school-community relations is likely to remain an important aspect of their role in coming years. For one thing, the local community has emerged as a new decision-making arena; local residents are playing a greater role in the governance of our schools through local school boards and advisory councils, a task previously left to professionals and a central board of education. Another change in recent years has been the increasing emphasis on utilizing community resources and problems in the curriculum and instruction process, the use of parent and community volunteers, the hiring of paraprofessionals, and the moving of learning into the community. Also, public expectations for the public schools are greater and more complex than ever before, a by-product of numerous changes in our society. It requires considerable skill for a principal to define those expectations accurately, to tailor educational programs responsive to those expectations, and to build and maintain community support. Similarly, racial, ethnic, and class conflicts continue to have important effects upon our schools; successful desegregation of our urban schools, for example, will remain an important leadership challenge for principals.

But to acknowledge the importance of school-community relations is far easier than practicing it. In these pages we address some of the major concerns that trouble school principals who are attempting to be more responsive to their school-communities. We will focus particularly on the political governance questions which the community revolution implies for the principal's role.

In my conversations with school principals on this subject, I find them raising recurrent questions:

What does community mean?

Will community involvement make schools more parochial?

Will community involvement lead to politics and abuses of power by community leaders?

What is the school principal's role in relating to the community, and how does this role differ in various contexts?

What forms can community involvement take?

How can the principal determine the members of the local community?

Is it possible to be accountable to the community and to the school system simultaneously?

These questions are taken up in turn below and provide the organizational framework for the chapter.

THE MEANING OF COMMUNITY

Many principals resist the concept of community involvement because they say there is no consensus about what the community is or what its relationship to the school ought to be. We can better understand why public school educators today find community involvement problematic if we sketch at the start some of the major historic forces

that have shaped the schoolman's concept of community. These ante-
cedents explain some of the cardinal precepts of the profession of educational administration and do much to explain prevailing attitudes.

The community ideal of the American public school probably dates
back to educational and political Progressivism. This social movement, which flourished between roughly 1917 and 1957, influenced
many of the essential features of today's schools. The Progressives were
middle-class reformers who removed control of public schools from
corrupt ward politics [2] by replacing the power of political machines
with the power of professional standards. They also weakened the
neighborhood orientation of boards of education by reducing the
number of members, recruiting civic leaders to the boards, and turning the role of the boards from administration to policy making.

American public education was to serve the needs of the community
broadly defined — cities as metropolitan centers of commerce and culture, states as important sovereignties, and the nation as the embodi-
ment of constitutional principles. The Progressives sought to erect a
public authority defended by cooperative, deliberating, rational people whose obligation was primarily to principles — equality of opportunity (or merit by achievement), compromise, freedom of choice,
progress, and the brotherhood of man — rather than to individuals. To
the extent that people constituted a community, they were to be
bound to one another on the basis of reasonable choices. It was to be
what Morris Janowitz has called a community of limited liability, governed by shared taste, specific needs, or common interests. People's
obligations to one another were not to depend on place of birth, national origin, race, sex, or any other ascribed trait. [3]

This search for the "Great Community," as John Dewey referred to
it, thrust upon the public schools the overwhelming responsibility for
creating a new national character. Whatever their past practices, public school educators were asked to intrude in the sphere of private relations in order to construct the kind of personal loyalties that would
support the public good. [4]

Dewey's approach to the public interest, as Richard Hofstadter has
remarked, was essentially sociopsychological rather than political. [5] He
epitomized the Progressive faith in education as the primary instrument for political reform, rather than in political institutions to help
citizens iron out their differences. American public education, while
sometimes accused of a lack of vision by critics, has been all too uto-
pian in some of its precepts.

What was equally important, Dewey and other Progressives saw in the role of communication an instrument vital to the public interest. Dissemination of information was to be used to create social consensus, or at least to eliminate social conflicts. In accord with their positivist faith in a rational, ordered universe, Progressives believed that experts — educators, scientists, and others — possess knowledge and judgment that represent truth and that they are obliged to convey this to the public. This left little room for laypeople to question experts or their knowledge.

At the same time that Progressives such as Dewey sought to create a uniform public culture through the schools, they remained strikingly ambivalent about the effect of technology, organization, and urbanization on the search for community. They saw in contemporary American cities a violation of many of their aspirations toward an "inclusive and fraternally associated public."[6] Dewey admired the immediate community of primary groups and believed that only in a neighborhood setting would it be possible to secure face-to-face communication, and, through it, "the diffused and seminal intelligence" that he sought.[7]

Out of a faith in the local community as an enterprise upon which to reconstruct a just social order, Dewey and other Progressives supported the ideal of the community school. In theory, at least, the neighborhood school was to be a social and recreational center for youth and adults, and the curriculum was to create an embryonic community within which the child would experience social awareness and acquire a sense of civic duty.

For Progressives, then, the commitment to community ran in two different directions. One path led to what Herbert Croly, the famous Progressive, called the national idea. It implied the eclipse of local affiliations in favor of a world community of universal brotherhood among men. Yet other Progressives embraced localism as a protection against the urbanization and nationalization of American life.

It is hard to imagine how this social theory could have had a more profound impact on the operation of American public schools. Progressive ideals, with all their attendant ambiguities and contradictions, served as the frame of reference for several generations of teachers and administrators socialized in teachers' colleges and graduate schools of education. Consequently, the operating culture of the schools — their decision structures, rules, procedures, and modes of interaction with the public — were imbued with the same social theory. It is this heritage that explains why many school administrators endorse the neighborhood school, yet frequently find themselves at odds with community groups whose platforms they find too parochial and self-ish. It explains the impulse away from ethnicity and pluralistic values and toward centralization and uniformity, which better serve the broader community and the business ideal of efficiency.[8] It explains why school professionals are preoccupied with communicating information to the public and searching for consensus at the same time that they have difficulty in accepting and coping with criticism and conflict as a legitimate form of expression in school government. It explains enthusiasm among many professionals for the PTA, which exemplifies government by discussion under professional guidance. It explains the tendency to protect the supposed neutrality of the expert and to guard jealously the public interest, even if such a stance yields diminishing returns by increasing community conflict.

It is important to remember this intellectual legacy when examining the realities of school-community relations today. Do the Progressive formulas, whatever relevance they may have had for another era, speak of today's social problems? These solutions were devised to miti-gate two perceived dangers. First, we have said, Progressives and the school reformers among them, were concerned about the privatizing and localizing of social relations; they sought to create a national cul-ture out of the diverse American nation. Second, they feared the poli-tical corruption and tyranny they associated with city and neighbor-hood politics, where self-interest and small factions ostensibly could frustrate the public interest.

Many school principals continue to voice these fears today. Certain-ly each of these perceived problems deserves careful consideration if school principals are to be brought closer to their communities.

THE DANGER OF PAROCHIALISM

Does making schools more community oriented necessarily make them more parochial if, by that word, we mean more opposed to change and resistant to broader societal influences? While there are clear dangers, the main thrust of the community revolution is actually to expand the citizen's role in public education, to make both profes-sionals and citizens more aware of one another's needs, and to give both a stake in making the schools succeed.

Merely drawing citizens into the educational decision-making pro-cess does not guarantee that they will shed their parochialism, but the complex nature of the governance process may well have that effect. It is inconceivable that local communities could achieve anything like the autonomy and power that was enjoyed a hundred years ago. The national economy and national culture have grown too pervasive, the communications media too influential, and state and federal governments too strong for all of this to reverse itself. An interdependence between local communities and broader institutions is inevitable. What we are moving toward, then, are not self-sufficient, Balkanized neighborhood communities, but, instead, a more democratic federalism with another layer of the political community created to empower more participants.

Lack of self-sufficiency is no basis for ignoring local communities as important components of a governance system. The interdependence of communities is a world-wide phenomenon. Cities increasingly look to states and the federal government for assistance, states look to the nation, small nations look to large ones, and even large ones to the small. Many technological forces have brought about this state of mutual dependence, and the need to develop governmental systems to cope with the growing interpenetration of communities is becoming apparent. Interdependence works in both directions. Efforts to revitalize local communities create social networks and power relationships that limit the abuses of centralized public and private power. In turn, the mere existence of powerful national forces provides a check on the parochial, elitist trends of localism.

That the search for a more effective structural pluralism in American society will not lead to the disintegration of national values can be illustrated by the character of ethnicity in American life. Milton Gordon explains that, while ethnic group identities have persisted, they have not done so at the expense of common values and beliefs central to the American character.[9] Just as cultural pluralism gave way to structural pluralism in ethnic affairs, the strengthening of structural pluralism through neighborhood units will not lead us back to a cultural pluralism that reverses national identities.

There are, of course, differences in the amount of autonomy and responsibility implied for local communities in different reform platforms. Decentralization offers greater protections against parochialism than pure community control models. For example, schemes to decentralize large-city school systems administratively and politically give local principals and the citizens in their communities primary but not exclusive authority. Other prerogatives are retained by a central bureaucracy and board. Thus, the local community is only one of several communities that interplay as the public interest emerges. Such decentralized arrangements now operate in New York City and Detroit, and, to a lesser degree, in cities such as Chicago and Los Angeles. The more extreme case of community control cannot be found in metropolitan areas at this time, for this would mean that local communities had exclusive governance rights. Even there, however, state and national influences would predominate because equitable funding bases would have to come from higher governmental levels. Also, the increase of black, Latin, and other minority officials in city-wide, state, and national positions will create a counterforce to demands for extreme decentralization. In fact, as American cities become increasingly dominated by nonwhite constituencies, local political leaders are less likely to support extreme community control, preferring, instead, to build a city-wide power base.

COMMUNITY POLITICS AND ABUSES OF POWER

School principals sometimes point out that community involvement makes the schools more political because it allegedly allows community leaders or politicians to dominate the schools. Professionalism, it is said, guarantees that experts capable of making objective decisions will protect the public interest. This mind-set began — to return to our theme — with the effort of Progressives to give superintendents many of the powers once exercised by boards of education and with their effort to purge schools of graft and other political influences.

Yet community involvement today is quite different from the neighborhood politics of a hundred years ago when urban political machines used the schools to pyramid political resources (jobs, contracts, special programs, etc.) and left the citizen dependent on politicians for favors and benefits. Today the citizen is at the center of efforts to change the direction of the schools. One example of the difference between the "friends and neighbors politics" of the old machines and the community movement today is the current emphasis on debate and conflict resolution through advisory councils. These governments in miniature have a rationalist imperative; whereas the citizen in the prereform era had no responsible role and was only a recipient of government services, postreform politics seeks to allow the citizen to be active and involved alongside professionals.

While politicians may not dominate community involvement today, some educators are still concerned that this trend will politicize decision making. Yet it must be remembered that all complex social organization is in a sense political. Individuals seek status, money, influence, power, knowledge, and other benefits, all of which are in short supply. This axiom applies equally to lay people and professionals, to communities and bureaucracies. The image of school professionals making completely objective and informed decisions is a myth. Both community leaders and professionals must exercise calculations of self-interest, and some among them will inevitably use their positions for advancement and gain. Within each group some individuals will be more prone than others to balance self-interest with altruism. To search for and demand purity of motive is a misplaced pursuit.

While community involvement need not introduce decision making by pressures and favors, it *should* add a new political dimension to schools that has been missing. The sharing of information, influence, power, and authority between professionals and laypeople is an inherently political process because it entails open deliberation and mutual effort. Its aim is the development of political trust as the cornerstone of public authority rather than mere obedience. Educators frequently have espoused this vision of democracy and conveyed it to their students in the classroom, but administrators have unfortunately been less inclined to incorporate this model into the governance of our schools.

Like their intellectual forebears, public school professionals have confused the search for an educational community with the need for a political community. We have traced this confusion to Progressives like John Dewey, who saw the expert as the key to establishing communication among laymen so that they would grow in "the method of intelligence." In his eyes there was no public concerned with the execution of social policy; instead, it was the expert's obligation to shape public opinion and to create a new civic morality.[10]

One problem with this view is the way it shades into a kind of elitism. Without the political machinery needed to allow community constituents to express their views, principals are inclined to attempt to mold a community interest in line with their own expectations. Moreover, the pervasive fear of minority factions among school administrators has made them ill-equipped to regulate community conflict and sometimes has inclined them to dismiss serious community grievances.

Another elitist impulse is inherent in this view that school-community interaction is no more than a matter of communication. Many educators believe that a parent or community participant should speak only for herself or himself, not for a group or constituency. This attempt to cleanse involvement of political overtones has left educators without any theory of public representation. Yet there is no way to involve the community effectively in decision making without some attempts to introduce representation into the process.

As long as educators continue to bypass the political process in education and attempt to convert it to a method of public education, they will find it hard to work well with communities. Administrators have asked too much of themselves, and misunderstood their proper mission, by interpreting their role as the personal guardians of the public interest.

THE PRINCIPAL'S ROLE IN RELATING TO THE COMMUNITY

Students of school administration, and practitioners as well, have traditionally viewed the activities of the school from a managerial rather than a political perspective, as if the functions of government are carried out at higher levels of the system. While educators rarely have seen schools as a part of the political community, we have suggested above that the schools inevitably fulfill this role. The most obvious illustration is the school's role in orienting children and youth to political life. Yet it is also true that the school is a political community in its relation to parents and other adults in the community. The local school must perform many of the same governance tasks which boards of education and central office administrators do, except in a different context. While the school does not obtain tax resources, it does have significant discretion in the allocation and deployment of resources. Similarly, school principals are increasingly accountable for evaluating the educational programs and services provided to the public. Also, schools must build public support in order to govern effectively . On the reverse side of this support function, the achievement of sufficient consensus to function well requires the ability to regulate competing values and interests within each community and to resolve disagreements and conflicts that might emerge from time to time. Each of these tasks—resource allocation, public accountability, development of support, and conflict management—is an important function of government in which the individual school shares. Insofar as a school principal must carry out political responsibilities, the principal acts as a political agent in the local community.

It is important to recognize, then, that many dimensions of the principalship are inseparable from issues of government. Consequently, the way a principal fulfills these governmental responsibilities cannot be determined by the dictates of personal preference and style. On the contrary, the same performance expectations that apply to other governmental institutions apply here. We expect elected government officials to seek out the opinions of their constituents and to respond to them whenever possible. When they are in disagreement, we demand an explanation, and if disagreement with the public's wishes is habitual, we normally question how well these officials represent us. Also, we expect to be kept informed by government officials of the problems which they are confronting and their approach to resolving these issues. Recently the public has come to have these same expectations for the schools and is unwilling to accept the once sacred assumption that schools are somehow separate from the realities of political life. Individual schools are undeniably an important link in the chain of educational governance and, therefore, subject to the same pressures.

In addition, the expectations by today's public that its government officials will be responsive is part of a fundamental shift in the way authority has come to be viewed in American society. Because of the acceleration of social and cultural changes in recent years, tradition is no longer the unchallenged foundation of public authority. And because of the many abuses of public trust by government officials, typified by the war in Vietnam and the scandals of Watergate, respect for expertise has been shaken as well. Public demands for responsiveness signify, at least for the immediate future, some basic shifts in the way government, including schools, will have to operate in a democratic society.

Apart from this reality, there are other compelling arguments for a principal to develop a leadership posture of responsiveness. The latter epitomizes personal rather than coercive authority. The problem with coercive authority, quite apart from philosophical conflicts it raises with democratic traditions of governance, is that coercion is the most alienating kind of power. Amitai Etzioni argues that there is a trade-off between control and consensus; the greater the consensus the less the need for control. But where consensus is imposed by coercive control, it increases resistance and lessens the capacity to act; this Etzioni refers to as an overly managed society or institution.[11] The alternative strategy of relying on personal authority has the advantage that controls may be imposed without resistance because the level of public trust is high. This, in turn, allows for a high level of activity by a principal.

The problem of how to act responsively to the community carries with it a host of philosophical and strategic dilemmas, of course. One of these (dealt with later) is that the demands on the part of one's administrative superiors, including the board of education, may conflict with responsiveness to the community. Another is that the community may not always be of a clear mind, or of one mind, about what it wants. Or what it wants may contradict the professional vision of the principal. Indeed, the community may have little immediate inclination to become involved for reasons of low self-confidence, a sense of powerlessness, indifference or apathy, or whatever. In such situations it is necessary to draw on another source of authority for the principalship, that of educator.

Much space has been devoted in these pages to critiquing the tendency of school administrators to interpret school-community relations as a strictly educational process, so it may seem odd to emphasize here the relevance of this perspective. Yet we wish to argue also that it would be equally mistaken for the principal to view himself or herself as a mere agent of the community's will; such formulas, we suggest, would wrongly absolve the principal of the obligation to exercise leadership in the community.

Where parents and other residents do not fully understand how to become involved in the school and how to assume a position of influence, it is the principal's responsibility to develop a leadership-training program and to initiate other efforts to close the gap between the school and the community. It is also the role of the principal to inform the community of educational problems and needs and to enlist its assistance in school improvement. It is the principal's role to build bridges between the faculty of a school and the members of the community. Equally important, the principal should engage the school in addressing the problems of the community that directly or indirectly affect education. While the school cannot solve all problems, it can demonstrate its commitment to work with residents to improve the community. In this regard, a school principal can help a community develop an understanding of how to improve the health of a neighborhood. According to Margaret Mead, a primary aim of the neighborhood is to offer a child the opportunity to develop trust, confidence, and autonomy so that he is able to bear the strange, the unknown, and the peculiar.[12] The ability to endure change and to prize diversity requires a definition of community which extends beyond the spatial boundaries of the typical American neighborhood. Thus, while a principal works within a community and is responsive to its immediate needs, he must also have the vision to test the boundaries of that community

And undeniably there is a tension in the exercise of the principal's political role as against his or her educational role. Perhaps the single greatest challenge in the principalship is to find a balance between these sometimes competing requirements, to somehow match a posture of receptivity and responsiveness to the community with an inclination to pose new problems and to engage the community in developing solutions. It is this juxtaposition of responsiveness and leadership that sets school administration apart from professions such as law, medicine, and even the ministry, for while the latter all serve and lead, none of these but our own serves an explicitly public function and is so closely tied to the political community. The principalship has embodied within it an alliance of these two great ideas of democratic government, but to find the common ground where they meet requires great skill and commitment.

ROLE DIFFERENCES IN VARIOUS COMMUNITIES

The principal's leadership role will take on different configurations, depending on the community setting of the school. To be an effective leader, the principal must have different goals depending on the community and must be prepared to respond to different expectations and problems. For the sake of illustration, we examine below six different types of community, each of which poses distinct challenges. In practice, there is much greater variety among communities, and we can only highlight some of the major considerations for a principal working in each context.

White ethnic working-class communities have traditionally had a high level of organization, and, until recently, the members have been deferential toward professional people and institutions. With the awakening of the "new ethnicity" in many of these communities, however, principals are encountering increased hostility toward the public schools. One challenge in these situations is to help the community become aware of the quality of educational programming rather than confining concern to building issues such as new paint for the halls, repairs to the boiler, and similar problems. The racial issue has also emerged as a major undercurrent in many ethnic communities, along with attempts to assert "traditional" American values. As educational advocates, principals must help their communities cope with social change and help find ways to steer that change in directions that are not reactionary and racist. The quality of educational leadership in such communities is crucial.

The racial issue is also very much a problem for *upper-middle-class city or suburban communities*. It tends to be less obvious, though, because the prospect of racial change in wealthier communities is not usually imminent. This gives principals the opportunity to address problems of race and inequality without arousing as emotional a reaction as might be encountered in another kind of community. The issue of greater immediate concern is the quality of the educational programs. Where urban programs do not compare favorably with suburban ones, the residents may flee to the suburbs. In part, then, the principal's role is to make educational programs attractive enough by drawing upon the resources of the city so that residents will remain in the city. In affluent suburban communities, the principal as educational advocate should seek to break down barriers artificially erected between suburbs and cities, cultivating an appreciation of heterogeneity as a counterweight to the self-imposed homogeneity of many suburbs.

In *unorganized poorer communities* the principal ordinarily confronts an organizational network dominated by professional service organizations rather than by viable indigenous organizations. The principal's role should be to build leadership in the community capable of making not only the public schools but also other institutions accountable to the community and to break down as many of the barriers as possible between school and residents so that, with encouragement, residents will begin to take a greater interest in the school. There is a need in such communities for the school to become a symbol of the neighborhood's aspirations for its children rather than a reminder of the community's failures. Since the community is not always vocal, the principal must seek to determine the community's wishes, act as its advocate within the school system itself, and take the initiative in restructuring the school to make it more responsive. At the same time there should be an attempt to build a leadership base that will advocate for itself.

As in other upper-middle-class and ethnic communities, the advocacy role of the principal in *organized poorer communities* is not so much to generate leadership as to respond to this leadership and to help give it direction. As educational advocates principals can help the community become aware of various options for increasing self-determination. The principal might operate as a consultant, investigating and proposing numerous programmatic options for putting into action the community's mandate. As in other communities, the principal should also point out unmet needs and unrecognized problems. Since organized poor communities tend to be most suspicious of the traditional role of the expert, it is important that the principal raise these issues in as nonthreatening a fashion as possible.

The efforts of school officials have usually had their most disastrous effects in the *racially changing communities.* As political agents they often have been unable to act effectively in a divided community because they have usually served as advocates for the traditional white culture rather than attempting to restructure the school to accommodate a changing, diverse population. Faculty attitudes constitute another obstacle, and principals must find ways to create enough positive incentives for the faculty to accept change or to guide pressure from the community to create such incentives. If the community should experience racial or economic imbalance in spite of efforts to accommodate each constituent element, then the principal plays a crucial role in preventing the school from sliding into a poor self-image. Principals must be more than key innovators. They must be public relations and human relations experts able to keep channels of communication open and able to calm tensions among the various antagonists.

The setting in *noncontiguous desegregated communities,* the last of the types to be sketched, provides scarcely less of a challenge than that in the racially changing one. During the initial phase of desegregation through the use of busing, a principal must find ways to involve both the receiving and sending communities in achieving peaceful social change. A basic aim is to create a common purpose among students and adults who may have had no previous contact with each other and who are likely to harbor strong stereotypes of each other. In this setting, too, the principal must find ways to help teachers and other administrators respond to changing student populations and new parental expectations. While the desegregation process undoubtedly taxes the school's resources enormously, the process poses rare opportunities for a principal to initiate innovative programming and to encourage cooperative planning among parents, students, and the community.

These represent just a few of the problems a principal faces in such communities, for each community varies in subtle ways. Heretofore principals have had little training in determining the strengths and weaknesses of a community, apart from immediate school issues. If principals are to be educational advocates concerned with the community, it is necessary to bring new analytical insights to the task. They must know how to assess such factors as the demographic make-up of a community, its patterns of social interaction, the degree of identification residents have with the community, ties between the community and other communities and institutions, as well as many other factors that influence educational needs and public expectations. Unfortunately, these skills have rarely been emphasized in principalship-preparation programs and may have to be acquired independently by a principal.

FORMS OF COMMUNITY INVOLVEMENT

There are at least six different avenues that community involvement at the school level can take. No one of these dimensions alone will constitute an adequate program for promoting school-community relations. In fact, each of the options outlined below provides a unique asset unavailable in the others, so that the more of these options that are utilized effectively, the more we might describe a school as a community-oriented institution. Of course, they should be structured and combined with the needs and preferences of the local community in mind rather than imposed rigidly from above.

Perhaps the most common attempt by school principals to involve the local community is through a program of *public information*. They prepare newsletters and schedule open houses. Sometimes they schedule speaking engagements with community and civic organizations. Where possible, they obtain cooperative ties with newspapers and the electronic media. The purpose of a good public information program is not merely to dispense positive information about the school but also to be candid about the problems and needs of the school. Moreover, information should be viewed not as a way to quiet and placate the public but, instead, to engage it in giving more honest feedback to the school and more participation. Public information is, in other words, the ground floor for greater involvement.

One of the most potentially significant innovations in many school systems has been the creation of *decision-making structures* such as regional school boards and local school councils. While many of these have been locally initiated, a variety of federal educational programs also require local structures, usually of an advisory nature. While the specific responsibilities and authority of these structures vary widely, their broad purpose is to give each local community influence over the policies and operations of schools. Within this wide mandate, such structures serve a number of other related functions. They are a mechanism for articulating community preferences and needs, so that the school's programs and instruction can fit these expectations more clearly. They are also channels for communicating information about the school to the community and thereby building community interest and support. Finally, they are a way by which school personnel and community can share responsibility for the educational process, so that the school is more accountable to those it serves and the community feels more committed to the school.

There are varied options for structuring and relating to these councils and boards; here we cite only some of the important considerations. The composition of the council should approximate the demographic characteristics of the community served by the school; a later section pertaining to the membership of the local community will address this more fully. The council should have democratic means for selecting its members, whether by election, nomination by local organizations, or whatever. Terms of office should be limited to assure the opportunity for changes in membership. The council or board should have written bylaws and operate according to democratic and open procedures. It should have multiple mechanisms for reporting back to the community so that members remain accountable to those they represent and so that members remain in touch with community sentiments. The council should have regular access to information about the school and should be able to meet periodically with administrators or members of the school board who are in a position to affect policy and operational changes. In some systems local councils relate to intermediate structures such as regional or community district boards or councils. In order to integrate various decision levels, overlapping membership might be considered.

One of the advantages of localizing decision making is that it becomes easier for citizens to translate their views into policy when they grow dissatisfied. The size of the body politic is small enough in the neighborhood community so that each person's complaints and concerns can be heard, and fewer organizational resources are necessary to effect change. Many citizen concerns in suburban school districts are handled at the local school level, although sometimes through informal means rather than by formal decision structures.[13]

It bears emphasis that these councils and boards are a means for sharing authority and influence with the community. Some administrators mistakenly view them as devices to co-opt the community and deflect responsibility away from the professional. Such Machiavellian tactics can only erode public trust of professionals and ultimately have a destructive impact on school-community relations.

Programmatic involvement is another way to involve the local community where the goal is to utilize parents and other community resources in the instructional process. One way is to bring parents and other interested citizens into the classroom. This strategy has important benefits. As parents become more involved and supportive, this can improve their children's motivation and achievement. Also, as teachers interact informally with parents, they may become more appreciative of parental values and community strengths. Without proper leadership from the principal, though, the interaction can reinforce stereotypes that parents and teachers have of one another. It takes time and effort to build an atmosphere of trust and respect once channels of communication are opened.

Two common methods for programmatic involvement are volunteer programs and the development of paraprofessional roles such as classroom assistants and community aides. The use of paraprofessionals will be discussed more fully in a later section.

Another approach to involvement is by *community education.* It has evolved in two major ways. One view of community education is that the school exists to serve community needs, typified by lighted schoolhouse and community schools programs. The other view of community education is that the school should build community resources into the curriculum through community learning programs that assign students to museums, businesses, government, and elsewhere. Occasionally, local neighborhood institutions and problems are the objects of study, although generally the broader community is the focal point of attention.

Both approaches can lead to major innovations in the character and quality of a school's programs, depending on their degree of acceptance by a school principal and by the school's faculty. Community schools programs normally involve the assignment of a faculty member or a community paraprofessional to develop after-school, evening, and weekend programs for all age groups. Properly implemented, community education programs bring various groups in the community into closer contact with the faculty through shared teaching-learning experiences. And the school comes to be seen as a community institution rather than an alien place because it addresses community problems and needs and reaches out to the community. The dividends for the school include greater support from tax levies, reduced school-community conflict, diminished vandalism to school property, and improved student achievement, to name only some. Community learning programs permit more flexible scheduling, increase public understanding of the role of the school, permit curricular innovation, and improve student motivation.

Such programs require strong administrative leadership. The principal must exercise community development skills by helping the community identify and address neighborhood problems, by strengthening its capacity for cooperative activity and effective community organization. In this community development capacity, the principal does not impose a prophetic vision on the community; instead, he or she works with the community as a facilitator and a partner.[14] If necessary, the principal must be prepared to speak as an advocate for the community in dealings with the school system and with other institutions.

Community needs assessment and evaluation is an area where public schools are beginning to follow the lead of some other social service institutions. Community needs surveys and consumer preference surveys are common in many service agencies and adult education programs. Where these are conducted periodically, they provide an opportunity to reassess whether existing programs are comprehensive, accessible, relevant, or otherwise beneficial. These assessment processes also can be incorporated into the ongoing involvement of residents through planning committees, hearings, and the like.

Students, parents, and other residents can be involved not simply in identifying needs and preferences, but in evaluating existing programs, too. And evaluation should include opportunities to make suggestions for program improvement. Ideally, community involvement in needs assessment and evaluation can be coupled or coordinated so that students and parents have some explicit standards for evaluation. Of course, effective evaluation by community participants assumes that they have easy access to information about the school so that they can make informed judgments.

While planning and evaluation traditionally have been dominated by professionals, both areas provide great potential for community involvement. These processes can easily be manipulated by an administrator to ratify personal preferences; thus, the principal must be committed to the premise that potential criticism can be used constructively to improve a school and to improve the attitudes of students and residents toward the school. Unless there is a willingness to hear both the good and the bad, this kind of community participation becomes an empty gesture.

The providing of *curricular options* in a school is still another way to guarantee that the school honors various student and citizen preferences. Here we draw on the work of public choice theorists who have attempted to apply principles of the economic marketplace to the operation of government.[15] We emphasize here not so much choice to move among school districts, nor even among schools, but parental-student opportunity to choose among alternative programs within a school. Mario Fantini suggests how such choices might look to parents about to enroll their kindergarten child.[16] After discussing their child's personal characteristics with staff members and observing for themselves the differences among a traditional kindergarten, a more informal open classroom, and a Montessori approach, parents would select the room most appealing to them. The older the student, the greater the role in helping to select a program alternative. The introduction of greater choice in school programs is, then, one way to try to respond to the preferences of individuals in the community served by the school.

Still another way to tailor a local school to its neighborhood community is through the creation of *grievance and advocacy mechanisms* for resolving complaints and problems experienced by students, parents, and other interested persons. Many school systems provide no such procedural protection for individuals (other than those required by the courts for student suspension or expulsion). The difficulties of obtaining satisfaction or even fair consideration are compounded as a school system grows larger. Written procedures for resolving complaints should be developed and publicized broadly, and these procedures may vary for students, parents, and others in the community. The procedures need not take on a legalistic, adversarial tone, either; their primary aim is to resolve problems in a fair and equitable fashion.

Another way of addressing citizen concerns is through the creation of *ombudsman roles* within schools. An ombudsman's task is to help individuals resolve problems they are having and to advocate on their behalf. School-community representatives have sometimes been given this task, although their authority to hear and investigate complaints has rarely been acknowledged explicitly. The utilization of ombuds-men has been adapted from Scandinavian countries and affords the citizen more representation than the right to register a complaint; there is someone with investigatory powers and the right to speak on the individual's behalf. This innovation is almost unknown as yet in American school systems, but it has great potential as an avenue for responding to community concerns.

It is important to reemphasize that no one of these kinds of commu-nity involvement would, by itself, constitute a strong program of school-community interaction. If they are developed in consort, on the other hand, they can complement one another. Decision-making structures offer opportunities for formal representation of the com-munity, while programmatic involvement offers the community a role in the instructional process. Similarly, community education pro-grams relate the school's curriculum to the community and broaden its mission to serve the whole community. Needs assessment and eval-uation programs are devices for allowing the community to share in shaping educational programs and can dovetail with decision struc-tures. Grievance structures and advocacy roles add still another di-mension by seeking to resolve problems experienced by individuals. Finally, public information provides a necessary base upon which the success of all other components depends. It is the school principal's re-sponsibility, in cooperation with the board of education or administra-tive superiors, to devise a comprehensive strategy for community in-volvement.

IDENTIFYING THE LOCAL COMMUNITY AND ITS MEMBERS

Another concern for the principal is determining the boundaries of the school-community. This is not as simple as it might seem, for the physical boundaries of a school-community are not always cotermi-nous with those of the neighborhood surrounding the school. Indeed, the school sometimes serves a community only in the loosest sense of the word. Neither students nor residents may see the attendance area of the school as a single community. Certainly principals working in schools that have been desegregated by the use of noncontiguous at-tendance boundaries face this reality every day. Schools also often en-compass several neighborhoods where members are isolated from each other by barriers of age, class, race, or ethnic background. The prin-cipal soon learns that, although the institution may define the school-community in a particular way, this is frequently an external imposition, a mere abstraction with little resemblance to the way citizens define their community.

This difference between the institutional and the real community is magnified by a lack of coordination with other social service institutions. Education, recreation, health, housing, welfare — all use different boundaries that frustrate professionals and citizens alike.

One way of looking at the membership of the local community is to remember that the only *direct* consumers of the public schools are students. In many institutions consumers and clients are synonymous. This is not so in schools, where consumers are rarely legal adults; hence, parents act as clients on behalf of consumers. These consumers and clients deserve the most to say, at least at the local school level, about the choice of programs, the type of personnel, and related matters.

It is not correct to define teachers, social workers, or other professionals working in the community as primary constituents. Principals should resist the temptation to use professionals in a way that diminishes the power of local citizens. Professional people are hired by public or private institutions to serve community residents. They are not necessarily subordinate to the community, but they are obligated to help the community achieve its objectives. To the extent that teachers or other professional people differ with the community, they should try to gain the support of the community. If they do not gain that support, they are obliged to carry out the will of the community.

There are, however, those who claim that other members of the community can participate. Then the principal must ask: Which members of the community deserve policy-making representation? Do businessmen or residents without children deserve recognition as legitimate participants? Should spokesmen who live outside the community be given a voice? What role should professional educators play in relation to residents? Should paraprofessionals live in the community?

Since education has benefits for other members of society besides parents and students, the interests of other social groups must be considered. Residents without children and businesses, for instance, pay taxes to support education, and they are affected by the quality of public education. Although they are not primary constituencies, they may deserve some representation on local school councils as secondary constituencies, in an effort to balance the dominant views of parents and students. Their interests presumably are represented elsewhere, on the board of education itself. The advantage of including business-people, teachers, ministers, and others in local school-community affairs is that they can offer needed support and resources. One solution is to include them on citizen councils but to give them a nonvoting role or to limit their numerical representation to a small fraction of the total membership. In this way they may feel themselves to be valued participants, but their power is kept within bounds. And, if any secondary constituency deserves priority on local school councils, it is teachers, who bear such a close relationship to the effectiveness of educational programming.

In defining who constitutes the local community, principals sometimes face criticism from "outside" elements, such as service professionals in other agencies or community organizers brought into the local neighborhood. Principals are inclined to react defensively and to define criticism from these sources as illegitimate, but it is wise to work with all spokesmen to the greatest extent possible. Because of the interdependence of communities and their ties to broader political forces, there will continue to be social movements and community elites whose support transcends the boundaries of local neighborhoods. In order for community leaders to achieve broad impact they often have to build constituencies in more than one community. While the principal's primary role is to build policy-making and programmatic participation from within the community, it is not wise to ignore outside leaders who have won support within the local community.

In assessing the sincerity of their critics, principals have at times impugned the motives of these leaders in the community, assuming that their critics do not consider the children's needs first. This is another unfortunate reminder of the intellectual heritage left behind by the Progressives. Community leaders must build a following, establish a track record, generate relevant issues, garner resources for their efforts, and the like. As Mancur Olson has argued, this is a particular problem in voluntary organizations, where people are inclined to avoid joining if they can enjoy the benefits of the organization without exerting any effort.[17] Unlike private goods, collective goods cannot be denied to those in the community who wish to enjoy them freely. This means that organizations must constantly work to build and maintain a membership.[18] Simply because an organization has few active members does not mean that it does not represent community viewpoints. Or because it concerns itself with many noneducational issues does not mean that there is no basis for raising an issue with the schools. Principals must become sensitive to these leadership dilemmas when they assess the actions of community leaders.

Another problem that confronts principals is how to treat paraprofessional aides who are members of the community and also work in the school. Should local residents be treated differently than other personnel the principal supervises, given their ability to use their knowledge of the school's problems to create ferment against the school? Some principals have acted on this fear by refusing to hire local residents as aides; instead, they only hire aides who live outside the immediate school-community. While this may protect the principal, it bypasses some of the main goals of the paraprofessional movement: to provide different adult models for children within the walls of the school, to increase the community's knowledge of the school and its problems, to provide local residents with employment that upgrades skills and offers the possibility of later advancement. Still other principals have tried to co-opt the most militant leadership in the community by offering them paraprofessional positions. While such political maneuvering can be dangerous, the skillful principal has much to gain by effective collaboration with paraprofessionals.

Some principals have all paraprofessionals (and new teachers) screened by community representatives before they are hired so that the representatives share the responsibility for employees' scuccess. Also, principals have observed that many teachers are nervous in the presence of paraprofessionals since community aides could pose a threat to their authority and autonomy as professionals. While the principal can do much to relieve this anxiety, the situation can also be used to hold teachers more accountable. Community pressure can be an asset in an attempt to transfer or release an incompetent teacher.

The inclusion in the school of paraprofessionals from the community may, instead, require that the principal direct his or her energies toward educating and reassuring the community aides, quite apart from the professional staff. Many aides bring traditional notions of education to their new work and must be persuaded to see the potential in experimenting with a variety of educational approaches appropriate to different children. The paraprofessional movement has made the principal's role more politically sensitive, but principals who are skillful, open with the community, and capable of leadership can turn the situation to the advantage of the school and the community.

THE PRINCIPAL'S DUAL ACCOUNTABILITY

In assessing their role, principals are quite legitimately asking how they are to reconcile their accountability to the community with accountability to the organization of which they are a part. Many have asked whether it is fair for them to be held accountable for decisions often out of their hands. Moreover, they question how they can represent effectively two different masters and maintain their legitimacy in the eyes of both. It is this very serious problem of the relationship between accountability and performance to which we finally turn.

Principals have faced demands for greater accountability in recent years from two directions, internal and external. The Russian-American missile race beginning in the late 1950's, the civil rights disputes of the 1960's, and rising educational costs as reflected in higher taxes— all led to greater demands on school officials to justify expenditures with measurable results. The movement of education toward becoming a behavioral science and the centrifugal forces of technological society also bear some responsibility for an increasing obsession with performance and accountability.

This same impulse has caused school boards and superintendents to entertain various management-by-objective schemes to appraise administrative performance. In addition, plans to decentralize large-city school systems administratively are intended to focus not only greater authority but also sharper responsibility on the principal's shoulders.

Community groups are also restively insisting on making school principals directly accountable to them rather than to the administrative structure. Many principals feel that they are being pulled in two directions by the accountability struggle. In one direction, which strengthens the hand of central boards and staffs, principals find that they must strive for goals handed down from above. The other direction requires that they look outward rather than upward, devoting their energies to working with community groups.

Principals are frequently caught between these conflicting pressures. Superiors tell them to work with community groups, but impose more and more controls that may conflict with community needs and preferences. Community groups find that the principal's new responsibilities are meaningless because they are not accompanied by sufficient authority to make independent decisions. Some principals use this power vacuum to avoid working with community groups; others find themselves constricted in their efforts to bring change in the community. Principals are in the unpleasant position of appearing to the community to be influential within the organization but untrustworthy, since organizational demands push them in other directions, or in the equally unpleasant position of being trusted by the community at the risk of sacrificing an image of influence within the organization. Unless willing to take an extreme position identified exclusively with either the community or the bureaucracy, a principal is able to satisfy neither constituency. This "catch-22" dilemma is built into the present role.[19]

What we have seen in recent years is a classic organizational response to environmental criticism. At the institutional and managerial levels of the organization, board members and superintendents are under intense pressure to reduce criticism of schools from various publics.[20] Rather than transfer any of their own power, they have been inclined to expand the number of power centers in the system by creating new administrative authority for community constituents. While central administrators and board members certainly have lost some autonomy previously protecting them, they have diffused power rather than transferring it since they still control much decision making.

For principals this has meant, generally speaking, increased responsibility without a commensurate increase in power and authority. Principals, whose main role heretofore has been to administer the operation of the schools on a day-to-day basis, are forced into a new set of responsibilities related directly to the governance of the institution—receiving demands from the environment, channeling them in proper directions, maintaining support, broadening participation in the learning process itself. If they prove inadequate to the task, central administrators and board members usually blame the principals and their training rather than the governance structure. In the attempt to use the principal as a buffer to protect their own roles, central office administrators and boards have not made the changes in the decision structure of the system that would allow the principal to be successful. A reasonable alternative is to ask whether there are not better institutional structures for making the principal's role more workable.

As long as power to promote and evaluate principals remains in the hands of central officials, however, principals will balk at such alliances, knowing full well that opportunities for advancement to better-paying jobs and more challenging responsibilities are threatened. Certainly community-oriented principals have been known to have been kept in a particular school for many years beyond their effectiveness.

There are at least two ways to remove this control mechanism from the organizational hierarchy of school systems. One is to give local community residents the right to interview and participate in the selection of prospective principals. Those with a good track record will be in demand when they wish to move to another school within the system. A second strategy would be to remove the barriers to lateral moves between school systems. A principal wishing to move from one city to another faces parochial entry requirements, rigid certification standards that vary greatly among states, uneven reciprocity arrangements among states, and the like. Reforms that open school systems to lateral movement for principals will also allow principals to be more independent in directly allying with community constituents. A third strategy is to reallocate resources within school systems so that principals have more time, staff, and budget to improve school-community efforts. More and more resources are needed in local schools so that principals and communities may decide how best to concentrate their energies and so that local schools have resources for school-community relations.[21] We need to invert the pyramids of authority in administrative bureaucracies and put principals and their communities at the top. In addition, many other reforms might be instituted at the local school level; these we have discussed.

Until various structural changes radically decentralize both administrative and political decision making to accommodate the wishes of local communities, principals may legitimately argue that they are being employed as lightning rods in an effort to ground public criticism. They are liable to see their power further eroded as community groups, realizing that principals are powerless, escalate their pressure up the hierarchy, where agreements will be reached without consulting the principal.

One way of viewing the present situation, then, is to point to the structural changes that are badly needed in most urban school systems. Yet we have emphasized here that many of the problems principals experience in school-community relations do emanate from their own perceptions. Thus, in spite of organizational constraints, principals can do a great deal at present to shape collaborative relationships with community groups. And this need not be accomplished by sacrificing their career advancement. Supervisory authority in school systems is remarkably weak, and principals have far more discretionary authority than most are willing to use.

No structural mechanisms will by themselves draw principals into closer harmony with the communities the schools serve. Structural reforms merely provide incentives and sanctions to influence behavior; ultimately, they can do little to change behavior unless principals have a value commitment to work with communities. Most parents, community leaders, and other residents in our school communities seek only to share authority and responsibility with professionals. This attempt to democratize authority has been central to the development of our public schools and to American government. It is this democratic vision, if principals will accept it, that today offers the potential for empowering both school principals and our communities as partners.

NOTES

1. The local neighborhood community should be understood to refer, throughout this chapter, to the local school's attendance area.

2. See Richard Hofstadter, *Anti-Intellectualism in American Life* (New York: Vintage Books, 1962). See also Robert H. Salisbury, "Schools and Politics in the Big City," *Harvard Educational Review*, 37 (Summer 1967), 408-424.

3. For a discussion of this issue, see Leonard J. Fein, *The Ecology of the Public Schools: An Inquiry into Community Control* (Indianapolis, Ind.: Pegasus, 1971).

4. For an excellent discussion of Dewey's views on this subject, see Wilson Carey McWilliams, *The Idea of Fraternity in America* (Berkeley: University of California Press, 1973), 526-536.

5. For a critique of the sociopsychological emphasis in Dewey's pedagogy, see Hofstadter, *Anti-Intellectualism in American Life*, 359-390.

6. John Dewey, *The Public and Its Problems* (New York: Henry Holt and Company, 1927), 109, 127, 131-134.

7. *Ibid.*, 217-218.

8. Raymond E. Callahan, *Education and the Cult of Efficiency* (Chicago: University of Chicago Press, 1962).

9. Milton M. Gordon, *Assimilation in American Life: The Role of Race, Religion, and National Origins* (New York: Oxford University Press, 1964).

10. Dewey, *Public and Its Problems*, 177.

11. Amitai Etzioni, *The Active Society: A Theory of Societal and Political Processes* (Glencoe, Ill.: Free Press, 1968), 352-369.

12. Margaret Mead, "Neighborhoods and Human Needs," in *Human Identity in the Urban Environment*, ed. Gwen Bell and Jacqueline Tyrwhitt (New York: Penguin Books, 1972), 245-251.

13. A discussion of this phenomenon is found in David W. O'Shea, "School District Decentralization: The Case of Los Angeles," *Education and Urban Society*, 7 (August 1975), 377-392.

14. For discussions of community development, see Lee J. Carey, ed., *Community Development as a Process* (Columbia: University of Missouri Press, 1970). See also William W. Biddle, *The Community Development Process: The Rediscovery of Local Initiative* (New York: Holt, Rinehart, and Winston, 1965).

15. One example of public choice theory is provided by Gordon Tullock, *Private*

Wants and Public Means: An Economic Analysis of the Proper Scope of Government (New York: Basic Books, 1970).

16. Mario D. Fantini, "The School-Community Power Struggle," *National Elementary Principal,* 54 (January-February 1975), 57-61.

17. Mancur Olson, Jr., *The Logic of Collective Action: Public Good and the Theory of Groups* (New York: Schocken Books, 1969).

18. For a discussion of this problem, see Paul E. Peterson, "Community Representation and the 'Free Rider,'" *Administrator's Notebook,* 22 (May 1974).

19. For a similar discussion of this dilemma facing community planners, see Martin L. Needleman and Carolyn E. Needleman, *Guerrillas in the Bureaucracy: The Community Planning Experiment in the United States* (New York: John Wiley and Sons, 1974), 89-92.

20. I borrow here from Talcott Parsons' distinction between the institutional, managerial, and technical levels of an organization. Simply stated, the institutional level accommodates environmental demands. The managerial level translates and coordinates these into organizational language and transmits them to the technical level, where the organization actually performs its tasks. See Talcott Parsons, *Structure and Process in Modern Societies* (Glencoe, Ill.: Free Press, 1960).

21. It may be that decentralization will prove more costly and will require additional resources. See John Callahan and Donna E. Shalala, "Some Fiscal Dimensions of Three Hypothetical Decentralization Plans," *Education and Urban Society,* 11 (November 1969), 40-53. These problems are, of course, less relevant to small suburban systems.

Chapter Six

Daniel U. Levine

The Social Context of Urban Education

Some characteristics of contemporary society have important implications for those who organize and operate urban schools, including principals, and analysis of the social context in which education functions can be helpful in the organization and operation of schools. It is often difficult, however, to delineate and agree on the practical implications of societal characteristics that affect education. Unless the practical implications are identified and contribute to the operation of the schools, they may contribute little but gaseous obfuscation to educational decision making.

STRATIFICATION, SEGREGATION, AND METROPOLITAN SUBCULTURES

Many of the social conditions that should or do influence the organization and administration of schools are associated with the stratification and segregation characteristic of metropolitan society in the United States. "Stratification," as used here, refers to the division of a population into distinct groups based on social class, race, age, and other fundamental social or cultural attributes. "Segregation" refers to the separation of groups so that members of one group have relatively little contact with members of another.

Stratification and segregation as they have developed in metropolitan areas, also follow a definite geographic pattern. Different groups frequently are separated not just by social distance but by physical space as well. For example, poor neighborhoods now predominate in many cities. In other neighborhoods youth congregate in large numbers in such settings as rock concerts that set them apart from the adult world. Racial or ethnic enclaves in the metropolitan area are also often large enough to constitute separate social systems, despite the mobility afforded by automobiles and communication provided through the mass media.

A group of people that is part of, but set apart from, a larger society tends to develop or maintain a subculture in the sense that the members who share many values and characteristics of the society also will display a configuration of values and behaviors distinctive to the group. Educational issues and problems connected with the existence of metropolitan subcultures go far beyond such obvious topics as de facto segregation in housing and the schools, drug use among adolescents, and violent assaults on teachers or administrators. Implications following from an analysis of the most important of these subcultures are discussed below.

Social Class and the Culture of Poverty

Socioeconomic status (SES), often referred to simply as social class, is a term frequently used in conversation but seldom defined. Social scientists have expended a great deal of effort in identifying the components, and, while they do not always agree, have succeeded in outlining the major dimensions. Porbably the most widely accepted work in this area is that of Lloyd Warner and his associates,[1] who concluded that others' perceptions of one's social class are determined by occupational prestige, income level, amount of formal education, and type of house and neighborhood in which it is located.[2]

Based on these four factors and related measures such as degree of participatioh in civic affairs and recreational preferences, individuals or members of a family can be classified within a number of social-class groupings as: upper class (or elite), upper middle class, lower middle class, upper lower class, or lower lower class. The social-class background of students is related, in nearly all countries around the world, to educational achievement and attainment. Lower-class students generally achieve at a lower level and do not remain in the educational system as long as higher-class students. Partly owing to relative lack of success within the educational system, individuals from lower-class backgrounds are generally employed in low-prestige, low-income occupations, and tend to remain at the lower-status level.

Sociologists disagree on whether there is more upward mobility (movement from lower to higher status) in the United States now than

there was years ago, but it would be difficult to dispute the following
set of central generalizations concerning social class and education in
metropolitan areas:

— Large sections of many metropolitan areas are inhabited primarily
  by lower-class families. This means that the neighborhoods in which
  they live rank low in terms of occupational prestige, educational attainment, housing value, and income, and rank high in terms of
  such related social characteristics as crime, percentage of families
  headed by females (because poverty encourages family disorganiza-
  tion, and husband-wife families earn higher incomes and move to
  more desirable neighborhoods), and percentage of housing units deteriorating or vacant (money and loans to repair deteriorating units
  are not available to low-status residents). In general, such areas
  tend to be concentrated in the older, inner-core sections of the city,
  and thus can be characterized as "inner-city" neighborhoods.

— Educational achievement in schools in inner-city or other lower-
  class neighborhoods generally is extremely low. By the sixth grade,
  for example, mean achievement in the inner city usually is one or
  more years below national norms, and by the eleventh or twelfth
  grade it is three or more years below the national average. This
  means, in turn, that large proportions of the students in inner-city
  schools terminate their formal education able to read only at the
  fifth- or sixth-grade level or below and thus are functionally incapable of obtaining many jobs that require higher levels of reading or
  other basic skills taught in the schools.

The relationship between inner-city location and achievement is illustrated in Figure 6-1, which delineates the separation between
inner-city, fringe, and mixed- or middle-status neighborhoods (measured by percentage of families below poverty level, percentage of
female-headed families, and percentage of housing units below
$10,800, by census tract) in most of the Kansas City metropolitan area
south of the Missouri River. Figure 6-2 shows the census tract location
of schools within the Kansas City Public School District, which had
sixth-grade achievement means of 5.9 or below in 1971. (The national
"norm" at the end of the sixth grade is 6.8.) Similar maps, with a similar amount of congruence between the two sets of data, could be prepared for many other metropolitan areas, particularly older and
larger ones.

— Partly because achievement in the inner city is so abysmally low,
  many students growing up in these neighborhoods have little chance

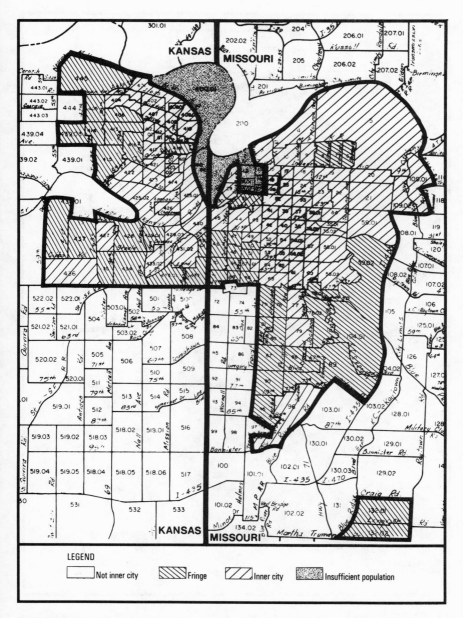

FIGURE 6-1. Classification of census tracts by inner-city location in major portion of the Kansas City metropolitan area, 1970

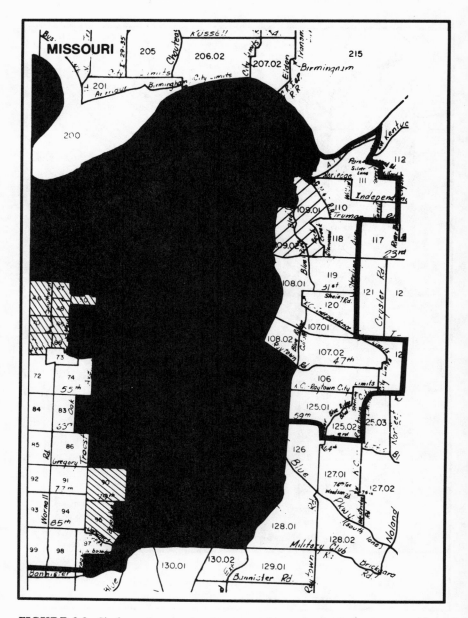

FIGURE 6-2. Sixth-grade school achievement in a school district in Kansas City, Missouri, 1971. (*Note:* The school district is outlined in black. Census tracts comprising elementary school attendance areas with achievement means 5.9 or below are darkened.)

to be upwardly mobile in the future. In a large proportion of cases, such students were born into low-status families, will remain in the inner city and retain low status as adults, and will transmit their low-status and inner-city location on to their children. From this point of view, it can be concluded that there is a permanently low-status population or "underclass" concentrated in the lower-class neighborhoods within our metropolitan areas.

One reason why achievement in inner-city or other lower-class schools is so low is because relatively large numbers of students from low status families have not been prepared at home to function successfully in the educational environment commonly found in the schools. At the same time, the schools have not been very successful in adapting instruction to teach low-status students more effectively. Despite the infusion of billions of dollars through Title I of ESEA, the Model Cities Program, and other federal and state projects, and despite gains made in some schools in the primary and middle grades, achievement levels at the sixth grade and above still are extremely low in inner-city schools throughout the country.

The existence of an underclass in the social structure of the United States has called attention to the question of whether there is a subculture (or culture) of poverty that perpetuates itself through the establishment and communication of values and behaviors that are separate from those of the larger society and help to perpetuate low social status. Indeed, one would expect that, given the social and geographic concentration of low-status families in relatively homogeneous neighborhoods, distinctive values and behaviors constituting a "culture of poverty" will tend to be developed, amplified, and transmitted from generation to generation among the individuals living in such neighborhoods.

Charles Valentine,[3] however, has examined evidence showing that low-status and middle-status individuals generally have similar aspirations and express agreement with many of the same ideals. He concluded that there is no true culture of poverty. Lower-class status is perpetuated, in his opinion, mainly by political, social, and economic oppression. Hyman Rodman,[4] on the other hand, has found that there is a "stretch" in the values of lower-class persons in the sense that their beliefs, and behaviors associated with those beliefs, are not always compatible with high aspirations. Many low-status individuals, for example, feel relatively powerless to control their environment or their future, and it is partly for this reason that they are unwilling or unable to work continuously toward achieving abstract or distant goals associated with success in the schools or other major social systems. Seymour Parker and Robert Kleiner, furthermore, have shown that some beliefs characteristic of the culture of poverty (for example, resignation, fatalism, present- as opposed to future-time orientation, and low versus high faith in human nature) are "functional" in the sense that they help the individuals who hold them adapt to the realities of failure and deprivation in a difficult environment.[5]

Low-status students, from this perspective, may be viewed as living in a culture of poverty that contributes to failure in school. Pessimistic about their chances for success in the first place, living in an environment in which it is difficult to study or pursue intellectual goals, and unaware of how to fulfill institutional expectations, students from low-status backgrounds thus fall victim to a cycle characterized by low achievement, an increased sense of hopelessness and defeat, and rejection of the operational values and beliefs required to succeed in the school.[6]

If the problems which inner-city students experience in school are indeed connected with low status characteristics such as feelings of hopelessness, lack of preparation for and failure in meeting teacher expectations beginning in the early grades, and difficulty in working toward distant, abstract goals, it follows that efforts to raise their achievement should aim specifically at increasing their sense of control over their future, reducing their sense of failure, building competence in planning and carrying out longitudinal tasks, and otherwise changing the school environment in accord with this diagnosis of their specific problems. Beyond this, a variety of steps should be taken to make the school more effective as an educational institution for inner-city students as well as students elsewhere in the metropolitan area, a goal discussed later in this chapter and in subsequent chapters.

Ethnic and Racial Subcultures

An "ethnic" group consists of people bound together in some way by common historical or cultural ties. Members of the group need not, as Berry points out, be uniform in their beliefs, experiences, or allegiance, but they do show a high degree "of adherence to certain basic institutions, such as family patterns, religion, and language," and they "often possess distinctive folkways and mores, customs of dress, art and ornamentation, moral codes and value systems, and patterns of recreation."[8]

By this definition, a social class could almost be considered an ethnic group, except that social classes are large groupings whose members tend to identify with family, friends, and neighbors, or with the larger society, rather than with other members of the class. Members of an ethnic group, by way of contrast, tend to perceive some degree of identity with others sharing characteristics of the group.

"Race" is even more difficult to define than ethnicity. It usually refers to people who share distinctive combinations of physical characteristics such as skin color, type of hair, or color of eyes. Except for such characteristics, members of a racial group may have little or nothing in common. Many black Americans, for example, have few or none of the cultural preferences or behaviors sometimes associated with "Black Culture," while many white Americans do exhibit such preferences and behaviors. Conversely, ethnic groups may include members of different racial groups, as, for example, Cubans and Hawaiians. From this point of view, race is not synonymous with ethnicity. Because members of racial groups tend to have shared historical and social experiences, however, there generally is considerable overlap between race and ethnicity.

Social scientists have had a difficult time determining whether there are racial subcultures separate from the social-class differences that characterize different racial groups. In the past few years, however, it has become clear that working-class whites and blacks (and other racial groups) do differ widely in attitudes and behaviors involving family structure, raising children, recreation, and other matters. The development of these patterns is associated with the unique history of each group and the social and geographical barriers that have divided one group from another.[9] At the middle-class level such differences become much less pronounced, perhaps because the media, the schools, and other institutions have a homogenizing effect in terms of developing somewhat standardized middle-class attitudes and behaviors. This finding suggests that there is a somewhat distinctive black subculture but in many respects it is characteristic primarily of lower-status blacks.[10]

Both race and ethnicity, in any case, frequently overlap with social class. In the United States, for example, disproportionate percentages of black Americans and Mexican-Americans are lower class in terms of socioeconomic status. Since it has already been asserted that school achievement is closely associated with the social-class level of students, the question arises as to whether race and ethnicity are associated with achievement and other educational outcomes, independent of social class.

The evidence currently available indicates that once social class has been taken into account, knowledge of students' racial and ethnic background does not enable one to greatly improve the accuracy of predictions concerning their achievement in school. The well-known study, *Equality of Educational Opportunity,* for example, found that race and ethnicity added little to the prediction of achievement after students' individual social-class background and the social-class composition of their schools had been statistically controlled.[11] It is true that several other studies have found relationships between racial or ethnic minority status and achievement even after accounting for social class, but these relationships generally have been modest and are greatly outweighed by the effects of social-class differences.[12]

In line with this conclusion, studies currently being conducted on achievement in big-city school districts clearly show that a limited number of social-class-related variables enable one to make excellent predictions concerning grade-level achievement means in elementary schools.[13] Table 6-1, for example, provides data on the relationships between six variables describing information on census tracts in elementary-school attendance areas in 1970 and grade reading means among sixty elementary schools in a middle-sized midwestern city in 1971. The five variables related to social class predict or "explain" 81

TABLE 6-1. Percentage of variance in sixth-grade mean achievement scores for 1971, explained by six census tract variables among sixty schools in a medium-sized midwestern city in 1970[a]

Variable	Squared multiple correlation[b]
1. Percentage of females separated	.64
2. Percentage of housing units with 1.51 or more people per room	.69
3. Percentage of elementary and secondary students in public schools	.73
4. Percentage of housing units vacant	.77
5. Percentage of males divorced or separated	.81
6. Percentage of population negro	.82

[a] The predictor variables in this analysis have been statistically transformed to take account of curvilinear relationships.

[b] Percentage of variance accounted for by independent variable.

percent of the variance in achievement scores, and adding knowledge of the percentage of Negro population in the school attendance areas adds only 1 percent to the prediction.

Table 6-2, similarly, shows the relationship between six census variables for 1970, percentage of black students enrolled in 1970, and sixth-grade reading means among 320 schools in a large midwestern city in 1971. In this case, the census variables predict or explain 78 percent of the variance in achievement, and knowledge of the percentage of students who are black adds nothing to the prediction.

TABLE 6-2. Percentage of variance in sixth-grade mean achievement scores for 1971 explained by six census tract variables and percent black enrollment among 320 schools in a large midwestern city in 1970[a]

Variable	Squared multiple correlation[b]
1. Percentage of families three times or more above poverty level	.67
2. Percentage of females separated	.73
3. Percentage of owner-occupied housing units less than $15,000	.75
4. Percentage female-headed families	.76
5. Percentage housing units with 1.51 or more people per room	.77
6. Percentage of rental housing units less than $80 per month	.78
7. Percentage of black students in the student body	.78

[a] The predictor variables in this analysis have been statistically transformed to take account of curvilinear relationships.

[b] Percentage of variance accounted for by independent variable.

This finding does not necessarily mean, however, that race and ethnicity are unimportant characteristics that one can neglect in the schools. Since race and ethnicity overlap with social class, cultural values and behaviors associated with ethnic group membership probably are confounded with the culture of poverty in affecting educational outcomes among low-status students in the public schools. This conclusion is supported by the finding of Martin Whiteman and Martin Deutsch that social-class-related deficits in educational performance begin in the early years and additional deficits associated with race become discernible later,[14] thus causing lower-class black youngsters to be "sequentially disadvantaged" educationally. In effect, the finding of Whiteman and Deutsch means that lower-class students in some minority subcultures face additional obstacles (as compared with lower-class whites) in school and society as a result of divergence from the larger culture in their beliefs and behaviors and of the inequality in social and economic opportunities available to members of these groups.

Implications of this conclusion are that, in attempting to improve the achievement of students with lower-status backgrounds, educators should study and identify beliefs and behaviors distinctive to students of differing racial or social background and should take these differences into account in designing instructional experiences appropriate to students of differing subcultures. It is likely, for example, that lower-class blacks differ from lower-class whites in some values and behavior patterns even though the differences are not "racial" in the sense that middle-class blacks do not differ in the same way from middle-class whites. Alternately, it is possible that middle-class members of some ethnic groups such as Mexican-Americans share certain distinctive beliefs and behaviors with lower-class Mexican-Americans and that these characteristics of their subculture are associated with relatively low performance in the public schools. In either case, it would be desirable to take such differences into account in providing educational programs particularly appropriate to the social background of each child in the schools.

Examples of ethnic, as opposed to social-class, values and behavior patterns that have been identified by social scientists and are thought to be related to outcomes in the public schools can be found in several sources dealing with the education of Mexican-American children and American Indian children. Audrey Schwartz, for example, found that Mexican-American children in a metropolitan area on the West Coast showed greater concern for parental approval and less independence from family authority than did groups of Anglo children comparable in social class.[15] Such findings suggest that educators might need to work even more closely with Mexican-American parents than with the parents of Anglo children in delivering educational services through the public schools.

Analogously, Robert Havighurst has cited several studies indicating that American Indian students are much more concerned than Anglo children with peer influence and reaction in the classroom, to the extent that Indian children may not respond to their teacher because it would be considered shameful to answer a question other students could not.[16] Since Indian children in urban areas probably are socialized, at least to an extent, in this type of pattern, urban educators should take it into account in assessing the classroom behavior of Indian students and planning instructional programs for them. James Mahan and Mary Criger further report that Indian children generally do not perform well when they are the center of classroom attention; for this reason, they recommend that teachers "avoid lessons that require the individual to stand out," instead using "student teams as much as possible for motivation and competition."[17] Research by several social scientists suggests that children from both American Indian and Mexican-American families may learn better in a cooperative than they do in a competitive classroom environment, as compared with students from white ethnic groups.[18] Such differences have obvious implications for instructional programming in the schools.

Although no formulas are available to help educators identify ethnic variations in values and behaviors of importance in educating the children with whom they work, sensitive observation in the classroom can provide useful insights. It sometimes has been claimed, for example, that black children have been taught to look away during conferences with adult authorities, and that white educators mistakenly interpret this behavior as a sign of disrespect. One observer familiar with Korean immigrant children has found that they are taught at home not to be overtly expressive with their emotions, feelings, and thoughts, and therefore "find it extremely difficult to express themselves in American classrooms."[19] Some observers familiar with Mexican-American family life believe that female teachers may have unusual difficulty keeping the attention of Mexican-American students because these youngsters have been taught to respect the authority of male rather than female adults. While such observations have not to my knowledge been fully documented in empirical research, concerned educators will look closely for signs of such differences associated with the ethnic background of the students with whom they work.

HOME AND NEIGHBORHOOD ENVIRONMENT, FAMILY CHANGE, AND EDUCATIONAL ACHIEVEMENT

The primary environments in which a child grows up are, of course, the home and the neighborhood; thus, it is no surprise to learn that home and neighborhood environments appear to be more directly related to educational achievement than social class, ethnicity, or other demographic constructs. This generalization makes a good deal of sense, after all, if one keeps in mind that values or behaviors associated with social class or ethnicity are learned in the home and the neighborhood and may be substantially modified in accord with a particular child's home and neighborhood situation.

Evidence concerning the close relationships that exist between neighborhood conditions and school-level achievement scores among big-city schools has already been presented. As regards home environment, Dave and Wolf have reported correlations of approximately .8 and .7 between home environment, on the one hand, and achievement and intelligence scores, respectively, on the other, whereas students' social class, as measured by parental occupation and income, typically correlates with achievement in IQ at about .6.[20] In further support of this conclusion, a study of students in two inner-city elementary schools in Kansas City found correlations as high as .46 between Dave and Wolf's Home Environment Scale and first-grade reading achievement, while parental social class and achievement were essentially uncorrelated.[21] The home environment scale used in these studies included measures of intellectual aspirations and expectations for the child, emphasis on correct language usage, the nature of rewards for intellectual accomplishment, opportunities provided by the parents for learning outside the home, and assistance to facilitate learning in a variety of situations.

Home environment has long been recognized as a determinant of children's behavior and success in the school, but changes in the role and importance of the family in preparing children to function in other social institutions, such as school and employment systems, are not always explicitly articulated.

To view these changes in their proper context, one must analyze them in terms of their connection with characteristics of modern urban society. Major characteristics of the emerging postindustrial society in which we now live have been summarized by Daniel Bell as:

Economic sector — the change from a goods-producing to a service economy;

Occupational distribution — the preeminence of the professional and technical class;

Axial principle — the centrality of theoretical knowledge as the source of innovation and of policy formulation for the society;

Future orientation — the control of technology and technological assessment;

Decision making—the creation of a new "intellectual technology."[22] Bell further delineates the change to postindustrial society by showing how, whereas the "axial" principal of preindustrial society was "traditionalism" and the axial principle of industrial society was economic growth, the central principle of modern industrial society now involves the "codification of theoretical knowledge."[23]

In one sense, the family is less important in preparing children for this type of society than it was in the traditional or industrial eras because it no longer functions, as it once did, to prepare children for filling inherited, often family-centered occupational roles such as farmer or craftsman. In addition, family "connections" and resources appear to be less important than they once were in helping young people establish or carry on small enterprises such as those that formed a central part of economic life during what Bell calls the "industrial" period. Instead, the main function of the family in preparing young people for economic roles in society is now to prepare them for school and other educational institutions where they can master intellectual and conceptual skills and gain the credentials required for success in a society based on control of communications-processing technology and "codification of theoretical knowledge."[24]

In another sense, however, the family has become even more important than it once was in preparing children for adulthood since mastery of skills in the educational system and, later, the economic system is related to successful preparation for school and adequate support thereafter. Institutions in industrial and postindustrial society are more "fragmented" than they were in traditional society, when religious, economic, education, and other institutions usually worked in conjunction with the family to prepare children for adult roles. Today what is formally and informally learned in the home is not effectively reinforced—indeed, it is often contradicted—by what children learn from the mass media, the school, the church, and other social institutions. From this point of view one can say that the family, and often other institutions as well compete with other forces in the attempt to socialize children for constructive adult roles. This is especially true in the inner city, where the family and the school reinforce each other even less strongly than they do elsewhere in the metropolitan area and where both institutions often function at cross-purposes with concentrated neighborhood influences associated with the "culture" of poverty.

Educators usually are well aware of how much children's home and neighborhood environments influence their behavior and performance in school. Both teachers and administrators, for example, often complain about how difficult it is to work with youngsters whose home environment tends to work against what is learned in school or whose friends and neighbors either fail to reinforce or directly contradict the values and expectations of the school. It is doubtful, however, whether this recognition generally does much good except to alleviate some of the frustration felt by those who have been unable to provide effective education for disadvantaged students.

Stated differently, one can react either defensively or constructively to the problem involved in educating children whose environment works against success in school. If one reacts defensively, the problem is acknowledged and used to explain failure in working with children from lower-class families or neighborhoods. If one reacts constructively, the problem is viewed as an extremely difficult one that requires redoubled efforts to build cooperation between the environment and the school, finding ways to overcome the educational disadvantages of students who grow up in lower-class homes and neighborhoods.[25] The advantage of the constructive reaction is underlined by a growing body of research suggesting that close involvement of parents is a prerequisite for the success of early childhood programs to improve the educational performance of educationally disadvantaged students.[26]

Types of Schools in the Metropolitan Area

Inner-city students are concentrated to a substantial degree in schools with a predominantly lower-class student body. Low achievement in these schools has become a major national problem, and much effort has been expended in trying to improve achievement levels there. Understanding the social roots of the problem, it is argued, can help in designing more effective programs.

There are, of course, many other types of urban schools that can be distinguished according to the social background of the students who attend them and the social characteristics of the environment in which they are located. Most big cities, for example, have several schools attended primarily by so-called white "ethnics" — lower-middle and upper-lower-class students from families of Eastern and Southern European extraction. Knowledge and understanding of the social background of students in these schools as in other types of schools, can help in making decisions about the organization and functioning of educational programs. In older neighborhoods with a substantial Italian-American population, for example, the family frequently is very cohesive, and children are taught to accept the authority of their parents. Effective teaching in such a community requires unusually close and continued contact with parents and community leaders in order to minimize conflict between the home and the school.

Using data dealing with the social characteristics and teaching conditions in elementary schools in a big city, Russell Doll identified this type of school as a "common man" school and contrasted it with "inner-city," "conventional," and "high-status" schools.[27] It is beyond the scope of this chapter to describe the characteristics of each of these or other types of urban schools and discuss their implications for educational programming, but such an analysis could well be carried out by the faculty of any school that serves a socially distinct community in the metropolitan area.

The Youth Subculture

One hundred years ago social scientists were not too concerned with the subculture of youth because most young people moved directly from school to work and were not clearly set apart from the rest of society. As in nearly all societies, however, young people tended to congregate together, often in church groups or neighborhood gangs. This means that individuals within a fairly narrow age range develop values and behaviors unique to the membership. This phenomenon has assumed more importance in recent times because schooling has been extended for many students until they are well into their twenties and there has been a heavier concentration of young people in larger high schools and institutions of higher education. Kenneth Keniston and others have identified "youth" as a "previously unrecognized stage of life" that, in contrast to previous eras, "is today being entered not by tiny minorities of unusually creative or unusually disturbed young men and women, but by millions of young people in the advanced nations of the world."[28] One defining characteristic of this stage of life, Keniston goes on to point out, is "the emergence of youth-specific identities and roles . . . [which] contrast both with the more ephemeral enthusiasms of the adolescent and with the more established commitments of the adult."[29]

Distinct to a substantial degree from other segments of society, many young people have been developing a pattern of beliefs somewhat different from those typical of society as a whole. Daniel Yankelovich, using data based on several years of surveys among college students and other groups of youth, has summarized the distinctive nature of this pattern of beliefs as follows:

placing emphasis on sensory experience rather than on conceptual knowledge;

de-emphasizing realms of knowledge illuminated by science; instead, celebrating the unknown, the mystical, and the mysterious elements of nature;

emphasizing cooperation rather than competition;

de-emphasizing detachment, objectivity, and noninvolvement as methods for finding truth; arriving at truth by direct experience, participation, and involvement;

rejecting mastery over nature, emphasizing harmony with nature;

de-emphasizing organization, rationalization, cost-effectiveness.[30]

This emerging subculture of youth by no means encompasses all or even most of the young people growing up in contemporary postindustrial societies such as that of the United States. Estimates of the proportion of young people adhering to beliefs defining the youth culture vary widely, but probably no more than 20 or 25 percent are firmly identifiable with the culture at the present, as Havighurst suggests in a recent analysis of "types" of young people fifteen to twenty-four years of age in the United States.[31]

Many members of the youth culture are, however, from upper-class and upper-middle-class families and thus can be found concentrated in upper-status schools in the wealthier parts of metropolitan areas. Because they subscribe to beliefs and behaviors somewhat different from those according to which schools traditionally have been established and operated, young people in this type of school have increasingly been demonstrating alienation not just from the larger society but from the school itself, particularly at the senior high school level.

The problem of alienation among middle-class high school students might seem relatively unimportant, except that in many ways these youngsters represent a segment of the population that is likely to grow both in numbers and proportion in future decades. Partly because the absolute number of persons aged fifteen to twenty-four is likely to increase by the end of the century, youth may be even more segregated from the rest of society during the coming decades than it is today.[32] The alienation originates in the problems middle-class youngsters encounter while growing up in relatively affluent communities that offer a wide range — possibly too wide a range — of alternatives routes to becoming an adult. If the proportion of working-class families in the population declines in the future, a higher percentage of young people may experience this middle-class alienation from the school and other major social institutions.

Implications for the schools are obvious. Many of the problems experienced by members of the youth culture center on the need to establish a stable and constructive identity amid the myriad possibilities for development available to young people in advanced postindustrial societies. Keniston has summarized the problems as "tension between self and society," "estrangement . . . [marked by] feelings of isolation, unreality, absurdity, and disconnectedness from the interpersonal, social and phenomenological world," and "refusal of socialization."[33] These are not the kinds of problems that have historically been given much attention in public school curricula, whether elementary or secondary, but urban school programming must take them into account in the future or face widespread rejection on the part of large numbers of youth who find the school irrelevant or debilitating. The need to put more emphasis on the social and personal development of young people in the schools has been aptly summarized by Frank Musgrove:

Our urban, industrial and technical society has been contrasted with non-literate societies in its requirement of ever longer formal education to maintain and develop its techniques and institutions. It is possible that our Western society requires a more thoughtful social preparation of the young; but this is precisely what the schools have, in general, failed to give. They have continued to place their major emphasis on the transmission of knowledge. And yet it is in just this respect that institutions of a literate society can afford to be more cavalier than the training system of a nonliterate people. Education in the sense of factual instruction and the memorizing of information is less necessary for the former than for the latter: if a generation of a primitive society fails to do its homework, the knowledge is irrecoverably lost.[34]

It is beyond the scope of this chapter to describe or argue for all the changes that might be introduced to make elementary and secondary instruction more appropriate for youth — particularly those wholly or partly representative of the youth culture. In the past few years several national commissions have analyzed the situation at some length and offered a series of promising recommendations for school reform that might achieve this goal. Interested readers can find these reports summarized in leading educational journals published in 1974 and 1975.[35] Elsewhere I have tried to spell out some of the educational implications of the widespread manifestation of identity problems among urban youth,[36] and they can be briefly summarized:

1. Educational experiences should be provided in a setting that brings young people into close and continuing contact with others of different social, racial, ethnic, and religious backgrounds.

2. Much of the curriculum, particularly in the social studies, should be concerned with the study of urban and metropolitan affairs.

3. Students should be immersed firsthand in the metropolitan environment.

4. Instruction and participation in urban and metropolitan studies should be fundamentally interdisciplinary.

5. Much more should be done to provide adolescents and young people with opportunities to perform socially important and personally meaningful work in urban communities.

6. Students should have more scope in choosing what to learn and how to learn it.

Complexity in the Urban Environment

No chapter on the social context of urban education would be complete without recognizing the complexity of modern urban society and discussing, if only briefly, its implications for school administrators, particularly school principals.

Organizations and living arrangements in industrial societies have grown enormously complex. From an agricultural nation with a few million people, the United States has become a highly industrialized nation with over 200 million people, the large majority of whom live in urban settlements of 2,500 people or more. Constantly bombarded by communications from a variety of media, surrounded by and dependent on machines of all types and descriptions, and brought into daily contact with people whose occupational titles fill a large dictionary, we have become accustomed to life in a complicated society where the internal workings seem ever more mysterious and invisible. Our cities now sprawl over thousands of acres of land and depend on gigantic infrastructures for transporting immense amounts of goods and energy. The main intersection of freeway routes in the city of Los Angeles, it has been said, covers more ground than the city of Florence at the height of the Renaissance.

Our social institutions have grown apace. Giant corporations function in a variety of industries not only throughout the nation but throughout the world. Large hospitals have been built staffed by hundreds of skilled and unskilled workers. Government office buildings are home eight hours a day for literally thousands of employees. Communications flow in increasingly steady streams from one end of the metropolis to another.

Schools, like other organizations, have grown in size and complexity. The typical elementary school in an urban area now has a professional staff of fifteen to twenty people at a minimum, secondary schools sometimes employ as many as two or three hundred teachers, and institutions of higher education are considered small if they have less than four or five thousand students. Frequently filled with modern equipment of all sorts, staffed by specialists who know little or nothing about each other's specialties, and coordinated by an administrative staff that comprises a small organization in its own right, schools have become as large and complex as other institutions established on the basis of a sophisticated technology.

One of the primary problems in large and complex organizations is that they tend toward a variety of dysfunctions. Inadequacy in personnel and supervision functions, for example, can mean that incompetent persons are hired and left to fend for themselves. Lack of appropriate equipment owing to delay in ordering or delivering supplies can paralyze the operation of an entire production department. Inefficiency in processing and responding to messages may leave members of the organization ignorant of information they need to do their job, and the size of the work force and work load may make it impossible to know who is responsible for major blunders in performance. At times the situation may appear so hopeless that we are tempted to start over from the beginning, as when New York City experienced severe problems with long-distance calls several years ago because its underground cables could take no more circuits, or when that city's police chief suggested pouring concrete over thousands of cars and beginning afresh after a massive four-hour traffic jam.

Urban schools, in their own way, are prone to the same type of malfunctioning and breakdown as other large organizations. How, for example, can one train and retrain a staff of thirty or forty teachers to work together in teaching hundreds or thousands of students? How can one ensure that the services provided by a central office staff of hundreds are of practical use to teachers in the field? How can an administrator make sure that instruction in ten or twenty or thirty classrooms is appropriate for the students enrolled there? How, above all else, can one ensure that the school is adjusting properly to the rapidly changing demands of an urbanized world?

Clearly, there are no instant or easy answers to such questions. From the viewpoint of the social analyst, however, it should be stressed that success in solving problems involving the complexity of urban schools and school systems will require a carefully worked out "systems" approach to organization and administration. Stated differently, the various segments and characteristics of the educational enterprise must be explicitly selected and established so that they fit together as a coherent and functional whole. In a society comprised of large numbers of interdependent organizational systems and subsystems, it is not enough to coordinate the operation of units and individuals working at cross-purposes or channeling their efforts in conflicting directions; one needs, instead, to establish and maintain organizations and programs that focus on the accomplishment of clearly understood objectives and that have a built-in capacity for solving the myriads of small and large problems that arise to block the attainment of goals.

This requirement, it should be obvious, it not unique to any type of school in the metropolitan area, but is endemic throughout the metropolitan educational system. Earlier in this chapter evidence was presented indicating that academic achievement levels in our schools are highly predictable from information about the types of neighborhoods in which schools are located and the social background of the students who attend them. Predictability of this magnitude suggests not only that we can forecast in advance where achievement levels will be very low; it also suggests that the great majority of urban schools are not very effective in terms of utilizing resources to help students attain higher academic goals than they would have achieved in accord with the advantages and disadvantages characteristic of their home and neighborhood environments. Students do learn a good deal in school, and for many school is an interesting and exciting experience. Few schools appear to be unusually effective, however, with respect to teaching skills measured by standardized achievement tests. The same generalization probably holds for other goals of schooling as well.

What would constitute a potentially successful systems approach for improving the effectiveness of urban schools? No single model could be appropriate for all or most of the schools in a metropolitan area, but there are already experiments that illustrate how such an approach might work in practice.

At the elementary level, for example, the Individually Guided Education (IGE) model appears to be providing a successful systems approach to instructional improvement in a number of urban schools. Major components of such an approach usually include:

—incorporation of teacher aides and volunteers so that the adult-pupil ratio in the classroom is one to ten or less, which, in turn, makes it more feasible to individualize instruction;

—arrangement of grade-level organization so that adults can function as teams in working with groups of students whose learning and behavioral characteristics are clearly recognized; and

—establishment of cabinet-type approaches to administration that allow teachers and other employees to join with the head administrator in pinpointing and solving organizational problems, both large and small.

At the secondary level, John Dewey High School in New York City has been developing a promising systems approach including the following interconnected components:

—a specially selected and trained staff of teachers and administrators;

—an eight-hour day that allows students opportunities for independent study and teachers more time to prepare instructional materials and work with students;

—regular computerized rescheduling and reorganization of classes so that students performing well in a subject can move on to advanced or different work, much of it independent, and class size thereby can be reduced for students performing poorly;

—substantial amounts of resources in learning centers for each major subject area, with instructional modules carefully prepared to facilitate students' independent study;

—opportunities for study in any subject of special interest to a group of students, made possible in part through the longer school day and the periodic reorganization of regular classes; and

—opportunities and encouragement to learn outside the school, again made more feasible by the flexibility and innovation inherent in the school's overall organization.

The importance of such experiments is not so much in the specific components as it is in the attempt to coordinate the components in an effort to achieve a functional whole. Only thus can we expect the urban school to function effectively in the complex environment of the modern metropolis.

NOTES

1. W. Lloyd Warner, Marchia Meeker, and Kenneth Eels, *Social Class in America* (New York: Harper and Row, 1960). Shinn and others have since found that occupation, income, and education account for nearly all of the variation in perceived social-class rankings. See Robert L. Hamblin, "Social Attitudes: Magnitude Measurement and Theory," in Hubert M. Blalock, Jr., *Measurement in the Social Sciences* (Chicago: Aldine Publishing Company, 1974), 61-120.

2. Educators interested in determining the social-class level of a local school popu-

lation can do so easily by using Hollingshead's Two Factor Index (Occupation and Education). See August B. Hollingshead, "Two Factor Index of Social Position" (New Haven, Conn.: n.p., 1957, mimeo).

3. Charles A. Valentine, *Culture and Poverty* (Chicago: University of Chicago Press, 1968).

4. Hyman Rodman, "Lower Class Value Stretch," *Social Forces,* 42 (No. 2, 1963), 205-215.

5. Seymour Parker and Robert J. Kleiner, "The Culture of Poverty: An Adjustive Dimension," *American Anthropologist,* 72 (No. 3, 1970), 516-527.

6. Robert E. Herriott and Ben J. Hodgkins, *The Environment of Schooling* (Englewood Cliffs, N. J.: Prentice-Hall, 1973).

7. This implication is particularly clear in view of Schwartz's findings that low faith in human nature and present-time orientation are associated with low achievement among both Mexican-American and Anglo lower-class youngsters. See Audrey J. Schwartz, "A Comparative Study of Values and Achievement: Mexican-American and Anglo Youth," *Sociology of Education,* 44 (No. 4, 1971), 438-462.

8. Brewton Berry, *Race and Ethnic Relations* (Boston: Houghton Mifflin Company, 1965).

9. For descriptions of the nature and origins of cultural patterns that have arisen among black families, see Andrew Billingsley, *Black Families in White America* (Englewood Cliffs, N. J.: Prentice-Hall, 1968); John Scanzoni, *The Black Family in Modern Society* (Boston: Allyn and Bacon, 1971).

10. Robert J. Havighurst and Bernice L. Neugarten, *Society and Education* (Boston: Allyn and Bacon, 1975).

11. James S. Coleman et al., *Equality of Educational Opportunity* (Washington, D. C.: U. S. Government Printing Office, 1966).

12. William G. Spady, "The Impact of School Resources on Students," in *Review of Research in Education,* ed. Fred N. Kerlinger (Itasca, Ill.: F. E. Peacock Publishers, 1973).

13. Daniel U. Levine et al., "Concentrated Poverty and Reading Achievement in Five Big Cities" (Kansas City: University of Missouri at Kansas City, Center for the Study of Metropolitan Problems in Education, 1977, mimeo).

14. Martin Whiteman and Martin Deutsch, "Social Disadvantage as Related to Intellective and Language Development," in *Social Class, Race, and Psychological Development,* ed. Martin Deutsch, Irwin Katz, and Arthur R. Jensen (New York: Holt, Rinehart, and Winston, 1968), 86-114.

15. Schwartz, "Comparative Study of Values and Achievement."

16. Robert J. Havighurst, "Minority Subcultures and the Law of Effect," in *Educating the Disadvantaged,* ed. Allan C. Ornstein et al. (New York: AMS Press, 1971), 3-12.

17. James M. Mahan and Mary K. Criger, "Culturally Oriented Instruction for Native American Students," *Integrateducation,* 5 (March-April 1977), 11-12.

18. Havighurst, "Minority Subcultures and the Law of Effect"; Lindel L. Nelson and Spencer Kagan, "Competition: The Star-Spangled Scramble," *Psychology Today,* 6 (No. 4, 1972), 53-57.

19. Hyung-chan Kim, "Education of the Korean Immigrant Child," *Integrateducation,* 15 (January-February 1977), 16.

20. Robin H. Farquhar, "Home Influences on Achievement and Intelligence: An Essay Review," *Administrator's Notebook,* 13 (No. 5, 1965), 1-4.

21. Daniel U. Levine *et al.,* "The Home Environment of Students in a High Achieving Inner-City Parochial School and a Nearby Public School," *Sociology of Education,* 45 (No. 4, 1972), 435-445.

22. Daniel Bell, *The Coming of Post-Industrial Society* (New York: Basic Books, 1973).

23. *Ibid.,* 117.

24. This change has been documented, to an extent, by a cross-cultural study in which Langton and Karns have shown that the economic and educational systems have transplanted the family, the church, and other early socializing institutions in preparing young people for adulthood in advanced societies as compared with traditional or economically developing societies. Kenneth P. Langton and David A. Karns, *A Cross National Study of the Relative Influence of School: A Causal Analysis* (Ann Arbor: University of Michigan, 1969). ERIC: ED 034 320.

25. Suggestions for administrative responses to the problem of incongruence in the school and home environments of educationally disadvantaged students can be found in Richard W. Saxe, *School-Community Interaction* (Berkeley, Calif.: McCutchan Publishing Corporation, 1975), and in Daniel U. Levine, "The Reform of Urban Education," *Phi Delta Kappan,* 52 (No. 6, 1971), 329-333.

26. Urie Bronfenbrenner, "Is Early Intervention Effective?" *Teachers College Record,* 76 (No. 2, 1974), 279-303.

27. Robert J. Havighurst and Daniel U. Levine, *Education in Metropolitan Areas* (Boston: Allyn and Bacon, 1971), 100-101.

28. Kenneth Keniston, "Prologue: Youth as a Stage of Life," in *Youth,* ed. Robert J. Havighurst and Philip H. Dreyer, Seventy-fourth Yearbook of the National Society for the Study of Education, Part I (Chicago: University of Chicago Press, 1975), 8.

29. *Ibid.,* 11.

30. Daniel Yankelovich, *The Changing Values on Campus* (New York: Simon and Schuster, 1972), 169.

31. Robert J. Havighurst, "Youth in Social Institutions," in *Youth,* ed. Havighurst and Dreyer, 126.

32. *Ibid.,* 127.

33. Keniston, "Prologue," 10-11.

34. Frank Musgrove, *Youth and the Social Order* (Bloomington: Indiana University Press, 1965), 26.

35. For example, see A. Harry Passow, "Reforming America's High Schools," *Phi Delta Kappan,* 56 (May 1975), 587-590.

36. Daniel U. Levine, "The Unfinished Identity of Metropolitan Man," in *Teaching about Life in the City,* ed. Richard Wisniewski, Forty-second Yearbook of the National Council for the Social Studies (Washington, D. C.: NCSS, 1972), 21-47.

Chapter Seven

Rodney J. Reed

Education and Ethnicity

It is participation and involvement in the school that creates and fosters pride and lends a sense of belonging. The relationship among participants and others involved in the workings of the school — students, teachers, administrative staff, parents, and interested members of the community — is vital to the success of the school as an educational enterprise.

In public schools where students tend to succeed, this interactive process is positive and constructive. Students, teachers, staff, and parents usually manifest a feeling of identification with the school and a sense of belonging to it. In some schools, however, the rate of failure among students is high. Such schools appear to lack successful interaction among participants, and the result is a negative, destructive influence that tends to breed a sense of vulnerability and isolation.

Seeds of conflict and mistrust within a school are nurtured when students are treated as unwelcome visitors, when teachers and other members of the staff resent being assigned to a school in a community where they feel uncomfortable, when teachers and administrators believe that students cannot or will not learn, or when parents feel that the school does not serve their children's needs. In most cases these conditions stem from a lack of understanding of ethnic minority-group cultures, a latent dislike for certain ethnic minority groups, a lack of understanding of different learning styles that demand different teaching styles, and a general lack of respect for ethnic minority

130

students and parents on the part of the school staff. Such conditions encourage the dysfunctional learning atmosphere that prevails in all too many schools attended by large numbers of ethnic minority students.

In urban school districts throughout the United States, Afro-American, Hispanic-American, and Native American students experience failure at alarmingly high rates. Asian-American students, with the exception of Chinese- and Japanese-American ones, also show a high incidence of failure in school. Is this because such students or their parents lack interest in the school or in education, as many people would have us believe? Or is it because these students do not feel that they are a part of the educational process? Is it their sense of isolation and vulnerability that promotes their failure?

Students must believe that the school staff is genuinely concerned about their educational development and is committed to the belief that they are capable of full educational attainment. This is perhaps more important for students from minority groups. They need to feel a genuine sense of belonging to, and identification with, the schools they attend if there is to be successful teaching and effective learning.

To belong is a crucial dimension of human development. The importance of the dimension is emphasized by Abraham Maslow,[1] who argues that a sense of belonging is a basic need that must be satisfied before higher-level needs and growth needs are activated. Sufficient satisfaction of the basic needs (physiological, safety and security, love and belonging, self-esteem, and esteem of others) and of the growth needs (meaningfulness, self-sufficiency, order, justice, and individuality) are necessary for the improvement, strengthening, and healthy development of the individual.[2] Satisfaction of these needs is also required for self-actualization, which has been described by Maslow as "the desire to become more and more what one is, to become everything that one is capable of becoming."[3]

Of course, school is not the sole institution within which students acquire the skills and experience necessary to satisfy the basic and growth needs defined by Maslow. School programs and practices can, however, increase the probability that minority-group students will feel they belong in schools that formerly have rejected them in many covert and overt ways. The actions of the entire classified and certificated school staff are vital in creating and maintaining an environment that builds upon the strengths of students and instills within them a respect for themselves and for human dignity. The total school staff must recognize the worth of all students and provide for their social and intellectual growth.

Conditions in the public schools associated with negative attitudes and behaviors toward minority-group students and thought to affect their school performance are examined in this chapter. The discussion focuses on the general effect that ethnic minority student representation in urban school districts has on staffing; the relationship of school staff attitudes, morale, transfer propensity, and teaching styles to the academic performance of ethnic minority students; parental involvement in the school; understanding ethnic minority-group culture and history; bilingual-bicultural programs; and respect for ethnic diver-

TABLE 7-1. Ethnic distribution of pupils by number and percentage of total enrollment in twenty-two selected urban school districts, Fall 1972

	Minority group enrollment					
	American Indian		Negro		Oriental	
School district	Number	Percent	Number	Percent	Number	Percent
Atlanta, Ga.	6	0.0	73,985	77.1	60	0.1
Baltimore, Md.	0	0.0	129,250	69.3	0	0.0
Cincinnati, Ohio	26	0.0	36,808	47.3	193	0.2
Chicago, Ill.	1,153	0.2	315,940	57.1	4,453	0.8
Cleveland, Ohio	319	0.2	83,596	57.6	248	0.2
Dallas, Tex.	523	0.3	59,638	38.6	298	0.2
Detroit, Mich.	213	0.1	186,994	67.6	540	0.2
El Paso, Tex.	55	0.1	1,866	3.0	361	0.6
Gary, Inc.	34	0.1	31,200	69.6	50	0.1
Houston, Tex.	157	0.1	88,871	39.4	819	0.4
Kansas City, Mo.	0	0.0	35,578	54.4	0	0.0
Los Angeles, Calif.	1,347	0.2	156,680	25.2	21,220	3.4
Memphis, Tenn.	28	0.0	80,158	57.8	171	0.1
Newark, N.J.	21	0.0	56,736	72.3	116	0.1
New Orleans, La.	37	0.0	77,504	74.6	141	0.1
New York, N.Y.	400	0.0	405,177	36.0	20,474	1.8
Oakland, Calif.	622	1.0	39,121	60.0	3,986	61.1
Philadelphia, Pa.	0	0.0	173,874	61.4	0	0.0
Richmond, Va.	31	0.1	30,746	70.2	107	0.2
San Francisco, Calif.	249	0.3	25,055	30.6	19,088	23.3
St. Louis, Mo.	54	0.1	72,629	68.8	99	0.1
Washington, D.C.	18	0.0	133,638	95.5	598	0.4

Source: Data compiled in Office for Civil Rights, *Directory of Public Elementary and Secondary Schools in Selected Districts, Enrollment and Staff by Racial/Ethnic*

sity—labeling, improving classroom and school-wide interaction processes, and getting to know the school community.

ETHNIC MINORITY STUDENT REPRESENTATION

Data compiled by the Office on Civil Rights in 1972 reveal that
more than three million Afro-American, Hispanic-American, Asian-
American, and American Indian[4] elementary and secondary school
pupils are concentrated in only twenty-two urban school districts.
These districts, along with the distribution of their students by ethnic
group, are listed in Table 7-1. The table indicates that American Indian students are found in relatively small numbers in those school districts, whereas black students are dispersed rather evenly throughout

Minority group enroll.		Total enrollment				
Spanish-American		Minority		Nonminority		Total number
Number	Percent	Number	Percent	Number	Percent	(N = 100 percent)
272	0.3	74,323	77.4	21,683	22.6	96,006
0	0.0	129,250	69.3	57,350	30.7	186,600
88	0.1	37,115	47.7	40,763	52.3	77,878
61,423	11.1	382,969	69.2	170,373	30.8	553,342
2,844	2.0	87,007	59.9	58,189	40.1	145,196
15,908	10.3	76,367	49.4	78,214	50.6	154,581
4,512	1.6	192,259	69.5	84,396	30.5	276,665
36,026	57.7	38,308	61.4	24,096	38.6	62,404
3,636	8.1	34,920	77.9	9,910	22.1	44,830
37,281	16.5	127,128	56.4	98,282	43.6	225,410
0	0.0	35,578	54.4	29,836	45.6	65,414
148,109	23.9	327,356	52.7	293,303	47.3·	620,659
48	0.0	80,405	58.0	58,309	42.0	138,714
11,981	15.3	68,854	87.7	9,638	12.3	78,492
1,622	1.6	79,304	76.4	24,535	23.6	103,839
298,903	26.6	724,954	64.4	400,495	35.6	125,449
5,412	8.3	49,141	75.4	16,048	24.6	65,189
9,550	3.4	183,424	64.8	99,541	35.2	282,965
40	0.1	30,924	70.6	12,901	29.4	43,825
11,511	14.0	55,903	68.2	26,067	31.8	81,970
203	0.2	72,985	69.1	32,632	30.9	105,617
818	0.6	135,072	96.5	4,928	3.5	140,000

Group, Fall 1972 (Washington, D.C.: U.S. Department of Health, Education, and
Welfare, 1972).

them. Spanish-speaking or Hispanic-American students are clustered in the East, the Southwest, and the Far West, and Oriental or Asian students are clustered primarily in the Far West.

Minority enrollment in the public schools often reflects societal policies and practices intended to confine ethnic minorities within certain geographic limits. One devastating result of such isolation is the generation of feelings of hostility and alienation. Barriers that lead to such perceptions have been removed for some, but they remain for many ethnic minority families.

Those urban districts where there is a heavy concentration of ethnic minority students are also marked by a high concentration of poverty, a high rate of unemployment, and a low average level of family income. The struggle for survival is constant, and the socioeconomic problems that surround the lives of many who live there are demeaning. Ethnic minority families are eager to break the cycle of poverty that surrounds their lives. They want more and better jobs, better housing, and better schools.

Recent efforts to remedy minority-group attendance patterns as a means of improving the quality of schooling have not been encouraging. As a result of court-ordered desegregation, for example, minority students have been bused or given the option of attending schools outside their neighborhoods. Clearly, these students often have not been welcomed. White parents and other citizens have demonstrated and protested vociferously, and many parents have removed their children from the public schools or moved to geographic areas where ethnic minorities are either nonexistent or so small in number as to eliminate the possibility of effective school desegregation. The message is clear: although some ethnic minority students may be tolerated outside the confines of their traditional neighborhoods, they are not welcome; they do not belong.

This message is strongly reinforced by housing patterns. Many whites move as soon as several, perhaps as few as three to five, ethnic minority families move into what they consider to be "their" neighborhood. Then there is the systematic denial of a full range of employment opportunities to members of ethnic minority groups in trades that require minimal skills, as well as in professions that require more technical skills, to reinforce the message. Such discrimination in employment has led to the enactment of affirmative action hiring policies at the federal, state, and local levels of government. The total impact of these policies, however, has been more cosmetic than substantive.

Given the above circumstances, it is understandable why ethnic minority groups often feel alienated. The elimination or reduction of some of the causes of such alienation must, of course, be linked to environmental circumstances outside the purview of public schools. Within the schools, however, the elimination of student alienation must begin with the school staff.

Many schools that have large enrollments of ethnic minority students also have high percentages of nonethnic minority teachers. (Table 7-2 illustrates that the majority of the urban school districts cited in Table 7-1, selected because of their high percentages of ethnic minority students, have high percentages of nonethnic minority teachers.) It is not surprising that many such schools come under attack by parents and students. Ethnically dissimilar teachers are often perceived as not relating effectively to minority-group students or to their parents. A comparison of the two tables clearly indicates that few school districts with high percentages of ethnic minority students have comparable percentages of ethnic minority teachers. This disparity is dramatically observed by comparing the percentages of Hispanic-American students and Hispanic-American teachers, and by comparing the percentages of Afro-American students and Afro-American teachers in these districts. Of the twenty-two selected school districts, only two show fairly close percentages of Afro-American students and Afro-American teachers. Comparison of Asian-American student-teacher percentages in the selected school districts reveals that these groups are more evenly matched than other ethnic minority groups. In only two of the selected districts are there significantly larger percentages of Oriental or Asian students than ethnically similar teachers. In a similar fashion, there is little discrepancy between percentages of American Indian students and teachers. Clearly the small number of Oriental or Asian and American Indian students enrolled in the selected districts provides an easier basis for matching the percentages of Asian and American Indian teachers and students than might otherwise be the case. In an atypical case, one school district in the Far West displays a higher percentage of Oriental or Asian teachers than the percentage of Oriental or Asian students. In contrast, note the small percentage of Asian teachers as compared to the large number of Asian students in another school district in the Far West.

In nearly all of the selected urban school districts, the percentage of
Afro-American and Hispanic-American students far exceeds the percentage of ethnically similar teachers. Though the evidence is incon-
clusive as to whether ethnic similarity is essential for effective teaching
and learning, it appears that, if students are to develop a sense of belonging in the schools and to become successful in them, they need
teachers who understand and respect them, who are able to use
teaching styles that match student learning styles, and who elicit a
warmer, more genuine response from both students and parents.

Many of the problems faced by ethnic minority students from poor
communities have never been experienced by members of traditional
school staffs. In order to understand fully the problems that surround
the lives of ethnic minority students, there is little substitute for the

TABLE 7-2. Ethnic distribution of teachers by number and percentage of total
number in twenty-two selected urban school districts, Fall 1972

	Teachers by ethnic origin					
	American Indian		Negro		Oriental	
School district	Number	Percent	Number	Percent	Number	Percent
Atlanta, Ga.	3	0.0	2,477	62.1	2	0.1
Baltimore, Md.	0	0.0	4,155	59.3	8	0.0
Cincinnati, Ohio	1	0.0	775	25.2	7	0.2
Chicago, Ill.	7	0.0	8,228	37.7	144	0.7
Cleveland, Ohio	1	0.0	2,068	40.2	11	0.2
Dallas, Tex.	3	0.0	1,800	28.5	4	0.1
Detroit, Mich.	52	0.5	4,563	46.5	39	0.4
El Paso, Tex.	10	0.4	87	3.3	9	0.3
Gary, Ind.	0	0.0	1,102	61.3	1	0.1
Houston, Tex.	0	0.0	2,975	36.0	24	0.3
Kansas City, Mo.	0	0.0	1,059	40.9	0	0.0
Los Angeles, Calif.	25	0.1	3,382	14.5	1,173	5.0
Memphis, Tenn.	0	0.0	2,370	42.9	2	0.0
Newark, N.J.	0	0.0	1,573	39.4	12	0.3
New Orleans, La.	1	0.0	2,262	57.3	6	0.2
New York, N.Y.	18	0.0	4,884	8.8	243	0.4
Oakland, Calif.	6	0.2	754	29.9	107	4.2
Philadelphia, Pa.	0	0.0	4,006	33.7	0	0.0
Richmond, Va.	0	0.0	1,068	54.6	1	0.1
San Francisco, Calif.	10	0.2	409	9.8	350	8.4
St. Louis, Mo.	1	0.0	2,128	53.7	9	0.2
Washington, D.C.	0	0.0	4,995	84.6	7	0.1

Source: Data compiled in Office for Civil Rights, *Directory of Public Elementary and
Secondary Schools in Selected Districts, Enrollment and Staff by Racial/Ethnic*

experience of having lived in a ghetto or barrio, or of having been victimized by the effects of discrimination and racism. Full understanding of the problems that inhere from such circumstances cannot be achieved through reading, conversation, or lectures. Most, if not all, ethnic minority teachers or administrators have experienced either discrimination or racism; most have experienced both. On the basis of that experience, they should have more insight into the problems many ethnic minority students face and greater empathy for the students. This would indicate that there should be *at least* proportional representation of ethnic minority teachers, administrators, and noncertificated staff in urban schools. There should also be ethnic minority teachers, administrators, and noncertificated staff in all schools, regardless of location, in numbers at least proportional to the ethnic

Teachers by ethnic origin				Total number of teachers
Spanish-American		Other		
Number	Percent	Number	Percent	(N = 100 percent)
3	0.1	1,506	37,8	3,988
0	0.0	2,856	40.7	7,011
0	0.0	2,297	74.6	3,080
259	1.2	13,170	60.4	21,808
9	0.2	3,060	59.4	5,149
129	2.0	4,388	69.4	6,324
58	0.6	5,109	52.0	9,821
606	23.3	1,886	72.6	2,598
40	2.2	655	36.4	1,798
203	2.5	5,053	61.2	8,255
0	0.0	1,532	59.1	2,591
660	2.8	18,078	77.5	23,318
2	0.0	3,155	57.1	5,529
130	3.3	2,281	57.1	3,996
13	0.3	1,669	42.2	3,951
1,239	2.2	49,404	88.6	55,788
58	2.3	1,620	63.7	2,545
0	0.0	7,893	66.3	11,899
0	0.0	886	45.3	1,955
183	4.4	3,239	77.3	4,191
5	0.1	1,822	46.0	3,965
25	0.4	875	14.8	5,902

Group, Fall 1972 (Washington, D.C.: U.S. Department of Health, Education, and Welfare, 1972).

representation in the overall population in order to help eliminate the barriers associated with misinformation and stereotyping. Further, the school staff must work constantly with other agencies to improve the physical and psychological environment in which many students are entrapped.

SELECTED STAFF ATTITUDES AND BEHAVIORS AND THEIR EFFECT ON THE ACADEMIC PERFORMANCE OF ETHNIC MINORITY STUDENTS

Many ethnic minority students in urban school districts are not matched proportionately to teachers who are ethnically similar. This same dissimilarity probably exists among the administrators and the noncertificated school staff. Given this ethnic dissimilarity, do staff attitudes affect student academic performance? Does the assignment of nonethnic minority teachers, administrators, and noncertificated staff to schools with large enrollments of ethnic minority students affect staff morale? Does a high incidence of staff transfers affect student performance? Do differences between teaching and learning styles affect student performance?

Staff Attitudes

The academic performance of minority students in schools where families have a low socioeconomic status (SES) falls further behind that of students in schools at the middle or upper SES level at each successive grade level.[5] This phenomenon of diminishing returns affects a significant number of minority students. It would appear that participation in the process of schooling is a destructive experience—one that has negative implications for the students' self-image and for their academic achievement, as well as for the academic expectations held for them by the school staff. The reasons for this phenomenon are not clear, but students who begin their formal educational careers at normal or expected levels of academic performance should not retrogress in schools that supposedly exist to increase learning and develop intellectual skills. In this regard, then, it is not unreasonable to question the relationship between teacher-pupil interaction and academic performance.

Positive interaction between teachers and students should result in more effective educational processes in the classroom. Positive interaction patterns between students and administrators, and between students and noncertificated staff are equally important and essential outside the classroom to create an atmosphere in which students can achieve at maximum educational levels. Students must feel that the entire school staff expects them to achieve academically. Students need encouragement, they require positive reinforcement inside and outside the classroom, and they must have the opportunity to enhance their awareness of self-worth and to gain a sense of human dignity. If so, they will progress academically.

The probability that academic performance will improve is greater in schools where students feel they belong, where they are expected to achieve, where the attitudes of the school staff are supportive, and where their self-concept[6] is positive. While most of these conditions fall within the purview of the school, the argument can be made that self-concept does not. Certainly the development of self-concept is not confined to the school, but "students who experience repeated success in school are likely to develop positive feelings about their abilities, while those who encounter failure tend to develop negative views of themselves."[7] To go one step further, "the teacher's attitude and opinions regarding his/her students have a significant influence on their success in school."[8]

Teacher-learner interactions must be constantly assessed so that negative self-concepts in students can be modified. Don Hamachek suggests that if we, as teachers, are to facilitate learning and self-esteem through self-concept enhancement, we must:

1. Understand that we teach what we are, not just what we know.
2. Understand that anything we do or say could significantly change a student's attitude about himself for better or worse.
3. Understand that students, like us, behave in terms of what seems to be true, which means that learning often is controlled, not by what the facts are, but by how they are perceived.
4. Be willing not just to teach subject matter, but to deal with what the subject matter means to different students.
5. Understand that we are not likely to get results simply by telling someone he is worthy. . . . One good way to start is to take time to listen to what the students have to say and to use their ideas when possible.
6. Understand that teacher behavior which is distant, cold and rejecting is far less likely to enhance self-concept, motivation and learning than behavior which is warm, accepting and discriminating.
7. Be willing to be flexible, to be direct or indirect as the situation and personality of the student demands.[9]

It follows, therefore, that many minority students experience school failure because teachers and administrators expect them to fail, an expectation conditioned by the past academic performance of similar students, by erroneous academic arguments regarding genetic inferiority and ethnicity that serve to stereotype minority students, and by characteristics of minority students that differ from those of teachers and administrators (speech patterns, language usage, reluctance to respond freely in the classroom, style of walking, SES levels, and so forth). If the recurring cycle of school failure is to be arrested and reversed, school staff must become aware of negative attitudes toward minority students and the effect such attitudes have on student performance.

Awareness can be stimulated by research efforts that demonstrate the effect of teacher expectancy[10] and that demonstrate negative classroom interaction between teachers and students.[11] Awareness, however, is only a first step. The willingness of teachers to change their attitudes toward minority students in a positive fashion is crucial. In the absence of change, minority students will continue to feel the current debilitating effects of the urban school experience. All students need to sense the sincerity, warmth, and respect of the entire school staff if they are to reciprocate with those same qualities. The effectiveness of both teaching and learning is minimized by negative attitudes and a hostile environment.

Staff Morale and Propensity for Transfer

Does the assignment of teachers, administrators, and other staff members to schools in poor urban communities result in lower staff morale and a higher incidence of transfer?[12] Do these conditions have an impact on students' willingness to participate fully in school learning? Many believe that new teachers and administrators serve an apprenticeship in economically disadvantaged urban schools and are later transferred to schools considered more desirable. The implication is clear: there is little prestige attached to being a teacher, an administrator, or a member of the noncertificated staff in an urban school attended primarily by ethnic minority students. To the extent that this view is accurate, the quality of inner-city urban schools attended by ethnic minorities is jeopardized. It also may suggest that many teachers, administrators, and school staff are unable to relate effectively to the students in those schools—hence, the desire to be transferred. Though the transfer of teachers who find it difficult to relate to ethnic minority students is desirable, the number of vacancies in schools thought to be more prestigious often is not equal to the demand. As a result, many staff members remain in inner-city schools where they are ill at ease and where they have little desire to serve. They manifest negative attitudes that exacerbate the frustration many students experience.

Such situations must be eliminated. As a first step in the process, only the best staff—those knowledgeable, creative, and sensitive to students; those who are respected by students and parents; those who show respect for students and parents; those who wish to work in schools attended primarily by ethnic minority students—should be selected. Teachers, administrators, and noncertificated staff must demonstrate pride in these schools through their commitment and their ability to relate to the students. Secondly, teachers, administrators, and noncertificated staff selected on the basis of the above criteria should view their assignment as being relatively permanent, with some commitment to continuing their professional careers in inner-city schools.

Inner-city schools must be considered the academic equivalent of schools attended by middle- to upper-income students. Inner-city schools must also no longer be viewed as dumping grounds for ineffective teachers and other staff members. A school staff that has neither the ability to be effective nor the desire to serve in a particular school exhibits low morale, and this is transmitted to students and their parents in such a fashion as to label the school as a failure, a place where students should not go if they wish to receive quality education. Inevitably, students who are extremely perceptive about the sincerity of adults retaliate by responding to the school with hostility. Staff members, for their part, request transfer to other schools. Effective schools demand effective school staffs.

Teaching Style

An important barrier to student academic performance is the failure of teachers to recognize cultural cues that stimulate learning. This dimension is frequently referred to in the literature as teaching-learning style or student cognitive style. While research is limited, it follows logically that conflicts arise and student academic achievement is impeded when cultural values and orientation of teacher and student differ.

Teacher-student conflict often erupts when teachers lack awareness of and refuse to accept differences in students' cultural values. For example, in comparing American middle-class and Mexican-American value orientations, Y. A. Cabrera reports several major differences involving individual value orientations and those of the family or group, time orientation in regard to material gain, and self-direction and control in contrast to accommodation to problems.[13] In an analysis of the cognitive styles of Afro-American children, Yolanda Jenkins notes major differences in the philosophy, values, and self-concept and the development of a cognitive style based on European and African descent.[14] J. S. Kleinfeld points out the intellectual strength of Eskimo children in figural ability. Accordingly, some of the socialization practices that may have influenced this strength include Eskimo child-rearing practices that emphasize independence and exploration, learning by watching adults rather than by receiving verbal instruction, and placing emphasis on observable information.[15] Among East Africans, higher levels of spatial ability are associated with environmental exploration.[16] Further indications that differential cultural strengths among various ethnic groups have an influence on learning style are suggested by Rosalie Cohen, whose research points out that some students are analytical in their approach to learning while others are relational.[17] Thus, fundamental cultural differences in such areas as competition and cooperation, learning styles, individual and group socialization patterns, time orientation, and self-direction and control must be understood if teachers are to reinforce cultural cues and build on pupil strength.

In a very provocative article, Wade Boykin posits that "there are at least three distinct but interrelated realms of one's home (and immediate ecological) environment that may aid in the characterization of some critical, adaptive cultural styles and strengths of Black children: the social-affective, the conceptual-informational and the vervistic." Boykin defines vervistic as "the level of spatial and temporal stimulus energy transformation and distribution in either an individual's exogenous or his proprioceptive environment." Boykin argues that affective, cognitive, and vervistic considerations ought to be taken into account in providing successful educational experiences for Afro-American children.[18]

Evidence of the effect of teacher style on student learning can be seen in the studies of Nancy St. John, who found that for Afro-American children, "child-orientation or interpersonal competence in teachers contributes significantly to reading growth."[19] Further evidence of the effect of teaching style is reported by Robert Heath, who concludes that: "the ability of teachers to relate to students is likely to vary substantially as a function of the ethnic background of the student group," and that "characteristics of teaching style contribute to ability-to-relate differentially in student groups of differing ethnic background."[20]

Differences in student learning styles are evident, though not thoroughly understood, in all school situations. This is particularly true in schools attended by multiethnic groups. These styles have cultural dimensions that teachers must recognize and adapt to their teaching techniques if they are to maximize student learning. Rigid teaching styles that utilize only one approach stifle the desire and motivation of some students for learning. It is important that teachers not view teaching as a uniform activity in which all students are expected to learn the same things, at the same time, and in the same manner. For the teaching-learning environment to be effective, teachers must value and understand the student's cultural background, must incorporate the student's culture into learning experiences, and must create a sense that the student belongs in the classroom. Essentially, students and teachers must have positive interactions based on trust. As described by R. P. McDermott, "trusting relations are framed by the contexts in which people are asked to relate, and where trusting relations occur, learning is a possibility. Where trusting relations are not possible, learning can only result from solitary effort."[21]

Overview

By virtue of their income, education, and occupation, school staff assume advantageous positions in comparison to parents and students in poor urban communities. To the extent that the school staff differs by ethnicity, cultural background may also contribute to conflicts between staff and students. To minimize these conflicts, staff members who are familiar with and who adequately understand and respect the students with whom they work must be selected. Consideration of ethnic-group similarity should lead to the hiring of school staff members who may have grown up in inner-city communities, who have a better understanding of problems in those communities, who are able to relate better to students and their parents, who have greater respect and understanding of the problems many minority students endure, who have higher levels of expectation for the minority students entrusted to their care, and who have a desire to strengthen and improve ethnic minority-group communities.

School staff selected on the basis of ethnic-group congruence alone, however, will not automatically ensure the selection of staff who display the foregoing characteristics. Staff members must be selected with ample consideration for background, attitudes, and behaviors toward ethnic minority students regardless of ethnicity. Importantly, those who are selected must not manifest attitudes and behaviors that are condescending and paternalistic. If staff members and potential staff members believe that ethnic minority-group students in urban schools cannot learn at high levels and if they evidence an avowed desire not to work in such schools, then they should not be hired or retained.

PARENTAL INVOLVEMENT

Teachers and administrators in schools located in the inner city frequently comment that parental involvement in school activities is minimal when compared to parental involvement in middle- and upper-class schools. The assumption that lack of parental involvement or participation in school activities indicates a general lack of interest or concern is incorrect. Parents at every social stratum and from every ethnic background tend to be vitally interested in the education of their children. Some parents, however, may not recognize the value of involvement in the school and may not participate because of attitudes about the school staff, because of family obligations, or because of time constraints. More specifically, lack of parental involvement may result from the poor reception accorded parents by the school staff, from a superior attitude, as expressed verbally or nonverbally by the school staff, from a language barrier, from the needs of young or sick children at home, from lack of energy or transportation to attend a meeting after working at demanding jobs, from work schedules that conflict with school activities, from a feeling that there is nothing parents can contribute to the school, or from a feeling that personal involvement makes little difference in the formal schooling process.

Parents can become involved in the school in a variety of ways: as paraprofessionals, teacher aides, instructional aides, volunteer helpers, tutors, room mothers, school advisory councilmembers, PTA members, or sponsors of special projects. They can also become involved through school visits and through teacher and administrator conferences.[22]

New school programs and new staff selection offer rich opportunities to utilize parents in the decision-making process. It is important that parents become partners in the educational enterprise with an opportunity to shape school programs, to ensure that new staff are sensitive to children, and to raise the image of the school. Participation and involvement create pride in the school and help to create an atmosphere conducive to feelings of belonging. The involvement of parents in the school may also be enhanced through organizational development. Parents receiving training in organizational development have been reported to have increased their participation in a variety of school activities.[23]

Despite the many options available to parents in inner-city schools, however, involvement continues at a low level, even though attitudes of the school staff toward the students they serve are likely to be more positive in schools where parents are heavily involved than in schools where they are not. Attitudes of the school staff appear to carry the greatest weight in explaining lack of parental involvement in the schools.

Support for this assertion is demonstrated by the relatively large number of parents who do attend school activities that directly involve the participation of their children (for example, concerts, athletic events, and dramatic presentations) and that provide a rewarding experience. This should be a highly visible indication to the entire school staff that parents are concerned about the education of their children, that they value education, that they expect their children to learn, and that they expect the school staff to be educationally and socially responsive to their children.

At another level, parental involvement appears to have some association with the academic performance of students. Some empirical evidence in this regard focuses upon the use of parents in the classroom as paraprofessionals or as teacher aides.[24] In classrooms where paraprofessionals have been used, there has been greater gain in reading and mathematics than occurs in similar classrooms where paraprofessionals are not used.[25] One explanation is that paraprofessionals enable students to receive more individualized instruction, thereby ensuring more effective teaching and learning. This reason is, of course, plausible. It should also be recognized, however, that paraprofessionals, as indigenous parents, also become surrogate parents for many students. Students witness, experience, and value the support and reinforcement of parents in their classes. As a result, their attitude toward school becomes more positive, and academic performance improves.

Teachers, administrators, and noncertificated personnel must work to eliminate the reasons for lack of involvement on the part of inner-city parents. In this regard, the use of paraprofessionals in the classroom has been effective in increasing parental involvement, in influencing better communication and attitudes between teachers and parents[26] and in enhancing student achievement. Parents are interested in the education of their children and will become more involved if teachers and administrators sincerely invite them to participate, solicit their input and help for very specific activities, offer flexible arrangements for involvement, and communicate with parents regularly and when necessary in the parents' first language. Further, the school staff must become more conscious of behaviors and attitudes toward parents and students that become barriers to effective communication. In short, the school staff must create an atmosphere in which parents as well as students feel they belong.

UNDERSTANDING HISTORY AND CULTURE

The entire staff (from building principal to custodian) of all schools (from kindergarten through the university) should develop an understanding of, and an appreciation and a respect for, all students, regardless of ethnicity or socioeconomic circumstances. One way to do this is to study the history and culture, including language usage, of ethnic minority groups through prescribed preservice and in-service training programs.[27] In California, such in-service programs are required for the staff in each school that has an enrollment where 25 percent or more of the students are from diverse ethnic backgrounds.[28]

Study of ethnic group history and culture can lead to reform of the entire educational system. The values of American Indians, for example, suggest that much of what is presently taught in the schools needs to be carefully reexamined.

The normative structure used to motivate whites is the antithesis of the Indian value system. American schools, reflecting American life, are built on competitiveness, individual achievement, rigid and regimented schedules, future orientation, dependency, obedience, and acquisitiveness. Life for Indian people revolves around the group, present orientation, flexible scheduling, cooperation, self-direction, and creative activities. This disparity in values becomes evident when we discover, for example, that in the Siouan and many other Indian languages, there is no word for time; yet most white Americans are fettered by the clock.[29]

It is unlikely that an American Indian student would experience success in the traditional school setting. Yet little effort has been made to change the schools that serve American Indian students so that their unique value system can be an asset in their schooling.[30] Many of the traditional values of American Indians—flexible scheduling, cooperation, self-direction, creativeness—are the same as those that have been the basis for "innovative" schools. Undoubtedly much more can be learned from the study of the American Indian culture, as well as the study of other ethnic group cultural traditions and customs.

Of course, school staffs must find ways to translate the study of history and culture into demonstrable feelings of understanding and respect for all students and, in turn, encourage students to reciprocate with mutual feelings of understanding and respect for themselves and for others. This could go far toward eliminating value conflicts between the cultures of minority students and the orientation of traditional public schools.

Bilingual-Bicultural Programs

Many ethnic minority children enter school with a limited knowledge of English. The fact that English is often not spoken at home places them at a distinct disadvantage in schools where their native language is not understood at all or is understood very little. Alienation, frustration, and failure are ensured unless the school program is flexible enough to meet the needs of such students, or unless at least some members of the school staff speak the students' language and can understand and appreciate their culture. Many schools attended by minority students do not, however, have staff members conversant with either the language or the culture of minority students. One solution proposed to alleviate such situations is bilingual-bicultural education.

According to David Ballestros,

bilingual education serves five positive purposes for the child and the school:
1. It reduces retardation through ability to learn with the mother tongue immediately.
2. It reinforces the relations of the school and the home through a common communication bond.
3. It projects the individual into an atmosphere of personal identification, self-worth, and achievement.
4. It gives the student a base for success in the field work.
5. It preserves and enriches the cultural and human resources of a people.[31]

Bilingual-bicultural education programs have been designed to increase the sense of belonging for students whose native language is not English and to encourage school personnel to become familiar with the cultural background of non-English-speaking students. Much of the impetus for bilingual-bicultural programs has come from federal funds available through the Bilingual Education Act of 1968.[32] While programs funded through this act may vary because of local conditions, several components appear to be basic for their effectiveness:
— utilization of the native language in the educational process to teach basic concepts and skills necessary for future learning;
— continued language development in the native language;
— development of subject matter in the native language;
— development of subject matter in the second language;
— development of a positive self-image and cultural identity;
— continued language development in the second language.[33]

Bilingual-bicultural programs are viewed as essential for maximizing the school performance of students who do not speak English and for reforming the monolinguistic, monocultural education traditionally associated with public schools.

While bilingual-bicultural programs have been tried with Spanish-speaking students, such programs are needed for all students who do not speak English fluently. Indeed, the findings in the Lau case indicate that exclusive teaching in English denies equal educational opportunity to non-English-speaking students.[34]

Bilingual-bicultural programs are also helpful for other students and members of the staff who, because of a lack of knowledge and familiarity with languages and cultures other than their own, tend to be insensitive to different ethnic groups. Such programs can be the foundation for a viable educational program that stresses the worth of all human beings.

RESPECTING ETHNIC DIVERSITY

We live in a multiethnic, multilingual, and multicultural world. Yet the public schools have traditionally perpetuated a monoethnic, monolingual, monocultural society. They have encouraged an assimilationist model that ignores ethnic, cultural, and linguistic characteristics. Such assertions as "I am color-blind" and "I treat all students the same" testify to this attitude. Such statements may be intended to denote a lack of preferential treatment for any student, but they indicate a lack of sensitivity to, or awareness of, obvious ethnic and cultural differences. Very conscious efforts must be made to see, to hear, and to respect the ethnic and cultural diversity of all people. The better goal is to strive for ethnic and cultural pluralism rather than assimilation.[35]

Avoiding Negative Labels

Much of the literature and many programs refer to ethnic minority students as "disadvantaged" or "deprived." While these designations have gained wide acceptance, they are frequently embarrassing to students. A study by Reginald Jones on the effect of the terms "culturally deprived" and "culturally disadvantaged" revealed that:

1. Regardless of socioeconomic or grade levels, children rejected the labels "culturally deprived" and "culturally disadvantaged" as descriptive of themselves.
2. Respondents perceived the terms as essentially negative.
3. Children who accepted the labels had more negative school attitudes.

4. Teachers' lowered satisfaction in work with young children was very closely tied to pupil satisfaction with school.
5. Counselors hold a very negative and stereotyped view of the "culturally deprived" group.[36]

The use of terms such as "culturally deprived" and "culturally disadvantaged" relate only to an arbitrary standard—that of the middle-income-class child. Designating the world of poor children, who are disproportionately minorities, as being devoid of cultural stimuli and, thereby, rendering the children deprived or disadvantaged is a fallacy.[37] Poor children are capable of learning at levels commensurate with children who are not poor. Pejorative labels placed on them serve only to limit their intellectual growth by the myopic expectancies of teachers and school staffs.

Improving Classroom and School-wide Interaction

Teacher behaviors that affect students in negative ways must be identified before classroom and interaction processes can be improved. Through the systematic use of audio- and videotaping, as well as interaction analysis techniques, such behaviors may be identified.[38] Once ineffective teaching behaviors have been isolated, in-service programs can be developed to eliminate them.

The role of the principal is crucial. He or she must ensure that opportunities exist for teachers to become aware of the dysfunctionality of their classroom behaviors. Importantly, the principal must maintain a nonthreatening school atmosphere that encourages and supports the desire for teachers to eliminate these behaviors. There are no simple and uniform ways to accomplish these ends, but it is clear that honest, open, warm, and sensitive leadership is mandatory.

Getting to Know the School Community

Another way of demonstrating sincerity and concern for students is to become acquainted with the neighborhood in which they live. Visiting their homes, attending church in the community, patronizing local businesses, and being present at some community affairs can yield rich dividends. By indicating to the community, to parents, and to students that the school staff is concerned enough to participate in activities important to them, the staff wins their respect. Further, the staff gains an awareness of some of the problems students and parents face and an appreciation of the tremendous strength that enables them to survive against great obstacles. Such participation may also provide an opportunity to interact informally with parents who may rarely visit the school.

Students in particular would react favorably to the sincere participation of the school staff in activities in their community. They would sense a measure of concern from their teacher's or principal's visits to their church or attendance at community functions. Staff manifestations of concern, when translated by students in the school setting, foster communication, respect, and the desire to participate more freely in the classroom. Such concern nurtures the sense that the student belongs in the school.

IN CONCLUSION

The school performance of ethnic minority students from inner-city communities can be improved by increasing the receptivity of the urban school to students from diverse ethnic backgrounds. While several strategies have been suggested, others also can be significant. One compelling strategy suggests that equalizing school economic input can bring about more equitable school outcomes.[39] Still another strategy has been to propose ability grouping. The evidence in this area is far from convincing, however. After reviewing experimental studies concerned with ability grouping and conducting a study themselves, Miriam Goldberg, Harry Passow and Joseph Justman state: "The general conclusion which must be drawn from the findings of this study and from other experimental grouping studies is that, in predominantly middle class elementary schools, narrowing the ability range in the classroom on the basis of some measure of general academic aptitude will, by itself, in the absence of carefully-planned adaptations of content and method, produce little positive change in the academic achievement of pupils at any ability levels."[40]

Still other strategies include early childhood education[41] and career education[42] programs. While all of these strategies have merit, the fundamental issue that they fail to address is the elimination of racism and the acceptance and respect of all ethnic minority groups throughout the structure of education.

Attitudes and behaviors of teachers, administrators, and noncertificated staff toward ethnic minority students and their parents represent a barrier that prevents or retards the development of a sense of belonging in the school. Many, if not most, ethnic minority students in inner-city schools perceive that they are tolerated rather than accepted; that many teachers, administrators, and noncertificated staff members feel that they cannot achieve academically at maximum levels; that school staffs do not understand and appreciate their cultural backgrounds or care about their communities. Thus, the frustration many ethnic minority students feel engender a feeling of alienation from the school, contribute to a lack of motivation for school achievement, and increase the probability of hostility toward schools and those associated with them. Elimination of school staff attitudes and behaviors that have a negative impact on ethnic minority students, therefore, is essential if we are to improve the learning environment, reduce student feelings of alienation, and improve the academic performance of students.

The recognition of ethnicity as an important and integral characteristic in the schools provides the initial basis for the development of the attitudes and behaviors of school staff and students that are necessary for healthy human growth and the creation of a culturally pluralistic society. Students must be accepted and respected without regard to their ethnicity. They must feel and know that they belong not only in the school, but also throughout the fabric of our society. While the schools have little direct and immediate impact on other societal institutions, they can affect the student socialization process (and parental resocialization, although to a somewhat lesser extent) so that racism, ethnocentricity, and ethnic insularity may be significantly diminished. In this process, it is important that the school staff be knowledgeable, sensitive, respectful, and accepting of ethnic and cultural differences.

Finally, longitudinal research on the effects of multiethnic staff and programs on student learning, attitudes, expectations, motivation, and success is needed. Such research can provide empirical bases for the development and implementation of school programs and practices that will ensure acceptance and respect for the diversity of people and the eventual elimination of inequality.

NOTES

1. Abraham H. Maslow, *Motivation and Personality*, 2d ed. (New York: Harper and Row, 1970).

2. *Ibid.*

3. Frank G. Goble, *The Third Force: The Psychology of Abraham Maslow* (New York: Grossman Publishers, 1970), 41.

4. Ethnic group designations used by the Office of Civil Rights included Negro, Oriental, Spanish surname. Clearly more accurate designations are desirable, such as black American, Afro-American, Chinese-American, Japanese-American, Filipino, Puerto Rican, Mexican-American, Chicano, or Hispanic, which we have used where appropriate.

5. For example, see "Evaluation Report of a Unified School District ESEA Title I Program," unpub. report prepared by Associates for Educational Analysis, Berkeley, Calif., 1972; Martin Deutsch, "The Role of Social Class in Language Development and Cognition," *American Journal of Orthopsychiatry*, 35 (January 1965), 78-88; James L. Coleman *et al.*, *Equality of Educational Opportunity* (Washington, D. C.: U. S. Government Printing Office, 1966).

6. For example, see the reviews of the literature by Perry A. Zirkel, "Self-Concept and the 'Disadvantage' of Ethnic Group Membership and Mixture," *Review of Educational Research*, 41 (June 1971), 211-225; see also William W. Purkey, *Self-Concept and School Achievement* (Englewood Cliffs, N. J.: Prentice-Hall, 1970), chap. 2, 14-27.

7. *Ibid.*, 26.

8. *Ibid.*, 47.

9. Don E. Hamachek, "Self-Concept Implications for Teaching and Learning," *School and Community*, 55 (May 1969), 18-19, 55.

10. Several studies have demonstrated a relationship between teacher expectancy and student achievement. For a comprehensive review of studies dealing with teacher expectancy, see J. Philip Baker and Janet L. Crest, "Teacher Expectancies: A Review of the Literature," in Janet D. Elashoff and Richard E. Snow's *Pygmalion Reconsidered* (Worthington, Ohio: Charles A. Jones Publishing Company, 1971). Specific studies on teacher expectancy are Jeremy D. Finn, "Expectations and the Educational Environment," in *Review of Educational Research*, 42 (Summer 1972), 387-410; W. Victor Beez, "Influence of Biased Psychological Reports on Teaching Behavior and Pupil Performance," in *Learning in Social Settings: New Readings in the Social Psychology of Education*, ed. Matthew W. Miles and W. W. Charters, Jr. (Boston: Allyn and Bacon, 1970), 328-334; Robert Rosenthal and Lenore Jacobson, *Pygmalion in the Classroom: Teacher Expectation and Pupils' Intellectual Development* (New York: Holt, Rinehart, and Winston, 1968). The methodology employed in the Rosenthal and Jacobson study has been severely criticized, thus raising some doubt about the validity of the findings. See Elashoff and Snow, *Pygmalion Reconsidered*.

11. For example, see U. S. Commission on Civil Rights, *Teachers and Students: Differences in Teacher Interaction with Mexican-American and Anglo Students*. Report V, *Mexican-American Education Study* (Washington, D. C.: the Commission, 1973).

12. Herriott and St. John examined a similar question in their analysis of data from the study of the principalship and found that some difficulties associated with teaching in low SES schools produce teachers who have relatively low morale as a group, as individuals are dissatisfied with many aspects of their job, and are relatively more eager to find different positions in the field of education. See Robert E. Herriott and Nancy Hoyt St. John, *Social Class and the Urban School* (New York: John Wiley and Sons, 1966), 84-97.

13. Y. A. Cabrera, "A Study of American and Mexican-American Cultural Values and Their Significance in Education," *Dissertation Abstracts* (1964), 25, 309.

14. Yolanda L. Jenkins, "Cognitive Styles of Black Children: An African Perspective," unpub. paper, University of California, Berkeley, March 1975.

15. J. S. Kleinfeld, "Intellectual Strengths in Culturally Different Groups: An Eskimo Illustration," *Review of Educational Research*, 43 (Summer 1973), 345.

16. R. L. Munroe and R. H. Munroe, "Effect of Environmental Experience on Spatial Ability in an East African Society," *Journal of Social Psychology,* 83 (February 1971), 15-22.

17. Rosalie A. Cohen, "Conceptual Styles, Culture Conflict and Non-Verbal Tests of Intelligence," *American Anthropologist,* 71 (October 1969), 828-856.

18. Wade A. Boykin, "Experimental Psychology from a Black Perspective: Issues and Examples," *Journal of Black Psychology,* 3 (February 1977), 35.

19. Nancy St. John, "Thirty-six Teachers: Their Characteristics and Outcomes for Black and White Pupils," *American Educational Research Journal,* 8 (November 1971), 646.

20. Robert W. Heath, "Ability of White Teachers to Relate to Students," *ibid.* (January 1971), 9.

21. R. P. McDermott, "Social Relations as Contexts for Learning in School, " *Harvard Educational Review,* 47 (May 1977), 199.

22. In schools that receive funds as a result of ESEA Title I, parents must be involved in determining the educational program. Several guides have been prepared that provide insight into how much parental involvement is required in Title I programs. For example, see *Parent Power and Title I ESEA* (New York: National Urban League, Education Division, n.d.); see also *Title I in Your Community* (New York: NAACP Legal Defense and Educational Fund, Inc., 1971).

23. Richard A. Schmuck, "Bringing Parents and Students into School Management: A New Program of Research and Development on Organization Development," *Education and Urban Society,* 6 (February 1974), 205-221.

24. For example, see H. M. Brickell, C. B. Aslanian, and B. J. Heinzen, *Paraprofessional Influences on Student Achievement and Attitudes and Paraprofessional Performance Outside the Classroom: A Study for the Board of Education of the City of New York in District Decentralized ESEA Title I and New York State Urban Education Projects in the New York City Schools* (New York: Institute for Educational Development, 1972); James Fey, "Classroom Teaching of Mathematics," *Review of Educational Research,* 39 (October 1969), 535-551; Alan Gartner, *Paraprofessionals and Their Performance* (New York: Praeger Publishers, 1971); Carol Lopate *et al.,* "Decentralization and Community Participation in Public Education," *Review of Educational Research,* 40 (February 1970), 135-150.

25. Brickell, Aslanian, and Heinzen, *Paraprofessional Influences.*

26. A study relating to this point is Charles B. Webb, "An Interaction Analysis of the Teacher-Paraprofessional Relationship as Influenced by an In-Service Training Program," unpub. diss., Walden University, Naples, Florida, 1973.

27. An excellent source book that can be used in these programs is James Banks, ed., *Teaching Ethnic Studies: Concepts and Strategies,* Forty-third Yearbook of the National Council for Social Studies (Washington, D. C.: NCSS, 1973). Several other excellent multimedia materials that are useful in increasing awareness and understanding are: *Confrontation: A Human Relations Training Unit* (New York: Anti-Defamation League, 1969); *Inner City Simulated Teaching Programs* (Chicago: Science Research Associates, n.d.); *Tense: Imperfect,* from a color series, "Critical Moments in Teaching" (New York: Holt, Rinehart, and Winston, n.d.); *Brotherhood of Man* (New York: McGraw-Hill Book Company, 1969); *Solving Multi-Ethnic Problems: A Simulation Game for Elementary and High School Teachers* (New York: Anti-Defamation League, n.d.).

28. California Education Code, Article 3.3, Sections 13345-13349. This article stipulates that each California public school in which 25 percent or more of the students are of diverse ethnic backgrounds "shall provide an in-service program designed to prepare teachers and other professional school service personnel to understand and effectively relate to the history, culture, and current problems of these students and their environment."

29. Bruce Bodner, "Indian Education: Tool of Cultural Politics," *National Elementary Principal,* 50 (May 1971), 22. Similar views are also found in: Francis McKinley, Stephen L. Bayne, and Glen P. Nimnicht, "Who Should Control Indian Education," in Glen P. Nimnicht and James A. Johnson, Jr., *et al., Beyond "Compensatory Education": A New Approach to Educating Children* (San Francisco: Far West Laboratory for Educational Research and Development, 1973); Rosalie Wax, "The Warrior Dropouts," *Trans-Action,* 4 (May 1967), 40-46; Miles Zintz, *The Indian Research Study: The Adjustment of Indian and Non-Indian Children in the Public Elementary Schools of New Mexico* (Albuquerque: College of Education, University of New Mexico, 1960).

30. An interesting study concerned with the impact of local control in ensuring that the cultural values of American Indians be incorporated in the schools serving these students is Janice J. Weinman, "Local Control over Formal Education in Two American Indian Communities: A Preliminary Step toward Cultural Survival," *Review of Educational Research,* 42 (Fall 1972), 533-539.

31. David Ballestros, "Toward an Advantaged Society: Bilingual Education in the 70's," *National Elementary Principal,* 50 (November 1970), 27.

32. Elementary and Secondary Education Act (79 Stat. 27), Public Law 89-10, 1965; Title VII Amendment, 1968.

33. Texas Education Agency, *A Resource Manual for Implementing Bilingual Education Programs; The Regional Educational Agencies Project on International Education* (Austin: Texas Education Agency, 1969), in Litsinger, *Challenge of Teaching Mexican-American Students,* 147.

34. *Lau* v. *Nichols,* 414 U. S. 563 (1974).

35. In this regard, several models or programs have merit for ensuring ethnic and cultural pluralism. For a description of several models, see Daniel U. Levine, ed., *Models for Integrated Education—Alternative Programs of Integrated Education in Metropolitan Areas* (Worthington, Ohio: Charles A. Jones Publishing Company, 1971). See also Banks, ed., *Teaching Ethnic Studies;* Dolores Escobar Litsinger, *The Challenge of Teaching Mexican-American Students* (New York: American Book Company, 1973).

36. Regionald L. Jones, "Labeling Children Culturally Deprived and Culturally Disadvantaged," in *Black Psychology,* ed. *id.* (New York: Harper and Row, 1972), 285-293. See also Jane R. Mercer, *Labeling the Mentally Retarded* (Berkeley: University of California Press, 1973; Erving Goffman, *Stigma: Notes on the Management of Spoiled Identity* (Englewood Cliffs, N. J.: Prentice-Hall, 1963).

37. For a discussion and critique of the studies surrounding the intellectual development of poor children, see Herbert Ginsberg, *The Myth of the Deprived Child: Poor Children's Intellect and Education* (Englewood Cliffs, N. J.: Prentice-Hall, 1972).

38. For example, see Robert F. Bales, *Interaction Process Analysis: A Method for*

the Study of Small Groups (Cambridge, Mass.: Addison-Wesley Publishing Co., 1950); Ned A. Flanders, *Analyzing Teacher Behavior* (Reading, Mass.: Addison-Wesley Publishing Co., 1970). An excellent anthology of observation instruments is Anita Simon and E. Gil Boyer, *Mirrors for Behavior in an Anthology of Observation Instruments* (Wyncote, Pa.: Communication Materials Center, 1974).

39. For example, see J. E. Coons, W. H. Clune III, and S. D. Sugarman, *Private Wealth and Public Education* (Cambridge, Mass.: Harvard University Press, 1971).

40. Miriam L. Goldberg, A. Harry Passow, and Joseph Justman, *The Effects of Ability Grouping* (New York: Teachers College Press, 1966), 167.

41. Some initial findings indicate the results of Head Start programs are only temporary. See Westinghouse Learning Corp., *The Impact of Head Start: An Evaluation of the Effects of Head Start on Children's Cognitive and Affective Development* (Washington, D. C.: U. S. Office of Economic Opportunity, 1969). However, the positive effects of the program were not sufficiently dealt with, as indicated by Marshall S. Smith and Joan S. Bissell, "Report Analysis: The Impact of Head Start," *Harvard Educational Review,* 40 (Winter 1970), 51-104. Early childhood education programs are viewed positively by many educators. See, for example, Millie Almy, *The Early Childhood Educator at Work* (New York: McGraw-Hill Book Company, 1975); California State Department of Education, *Early Childhood Education: Report of the Task Force on Early Childhood Education* (Sacramento, Calif.: Bureau of Publications, 1972); Edythe Margolin, *Sociocultural Elements in Early Childhood Education* (New York: Macmillan, 1974); George S. Morrison, *Early Childhood Education Today* (Columbus, Ohio: Charles E. Merrill Publishing Co., 1976).

42. Career education is viewed as a program that will ensure that each student will develop a marketable skill in the public school setting. See Sidney P. Marland, *Career Education: A Proposal for Reform* (New York: McGraw-Hill Book Company, 1974); Kenneth Hoyt, Rupert Evans, Edward Mackin, and Garth Mangum, *Career Education: What It Is and How to Do It* (Salt Lake City: Olympus, 1972). For an interesting criticism of career education, see W. Norton Grubb and Marvin Lazerson, "Rally 'Round the Workplace: Continuities and Fallacies in Career Education," *Harvard Educational Review,* 45 (November 1975), 451-474.

Chapter Eight

Staten W. Webster

Development of a Program

Two questions preface this chapter: What should the urban principal know about curriculum development, that is, the development of an educational program? How can principals function to guide development and to promote change in their institutions?

Before proceeding, however, it is necessary to define the term "program," which in its educational sense is known as "curriculum"—those learning activities and experiences selected by the school to achieve specific educational goals and objectives that may or may not be the same for all students. (In this chapter the terms "curriculum" and "program" are held to be synonymous.) This definition includes academic and nonacademic, as well as curricular and cocurricular, activities used in the pursuit of predetermined goals or objectives. The program of a school also represents a series of solutions to the problems of student learning. At some point in time, for example, a principal, teacher, or committee recognized the existence of a problem and shaped their conception of the best solution to it. Both the way or ways in which the problem was originally perceived and the resulting solution or solutions were influenced by the frames of reference or curriculum theory held by those responsible for solving it. We all act in terms of our values, beliefs, and feelings, whether engaged in curriculum development or other matters.

There are two basic assumptions that underlie the following discussion. One is that the traditional perception of the principal as all-knowing curriculum or program leader of the school is outdated. It is almost impossible for any urban principal to be as knowledgeable about all of the many changes taking place in the curricula of schools. Modifications in specific subject matter areas, both instructional and organizational, have occurred simultaneously. Some changes are open classrooms, nongraded structures, differentiated staffing patterns, learning centers, flexible modular scheduling, alternative schools, and schools without walls, to mention just a few.

The second assumption is that certain basic program- or curriculum-related competencies are needed by all principals, regardless of the school setting. In other words, the principal of a middle-class, largely Anglo-populated suburban school needs a frame of reference, a body of knowledge, and relevant skills that do not differ substantially from those of a peer in an inner-city, largely black ghetto school.

There are forces that suggest the need for a new look at the role of the principal as it affects the school program.[1] For one thing, most urban schools have failed to educate large numbers of socially disadvantaged students. This failure has turned the spotlight of public criticism on the schools and has brought mounting pressure to bear on urban principals and their staffs, including demands for local control or at least greater involvement in school affairs, personnel reeducation or transfer, and curricular changes (for example, ethnic studies, bilingual education, and a reemphasis on basics). In response to public criticism, state and federal agencies have also entered the realm of the schools.

There has been a need to minimize the negative effects of large, urban school systems that has encouraged administrative decentralization. Power and responsibility have, in some instances, been shifted from the central office to smaller administrative units. In terms of the curriculum this has meant that principals and their staffs have gained greater latitude in developing school programs. More power and increased discretion frequently require modification of the traditional roles played by teachers and administrators involved in the instructional program. Diversified staffing patterns, for example, have changed the principal's role as it relates to the school program. As Clinton Boutwell has stated:

Differentiated staffing, then, deals primarily with teaching staffs; and, obviously, if a district gives more decision-making prerogatives to the teaching staff and establishes a hierarchy which allows for direct participation in leadership, some adjustments must

be made in administrative positions. The administrator becomes a colleague and for
the most part becomes a manager and orchestrator of the school plant and program.
His major responsibilities lie within the area of facilitating the decisions made by those
ultimately responsible for curriculum and instructional programs. . . .[2]

Another force operating to modify the principal's role regarding the
program is the new, more powerful status of teachers as a professional
group. Fenwick English contends that, to some extent, the demands of
administrators and their professional groups for improved teacher
education have backfired. Colleges and universities, in reacting to criticism, have modified their programs, and, according to English, have
"produced the highest caliber of teaching excellence yet known, and
impetus for teachers to challenge the organizational rules which lock
them out of decision-making and ignore their specialization."[3] Many
teachers, like numerous other Americans, have come to feel that they
should have some form of direct participation in, or influence over,
matters that affect their lives and destinies. Thus, teachers and their
organizations have become more willing to challenge school administrators and districts through a variety of means, including strikes.

A final factor pressing for change in the principal's traditional role
is the growing demand for accountability. As the cost of education has
escalated, along with almost everything else, so have the tax bills
needed to support it. A heavily taxed public, finding itself reminded
continuously of the failure of schools, increasingly demands its
money's worth from the educational establishment.

At the individual school level these pressures fall largely on the
shoulders of the principal as program leader. It is, then, the flood of
new curricular materials, the appearance of new instructional strategies, the modifications in organizational structure, the public's dissatisfaction coupled with demands for accountability, the increase in
teacher militancy and strength, and the greater involvement of governmental units in education that are operating to change the principal's role as it relates to the school program.

We return to the first of the questions that began this chapter:
What should the urban principal know about curriculum development, that is, the development of an educational program? A curriculum model will be used to integrate material regarding what the urban principal needs to know about the program (curriculum), and the
following diagram will serve to introduce the various components of
the model:

FORMING CURRICULUM THEORY

One essential task that every principal who works in curricular activity must complete successfully is the determination of a theory of curriculum. An excellent definition of this concept has been given by Hilda Taba:

A theory of curriculum is a way of thinking about matters that are important to the curriculum development: what the curriculum consists of, what its important elements are, how these are chosen and organized, what the sources of curriculum decision are, and how the information and criteria from these sources are translated into curriculum decision. [4]

Or, in the words of J. M. Gwynn and John Chase, curriculum theory is:

a set of beliefs that, when accepted and internalized by the individual, serve[s] as a basis for decision making in curriculum development and implementation. [5]

The important implication of these definitions is that all educators must recognize that they bring to any curricular task a predetermined set of personal beliefs, habits, and so forth that influence and shape their perceptions and decisions. An awareness of one's theory of curriculum is vital, for a problem involving curriculum that commands the attention of a principal (Time 1) will be filtered through that belief system. In the process this perception of the problem will be modified (Time 2), as shown in Figure 8-1.

Determinants of Curriculum Theory

One of the most salient factors contributing to one's system of beliefs is prior life experiences relevant to the problem at hand. The same is true for beliefs related to school programs.

Consider, for instance, a hypothetical situation in which an urban principal at a multiethnic junior high school is approached by several teachers who feel that the interracial hostilities and isolation among students are undesirable conditions in a school. They ask the principal to explore ways of changing the school program to promote improved intergroup relations. One factor that could influence the principal's

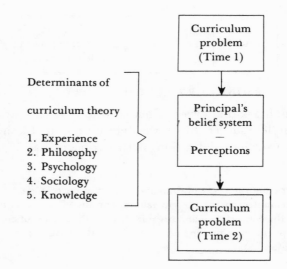

FIGURE 8-1. Diagram of a problem in curriculum theory

perception of the problem might be prior experience in multiracial settings. A principal with limited interracial experiences who had been socialized in a setting that was racially homogeneous and that sanctioned racial segregation might, for example, be disposed to feel that no programmatic efforts to promote change were required. Had the principal's life experiences been different, the response to the problem might have been more positive.

Another determinant of curriculum theory is one's philosophy of life, as well as of education, but it is education that concerns us here. Most perceptions of what the goals of education should be can be grouped under three basic social functions: conservative, adaptive, and creative (or reconstructive). The one view of the purposes of education that might be difficult to fit under this umbrella might be the existentialist one, for it tends to be almost completely person-oriented.

The conservative function sees the primary task of education as conserving the best of man's thought and accomplishments. The adaptive function sees that task as preparing persons to adapt themselves to the realities of life without too much disruption, a view that is present- and adjustment-oriented. While respecting the importance of both past and present, the creative or reconstructive view sees the primary goal of education as concentrating on the development of persons who can wisely change society as needed. Principals faced with a potential curriculum problem in the human relations area such as the one cited above would view the educational relevance or significance in light of what they see as the primary function of education. Those with a reconstructive orientation would probably be more receptive to the teachers' perceptions of the school's race problem than principals with a conservative view of the goals of education.

Another determinant of curriculum theory comes from the field of psychology. Questions involving the nature of the learner and salient aspects of the learning process—concepts of intelligence or mental ability and the process of learning; matters such as readiness, motivation, or reinforcement; and behavior modification—influence curricular decisions. Principals whose curriculum theory or psychological foundations have led them to conclude that prejudicial attitudes cannot be modified would perhaps react to the human relations situation sketched above in a way different from the principal who rejects this belief. Much more remains to be said regarding the psychological components of curriculum theory at a later time, when the teaching and learning act is discussed.

There are also sociological determinants of curriculum theory. The school is a social institution, and educators must be successful students of their society and its culture. Curriculum goals and objectives should reflect a high level of sociocultural awareness if they are to be relevant and to gain public support. Principals whose sociological beliefs are such that they feel that in-group versus out-group hostilities are natural human behaviors and that the school cannot and should not tamper with this phenomenon would provide little support for programs concerned with intergroup relations.

A final determinant of curriculum theory is generated by one's perception of the nature and structure of knowledge. Key issues in this area involve the question of how the subject matter of the school should be treated: Are subjects discrete bodies of knowledge, or should they be integrated or fused to seek certain educational goals? Do certain subjects deserve being included in the curriculum while others do not? Principals who feel that only "American history" should be taught in the school might oppose adding courses or units on black or Native American history.

Determinants of curriculum theory do not stand in isolation. There must be considerable correlation among the variables, as the following passage demonstrates:

one's philosophical belief of reality or one's belief of what is of value might be so compartmentalized that it is impossible to relate these beliefs to the beliefs one holds about the needs of society or the validity of certain societal customs. This impossibility may be illustrated by the conflict that would exist if one accepted the philosophical belief that the child is capable of making choices and that which is of value to the child is that which the child chooses from alternatives, but also accepted the belief that the child's choices of behavior as expressed in societal customs and mores were not good for the welfare of society. In this case, the individual experiences conflict between his beliefs about the freedom and ability of the child to choose and the belief that the child must be made to conform to certain behavior patterns for the welfare of society. Such a conflict in beliefs is transferred to the process of curriculum planning and consequently into the classroom as decisions are made governing the student's role in making choices about content and process in learning. In turn, conflicts in belief generate inconsistent behavior, laissez-faire behavior, or no action at all.[6]

Improving Curriculum Theory

To paraphrase Dewey, education is the constant reconstruction of one's experiences. Any principal engaged in developing or implementing a curriculum must constantly reexamine and reconstruct curriculum theory as change becomes necessary. What are some essential factors that should be included in this process of reeducation? The following suggestions are offered:

Knowledge of the Past. One competency that I consider essential to the development of a sound curriculum theory is the possession of a knowledge and understanding of history as it relates to the institution of the school. Principals need to be aware of the evolutionary development of education in this country. Further, they should be aware of forces and stresses that have produced educational change.

Such knowledge and the insights it affords serve several purposes. First, the principal gains a sense of where the institution of the school stands in its development. Second, the educator develops an ability to weigh more accurately new ideas or educational approaches. The student of the history of education realizes that such currently controversial proposed practices as local control of schools by ward-type boards of education are not new.[7] That person would also be aware that individualized, nongraded instructional programs and forms of peer tutoring were practiced early in the history of schools in this country. Knowledge of earlier applications of educational practices, as well as their success or failure, can broaden the perspective of the principal faced with a curriculum problem. Knowledge of history can also help in the anticipation of possible future needs both on the part of society and on the part of its schools.

In addition to mastering the history of the broader society and of education, urban principals should acquire a knowledge and an understanding of the histories unique to ethnic minority groups present in society—information essential for principals in multiethnic socio-economically diverse schools. In addition to recorded history, educators need to be aware of essential subcultural influences and of matters related to class differences.

The Value of Research. Ralph Tyler encourages curriculum workers to be more aware of the nature of research and to make better use of it in their activities.[8] While not addressing himself specifically to the improvement of curriculum theory, several of his ideas seem to apply. In his words: "It was found in a recent study that very few school superintendents in major cities could name any research that they had utilized in their decision-making, though doubtlessly they were using some." The same could probably be said about many principals.

Three types of knowledge, according to Tyler, are produced by research: facts, concepts, and generalizations. Of the three, he contends that concepts have the broadest applicability, and he encourages educators (we are stressing principals here) to become aware of research findings in relevant disciplines and to make particular use of concepts in their work. The following table summarizes and illustrates how Tyler feels research-generated concepts can be of value to curriculum workers.

Discipline	*Concept(s)*	*Applicability to education*
Anthropology	Culture-subculture	If socially disadvantaged persons are seen to be possessors of a culture that has worked successfully for them in other settings (for example, rural, agrarian, Appalachian), but that is at variance with the cultural solutions of urban settings, then the school and the curriculum must be modified to account for those differences.
Social psychology	Peer group	This is seen in forms of group learning, peer tutoring, and so forth.
Personality psychology	Human needs, self-concept	Moral education, character education, identity education, action learning should be considered.

Sociology	Social stratifica-	Career education and curriculum
	tion, social	should be designed to reeducate
	class, social	persons as required by developing
	mobility	technology and other changes.

In addition to suggesting greater mastery and utilization of the fruits of research efforts, Tyler makes other suggestions relevant to the modification of curriculum theory. For one thing, he calls for educators, in their own work, to adopt the way researchers study questions. This requires clear specification of the problem and deciding the best way to attack it through obtaining, summarizing, interpreting, evaluating, validating, and reexamining relevant data. Tyler further encourages curriculum workers, including principals, to develop the objective attitude of researchers toward facts characteristic of the researcher. Says Tyler: "We must assume a commitment to finding out what the facts are, even though they are unpopular. I've heard my friends say they don't want to know how well kids are doing because it will embarrass the school. The attitude of research is that one is never embarrassed by knowledge. It only gives a more intelligent basis for knowing what to do about a situation."[9]

Awareness and Acceptance of Change. It is essential, as has been implied by Tyler, to emphasize the importance of the principal's ability to understand, accept, and react appropriately to the forces of change affecting all of human existence. A person convinced that he or she has the ultimate answer to the problems of life is no longer capable of growing to the point of even considering new possibilities. There can be no change or growth.

CURRICULUM THEORY TO POSTULATES TO PLANS

If one goes back to Figure 8-1 and adds components of postulates and plans or objectives, a new, more complex diagram results (see Figure 8-2).

Theory into Postulates

Curriculum theory, or one's basic beliefs, intimately manifests itself in postulates or subtheories that guide the curriculum worker's behaviors and decisions. It is vital that principals and other educators are aware of the fact that much of what they do often rests on unverbalized postulates or assumptions. In the ideal curriculum or program development procedure the persons engaged in curricular activity are

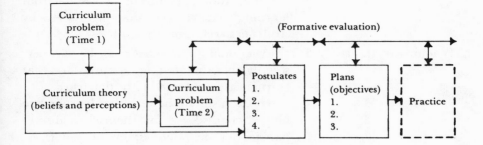

FIGURE 8-2. Diagram of a problem in curriculum theory, with components of postulates and plans or objectives

fully aware of their own assumptions that could ultimately influence any plans that are developed and any practices that result from them. In the case of the hypothetical principal mentioned earlier, that person's perception of the problem presented by the teachers (Time 1) would be modified as it passed through the filter of his curriculum theory. The extent to which the issue was seen as a problem would be influenced and modified (Time 2) by the belief system.

Assuming that the principal agreed that the school should try to do something about the race relations problem, this would or should lead to the identification of relevant beliefs and the specification of specific postulates that would serve as a guide to the development of plans. To illustrate this point, let us identify some possible beliefs and see how they might manifest themselves in postulates:

Basic beliefs:
1. In a democratic society race prejudice is an undesirable form of human behavior.
2. People can be helped to change their attitudes, values, and beliefs.
3. People learn best by doing.

These three beliefs reflect a certain perception of society, education, and human nature. They, in turn, serve as the starting point for the generation of specific postulates (see Figure 8-2), such as:

Area of concern   *Postulates*

Curriculum design
1. Instruction must be such that students are exposed to content that is relevant to their situation in the school.

2. Greater student involvement results from learning experiences that are seen by students as relevant to their lives.

Teaching methods

3. Instructional approaches must be of a personally nonthreatening nature, so that learners are not forced to be defensive.

4. Instruction should be such that learners are helped to discover for themselves discrepancies in their value system and beliefs.

Evaluation

5. Evaluation must not only be at the cognitive-knowledge level, but must include affective and overt behavior dimensions.

Postulates into Objectives or Plans

As indicated above, the progression of beliefs to postulates to plans should be followed by principals and other curriculum workers. For our purposes, plans are best classified as objectives. In this immediate section we will focus on several factors related to educational objectives that should be known and understood by all principals concerned with the school program or curriculum.

Before looking at specific types of educational objectives, it is important to consider David Krathwohl's comments on this subject.[10] According to him, we need educational objectives on three levels of specificity. The first of the levels involves what might be called goals, which are broad general statements useful in the development of programs of instruction or courses. Goals are outcomes that involve considerable periods of time—for example, junior high school years.

Level two involves behavioral objectives that are the building blocks of goals and are used in connection with specific learning experiences or units. The third level involves instructional materials, and, according to Krathwohl, "brings into focus the objectives of specific lesson plans, and the level of achievement required for each goal or objective if successful accomplishment of the next goal is to be achieved." Objectives at this level are concerned with the characteristics of individual learners in relation to the demands of the learning situation. Thus, entry levels of ability or proficiency must be known for each student, and instructional strategies and levels of expected terminal performance must be individualized.

Schools seek to realize three types of educational goals or objectives:

Cognitive — dealing with knowledge and related skills;

Affective — dealing with feelings, emotions, appreciations, and so forth; and

Psychomotor — physical skill performances with a psychological component.

Traditionally, most of the school's curriculum focuses on objectives in the cognitive area.

In recent years emphasis on procedures such as program planning and budgeting systems (PPBS), cost accounting, programmed instruction, performance-based education, and accountability schemes have stressed the need for a much more specific statement of educational objectives. This has led to the great controversy over behavioral objectives.[11]

There are three major components or attributes of behavioral or performance objectives: they describe the learning conditions or experiences involved; they clearly state what the student will be able to do after the learning experience; and they clearly state the level at which the learner, if successful, will be able to perform. As might be expected, demands for such specificity in terms of educational objectives have roused considerable controversy. James Popham has produced a comprehensive list of the pro and con arguments.[12] Selected items from that list appear below and illustrate some of the key issues.

Con	Pro
1. Trivial learner behaviors are easiest to operationalize; hence, the really important outcomes of education will be underemphasized.	Explicit objectives make it far easier for educators to attend to *important* educational outcomes.
2. Prespecification of explicit goals prevents the teacher from taking advantage of instructional opportunities unexpectedly occurring in the classroom	Specification of ends does not mandate the specification of mean.
	Serendipity in the classroom is always welcome, but it should always be justified in terms of its contribution to the learner's attainment of worthwhile objectives.
3. Besides pupil behavior changes, there are other types	The school's primary responsibility is to its pupils. Hence all modi-

of educational outcomes that are important, such as changes in attitudes of parents and the professional staff, community values, and so forth.

4. It is undemocratic to plan in advance precisely how the learner should behave after instruction.

fications in personnel or external agencies should be justified in terms of their contribution toward the achievement of desired pupil behavior changes.

Instruction is by its very nature undemocratic and to imply that a freewheeling democracy is always present in a classroom would be untruthful.

If schools allowed students to "democratically" deviate from societally mandated goals, the institution would cease to receive society's approbation and support.

Regardless of how a principal may feel about behavioral objectives, it is probable that much educational practice in the future will be directed by such specific formulations.

TAXONOMIES AND EDUCATIONAL OBJECTIVES

A taxonomy is a framework or a structural system designed to assist educators in analyzing and developing educational objectives. Every principal interested in the school curriculum or program should know and be able to use the taxonomies of educational objectives as developed by B. S. Bloom (cognitive), David Krathwohl (affective), and their colleagues.[13]

According to Krathwohl, the taxonomy of educational objectives was developed to meet the needs of curriculum workers at the University of Chicago in their efforts to improve communication between persons engaged in curricular activities. To quote Krathwohl,

Basically the taxonomy grew out of our attempt to resolve some of the confusion in communication which resulted from the translation of such general terms as "to understand" into more specific behaviors. Thus the "understanding" of Boyle's law might mean that the student could recall the formula, tell what it meant, interpret the particular meaning of the law in an article about it, use the formula in a new problem situation he had never met, or think up new implications of its relationship.[14]

This statement introduces the six stages of the taxonomy in the cognitive domain:

Knowledge   1. Knowledge (recall of information)

- -

Intellectual skills   2. Comprehension (understanding)

3. Application (use of abstractions in particular concrete situations)

4. Analysis (breaking a communication into its parts so that organization of ideas is clear)

5. Synthesis (putting elements into a whole)

6. Evaluation (judging the value of material for a given purpose)

Before presenting the components of the affective domain taxonomy, a method suggested by Newton Metfessel[15] demonstrates how the cognitive domain elements can be used in developing educational objectives:

Level	*Component*	*Objective*
1	Knowledge (recall)	The student, if asked to respond, can accurately identify the five largest standard metropolitan areas in the United States.
6	Evaluation	Given a brief of a hypothetical civil rights case, a student will be able to identify at least five of six constitutional issues contained in the document and be able to defend that selection.

The objective above, at level 1, requires simply that the student recall information regarding standard metropolitan areas. The objective at level 6, however, requires that the student engage in cognitive activity at a much higher level. One of the important contributions of the taxonomies is that they help the teacher or curriculum developer recognize the cognitive level or levels at which instruction and learning might be taking place. Considerable data from observation studies of classrooms indicate that a great deal of education focuses on the lower elements of the cognitive hierarchy.[16]

The elements of the affective taxonomy are:

1.0. Receiving (attending)
    1.1. Awareness
    1.2. Willingness to receive
    1.3. Controlled or selected attention
2.0. Responding
    2.1. Acquiescence in responding
    2.2. Willingness to respond
    2.3. Satisfaction in response
3.0. Valuing
    3.1. Acceptance of a value
    3.2. Preference for a value
    3.3. Commitment (conviction)
4.0. Organization
    4.1. Conceptualization of a value
    4.2. Organization of a value system
5.0. Characterization of a value or value complex
    5.1. Generalized set (views all problems in terms of their aesthetic aspects/or readiness to revise judgments and to change behavior in light of evidence)
    5.2. Characterization (develops a consistent philosophy of life)

The affective domain was much more difficult to develop than the cognitive domain. Further, application of the former in educational planning and practice is much more difficult. What is attempted in the affective domain is best described, again, by Krathwohl:

By seeking the unique characteristics of the affective domain, it was hoped that the additional principles needed to structure an affective continuum would be discovered. Analysis of affective objectives showed the following characteristics which the continuum should embody: the emotional quality which is an important distinguishing feature of an affective response at certain levels of the continuum, the increasing automaticity as one progresses up the continuum, the increased willingness to attend to specific stimulus or stimulus type as one ascends the continuum, and the developing integration of a value pattern at the upper levels of the continuum.[17]

Two examples of possible objectives that could be developed through the use of the affective domain taxonomy follow:

Level	Component	Objective
1	Receiving	Students will provide evidence of their active involvement in a human relations experience by their abilities to differentiate between prejudiced behaviors and democratic-type behavior.
5	Characterization	Students in their behavior toward each other consistently avoid name-calling, segregation, or physical aggression.

An interesting, somewhat divergent view of the types of objectives needed in education has been introduced by Elliot Eisner, who called for the introduction of two new instructional objectives. Eisner does not oppose the use of objectives, as evidenced by his comment that: "The rationale for their use is straightforward: one must know what it is that a student is able to do in order to determine the effectiveness of the curriculum."[18]

One of Eisner's suggestions involves the *expressive objective* which is "the outcome of an activity planned by the teacher or the student which is designed not to lead the student to a particular goal or form of behavior but, rather, to forms of thinking-feeling-acting that are his own making."[19] Emphasis in the case of such objectives is on the expressive behavior of the learner. The teacher does not look for the realization of a particular criterion score, but, rather, to what happened to the student during the learning process (What creative, personalistic utilization of skills took place?).

Eisner's other suggestion is what he calls *Type III Objectives,* where the problem is known but the solutions are not. What does one look for in evaluating learning activities keyed to these objectives? According to Eisner, "Ingenuity of solution, appraised on the basis of the parameters as specifications of the problem, is the ideal." Educational problems used in the pursuit of Type III objectives resemble tasks given to architects, engineers, designers, and commercial artists. The problem is specified, along with the overall demands of the solution, but the range of solutions is left open.

Both instructional objectives introduced by Eisner, if used to guide curriculum development, would have a profound effect on the teaching-learning act.

CURRICULUM PLANS TO PRACTICE

This section is an attempt to call to principals' attention essential information, concepts, and practices involved in program or curriculum development or implementation. Further additions to the curriculum model (Figures 8-1 and 8-2) are needed to accommodate the concerns of practice (see Figure 8-3). As used here, practice is held to be descriptive of the teaching and learning act (TLA).

Situational Variables

The teaching and learning act is influenced greatly by salient factors in the environment in which it takes place. The resources available to a staff can limit or enhance program efforts. Likewise, the characteristics of the instructional staff in terms of abilities, training, values, and attitudes also can have great impact on the teaching and learning act, along with important situational characteristics: student characteristics, administrative climate, community attitudes and degree of involvement with the school, and legal requirements. Because the focus of this chapter is on the principal and the program, these factors are briefly mentioned. It is obvious, however, that the principal must know, understand, and be able to deal with problems associated with these situational variables if the goals of the program or curriculum are to be realized.

Learning Theories

The ultimate goal of learning is modification of the behaviors of students in terms of specified, desired objectives. Another perception of learning offered by Robert Gagné held that "learning is a change in a human disposition or capability, which can be retained, and which is not simply ascribable to the process of growth."[20] Some information regarding selected perceptions and theories of the learning process is essential for principals who work with programs.

Learning theory is often divided into two major schools or camps. The mechanistic one seeks to explain the phenomenon of learning in mechanical terms. The factors (such as stimuli) that produce learning, while acting upon and within the learner to produce responses, are viewed as being entities in their own right. The organismic school gives learners a more important role in the modification of their behavior.

Associationism is one example of a mechanistic view of how learning takes place. E. L. Thorndike was one of the leading proponents of this school.[21] The two key concepts involved are stimulus and re-

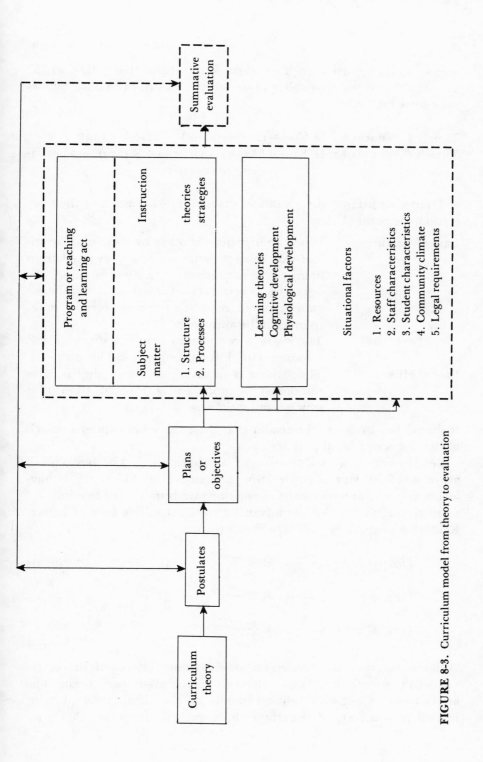

FIGURE 8-3. Curriculum model from theory to evaluation

sponse, and they are identified in the illustrations that follow as "S" and "R." Here learning takes place when a desired response follows the selected stimulus.

Time 1 ("What is 4 x 4?"S) ⟶ (No response) ⟶ No learning
Time 2 ("What is 4 x 4?"S) ⟶ (Association or ⟶ R [16]) ⟶ Learn-
                                          ing connection

Thorndike offered three sublaws that summarize much of the associationistic point of view:

Law of readiness: When an organism is ready to respond, discomfort will be experienced if it is prevented from doing such; conversely, if ready to respond, the organism experiences satisfaction, and if the organism is not ready to respond, forcing a response will be annoying.

Law of exercise: The more a connection between stimulus and response is used, the stronger it will become.

Law of effect: That which is satisfying to learn (that is, give responses) is more easily learned than that which is not satisfying.

It should be obvious to the reader that these three laws underlie much of current educational practice.

Behaviorism is a modification of associationism. The best-known advocate of this view of the learning process is B. F. Skinner.[22] Behaviorism concentrates on efforts to elicit certain responses or to eliminate them through the principle advanced by Thorndike's Law of Effect. Reinforcement is a key concept in this theory.

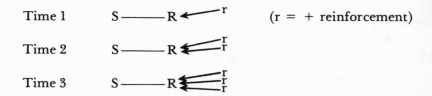

In the diagram, the desired response is immediately reinforced (rewarded) thereby enhancing its chance of being made permanent. The application of negative reinforcements or the elimination of reinforcement can be used to extinguish or weaken the chance that a response will follow an associated stimulus. These key principles under-lie programmed instruction and behavior modification movements.

Individuals who entertain the organismic view of learning claim that associationism and its offspring, behaviorism, are too mechanistic to explain all of learning. Advocates of this view see learners as playing a more significant, personal role in modifying their behavior. Typical-ly, Gestalt psychologists[23] and field theorists[24] take this point of view. Insight, intuition, and problem solving are viewed as sources of learn-ing that do not follow the mechanistic patterns of $(S \longrightarrow R)$ psychol-ogy, and both Gestalt psychology and field theory are concerned with aspects of perception. How an individual responds to problems or sit-uations is a product of psychophysical factors within the person, past experiences, and salient factors in the environment. This organismic view sees man as being in constant pursuit of increased comprehen-sion, closure, order, and self-fulfillment, rather than as an object sit-ting and waiting for a stimulus to be, as it were, turned on.

Gagné contends that these two divergent views of learning are per-haps related.[25] While admitting that most learning involves various combinations of stimuli and responses, Gagné offers a synthesis in his eight varieties of learning:

Gestalt psychology and field theory	8. Problem solving—combining old princi-ples into new ones
	7. Principle learning—basic idea; chain of two or more concepts involved in a relation
	6. Concept learning—responding to S in terms of abstracted properties
	5. Multiple discrimination—ability to make complex dis-criminations from among multiple $S \longrightarrow R$'s
	4. Verbal association—a more complex form of chaining
$S \longrightarrow R$ association	3. Chaining $\rightarrow S \rightarrow R$ Connecting $S \rightarrow R$'s $S \rightarrow R$ in a sequence

2. Stimulus-response learning—S→R
1. Signal learning—involuntary S→R learning

The principal who wishes to work effectively in curriculum needs a solid mastery of the various perceptions of learning.

Theories of Cognitive Development

In addition to understanding the nature and conditions of learning, educators also need to be aware of the theories of cognitive or intellectual development advanced by such researchers as Jean Piaget, Barbel Inhelder, and Jerome Bruner.[26] Findings that stages of cognitive growth and development exist almost universally, regardless of cultural differences, have influenced greatly our perceptions of intelligence, learning, and the total process of education. Educators should become aware of Lawrence Kohlberg's emerging work, which indicates that, like cognitive development, there are stages of moral development. If these findings continue to be replicated, they will have great import for curricular practices.

Content or Subject Matter Considerations

Two terms that have had a profound effect upon curriculum and its development have been "structure" and "process." Stated simply, structure raises the question of how knowledge can best be organized for teaching and learning. Process or processes involve the various ways in which we operate cognitively in using knowledge.

The educational revolution of the late 1950's and the 1960's brought to the forefront the idea of structure. Bruner's book, *The Process of Education,*[27] played a major role in getting scholars in the various disciplines and school personnel together in a much-needed re-evaluation of all aspects of the school program.

There are many views of what constitutes structure, including those by Harry Broudy, Philip Phenix, Robert Heath, and Stanley Elam.[28] All educators do not agree with the emphasis on structure, as is evidenced by the views of James Hullett.[29] For our purposes, two views of the nature of the structure of knowledge are presented.

In one view the social sciences constitute a body of knowledge that is typically assigned to six disciplines (sociology, history, anthropology, and so forth). One possible schema for understanding the structural elements of these disciplines might make use of the following components.

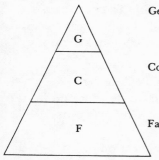

Generalizations: Principles, laws, hypotheses that seek to explain phenomena. Such formulations involve two or more concepts.

Concepts: Verbalized abstractions that can be used to identify classes of phenomena, for example, democracy, capital, labor, tree.

Facts: Propositions that are either true or false; for example: George Washington was the first president of the United States of America.

In this framework, the primary or base unit of knowledge is the fact. It is out of a collection of facts, coupled with much analysis and comparison, that concepts are born. These verbal, shorthand-type units facilitate communication. As an example, mastery of the core concept of "democracy" would facilitate a discussion during which the ideas of limited, direct, or representative democracy were used.

The second view of the structure of knowledge is held by John Michaelis and his colleagues, and takes what they call an operational approach to the discrimination of structure. Concepts and concept clusters within various subjects are viewed as the basic structural unit. Their schema is conceptualized as follows:

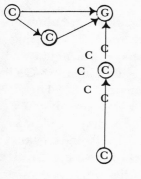

Generalizations: Statements of broad applicability that indicate the relationship between concepts.

Concept clusters: A set consisting of a basic or root concept and the concepts that are related to it and that are needed to give it depth and breadth of meaning.

Concepts: Categories or classifications, abstractions that apply to a class or group of objects or activities that have certain qualities in common.

Some examples of concept clusters given by Michaelis and his colleagues follow:[30]

Field	Cluster
Earth science	*Type of rock:* metamorphic, sedimentary, igneous

Economics   *Functions of money:* medium of exchange, stan-
                                               dard of value, store of value
Music   *Elements of music:* rhythm, melody, harmony
Geography   *Climate:* temperature, precipitation
                             ↓ (add and connect later)↓
                       Land forms: elevation, latitude, mountain sys-
                                tems, winds, ocean currents

Concept clusters are used to guide both the selection of content and
modes of instruction and inquiry. "A key point here is that concept
clusters are not absolutes to be memorized and treasured for their own
sake. They are sets of concepts which are selected and used to guide
study and inquiry, and they are adapted and changed to serve changing purposes of inquiry."[31]
    A number of positive arguments offered in support of the idea of us-
ing structure in curriculum development are:
    1. The use of structure promotes economy of learning.
    2. Greater focus is placed on fundamental ideas.
    3. Greater transfer of training is encouraged.
    4. Closer liaison between educators and scholars is possible.
    5. A teaching strategy is linked with essential modes of inquiry.
    6. Learners display higher levels of motivation because discovery is
        promoted.[32]
The second important content-related component of curriculum involves processes or modes of inquiry that are used in acquiring, using,
and evaluating knowledge. The idea that process was of equal and
perhaps greater importance than content was advocated by Cecil
Parker and Louis Rubin in their book, *Process as Content.*[33] Therein
they argued that, while content is important, the emphasis in education should be on teaching students ways to acquire and use knowledge, for, as they argued with some levity, it is well known "that
knowledge keeps little better than fish." Examples of processes are observing, analyzing, comparing, inferring, and synthesizing.
    In moving their plans into practice in the crucible of the teaching
and learning setting, principals must be aware of the significant roles
that structure and process can play in determining the extent to which
goals are realized.

Instructional Strategies

Another major component of the teaching and learning act involves
modes of instruction. While Bruner[34] and others point out that we do

not possess a valid unified theory of instruction, there are conceptualizations of the instructional process that can be considered.

N. L. Gage offers a schema for looking at the teaching and learning process that first focuses on what the teacher does during the teaching and learning act.[35] Second, attention is given to the specific objectives pursued in the act. Third, the activities of the teacher are articulated with components in the learning process as follows.

Components of learning	*Teacher acts*
1. Drive (motivation)	1. Producing motivation
2. Cue	2. Producing perception
3. Response	3. Eliciting response
4. Reward	4. Providing reinforcement

Finally, attention is given to selection of the most promising theories of learning (associationism, behaviorism, identification theory).

To illustrate how Gage's ideas can be used to structure the instructional component of the teaching and learning act, two examples are presented.

Example 1   (Cognitive domain)
Objective: Teacher wants students to master the process of extrapolation, to be able to detect trends which go beyond the data given.
Teacher activity (major):   Explaining
Key component of learning process: Perceptual. The teacher's primary function is that of directing the students' attention to salient aspects of their environment, that is, data.
Appropriate learning theories: Involves cognitive restructuring via the use of processes. The teacher manipulates the cognitive field (data) either verbally or physically (for example, on the board). Actually elements of stimulus-response theories plus Gestalt and field theory concepts would be used.

Example 2   (Psychomotor domain)
Objective: To help young children to learn to write the letter "Z."
Teacher activity (major):   Demonstrating

| Key component of learning process: | Response. The teachers' primary function would be that of eliciting the desired response in the form of acceptable "Z's." |
| Appropriate learning theories: | Identification theory. Students identify with the proper "Z's" demonstrated by the teacher. Practice would involve applications of the stimulus-response laws of exercise and perhaps effect. |

The above ideas of Gage and those that follow are intended to help the principal see the importance of developing appropriate ways of observing and understanding instruction in teaching and learning. Bruce Joyce and Marsha Weil have suggested that models of teaching can be used to conceptualize essential variables in instruction.[36] They have suggested four models:

Social Interaction Sources. Models in this family focus on person-to-person or person-to-society relations. These instructional strategies give priority to social relations and the creation of a better, more democratic society. Examples: group investigations by students, T-groups, social inquiry.

Information-Processing Sources. Models in this school are concerned with helping the learner to become a more effective processor of information (facts and so forth). Some models are concerned with improving the learner's ability to solve problems. Other models concentrate on creativity and general intellectual ability. Examples: inquiry training, *Man: A Course of Study,* Taba's inductive model.

Personal Sources (the self). Models in this area focus on the individual person as the primary source of educational ideas. Stress is placed on the development of such things as personal courage, the self-concept, and a more realistic view of one's self. A great deal of importance is placed on pupil-teacher relations. Examples: nondirective teaching, synectics, awareness training.

Behavior Modification as a Source. Models in this camp seek to develop efficient systems of learning through the sequencing of learning activities and the shaping of behavior by manipulating reinforcements. Models of this type are associated with Skinner and concentrate on operant conditioning. Examples: Programmed instruction, operant conditioning.

Joyce and Weil[37] also offer a structure that can be used to analyze particular models or approaches to teaching. One important variable is the orientation of the model, which is to say its key thesis or major emphasis, wherein one should find the goals of the model's developers, specifications of the best means of achieving the goals or objectives, and descriptions of important environmental factors.

The second variable is the syntax or phasing used in the model. Simply stated, this is a description of the model in action. An example is the syntax of an "advanced organizer" model.

Phase 1	*Phase 2*	*Phase 3*
Presentation of high-level concept verbally	Presentation of related data	Relating data to initially introduced concept

The third variable involves the roles or reactions of teachers or other agents to the pupils' activities. In the above model, the teacher's role involves introducing the initial concept and reinforcing student responses, which relates to the advanced organizer or conceptual idea.

The social system characteristic of the model constitutes the fourth variable. Of concern in this area are the roles of teachers and students in teaching and learning. In order to determine whether these are hierarchical or authority related, it is necessary to learn the behavior norms that were expected and rewarded in the situation.

Necessary support systems are another factor that should be considered in viewing a particular model of teaching, and a final variable is the values of the model. According to the authors a particular approach to instruction has both instructional effects and indirect or nurturant effects. The former are the outcomes of the instructional process, while the latter come from being in the environment created by the model. Any model of teaching should be questioned as to the value it holds for both instruction and nurturance.

EVALUATION

In this final section relating to the question of what the principal needs to know regarding the school's curriculum we will focus on selected views of the role of evaluation in educational practice. The field of evaluation in education is growing rapidly, and there are differing points of view and approaches.

In this discussion we will focus on the ideas of Michael Scriven,[38]

Daniel Stufflebeam,[39] and Edward Karns and Marilyn Wenger.[40] In
the chart that follows, two of Scriven's perceptions of evaluation can
be seen. These are formative and summative evaluation.

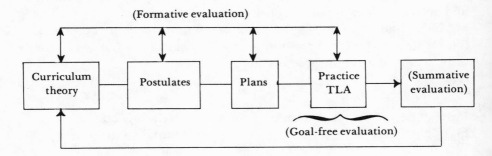

Scriven has argued that Tyler's definition of evaluation— determining whether objectives have been achieved—is much too narrow.
Scriven contends that two types of evaluation are needed:

Formative evaluation: This form of evaluation is a part of the
                          curriculum development process. This form
                          of evaluation is concerned with what hap-
                          pens during the course of program imple-
                          mentation of product development. This is
                          viewed as a form of internal evaluation car-
                          ried on by those engaged in the curriculum
                          effort.

Summative evaluation: This evaluation takes place typically after
                          the curriculum has been moved from theory
                          to practice. It seeks to provide answers as to
                          the merit of the venture. Often this evalua-
                          tion is carried on by outside parties or agen-
                          cies.

Scriven, according to Stufflebeam,[41] conceptualizes two other forms
of evaluation. These are intrinsic and payoff evaluation. The former
appraises the qualities of the teaching instrument (teacher, machine,
or program), regardless of its effects, by looking at such factors as content, goals, grading procedures, materials, and teacher attitudes.
Payoff evaluation is not concerned with the teaching instrument but

with its specific effects on students. For Scriven, both intrinsic and payoff evaluation can serve formative and summative roles.

Another controversial evaluation idea introduced by Scriven[42] involves goal-free evaluation (GFE). This concept of evaluation is one in which the evaluator is an outsider who is not apprised of the goals that the program claims to be seeking to achieve. It is his contention that such conditions will reduce biases on the evaluator's part and enhance the possibility of discovering important and unanticipated effects that goal-based or focused evaluators might not see. The serious administrator might find this form of evaluation a useful supplement to traditional approaches.

Stufflebeam,[43] on the basis of his work evaluating Title I ESEA projects, developed a system of curricular evaluation known as the CIPP (Context, Input, Process, Product) Model. His original schema was modified by the work of a Phi Delta Kappa Study Commission, of which Stufflebeam was a member. The definition of evaluation that provides the underlying theme for CIPP is: "Evaluation is the process of delineating, obtaining, and providing useful information for judging decision alternatives."[44] This conceptualization sees curricular or program evaluation as involving four major decisions, each of which is associated with a particular type of evaluation.

Decisions		*Type of evaluation*
1. Planning	Context:	Planning decisions by the identification of unmet needs, unused opportunities, and underlying problems.
2. Structuring	Input:	Structuring decisions by projecting and analyzing alternative procedural designs.
3. Implementing	Process:	Serving implementing decisions by monitoring project operations.
4. Recycling	Product:	Serving recycling decisions by identifying and assessing project results.

Stufflebeam contends that CIPP can be used as both a formative and summative form of evaluation. If used in decision making, the application is formative, and if used in accountability determination it is summative.

Across all of the four types of evaluation, three specific steps produce a framework that can be used to design evaluation studies of programs. They are:

	Context	Input	Process.	Product
	↓	↓	↓	↓
Delineating	(What questions will be addressed?)			
	↓	↓	↓	↓
Obtaining	(How will needed information be obtained?)			
	↓	↓	↓	↓
Providing	(How will the obtained information be reported?)			

"Evaluation designs and reports making use of the CIPP model should be judged in terms of three standards: *technical adequacy* concerns validity, reliability, and objectivity; *utility* involves the relevance, scope, timeliness, importance, pervasiveness, and credibility of the evaluation; *cost effectiveness* constitutes the final standard."[45]

The viewpoints presented here may be difficult to understand. Principals who want to improve their proficiency in the area of program evaluation must, however, try to master these and other conceptual frameworks. Karns and Wenger make several practical points in an article on "corrective evaluation" which I feel all principals should be aware of. The authors liken the problem of evaluation to the teaching act, which should involve a preassessment of problems or needs and program development, actual teaching in terms of the objectives, posttest assessment to measure progress toward goals, and reteaching that which has not been mastered. The authors call the last phase the "prescriptive phase" and contend that all too often it has been ignored in educational evaluation.[46]

Corrective evaluation feeds useful information back in a consistent fashion so that changes can be made in a program. Karns and Wenger argue that too much evaluation is done on an annual basis and that many of the data produced go unused. In a strong statement they make an important suggestion:

Constraints should be written into the [educational] program whereby evaluation may [must] take place at more frequent intervals. A year is a long time in the life of a boy or girl to be subjected to an error in the learning process.[47]

In closing their article, the authors present useful criteria for sound corrective evaluation:

Relevance:	Is the information produced related to program objectives?
Applicability:	Does it have import for actual instructional procedures?
Timeliness:	Is it timely and available in order for teachers and curriculum planners to use the data?
Variety:	Does it provide broad information?
Clarity:	Is it clear as to what is being evaluated?
Ongoingness:	Is the process of evaluation continuous?
Validity and objectivity:	Does the evaluation relate to the actual process of growth and development?
Consistency— longitudinal:	Are data such that they can be used throughout the system and over time?

These approaches to program evaluation constitute but a sample of what is available. Principals involved in curricular activities should also be aware of other aspects of evaluation, especially in the area of testing, including criterion-referenced testing, doman-referenced testing and associated matrix-sampling techniques, performance tests, and the traditional norm-referenced achievement and aptitude measures.

SUMMARY

In this somewhat extended chapter, an attempt has been made to introduce information regarding the school curriculum or program that seems to be essential for principals. Initially, the problem of a curriculum theory was presented, and an attempt was made to demonstrate how beliefs translate into postulates and plans. Major emphasis was placed on selected elements of the teaching and learning act and related psychological considerations. Finally, some examples of contemporary thought regarding evaluation of school programs were introduced.

NOTES

1. Fenwick English, "The Ailing Principalship," *Education Digest,* 34 (No. 6, 1969), 13-16.

2. Clinton Boutwell, "Differentiated Staffing as a Component in a Systematic Change Process," *Educational Technology,* 12 (August 1972), 20-24.

3. English, "Ailing Principalship."

4. Hilda Taba, *Curriculum Development: Theory and Practice* (New York: Harcourt, Brace, 1962), 420.

5. J. M. Gwynn and John B. Chase, *Curriculum Principles and Social Trends* (New York: Macmillan, 1969), 583.

6. *Ibid.*, 582-583.

7. Robert F. Lyke, "Political Issues in School Decentralization," in *The Politics of Education at the Local, State, and Federal Levels*, ed. Michael Kirst (Berkeley, Calif.: McCutchan Publishing Corporation, 1970), 111-132.

8. Ralph W. Tyler. "Utilizing Research in Curriculum Development," *Theory into Practice*, 13 (February 1974), 5-10.

9. *Ibid.*, 6.

10. David R. Krathwohl, "Stating Appropriate Educational Objectives," in *Curriculum Evaluation: Commentaries on Purpose, Process, Product*, ed. David Payne (Lexington, Mass.: D. C. Heath and Company, 1974), 69-80.

11. R. F. Mager, *Preparing Objectives for Programmed Instruction* (San Francisco: Fearon Publishers, 1962).

12. W. James Popham, "Probing the Validity of the Arguments against Behavioral Objectives," in *Current Research on Instruction*, ed. Richard C. Anderson *et al.* (Englewood Cliffs, N. J.: Prentice-Hall, 1969), 66-72.

13. B. S. Bloom *et al.*, *A Taxonomy of Educational Objectives: The Classification of Educational Goals*. Handbook I, *The Cognitive Domain* (New York: Longmans, Green, 1956); Handbook II, *The Affective Domain* (New York: David McKay Company, 1964).

14. Krathwohl, "Stating Appropriate Educational Objectives."

15. Newton S. Metfessel, William Michael, and Donald Kirsner, "Instrumentation of the Taxonomy of Educational Objectives in Behavioral Terms," in *Curriculum Evaluation*, ed. Payne, 81-87.

16. B. O. Smith and Milton Meux, "A Study of the Logic of Teaching," in *Teaching: Vantage Points for Study*, ed. Ronald T. Hyman (Philadelphia: Lippincott, 1968); James J. Gallagher and Mary Jane Ashner, "A Preliminary Report on Analyses of Classroom Interaction," *Merrill-Palmer Quarterly*, 9 (July 1963), 183-194; Ned A. Flanders, "Teacher Influence in the Classroom," in *Theory and Research in Teaching*, ed. Arno Bellack (New York: Teachers College Press, 1963), 16.

17. Krathwohl *et al.* *Taxonomy of Educational Objectives*. II, *Affective Domain*.

18. Elliot Eisner, "Emerging Models for Educational Objectives," *School Review*, 80 (August 1972), 573-590, esp. 580.

19. *Ibid.*

20. Robert Gagné, *The Conditions of Learning* (New York: Holt, Rinehart, and Winston, 1966), 5.

21. E. L. Thorndike, *Animal Intelligence: An Experimental Study of the Associative Process in Animals*, Monograph Supplement to *Psychological Development*, 2 (No. 4, 1898).

22. B. F. Skinner, *The Behavior of Organisms: An Experimental Analysis* (New York: Appleton-Century-Crofts, 1938).

23. Max Wertheimer, *Productive Thinking* (New York: Harper and Row, 1945); W. Kohler, *Gestalt Psychology* (New York: Liveright, 1929).

24. Kurt Lewin, *Principles of Topological Psychology* (New York: McGraw-Hill Book Company, 1936).

25. Gagné, *Conditions of Learning*, 5.

26. Jean Piaget and Barbel Inhelder, "Diagnosis of Mental Operations and Theory of Intelligence," *American Journal of Mental Deficiency*, 51 (No. 3, 1947), 401-406; Jerome S. Bruner, *Toward a Theory of Instruction* (Cambridge, Mass.: Harvard University Press, 1966).

27. Jerome S. Bruner, *The Process of Education* (Cambridge, Mass.: Harvard University Press, 1961).

28. Harry S. Broudy, *Building a Philosophy of Education* (Englewood Cliffs, N. J.: Prentice-Hall, 1954), 144-196; Philip Phenix, *Realms of Meaning* (New York: McGraw-Hill Book Company, 1964); Robert W. Heath, ed., *New Curricula* (New York: Harper and Row, 1964); Stanley Elam, ed., *Education and the Structure of Knowledge* (Chicago: Rand McNally and Company, 1964).

29. James Hullett, "Which Structure?" *Educational Theory*, 24 (Winter 1974), 68-72.

30. John U. Michaelis, Ruth Grossman, and Lloyd Scott, *New Designs in Elementary School Curriculum* (New York: McGraw-Hill Book Company, 1967), 32.

31. *Ibid.*, 33.

32. *Ibid.*, 11-12.

33. J. Cecil Parker and Louis J. Rubin, *Process as Content: Curriculum Design and the Application of Knowledge* (Chicago: Rand McNally and Company, 1966).

34. Bruner, *Toward a Theory of Instruction*.

35. N. L. Gage, ed., *Handbook on Research on Teaching* (Chicago: Rand McNally and Company, 1963).

36. Bruce Joyce and Marsha Weil, *Models of Teaching* (Englewood Cliffs, N. J.: Prentice-Hall, 1972).

37. *Ibid.*

38. Michael Scriven, "The Methodology of Evaluation," in *Perspectives on Curriculum Evaluation*, AERA Monograph Series on Curriculum Evaluation, No. 1 (Chicago: Rand McNally and Company, 1967).

39. Daniel Stufflebeam, "Alternative Approaches to Educational Evaluation: A Self-Study Guide for Educators," in *Evaluation in Education*, ed. W. James Popham (Berkeley, Calif.: McCutchan Publishing Corporation, 1974), 116-143.

40. Edward A. Karns and Marilyn J. Wenger, "Developing Corrective Evaluation within the Program," *Educational Leadership*, 30 (March 1973), 533-535.

41. Stufflebeam, "Alternative Approaches to Educational Evaluation."

42. Scriven, "Methodology of Evaluation."

43. Daniel Stufflebeam *et al.*, *Educational Evaluation and Decision-Making* (Itasca, Ill.: F. E. Peacock Publishers, 1971).

44. Stufflebeam, "Alternative Approaches to Educational Evaluation," 121.

45. *Ibid.*, 123.

46. Karns and Wenger, "Developing Corrective Evaluation within the Program," 534.

47. *Ibid.*

Chapter Nine

Michael E. Manley-Casimir

Students' Rights

THE CRUCIBLE OF CONFLICT

The case of trouble, again, is the case of doubt, or is that in which discipline has failed, or is that in which unruly personality is breaking through into new paths of action or of leadership, or is that in which an ancient institution is being tried against emergent forces. It is the case of trouble which makes, breaks, twists, or flatly establishes a rule, an institution, an authority. Not all such cases do so. There are also petty rows, the routine of law-stuff which exists among primitives as well as among moderns. For all that, if there be a portion of a society's life in which tensions of the culture come to expression, in which the play of variant urges can be felt and seen, in which emergent power-patterns, ancient views of justice tangle in the open, that portion of the life will concentrate in the case of trouble or disturbance. Not only the making of new law and the effect of old, but the hold and the thrust of all other vital aspects of the culture, shine clear in the crucible of conflict.[1]

Karl Llewellyn and Adamson Hoebel made this discerning comment in their study of law and custom among the Cheyenne, but their comment has force transcending the Cheyenne. It captures the quintessence of the relationship between law and social change — the catalytic role of law in effecting social change — and so it is as relevant now as it was then. Indeed, were Llewellyn and Hoebel writing today, they might well characterize and interpret current developments in school law in a similar vein. In the last two decades we have witnessed a spate of landmark judicial decisions[2] involving the public schools, decisions arising from cases of trouble where unruly personality and emergent forces have challenged the customary practice of that ancient institution — the public school. In many respects the public school has become the crucible of conflict wherein ancient views of justice have yielded to emergent power patterns, and customary practice to new law.

While judicial decisions reflect this new law, they also reflect social changes and cultural shifts impinging on the school. Thus, the case of *Tinker* v. *Des Moines Community School District*,[3] important for its affirmation of students' constitutional rights, also reflects the social dissent of the late 1960's and the increasing assertiveness of youth. Other cases similarly reflect other vital and changing aspects of the culture. While each decision is intrinsically important, the cumulative effect is tantamount to a paradigmatic shift in the administration of public schools. Much that was traditional in the schools has yielded, through judicial scrutiny, to an innovative view of the school as a social institution, of the nature of school administration and the role of the principal, and of role expectations and role relationships within each school. The direction of change is away from the traditional definition of the student-school relationship as in loco parentis, with its attendant wide discretionary power, and toward recognition of the need for constitutional protection, with consequent checks on discretionary power. This argument requires more precise form and substance, however, as do the administrative implications of the shift.

Accordingly, this chapter has three main purposes. The first is to document and develop the argument that the cumulative effect of recent judicial decisions represents a paradigmatic shift in the conception of a school. The *Tinker* decision and *Goss* v. *Lopez*[4] are the two primary cases used to develop this argument, and the discussion demonstrates the need for the school principal to view the school as a system of rights and identifies the dimensions of that system. The second purpose is to consider the basic choice open to the principal and to discuss the constraints or barriers to administrative responsiveness inherent in the existing structure of the school. The third purpose is to identify and discuss some ways to overcome the strong tendency toward institutional inertia in favor of institutional renewal, and that discussion argues the need for affirmation of leadership by the principal, for effective in-service training probably using organizational development techniques, and for restructuring administrative leadership-training programs.

THE SCHOOL AS A SYSTEM OF RIGHTS

The argument that the public school principal should view the school as a system of rights draws its force both from philosophical premises and judicial decisions. Philosophically, the argument rests on the correlative nature of a right — that is, if X is said to have a right, then Y has a correlative duty to respect X's right and an affirmative responsibility to allow X the full exercise of his right. Thus, in the case of a public school, if a student is said to have a right, then the principal (as well as teachers and other students) has the correlative duty to respect the student's right and to ensure that no administrative action negates the right in question. Judicially, the argument draws its validity from an increasing number of judicial decisions involving both the substantive and procedural rights of students under the Constitution. These decisions, by affirming the rights of students, directly imply the correlative duty of the principal to respect and to permit the free exercise of these rights in school, within the constraints imposed by the courts and by the special nature of the school.

The Rights of Students: Tinker and Goss

Judicial recognition of the general protection of the Constitution for public school students is not new. In *West Virginia* v. *Barnette* (the case concerning the salute to the flag) the Supreme Court affirmed the applicability of the Fourteenth Amendment to students:

The Fourteenth Amendment, as now applied to the States, protects the citizen against the State itself and all of its creatures — Boards of Education not excepted. These have, of course, important, delicate, and highly discretionary functions, but none that they may not perform within the limits of the Bill of Rights. That they are educating the young for citizenship is reason for scrupulous protection of Constitutional freedoms of the individual, if we are not to strangle the free mind at its source and teach youth to discount important principles of our government as mere platitudes.[5]

It was again the decade of the sixties that saw a flood of cases involving students' rights in the courts. Many of these cases broke new ground in affirming the specific claims of students to constitutional protection, but the *Tinker* decision, in particular, marks the beginning of the shift in judicial thinking regarding students' rights and the corresponding change in the administration of schools. The more recent *Goss* decision, like *Tinker,* has important implications for the administration of public schools and, derivatively, for the role of the principal. Also, both decisions include dissenting opinions attesting to and opposing the shift represented by the majority opinions.

The Tinker *Decision.* In *Tinker,* the Supreme Court held that the wearing of black armbands to school by three students to protest the Vietnam War was entirely divorced from actually or potentially disruptive conduct and was closely akin to "pure speech" and, hence, protected under the First Amendment. The Court unequivocally affirmed the rights of students under the Constitution:

School officials do not possess absolute authority over their students. Students in school as well as out of school are "persons" under our Constitution. They are possessed of fundamental rights which the State must respect, just as they themselves must respect their obligations to the State. In our system, students may not be regarded as closed-circuit recipients of only that which the State chooses to communicate. They may not be confined to the expression of those sentiments that are officially approved. In the absence of a specific showing of constitutionally valid reasons to regulate their speech, students are entitled to freedom of expression of their views.[6]

Moreover, the Court emphasized that the rights of students are not confined to classroom hours:

A student's rights, therefore, do not embrace merely the classroom hours. When he is in the cafeteria, or on the playing field, or on the campus during the authorized hours, he may express his opinions, even on controversial subjects like the conflict in Vietnam, if he does so without "materially and substantially interfer(ing) with the requirements of appropriate discipline in the operation of the school" and without colliding with the rights of others. . . .[7]

This decision delineated more precisely than before those aspects of school life over which school authorities could exercise control and placed beyond the pale of school regulation those aspects of student autonomy protected by the Constitution, and it established an important and administratively useful standard — that of "material and substantial interference." By using this standard the Court firmly established a yardstick to guide school principals and other school officials in the regulation of student conduct.

The dissent of Justice Hugo Black is particularly noteworthy. The tenor of his dissent is reflected in his first sentence:

The Court's holding in this case ushers in what I deem to be an entirely new era in which the power to control pupils by the elected "officials of state supported public schools . . ." in the United States is in ultimate effect transferred to the Supreme Court.[8]

Quite apart from the explicit recognition in this comment of the shift in the traditional role of the Supreme Court, there is here, and later in the dissent, implicit recognition of the change in the conception of a public school attendant upon the affirmation of students' rights. Justice Black concludes his dissent with a touch of hyperbole:

This case, therefore, wholly without constitutional reasons in my judgment, subjects all the public schools in the country to the whims and caprices of their loudest-mouthed, but maybe not their brightest, students. I, for one, am not fully persuaded that school pupils are wise enough, even with this Court's expert help from Washington, to run the 23,390 public school systems in our fifty states.[9]

What is important in this passage is the recognition that this decision dramatically alters the status of the public school student and, hence, the relationship between student and the school — teachers, principal, and administration generally. In effect, the *Tinker* decision by itself requires school principals to ensure that the administrative practices in a public school are compatible with the constitutional rights of students. But, contrary to the claim of Justice Black, this decision does not surrender control of the public schools to students. As the majority opinion pointed out:

the Court has repeatedly emphasized the need for affirming the comprehensive authority of the States and of school officials, consistent with *fundamental constitutional safeguards*, to prescribe and control conduct in the schools.[10]

Thus, what is distinctive about this decision is the affirmation of students' rights and the correlative duty attaching to school principals, among others, to respect and allow students the full exercise of those rights within the constraints of the special nature of the school.

The Goss *Decision.* The next landmark decision for students' rights, *Goss* v. *Lopez*,[11] established the right of students to procedural due process in discipline cases involving suspensions for ten days or less. In this case, the Supreme Court upheld the decision of the district court that nine students suspended from the Columbus, Ohio, Public School System in 1971 were denied due process. The Supreme Court, reiterating that "the Fourteenth Amendment forbids the State to deprive any person of life, liberty or property without due process of law," held that Ohio State law entitled students between six and twenty-one years of age to a public education and that this constituted a property interest for the student, hence falling under the protection of the Fourteenth Amendment. The Court found further that students have a liberty interest in their reputation, again entitling them to the protection of the Fourteenth Amendment.

School authorities here suspended appellees from school for periods of up to ten days based on charges of misconduct. If sustained and recorded, those charges could seriously damage the students' standing with their fellow pupils and their teachers as well as interfere with later opportunities for higher education and employment.[12]

On the issue of whether or not students were entitled to procedural due process the Court concluded by saying:

A short suspension is of course a far milder deprivation than expulsion. But, "education is perhaps the most important function of state and local governments" *(Brown* v. *Board of Education,* 347 U. S. 483, 493) . . . , and the total exclusion from the educational process for more than a trivial period, and certainly if the suspension is for ten days, is a serious event in the life of the suspended child. Neither the property interest in educational benefits temporarily denied nor the liberty interest in reputation, which is also implicated, is so insubstantial that suspensions may constitutionally be imposed by any procedure the school chooses, no matter how arbitrary.[13]

Having established the applicability of due process to students, the Court then turned its attention to the nature of due process and its requirements in school disciplinary proceedings. Recognizing that "judicial interposition in the operation of the public school system of the Nation raises problems requiring care and restraint . . . ,"[14] the Court held that:

At the very minimum, therefore, students facing suspension and the consequent interference with a protected property interest must be give *some* kind of notice and afforded *some* kind of hearing.[15]

Furthermore, the Court observed:

Students facing temporary suspension have interests qualifying for protection of the Due Process Clause, and due process requires, in connection with a suspension of ten days or less, that the student be given oral and written notice of the charges against him and, if he denies them, an explanation of the evidence the authorities have and an opportunity to present his side of the story. The clause requires at least these rudimentary precautions against unfair or mistaken findings of misconduct and arbitrary exclusion from school.[16]

The Court noted that "[t]here need be no delay between the time notice is given and the time of the hearing." Prior notice and hearing, however, cannot be insisted upon with "[s]tudents whose presence poses a continuing danger to persons or property or an on-going threat of disrupting the academic process . . . ."[17] These students may be immediately removed from the school with the requisite notice and hearing following as soon as practicable.

In reflecting on its decision the Court observed that "we do not believe that we have imposed procedures on school disciplinarians which are inappropriate in a classroom setting. Instead we have imposed requirements which are, if anything, *less than a fair-minded school principal would impose upon himself in order to avoid unfair suspensions.*"[18] The Court, moreover, explicitly stopped short of requiring that hearings in connection with short suspensions allow the student "to secure counsel, to confront and cross-examine witnesses supporting the charge or to call his own witnesses to verify his version of the incident."[19]

The Court concluded its opinion by setting out a rationale for the decision based essentially on the need for fairness in the administration of discipline:

Requiring effective notice and informal hearing permitting the student to give his version of the events will provide a meaningful hedge against erroneous action. At least the disciplinarian will be alerted to the existence of disputes about facts and arguments about cause and effect. He may then determine himself to summon the accuser, permit cross-examination and allow the student to present his own witnesses. In more difficult cases, he may permit counsel. In any case, his decision will be more informed and we think the risk of error substantially reduced.[20]

So the Court justified its decision not only in terms of constitutional law and precedent but also in terms of "informing the discretion" of the disciplinarian and so reducing the likelihood of injustice to the student.

Four justices dissented from the majority opinion. Their dissent, written by Justice Lewis Powell, draws attention to the basic shift in the status of public school students and in the relationship of the student to the school. The basis of the dissent was legal: Justice Powell argued that, whatever infringement on a student's property interest there is, "it is too speculative, transitory and insubstantial to justify imposition of a *constitutional* rule."[21]

Justice Powell subsequently argued the need for suspension as a disciplinary technique, the commonality of interest between state and student in the educational process, and the utility of discipline as a means of teaching students the necessity of rules and obedience to them. He concluded his dissent with the following critically important observation:

No one can foresee the ultimate frontiers of the new "thicket" the Court now enters. Today's ruling appears to sweep within the protected interest in education a multitude of discretionary decisions in the educational process. Teachers and other school authorities are required to make many decisions that may have serious consequences for the pupil. They must decide, for example, how to grade the student's work, whether a student passes or fails a course, whether he is to be promoted, whether he is required to take certain subjects, whether he may be excluded from interscholastic athletics or other extracurricular activities, whether he may be removed from one school and sent to another, whether he may be bussed long distances when available schools are nearby, and whether he should be placed in a "general," "vocational," or "college-preparatory" track.

In these and many similar situations claims of impairment of one's educational entitlement identical in principle to those before the Court today can be asserted with equal or greater justification.[22]

There seems little doubt as to the accuracy of Justice Powell's prediction. Affirming the "property" interest of public school students in education certainly marks a major change in the claim of students to a public education and will certainly subject to judicial scrutiny many of the discretionary decisions mentioned here. Some of these decisions, particularly those involving the classification of students, are already receiving attention from the courts and educational policy analysts.[23] What the *Goss* decision does is to require that decisions of this kind — decisions affecting a substantial "property" interest of a student in education — be procedurally fair. The area *is* a thicket, but the claim of students to substantive and procedural fairness in decisions affecting their property interest in education is such that the thicket must be entered.

The Effect of Tinker *and* Goss. These two decisions are good examples of Llewellyn and Hoebel's cases of trouble. In both decisions the customary practice of school administrators in regulating student behavior tangles with and yields to the emergent claim of students to constitutional protection. The dissenting opinions, moreover, suggest strongly that these will not be the last cases involving students' rights to reach the Supreme Court. There are yet other emergent issues in students' rights on the horizon, issues that will challenge even further the customary practice of that ancient institution — the school. Thus, in *Wood* v. *Strickland* the Supreme Court held that:

in the specific context of school discipline, . . . a school board member is not immune from liability for damages . . . if he knew or reasonably should have known that the action he took within his sphere of official responsibility would violate the constitutional rights of the student affected, or if he took the action with the malicious intention to cause a deprivation of constitutional rights or other injury to the student.[24]

And, further, in *Baker* v. *Owen* the district court, relying on *Goss,* held that a student has a liberty interest in avoiding corporal punishment and that, if corporal punishment is to be administered, the elements of procedural due process must be observed.[25]

The *Tinker* and *Goss* decisions, then, are milestones in the constant paradigmatic shift affecting the administration of public schools. For the principal this shift is from a condition of almost unlimited discretionary power to one where discretionary power is substantially checked, from voluntary recognition of students' rights and interests to judicially required recognition, from a traditional authority relationship defined in terms of adults and students to a relationship based on the idea of students as "persons" with rights, and from a custodial concept of student governance to a more humanistic orientation.[26] The student, who was organizationally impotent, has gained constitutional protection.

The overall effect of the *Goss* and *Tinker* decisions is to require school administrators, most particularly, school principals, to examine very carefully both the administrative and educational practices in their schools and bring them into line with judicial requirements, thus ensuring that school policies, procedures, and practices respect the constitutional rights of students in both substantive and procedural terms.

THE PRINCIPAL'S RESPONSE

The basic choice facing the school principal is whether or not to comply with judicial decisions affirming the constitutional rights of students and so reform or modify school policy, procedures, and practices to reflect the directions charted by the courts. Although the courts may require school principals to render their school governance compatible with judicial decisions, there is no assurance this will happen. Richard Mandel, in his discussion of the effectiveness of the judicial process as a mechanism of change in public schools, cites the findings of the New York Civil Liberties Union Report on the first two years of its Students' Rights Project. This project, in which the extent of administrative compliance with the New York City Board of Education's newly promulgated suspension and expulsion procedures was investigated, showed that in many cases "almost every protection granted by the Board of Education to the students had been violated."[27] Similarly, Mandel reports that in other areas the project found considerable administrative violation of students' rights. Nor does a student winning a lawsuit necessarily induce administrative compliance. Again, Mandel cites the case of a public school principal refusing to allow the distribution in his school of a court order reinstating a suspended student when the school had agreed not to interfere with students exercising their right to distribute literature on school property. These data, combined with analysis of the relevant literature — in particular, the extensive record of administrative noncompliance with the prayer and Bible reading decisions, led Mandel to hypothesize:

The judicial process is largely ineffective in bringing about change in public school organizations; court decisions which, if implemented would change existing modes of organizational behavior will not be complied with.[28]

Why is this the case? Why is it that those charged with the responsibility of preparing youth to enter society as adults do not immediately adopt judicial precedents as guides to action? What are the barriers mitigating against administrative responsiveness to judicial decisions?

Barriers to Administrative Responsiveness

There is no systematic analysis of the barriers confronting the school principal when a court decision requires changes in the policies, procedures, and practices of the school. Hence, what follows are tentative but plausible explanations of the factors that may operate as barriers to implementation of judicial decisions: philosophical-ideological, political-legal, and organizational-administrative.[29]

Philosophical-Ideological Barriers. Barriers to administrative responsiveness in the philosophical-ideological domain seem to have their origins in the clash between traditional and emergent views of the status of the child and student and derivatively of the nature of the school as a social institution. The chief barrier seems to be concerned with the changing status of the child and student in the culture. There is a tension between the traditional view of the child and student as a dependent, impotent individual in need of care and protection and the emergent view of children as "persons" under the Constitution with attendant rights.[30] For those school principals familiar with and ideologically committed to the traditional view (standing in loco parentis) accommodating the emergent view and incorporating it into their personal philosophy and administrative practice may be difficult, if not impossible. So the first and most important barrier may be the philosophy and ideology of the school principal. If he or she is not committed to the emergent view of children and students as "persons" with rights under the Constitution then the likelihood of bringing administrative practice into line with the *Tinker* and *Goss* decisions seems slim.

There is a corollary to this, one concerning the nature of the school itself. Recognizing the emergent view of children and students implies changing the policy, procedures, and practices of the school, changing the school from the often characterized authoritarian bureaucracy to a more representative bureaucracy. Michael La Morte characterizes the change as a movement away from the traditional, custodial concept of student governance toward a more humanistic orientation:

In its exaggerated form, the custodial concept is manifested by administrative behavior which tends to be authoritarian, punitive, generally distrustful of students, highly impersonal, and overemphasizing order. The humanist orientation, on the other hand, may be characterized by the following: a school atmosphere is promoted which allows for a high degree of individual differences in conduct allowed students; administrators may not necessarily have the final word determining what constitutes disruptive behavior; students are treated with dignity by the professional staff in their regulation of student conduct; clear relationships are shown between rules governing student conduct and educational objectives; and students have certain Constitutional protections which must be observed.[31]

Creating and administering a humanistic school may well present a signal difficulty for principals with traditional values and accustomed to the custodial concept of student governance. Although Donald Willower, in his review of research conducted using the Pupil Control Ideology instrument, reports that principals and counselors are more humanistic in orientation than teachers,[32] Ray Helsel found that traditionalism in educators' values is positively related to custodialism in pupil control ideology.[33] And so, where school administrators hold traditional values, they will tend to be custodial in orientation to student governance and will probably find the humanistic emphasis in judicial decisions to be both antithetical to their philosophy and ideology and alien to their professional training and experience. For school principals holding traditional values, then, changing their professional ideology and administrative style to a more humanistic orientation is likely to be as difficult as passing through the eye of a needle.

Political-Legal Barriers. Two possible explanations for the principal's reluctance or inability to accommodate the emergent status of students lie in the political and legal domain. Politically, it may simply not be feasible to alter the structure of the public school because principals may lack the support of senior administrators, the community, and teachers in the school. They may in fact be so constrained as to be administratively powerless.[34] Given the bureaucratic relationship between the individual school and the system of which it is part, a principal would be unwise to restructure a school's organization without the support of an immediate superordinate. With the increasing power of school-community councils, the principal would be unwise to move without their support as well. Similarly, the support of teachers and other members of the school staff are critical to the success of the change. Any or all of these reference groups can support or oppose the change. For any particular principal, these groups may serve as assets or liabilities.[35]

Legally, the fact that the principal is accountable for the organization and administration of a school may deter him from high-risk leadership. The annals of educational leadership are punctuated by the oustings of superintendents and principals who dared to exert high-risk leadership in accepting the challenge of change.[36] Not only does the principal receive plaudits; he also receives political and professional criticism, and pressure from various groups in the community seeking to advance their own interests. Legally accountable as he is, the principal may prefer a low-risk option and move very slowly and cautiously, if at all.

Organizational-Administrative Barriers. Perhaps the most potent barriers to administrative responsiveness have their source in the organizational-administrative domain, and emanate particularly from structural characteristics of the school.

One of the main barriers to administrative responsiveness stems from the conflict between traditional and emergent views of *authority relationships* in school. The traditional pattern of authority in the public school vests authority in the adults. Teachers and administrators stand in loco parentis to the student and possess extensive discretionary power in the school. The principal, as the legally accountable executive of the board, has most of the discretionary power conferred by statute, board policy and custom. The teacher, as the individual charged with classroom teaching and management, has extensive autonomy and discretion within the confines of the classroom.[37] While the principal is responsible for the administration of the school as a whole, it is the classroom teacher who deals directly with students each day. In contrast to the principal and teachers, students are pawns. They are powerless, possessing little or no personal autonomy or discretionary power. It is salutary to recall here Willard Waller's classic characterization of the teacher-pupil relationship:

The teacher-pupil relationship is a form of institutionalized dominance and subordination. Teacher and pupil confront each other in the school with an original conflict of desires, and however much that conflict may be reduced in amount, or however much it may be hidden, it still remains. The teacher represents the adult group, ever the enemy of the spontaneous life of groups of children. The teacher represents the formal curriculum, and his interest is in imposing that curriculum upon the children in the form of tasks; pupils are much more interested in life in their own world than in the desiccated bits of adult life which teachers have to offer. The teacher represents the established social order in the school, and his interest is in maintaining that order, whereas pupils have only a negative interest in that feudal superstructure. Teacher and pupil confront each other with attitudes from which the underlying hostility can never be altogether removed. Pupils are the material in which teachers are supposed to produce results. Pupils are human beings striving to realize themselves in their own spontaneous manner, striving to produce their own results in their own way. Each of these hostile parties stands in the way of the other; in so far as the aims of either are realized, it is at the sacrifice of the aims of the other.[38]

The emergent, humanistic orientation of recent judicial decisions seriously undermines and directly challenges the traditional concept of student governance and, thereby, the traditional relationships between schools, principals, teachers, and students. The emergent view, by upholding the constitutional rights of students, negates the role of student as *pawn* and affirms the role of student as *person* — not necessarily fully adult in capacity but with the potential of becoming adult — and thereby confers upon the student the protection of the Constitution, including avenues for redress of grievance. This marks a dramatic shift toward a balance of power in public schools. In the light of this shift and given Waller's characterization of the teacher-pupil relationship, overstated though it may be, it should not be surprising to find that teachers themselves may be a barrier to administrative responsiveness and may oppose the affirmation of students' rights in school on the grounds that it reduces their traditional authority and fundamentally changes the teacher-pupil relationship. In particular, teachers may oppose the implementation of judicially compatible policies, procedures, and practices because they may see this move as limiting the capacity of the principal (or his designee) to support their authority when challenged by the student. Teachers generally hold a strong normative expectation that the principal should uphold their authority regardless of circumstances.[39] They may well construe any attempt on the part of the principal to redefine their role or relationship with respect to students as a threat and so oppose it.

A second barrier mitigating against administrative responsiveness in schools is the organizational *press for control* of student behavior. Press for control seems to have its source in a number of structural characteristics of schools. The relationship between school and client is mutually mandated leading Richard Carlson to characterize public schools as domesticated organizations along with prisons and mental hospitals.[40] The fact that neither schools nor clients have a choice in the matter of who attends or whether to attend, together with the fact that domesticated organizations are generally concerned with maintenance of the social system and hence slow to change and adapt, begins to explain the press for order and control of student behavior in the school. Add to this the absence of clearly stated objectives for the public school, the endemic uncertainties facing teachers,[41] the massive imbalance of power in the teacher-pupil relationship,[42] the "structural looseness" of the school,[43] and the incentive structure for administrators to maintain the system,[44] and the origins of the press for control become clearer and the resistance of administrators and teachers to change becomes more intelligible.

These barriers, philosophical-ideological, political-legal, and organizational-administrative, suggest some of the factors mitigating against administrative responsiveness and contributing to institutional inertia in schools. These barriers in large part derive from the traditional structure of the school as a formal organization and may be immutable. Still, if the principal is to adminster a school that recognizes the rights of students, he must find ways of coping with these barriers. The challenge is to find strategies contributing to institutional renewal.

STRATEGIES FOR INSTITUTIONAL RENEWAL

The challenge facing the public school principal is demanding. Not only must he organize a school that is educationally effective, professionally fulfilling, and responsive to community wishes, but this must be done in a manner compatible with judicial decisions. What is needed is not only "a new model of norms with supporting values which are within judicially defined perimeters . . ."[45] but also a repertoire of strategies for anticipating and overcoming the traditional inertia of the public school. In this regard three strategies bear further scrutiny: the first involves the affirmation of leadership, the second relates to the provision of in-service training; and the third concerns the restructuring of administrative leaderhip-training programs.

Affirmation of Leadership

The insistence that the public school principal affirm leadership may seem strange at first glance. It does, however, carry some important implications. Affirming leadership implies a conscious and deliberate intent on the part of the principal to set a clear direction for the school; it implies the presence of a coherent, integrated philosophy; it implies evidence of moral deliberation and moral maturity. As

Donald Barr notes: "What youngsters, even adolescents, need to see is not a system grinding out decisions but a man making moral choices. How else will they learn to become men and make moral choices."[46] Ultimately, of course, it requires that the principal decide what kind of schools he or she is going to have — whether decision making will be autocratic or democratic, unilateral or consensual, closed or open; whether students, teachers, and parents participate in making decisions affecting their lives and interests; whether the governance of the school be like that of an authoritarian bureaucracy or be predicated on recognition of constitutional rights in school, and thereby compatible with judicial decisions in these matters.

I have argued elsewhere that the notion of discretionary justice provides a judicially compatible approach for school governance. Such an approach, focusing as it does on the exercise of discretionary power in terms of the substantive and procedural fairness to affected parties, would go far toward recognizing the rights of students in school. In fact, this approach is compatible with the conception of a school as a system of rights affecting all interested parties — students, teachers and parents in the schooling process — their rights and interests, both substantive and procedural, are explicitly accommodated in this approach to school governance.[47]

Adopting such an approach may not, however, be feasible for some principals. It may be too time consuming to work out in practice, too legalistic to seem useful, or too idealistic to fit their knowledge and perception of the school. An alternative way of affirming leadership through the recognition of students' rights is for the principal to adopt in his school the sample Student Code developed by Phi Delta Kappa's Commission on Administrative Behaviors Supportive of Human Rights.[48] This code lays out simply and clearly policy guidelines governing and regulating student behavior in a manner consistent with the requirements of the courts.

Yet a third alternative is to adopt the approach discussed so well by Edward Ladd.[49] He argues forcibly that schools and school officials tend to exert unnecessary and countereducational control over student behavior and that they should only control those aspects of student behavior necessary for *law enforcement* (enforcement of public laws in school), *housekeeping* (regulation of organizational life and procedures), and *protection* (prevention of serious injuries, health hazards, personal assault, property damage, and infringement of rights). Ladd goes on to advocate a totally different set of governing assumptions for the operation of public schools, assumptions involving widely divergent views of the extent and kind of freedom (in contrast to orderliness) required to enable education to take place. In effect, Ladd advocates a view of "education as freedom" and discusses the implications for regulating student conduct in a manner compatible with the rights of students, the demand for institutional regulation, and the educational value of "disruptive" behavior.

Before adopting any or all of these approaches, the principal would be wise to inform himself or herself about the barriers to compliance, to develop an understanding of the forces inducing bureaucratic inertia, and to marshal resources to overcome resistance to change. In either case the decision to recognize students' rights is an important organizational change and will require careful planning and implementation to be successful.

The Need for In-Service Training

In-service training is central to the effective implementation of a new policy on students' rights. Continuous in-service training with all members of the school staff — administrators, disciplinarians, counsellors, teachers, paraprofessional and support staff — is necessary if the actual practices of the school are to reflect the intent of the policy. What makes the translation of policy into practice problematic is that it will involve changing the attitudes and behavior of some members of the school staff. To effect these changes requires more than promulgating a new policy, specific and defensible though it may be; it requires systematic, extensive, and continuing effort on the part of the principal to shape the practice of the school so that students do in fact have rights and are able to exercise them.

Such a program of in-service training should certainly involve parents, teachers, students, and the community at large, as well as other members of the school staff. To increase the likelihood of acceptance it may be necessary and desirable to bring in a consultant knowledgeable about organizational development to work in the school and to assist in the process of restructuring the school.

Administrative Leadership Training Programs

To make public schools responsive to judicial decisions concerning students' rights requires shifts of emphasis and changes of direction in administrative leadership-training programs. To organize and administer schools in a manner consistent with the rights of students requires that prospective and practicing school administrators recognize the existence of a need in this area, gain a working knowledge of the statute and case law governing students and their rights, and acquire the conceptual-analytic skills necessary to move from precedent and principle to practice. Training programs for administrators can contribute to the acquisition of these skills. Courses in school law[50] and seminars in students' rights[51] can provide prospective and practicing administrators with the conceptual perspective and substantive knowledge of the field. Evidently many secondary school principals are not aware of recent court decisions involving students' rights. Michael Kirsch reports that of twenty randomly selected suburban high school principals only eleven (55 percent) had any knowledge of the *Tinker* case.[52] If these principals are in any sense representative of secondary principals across the nation, there is clear need for more intensive and extensive exposure to current developments in students' rights. It is not enough, however, merely to disseminate information, though this is important; training programs must also attend to the processes of knowledge utilization and to the process of policy formation.[52] The translation of knowledge into administrative action is a focus requiring explicit attention and practice. Internships and practicums can provide prospective administrators with actual experiences in creating and sustaining organizational change, in working with policy development and formulation, in coping with conflicting community pressures, and in clarifying a personal philosophy of administration. If, however, there is a serious concern with making schools responsive to judicial decisions, then systematic attention needs to be directed toward strategies of implementation in training programs for administrators.

THE ARGUMENT RESTATED

In the last decade the public schools have become crucibles of conflict as students have pressed their claims to constitutional protection. In many cases the Courts have upheld their claims and affirmed their rights; these decisions, especially those of *Tinker* and *Goss*, constitute a paradigmatic shift for the administration of schools—a shift emanating from the changing conception and status of the child in the culture. There are, however, substantial barriers to administrative responsiveness inherent in the existing structure of the school. To overcome these barriers—to overcome the institutional inertia of schools—requires the affirmation of leadership by public school principals, and corresponding modifications and shifts of emphasis both in training programs for administrators and in organizational development.

NOTES

1. Karl N. Llewellyn and E. Adamson Hoebel, *The Cheyenne Way* (Norman: University of Oklahoma Press, 1941), 28-29.

2. Edward C. Bolmeier, *Landmark Supreme Court Decisions on Public School Issues* (Charlottesville, Va.: Michie Company, 1973).

3. *Tinker* v. *Des Moines Community School District*, 393 U.S. 503, 89 S. Ct. 733 (1969).

4. *Goss* v. *Lopez*, 95 S. Ct. 729 (1975).

5. *West Virginia State Board of Education* v. *Barnette* 319 U.S. 624 (1943), 637.

6. *Tinker* v. *Des Moines Community School District*, 393 U.S. 503, 511.

7. *Ibid.*, 512.

8. *Ibid.*, 515.

9. *Ibid.*, 525-526.

10. *Ibid.*, 507 [emphasis added].

11. *Goss* v. *Lopez*, 95 S. Ct. 729 (1975). See also Robert E. Draba, "Short Suspensions: The Goss Decision Establishes a Student's Due Process Rights," *Administrator's Notebook*, 23 (No. 4 [n.d.]). This decision deals only with short suspensions of ten days or less. By affirming the right of students to due process in short suspensions, the Court implicitly acknowledged constitutional protection for students in discipline cases involving longer suspensions. The Court noted, "Longer suspensions or expulsions for the remainder of the school term, or permanently, may require more formal procedures" (95 S. Ct. 729, 741).

12. *Ibid.*

13. *Ibid.*, 737.

14. *Ibid.*, 738.

15. *Ibid.*

16. *Ibid.*, 739-740.

17. *Ibid.*, 740.

18. *Ibid.* [emphasis added].

19. *Ibid.*

20. *Ibid.*, 741.

21. *Ibid.*, 742.

22. *Ibid.*, 747-748.

23. David Kirp, "Student Classification, Public Policy, and the Courts," *Harvard Educational Review*, 44 (February 1974), 7-52. See also D. Parker Young and Donald D. Gehring, "The Other Side of the Coin: Due Process in Academic Affairs," *NOLPE School Law Journal*, 1 (Spring 1971), 32-38.

24. *Wood* v. *Strickland*, 95 S. Ct. 999 (1975), 1001.

25. *Baker* v. *Owen*, 395 F. Supp. 294 (1975).

26. Michael W. La Morte, "The Courts and the Governance of Student Conduct," *School and Society*, 100 (February 1972), 89-93. See also Edward T. Ladd, "Regulating Student Behavior without Ending Up in Court," *Phi Delta Kappan*, 54 (January 1973), 304-309. Both La Morte and Ladd recognize the shift in student governance contingent upon judicial decisions. They do not, however, label it a "paradigm shift."

27. Richard L. Mandel, "Judicial Decisions and Organizational Change in Public Schools," *School Review*, 82 (February 1974), 331. See also David L. Kirp, "The Role

of Law in Educational Policy," *Social Policy* (September-October 1971), 42-47, for a discussion of the effectiveness of law as a vehicle for changing educational practice.

28. Mandel, "Judicial Decisions and Organizational Change in Public Schools."

29. These general rubrics are similar to those used by Stephen P. Hencley, "Impediments to Accountability," *Administrator's Notebook,* 20 (December 1971).

30. Richard Farson, *Birthrights* (New York: Macmillan, 1974).

31. La Morte, "Courts and the Governance of Student Conduct," 89.

32. Donald J. Willower, "Some Comments on Inquiries on Schools and Pupil Control," unpub. paper presented at the Annual Meeting of the American Educational Research Association, Chicago, April 1974, 4.

33. A. Ray Helsel, "Value Orientation and Pupil Control Ideology of Public School Educators," *Educational Administration Quarterly,* 7 (Winter 1971), 28. Helsel found the relationship between traditionalism in values and custodialism in pupil control ideology to hold for each of his five organizational positions: elementary teacher, secondary teacher, counselor, elementary principal, and secondary principal.

34. Donald A. Erickson, "Moral Dilemmas of Administrative Powerlessness," *Administrator's Notebook,* 20 (April 1972).

35. William L. Smith, "Cleveland's Experiment in Mutual Respect," in Danforth Foundation and Ford Foundation, *The School and the Democratic Environment* (New York: Columbia University Press, 1970). Smith provides a brief overview of an experiment in his school where the operational principles of administrative action were "mutual respect" and "justification."

36. As an example, see R. Bruce McPherson, Steven Daniels, and William P. Stewart, "Options for Students in Ann Arbor," *Phi Delta Kappan,* 54 (March 1973), 469-472; L. R. Dolph, "Why Ann Arbor's School Revolution Failed," *ibid.* (June 1973), 683-686.

37. Dan C. Lortie, "The Balance of Control and Autonomy in Elementary School Teaching," in *The Semi-Professions and Their Organization,* ed. Amitai Etzioni (New York: Free Press, 1969), 9; W. S. Simpkins and David Friesen, "Discretionary Powers of Classroom Teachers," *Canadian Administrator,* 9 (May 1970), 35-38.

38. Willard Waller, *The Sociology of Teaching* (New York: John Wiley and Sons, 1967), 195-196.

39. Howard S. Becker, "The Teacher in the Authority System of the Public School," in *Complex Organization,* ed. Amitai Etzioni (New York: Holt, Rinehart, and Winston, 1965), 246.

40. Richard O. Carlson, "Environmental Constraints and Organizational Consequences: The Public School and Its Clients," in *Behavioral Science and Educational Administration,* ed. Daniel E. Griffiths (Chicago: University of Chicago Press, 1964), 266.

41. Dan C. Lortie, *School Teacher* (Chicago: University of Chicago Press, 1975), 134-161.

42. Philip W. Jackson, *Life in Classrooms* (New York: Holt, Rinehart, and Winston, 1968), 28-33.

43. Charles E. Bidwell, "The School as a Formal Organization," in *Handbook of Organizations,* ed. James G. March (Chicago: Rand McNally and Company, 1965), 976.

44. James S. Coleman, "Incentives in American Education," *Educate,* 11 (September 1969), 18-19.

45. Mandel, "Judicial Decisions and Organizational Change in Public Schools," 344.

46. Donald Barr, *Who Pushed Humpty Dumpty?* (New York: Atheneum, 1917), 122.

47. Michael E. Manley-Casimir, "School Governance as Discretionary Justice," *School Review*, 82 (February 1974), 347-362.

48. Commission on Administrative Behaviors Supportive of Human Rights, "A Sample Student Code," *Phi Delta Kappan*, [56] (December 1974), 236-242.

49. Edward T. Ladd, "Toward an Educationally Appropriate Legal Definition of Disruptive Student Behavior," *Educational Administration Quarterly*, 7 (Autumn 1971).

50. Robert E. Phay, "The Teaching of School Law," Results of a Survey of Schools of Education and Law Schools (Topeka, Kans.: National Organization on Legal Problems of Education, January 1972). This survey showed that school law is increasingly being taught in both schools of education and schools of law.

51. William W. Van Alstyne, "A Suggested Seminar in Student Rights," *Journal of Legal Education*, 21 (No. 5, 1969), 547-558.

52. Michael G. Kirsch, "Are Secondary School Principals Ignoring *Tinker?*" *Phi Delta Kappan*, [56] (December 1974), 286.

53. Jean Hills, "Preparation for the Principalship: Some Recommendations from the Field," *Administrator's Notebook*, 23 (No. 9, 1975).

Chapter Ten

Francis Schrag

The Principal as a Moral Actor

Inasmuch as the decisions of the school principal affect the welfare and the interests of other people, it is possible to view those decisions from a moral perspective.[1] The principal may also feel a need to consider alternatives from the moral point of view. But what is meant by the moral point of view? What considerations must a person entertain if he wishes to be a conscientious moral actor? Upon what principles does he distinguish between alternative courses of action? The moral philosopher addresses such questions in a way that may help an administrator in his deliberations, but the philosopher cannot supply any magic formula for making "correct" decisions. His contribution is probably limited to outlining the major principles and considerations that the administrator must countenance.

THE MORAL POINT OF VIEW

What, then, is involved when one takes a moral point of view? Philosophy has not produced, and is not likely to produce, a definitive answer to this question. A number of philosophers would, however, agree that any complete list would include the following features:

1. A moral agent must base his decisions on principles that apply to classes of situations, not on a whim of the moment or a predilection for one particular kind of situation. These principles must be meant for all human beings; they should not benefit or burden any group or class within the society. The principles must also be impartial, or, stated another way, the effect must be reversible. This means that an

actor must be willing to adhere to the principle even if his role in the moral situation were to be reversed and he were the one to whom the principle was being applied.

2. A moral agent should consider the welfare and interests of *all* who stand to be affected by his decision or action, including himself.

3. A moral agent has the obligation to base his decision on the most complete information relative to the decision that he can obtain.

4. A conscientious moral agent's moral judgments are prescriptive. He must acknowledge that, when he has fully examined a situation calling for his decision and reached a conclusion, he has thereby answered the question: What ought I to *do*? If he acts otherwise, it is through weakness of will or through failure to take the moral obligation seriously.

These conditions may be said to define the moral point of view or attitude, but they do not and are not meant to give a person specific guidance in a moral situation. They are, rather, standards that a man must meet if he wishes to make a decision on moral grounds.[2]

In this chapter the discussion will focus on the analysis of a concrete situation of the kind an inner-city school principal might confront. The analysis will reveal the situation to be perhaps *more* complex, its resolution *more* difficult, than the reader expected. The aim here, however, is not to simplify decision making but to illuminate the various facets of moral situations in all their complexity.

THE SITUATION

The Abraham Lincoln Elementary School is located in the inner core of Monroe City, a city inhabited by close to a million people. The population the school serves is virtually all black from lower- middle-class and lower-class socioeconomic backgrounds. The staff is integrated, and the principal, David Palmer, is white. There is a Black Parents League, composed primarily of parents of children in the Lincoln School, that became active in 1967 and has been working for several years to gain a voice in determining the school's policy and program. The parents are determined to improve the education of their children, which they perceive to be inadequate.

A delegation of parents from the Black Parents League has met with Mr. Palmer to complain about one of the teachers, Mrs. Doris Newsome, a second-grade teacher new to Monroe City's school system but with ten years of experience in another state. Mr. Palmer had been receiving complaints about Mrs. Newsome, a white woman, ever since the school year had begun two months ago, and the same complaints were now being voiced by the delegation. The group claimed that Mrs. Newsome was prejudiced toward black children and did not consider them capable of learning. Two parents of children in her class contended that she had, according to reports from the children, more than once told a child that he or she was "stupid" or "ignorant." The members of the delegation had not come merely to complain about Mrs. Newsome, however; they were demanding that she be transferred to another school and replaced by Wilma Reed, a black teacher, who frequently substituted for absent teachers at Lincoln. Mrs. Reed does not have a master's degree (Mrs. Newsome does), but she knows the neighborhood and its children well. She was even a member of the Black Parents League while her son was in elementary school. At the conclusion of the meeting Mr. Palmer promised to reply to the league parents within three days.

After school he spoke with Mrs. Newsome and told her of the accusations made against her. She said that the parents were probably agitated because she had sent notes to some of them informing them of their children's inadequate behavior and performance in school. Although she had been assigned to Lincoln School by the central office, Mrs. Newsome said she felt comfortable in the school and had no desire to transfer. In fact, she was indignant at Mr. Palmer's suggestion that she consider the possibility of a transfer rather than risk continued hostility from the league. This left Mr. Palmer confronted by the league's demands, on the one hand, and by Mrs. Newsome's categorical denial of the legitimacy of those demands, on the other. What should he do?

The fact that he posed this question to himself does not necessarily mean that Mr. Palmer sees the issue in moral terms. The question "What ought I to do?" may be conceived as a purely self-interested one. From that point of view, the principal is concerned only with what is in his own interests (What course of action is least likely to prejudice my position? What course is most likely to win praise from my superior?). Or, the principal may take the question to mean: How can I mediate the conflict between the two parties and negotiate a settlement that both sides can live with? This approaches a moral view of the dilemma in that the principal is not primarily concerned with his own interests but with those of the parties to the dispute as well. Although this is a disinterested view, it is not yet an adequate moral one because it fails to consider the interests of others who, though not parties to the dispute, will be affected by the decision. Another reason that it is still inadequate morally is that, even if a compromise agreeable to both the league and Mrs. Newsome could be worked out, there is still some question as to whether such a compromise would be morally just or whether either or both parties ought morally to have to accede to the demands of the other at all. An example will make this clear. When a person is accused of a crime, the prosecuting and defense attorneys frequently try to strike a bargain in which the accused pleads guilty to a lesser charge in return for a light or suspended sentence. An innocent defendant may be willing to make such a bargain because the alternative (if he is poor) could be that he would spend a long time in prison awaiting trial. Such a bargain is not morally sound because no person ought to be asked to plead guilty to a crime he did not commit.

THE PROCESS OF CONSIDERATION

How might Mr. Palmer proceed to determine the moral thing to do? The following procedure is plausible: try to anticipate the consequences of each of the alternatives, weigh the consequences against each other, and choose the course that maximizes the beneficial consequences. This procedure is much more difficult to follow than it sounds. First, it requires that the notion of beneficial and harmful consequences be defined. Is good defined in terms of simple pleasure, or with respect to some more encompassing notion such as happiness or self-realization? If the latter, how does one define happiness or self-realization? If the former, how does one measure and calculate pleasure? For example, are kinds or qualities of pleasure distinguishable, and, if so, on what basis? Next, Mr. Palmer must determine whose benefits to consider. Certainly, the satisfaction or suffering incurred by Mrs. Newsome and the parents in the league must be considered — and probably the good and bad effects on the children in Mrs. Newsome's class. Perhaps the effect on overall morale among the faculty might be a consideration, and still other considerations may be deemed relevant. But will there be an effect on Mrs. Newsome's husband, or will feelings of satisfaction and dissatisfaction be engendered among different segments of the community? Then there is the difficulty of estimating the probability of outcomes. Will the Monroe City Teachers Association see Mrs. Newsome's transfer as a violation of teachers' rights and threaten to take major action, even walk out to dramatize its opposition? Finally, the task of measuring and comparing consequences is also beset with innumerable practical and theoretical difficulties. How, for example, does one compare the mild satisfaction experienced by many members of the league with the intense suffering experienced by Mrs. Newsome, both of which might be the consequences of opting to transfer her against her will? And, how does he weigh the relative values of immediate and long-term benefits?

I do not wish to belabor these difficulties because there is a more profound objection to the entire procedure, namely, that it violates some of our strongest intuitions about what is moral and immoral. Let us imagine that the charges brought against Mrs. Newsome are without foundation, that her removal will have little effect on the other teachers, and that the pupils will be neither worse nor better off if she is replaced by Mrs. Reed. Now, assume that the total satisfaction her removal affords the two hundred members of the league far outweighs the suffering experienced by Mrs. Newsome alone. If the decision procedure is simply to maximize total satisfaction, then Mr. Palmer has no choice but to transfer Mrs. Newsome. But this will strike most of us as immoral because it is unjust. If Mrs. Newsome is innocent she deserves to keep her position and her removal cannot be morally defended by appealing to the satisfaction it will bring to those who have slandered her. There are, then, considerations of justice or fairness or what people deserve which the principle of maximization of benefits fails to acknowledge.

We feel strongly that, given the assumption just mentioned, it would be wrong for Mr. Palmer to accede to the league's demands; it would be unfair to Mrs. Newsome who deserves to retain her position. But, suppose (and this is plausible) that the charges can neither be proven nor disproven beyond a reasonable doubt and that Mrs. Newsome argues, in the absence of convincing proof of her wrongdoing, that it would be unfair of Mr. Palmer to transfer her. It is unfair on two counts: the first on the grounds that it would constitute punishment of an innocent person, and the second that it would violate the conditions of her contract, conditions binding on all members of the school system. The league members argue, however, that, even if her guilt cannot be proven, Mrs. Newsome, having lost the parents' confidence, does not deserve the job. They also claim that, since a class of children is more important than a single teacher, it is not fair to retain Mrs. Newsome. The fact that both parties to the dispute believe justice is on their side suggests that the notion of what is fair or just or deserved is itself a complex one requiring examination.

The question of justice may arise whenever there is an allotment to be made of things considered desirable (for example, goods, positions, resources) or undesirable (for example, penalties). A just distribution is one where everyone gets his due. But how is one to know when he has given people their due? Any answer to this depends on finding an adequate criterion of distribution on which to decide a particular case. Many of the philosophical discussions of justice are devoted to the discovery, formulation, and assessment of alternative criteria, which will be discussed further a bit later. An actor in a situation like Mr. Palmer's, however, cannot simply decide on some criterion for awarding teaching positions and then see whether Mrs. Newsome or Mrs. Reed is more deserving according to that criterion. Giving people their due involves more than that. For Mr. Palmer, as any person faced with a difficult decision, has existing commitments to people, commitments that he must honor if he is to act justly. His first task in attempting to act justly, then, is retrospective rather than prospective: to discover the obligations he already has and the basis for these obligations.

Obligations and Rights

What are Mr. Palmer's existing obligations to Mrs. Newsome and to others involved in the situation? (We are now assuming that the leagues's accusations cannot be conclusively proven.) A few preliminary observations of a philosophical nature are in order. The philosopher Kurt Baier has analyzed the notion of obligation in a way that is useful for our purposes:

Obligation has three logical dimensions, "the partner," "the ground," and "the content" of the obligation. We mention the partner of an obligation when we answer the question "to *whom* is A under an obligation?"; the ground when we answer the question "*On account of what* is A under an obligation to B?"; and the content when we answer the question "*what* does A's obligation to B *consist in?*"[3]

It is useful also to point out that rights and obligations are considered by most philosophers to be correlative terms. If one person has a right, then someone else has an obligation. If I have a right to speak, then you have an obligation not to prevent me from speaking. If the government has a right to collect $500.00 in taxes from you, then you have an obligation to pay that amount. From the fact that A has a right, it follows logically that someone has an obligation, but this does not mean that a question cannot arise as to who has the obligation. We may agree for example, that any person has a right to a guaranteed minimum income, but we may disagree about who is obliged to provide that income.

What, then, are Mr. Palmer's obligations? Once a teacher has signed a contract and has been assigned to his school, he is obliged to honor that contract unless the teacher's actions violate that contract or "conflict with the instructional requirements and best interests of the school district and the pupils."[4] He is therefore obligated to retain Mrs. Newsome unless there is cause for her removal. The basis for this obligation is his own agreement to abide by the contract between the Monroe City Board of Education and the Monroe City Education Association, and the contract bears witness to that agreement.

Most of us would also say that Mr. Palmer has an obligation to protect his teachers from undue parental interference. The ground of this obligation lies in certain common expectations and shared assumptions about the nature of schooling. Teachers expect such protection from the principal and feel demoralized when it is not forthcoming. Most parents, in turn, accept the view that teachers are more or less qualified professionals who cannot be expected to perform their function unless granted a reasonable degree of autonomy, and they expect the principal to prevent (other) parents and outsiders from disrupting the educational process. Although there is no explicit promise by the principal to protect his staff, such protection is nevertheless understood by all to be one of the functions of his role in the institution. Were he to accede to the demands of the league, his staff (and no doubt others) would see him as failing to meet his obligations.

Does the principal have an obligation to the parents of children in the school? Our society would answer in the affirmative. The school is the agent of the entire community, but, in the dominant view, the community has no rights over individual children other than those the parents have agreed to entrust to it. The school is commonly seen as acting in loco parentis, that is, for the parents. It is possible to take a different view of the rightful authority of parents, to hold that the community or even the state has prior rights over children, in which case the principal of a school would have a prior obligation to the whole community, not to the parents alone. But such a view finds few adherents. Indeed, the movement for "community control" is really an effort on the part of parents to recapture a strong voice in determining their children's education. What, then, is the ground of the principal's obligation to parents? Once again, it rests not on any conscious promise or pledge by him but on public acceptance of the fact that the existence of schools does not relieve parents of either their primary rights or their responsibilities for the education of their children. What is the content of the principal's obligation to parents? One could answer: the instruction of the children in those areas that are considered vital and within the school's jurisdiction. This does not tell us very much unless one can agree on what is vital and on what is within the school's jurisdiction. Can we agree? I defer consideration of this question until later.

Just as parents have rights over children until they reach maturity, which means that the principal has an obligation toward parents, so the larger community has rights also, for it has a legitimate interest in the education of children. The ground for saying this interest is legitimate, which is the same ground for saying that the principal has an obligation to the wider community, is twofold: first, all adult members of the community contribute through their taxes to the support of the school and so ought to have some voice in the education of its children; second, the consequences, fortunate and unfortunate, of children's education are borne not only by their own parents but by the whole community and, indeed, by other communities as well. And we may assume that a person has a right to a voice in decisions that affect him.

The principal as a civil servant and a citizen also has an obligation to respect and obey the laws and statutes. In a just society these laws and statutes would never run counter to the interests of the community. But in any actual society it is possible that duly elected and appointed officials fail to represent the will of all or even of a majority of the citizens they are chosen to represent. The interests of many or even all parents within a school district may, moreover, diverge from those of the majority at another level of jurisdiction, say, county, state, or nation. At times the laws themselves will reflect this divergence so that a principal may be required by local statute to do that which a federal judge forbids. Laws are human instruments for rendering the affairs of men more just and predictable than they would be in the absence of laws. One can recognize a strong obligation to obey the law and yet allow for exceptional situations in which a person has a moral right, some would say even a duty to refuse to obey the law. Administrators in particular ought to be aware that the fact that some proposed course of action is legal or illegal does not always definitively settle the issue of whether that action ought or ought not to be taken. We reject the notion that a school principal be a mere tool of the state.

I have left for last what many will have thought of first — the principal's obligation to the children in his school. What is the content of this obligation? An immediate answer might again be: to provide the children with whatever instruction is vital and within the school's jurisdiction. That begs the question, however, of who is going to determine what is vital. If we say that it is the parents who should make the determination, we are in effect saying that the principal has no obligation other than to carry out the parents' wishes. But are we prepared to let the principal become a mere instrument of the parents, allowing the latter complete discretion? Suppose the parents are uninformed about what is in their children's interest, or suppose they wish to use the children as instruments for their own purposes? The principal, we said, should not be a mere tool of the state; no more should he be a mere tool of the parents. On the other hand, if we take the view that the principal's primary obligations are to the children, not to their parents, who determines the content of this obligation? And perhaps more difficult still, what is the ground of this obligation? And perhaps more difficult still, what is the ground of this obligation? One could argue that the ground lies in the entire community's selection of the principal as its representative to use professional judgment, wisdom, and foresight to govern the school in the children's best interests. This position assumes that the principal, as a competent professional educator, is better able than the parents to determine the content of the obligations to the children. More important, this position depends on a crucial assumption that there is some objective, nonpartisan answer to the question of what is in children's best interests. Once again, I defer discussing this assumption until the end of the chapter. Despite the difficulties this position encounters, I think most of us will be prepared to acknowledge that a principal (or teacher) has a direct obligation to the children, independent of any obligation to parents, community, or state.

We have now identified five of Mr. Palmer's obligations: to Mrs. Newsome by virtue of promises made and recorded through contracts; to the teaching staff by virtue of the principal's role in the organization; to the parents by virtue of our common acceptance of the primacy of parental rights; to the wider community by virtue of their sharing in both the support and the effects of schooling; and, to the children themselves by virtue of the principal's role as educator in the community. Mr. Palmer cannot, as a conscientious moral agent, deny the legitimacy of any of these obligations. All arise from his position as principal of an elementary school. They do not of course replace, or in any way weaken, the other obligations he shares with all moral agents, obligations to tell the truth, keep promises, act justly, and so forth.

There seems to be a conflict of obligations here, but the conflict can, I think, be resolved. Recall that Mr. Palmer is not obligated to retain a teacher under all circumstances; he is only obligated if retention does not conflict with "the instructional requirements and best interests of the school district and the pupils." Mr. Palmer's obligation to protect teachers is also justified in terms of the need for teachers to enjoy at least partial autonomy in the educational process. Even the Black Parents League defended its demands, not on the basis of parental rights per se but on the basis of its concern for the education of its children, and even if the league represents the view of all the members of the community (which it well may not), Mr. Palmer's obligation to the community is again based on the community's legitimate interest in the education of its children. Although the ground of this obligation is unclear, Mr. Palmer's primary obligation, since it is the basis on which the other obligations rest, is his obligation to the children.

It is important to understand that, although we have now reduced the question to that of whether Mr. Palmer can best meet his primary obligation to the children by retaining Mrs. Newsome, Mr. Palmer's analysis of what he ought to do was not and should not have been confined to an examination of that question. For that question presupposes that he has already assessed his obligations to the children vis-a-vis his existing obligations to other parties to the dispute. We must be careful here. We have said that Mr. Palmer has a primary obligation to the children, but that does not abrogate his obligation to Mrs. Newsome. He is morally entitled to transfer her only when it is established that her presence in the classroom is detrimental to the best interests of the children. Is there any way of establishing this assertion?

Criteria of Distribution

To better deal with the essential question and to make our story as plausible as possible we shall modify the original situation a bit. Seeing the impossibility of proving that Mrs. Newsome really made the damaging statements attributed to her, the league abandoned its demand for her immediate transfer and asked that she be removed from the school at the end of the school year and that her position be filled the following year by Mrs. Reed. The league parents argued that it was essential for their children to be taught by members of their own race who could relate to them. Mrs. Newsome welcomed the retreat of the league, but reasserted her intention to remain at the school unless she was thrown out. Does Mrs. Newsome deserve the position? Is it right to give the job to Mrs. Reed?

A natural way Mr. Palmer might tackle these questions is by attempting to determine which of the candidates is better qualified for the position. Supporters of Mrs. Newsome may assert that her graduate training in remedial reading certainly constitutes a relevant qualification, whereas the color of a person's skin, his race, is surely irrelevant. Now race is certainly irrelevant to performance in many occupations, but it may be related to successful teaching in at least two ways. If one assumes that children's learning is enhanced by their ability to identify with and model themselves on adults, then it is plausible that black children may identify better with members of their own race. One could also argue that successful teaching depends on an understanding of the resources and privations of the students and that a black person, especially one who has lived in the community and knows many of its parents and children, has an asset that any white person, especially a newcomer, lacks. On the other side, it is also plausible that training in the diagnosis and remediation of reading problems is relevant to the successful teaching of reading. All of these assertions are plausible, yet this is not to say that any is demonstrable. Adequate research evidence demonstrating beyond doubt the warrantability of these hypothesized relations may not yet exist, and, even if it did, this would not necessarily settle the question of who deserved or even who was more qualified for the position. Why not?

It is quite possible that both race and preparation in remedial reading are positively related to the academic achievement of students so that, to choose between two teachers, one would still need to look for other bases for determining who deserved the position. But let us assume that there is a statistically significant correlation between the degree of teacher training in remedial reading and student performance on academic achievement tests and no relationship between the race of the teacher and the performance of students of like (or different) race. The question of whether Mrs. Newsome or Mrs. Reed is better qualified is still not settled. The generalizations do not hold in every single case; moreover, every individual is a unique constellation of traits, attitudes, competences, and other qualities—all of which may have some bearing on student performance. Mr. Palmer is choosing between two people, not two races or educational histories, so that no amount of research evidence will eliminate the need for deliberation and judgment on his part.

The entire discussion so far has been treating the question of qualification as if it were a factual issue and not a normative one. Once it is agreed that student academic performance is the measure of teaching success, then the question of whether certain attributes are relevant to being qualified to teach is, indeed, reduced to an empirical one. But suppose that there is not agreement at this level. Suppose that the league's views of what teachers and schools ought to be doing is at variance with that of other parties to the dispute. Given the league's view of the primary purposes of schooling, whether a candidate has had training in remedial reading may not even be relevant to whether she is qualified. The league, that is, may acknowledge that training in remedial reading is associated with student academic achievement, but because it places (let us imagine) a lower value on academic performance, the league may yet deny that this makes Mrs. Newsome more qualified than a person without such training. The concept of relevance is tricky. Statements of relevance contain both a factual and a normative component although the latter is at times concealed.

I have promised to discuss the question of alternative educational ideals at the end of the chapter. For the moment, in order to advance the examination of Mr. Palmer's dilemma let us assume that he sees no reason yet to abandon his belief that all parties are operating within the same normative framework: that he finds it plausible to consider both Mrs. Newsome's training and Mrs. Reed's blackness relevant qualifications and that he finds both individuals equally qualified. (We will assume that as a conscientious moral actor he is willing to consider race a relevant qualification, not only in this case but in other cases, even if the race of the teacher and students were reversed.) Are there any other grounds for holding that one of the two candidates deserves the position?

There are, indeed, two further bases on which a person could contend that one of the candidates deserved the position: as a reward for past services and as compensation or reparation for previous injury. Suppose, for example, that, although it is not widely known, Mrs. Newsome has been working diligently for the children in the community. She has recently organized and is running an after-school study center for all neighborhood children without receiving any additional remuneration, whereas Mrs. Reed has not done anything notable for the school or its children. Mrs. Newsome's backers may claim that she deserves the position in recognition of past services. This argument carries weight only if the two candidates are equally qualified; otherwise it should not be an important consideration because we have already agreed that Mr. Palmer's primary obligation is to the children. Were he to offer Mrs. Newsome a position by virtue of her previous contribution to the school, although he believed Mrs. Reed to be a better teacher, he would be violating that obligation.

Mrs. Reed's backers have an additional argument in support of their candidate. They argue as follows: "Blacks have for years been denied employment on the basis of their color. In recent years after official discrimination was finally ended, more subtle ways have been found to exclude blacks; for example, an oral reading test was devised to ensure that teachers had command of 'correct grammar and pronunciation.' This test was in fact used to systematically discriminate against blacks. Mrs. Newsome is a member of the oppressor race and hence has no just claim to this position. Mrs. Reed is every bit as good a teacher as Mrs. Newsome. She deserves the position as reparation for the centuries of degradation visited upon the black man in America." This argument and others like it possess a measure of cogency, but they are less convincing than they seem. The history of injury and oppression of blacks by whites that the argument alludes to is not in question. What is in question is how that history of the moral relations between two racial groups can help us settle a moral question concerning two individuals, each of whom is a member of one of those groups. If there were a time in the past when Mrs. Newsome personally discriminated against Mrs. Reed, there would not be any difficulty. If it could be documented that Mrs. Reed (or even her husband or children) were actually victimized by whites on the basis of race and that Mrs. Newsome herself discriminated against blacks or even knowingly benefited from the discrimination of others, a case for reparations would be plausible. But suppose that, although there is reason to believe that Mrs. Reed has been unjustly burdened by virtue of her race, Mrs. Newsome has never played any part in nor condoned in any way the oppression of blacks. On what moral basis ought she to be asked to make reparations to Mrs. Reed? Is it simply because her skin is white, a fact over which she had no control? It is true that many blacks have suffered at the hands of many whites. The difficulty with the notion of racial reparations lies in its application to specific cases. How does one calculate what is due any particular black person? What about blacks who have benefited from being black? How does one calculate what price ought to be exacted from any particular white person? What about whites who have themselves been victimized by other whites or whose forbears have been oppressed and discriminated against as much as the ancestors of some blacks? If the idea of reparations is applied indiscriminately to black or white, regardless of injuries personally suffered or inflicted, the results must be unjust.

There is one other basis on which it might be argued that one of the candidates, Mrs. Newsome let us say, deserves the job, and that is on the basis of need. Let us suppose that Mrs. Newsome provides the sole support for her widowed mother, her invalid husband, and her four children, whereas Mrs. Reed's husband earns a handsome income which is ample for themselves and their two children. It is perhaps misleading to say that Mrs. Newsome deserves the job on account of her greater need, for she has not done anything to deserve it. We might more accurately say that, even though she is not more deserving than Mrs. Reed, she ought, nevertheless, to get the job on account of her greater need. There are cases where the prime basis for distributing resources ought to be need (for example, medical attention), but this does not seem to me to be one of them. We must again recall that Mr. Palmer's primary obligation remains to the children. The needs of the candidates for the position become relevant only after he has assured himself that neither candidate is more qualified than the other.

Several bases for considering whether a person ought to be given a teaching position have now been discussed: qualification, reward for prior services, compensation for previous injury, and need. The first ought to take priority, I have argued, because the principal's primary obligation is to meet the educational needs of the children. In any actual contest for a position, however, it may be difficult to determine which of the candidates is better qualified. In that case, the other criteria warrant consideration although, as we saw in our example, these criteria need not point toward the same candidate. And, even if they did, that would not be an end to the matter. One must still take into account the overall consequences for all those affected by the decision. I said at the beginning that one could not confine the decision process to a weighing of the total good and bad consequences of each option. That does not mean, however, that one can exclude consideration of total consequences. The claims of justice have to be balanced against the claims of good consequences, or what philosophers call utility. In our own society we generally hold that the claims of justice take priority, but this does not mean that the claims of utility can never override those of justice. Where the claims of justice are themselves unclear, considerations of the utility of an action become all the more important.[5]

Throughout our discussion we have repeatedly faced and avoided saying anything about the goals or purposes of education. Yet Mr. Palmer cannot assess the beneficial and harmful consequences for the children of appointing Mrs. Newsome or Mrs. Reed without assuming some standard of valuable educative experience. Nor can he determine the content of his obligation to the children without committing himself to some conception of the ends of education. And, finally, he cannot decide which of the candidates is more qualified unless he has a view of what teachers and schools ought to be about.

If there is a consensus about the purposes of education, there is hope that, despite the enormous difficulty of balancing the myriad considerations, already adduced, a decision can be made that will be acceptable to, if not welcomed by, all interested parties. There is some reason to believe, however, that such a consensus will not be found in the urban milieu we are focusing on. The main participants are white and black teachers and administrators and militant black parents. Other participants may range from lower-class blacks to establishment whites, from establishment blacks to radical whites. Representatives of such diverse groups are likely to hold quite divergent values and aspirations for their children and their community. These individuals may therefore fundamentally disagree about what the mission of the school ought to be.

ALTERNATIVE CONCEPTIONS OF EDUCATION

It has been one of the traditional tasks of the educational philosopher to lay out the alternative answers that have been given to this question of what the aims and nature of education ought to be. These answers can be found in innumerable education textbooks under headings such as "perennialism," "existentialism," and "reconstructionism," among others. I think it can be fairly said that neither participants in the schools nor observers and critics of schools have found that either their own or others' actions are in any way guided by these "philosophies." In reaction to this sterile mode of philosophizing, one well-known contemporary philosopher of education has suggested that talk about the ultimate ends of education is misleading and unnecessary.[6] This will not do. I agree that no useful purpose is served by pretending that participants in the educational arena can be grouped according to whether they are, for example, existentialists or reconstructionists. Nevertheless, the question of ends cannot be dodged. I think, moreover, that those who are concerned about education, whether as professionals or citizens, do operate with some notions, however inchoate, of what the mission of schools and teachers ought to be. Those who speak most vociferously about schooling are usually dissatisfied with the status quo. The word "philosophy" suggests to some a relatively stable, systematic, and coherent set of norms, assumptions, and beliefs, and few of us have a "philosophy of education" in this sense of philosophy. I think the word "posture" is useful in suggesting a prevailing attitude or ethos rather than a rigorous doctrine.

In reviewing the current literature about schools, what they are and what they should be, I have identified three characteristic postures taken by authors. I do not claim that the daily work of professionals in the schools is informed by any one of these postures. Indeed, it is possible to move through the daily rounds in school without adopting any posture at all. One does what needs to be done; that is all. But for those who try to set themselves apart from the daily life of the school, whether to see what is wrong with the institution or to plot its future direction, I would argue that they tend to assume one of the following postures, though not perhaps in its extreme form. Whether these three exhaust the possibilities is not my main concern. What I wish to show is the relationship of the dilemma facing Mr. Palmer to some conception of the educational ideal. First, however, I shall try in a few broad and necessarily crude strokes to depict each of the postures.[7]

Those who adopt the first posture believe school ought to be concerned with all areas of human development. The mission of the school is to nourish each individual's growth to enable him to live the best life of which he is capable. No dimension of human competence can or should be singled out for attention. Emotional growth in particular should not be sacrificed for growth in intellectual mastery. Thus those who hold this view deplore the fact that, in the conventional school,

> the classroom walls and prisonlike buildings narrow the teacher's outlook, and prevent him from seeing the true essentials of education. His work deals with the part of a child that is above the neck; and perforce, the emotional, vital part of the child is foreign territory to him.[8]

This view of the ends of education is typically accompanied by a certain view of children: they are incommensurable and indivisible. One cannot measure, evaluate, and classify children in order to "treat" them:

> A reading problem, in short, is not a fact of life, but a fact of school administration. It does not describe Jose, but describes the action performed by the school, i.e., the action of ignoring everything about Jose except his response to printed letters.[9]

Proponents of this view of children usually also share a view of growth or learning as a natural activity of the young. Adults may be needed to enhance or facilitate this natural propensity, but they do not have to engineer it. When adults do try to engineer specific kinds of learning they succeed only in vitiating the child's natural growth. "There is no such thing as learning except (as Dewey tells us) in the continuum of experience."[10]

The vision of school which follows such a conception of the nature of children and the aim of education is that of a "free" community. This implies at least that children choose from among a variety of activities and resources available to them. Conventional divisions between school and home, one academic subject and another, one grade and another, work and play, are seen as "artifical barriers" to be broken down. Children are to be treated with respect as individuals and the status difference between adult and child is to be minimized if not eliminated.

> The continuum of experience and reality of encounter are destroyed in the public schools (and most private ones) by the very methods which form the institution itself—the top-down organization, the regimentation, the faceless encounters, the empty professionalism, and so on.[11]

A second posture defines the ends of schooling in terms of the mastery of specifiable intellectual competences. One writer's initial proposal for reforming schooling is as follows: "Restrict the responsibility of the schools entirely to training in well-defined, clearly teachable skills."[12]

This conception of the ends of schooling is accompanied by a conception of students as more or less interchangeable "learners" whose cognitive activities and characteristics can be clearly distinguished from other dimensions of human living. The proponents of this posture do not deny facts of individual differences, but they do deny that the nature of these differences is such as to preclude the development of an instructional technology adaptable to any student.

Those who take this posture also share a view of learning. The particular skills they are concerned with can best be learned, they contend, in a program deliberately engineered for that purpose. These attitudes toward learning are illustrated in such passages as:

> Learning involves the modification of behavior. The instructor's goal is to modify student behavior with respect to subject matter stimuli . . . . In the training situation, the instructor attempts to: (a) bring new stimuli to control the learner's behavior, (b) guide the learner's response to subject matter stimuli, (c) arrange for reinforcing consequences of behavior.[13]

A third posture taken by segments of certain minority groups sees the creation of community as the central purpose of schooling. A child must be imbued with a new sense of group pride, but that is not sufficient; he must become a "new man" totally committed to, and identified with, the struggle of his group or race.

Those who adopt this posture do not contend that intellectual skills are unnecessary, but the development of such skills is subsidiary to the development of a new identity. "The content of the curriculum is always viewed as a vehicle for teaching or demonstrating a revolutionary truth."[14]

Nor do those who take this view deny the need for freedom and for total human development. But they clearly wish to differentiate themselves from those who adopt the first posture.

> It is especially important that we raise the standard of correct discipline against the decadent cries of "freedom of self-expression," and "freedom of the individual." We must raise our children in an environment which demonstrates the power and purposefulness of the disciplined life and correct revolutionary struggle.[15]

Advocates of this posture conceive of the child as malleable material to be molded. The school would ideally be a total institution free of the corrupting influences of the wider society. And the teacher is neither a relatively passive facilitator nor an engineer.

> The revolutionary teacher must understand that his total life—in and out of the classroom—is an object lesson not only for his students but for everyone with whom he comes in contact. In short, he must teach precept and be example . . . . The revolutionary teacher may be summed up as the vanguard of correct struggle on the basis of Truth.[16]

Let us return to our discussion of Mr. Palmer's dilemma over personnel selection. I think it will be evident that the conception he has of the mission of the school will affect his decision in favor of one or the other candidates. If, for example, he leans toward the second posture, then the race of the candidate becomes somewhat less important than her training in diagnosing and remedying reading difficulties. If he adopts the third posture, the opposite is true. Similarly the sorts of consequences he will attend to and the weight he assigns to those consequences when considering alternatives will be determined in part by his conception of schooling.

It is possible, perhaps probable, that not all participants in the dispute share the same posture toward the nature and ends of schooling. The Black Parents League may favor the third; Mrs. Newsome, the second; and some of the other parents and staff may lean toward the first. This raises the question of whether there are any rational or moral grounds for either reconciling conflicting postures or preferring one posture to another. Someone may say that people assuming different educational postures do not really disagree about ends but only about means so that one could in principle test to see which means are most effective in reaching desired ends. But the conflict envisaged here cannot be so interpreted. People assuming conflicting postures may disagree about ultimate ends — the kind of society worth living in and the ideals of human excellence to which one ought to aspire. I do not think such disagreements are reconcilable through reasoning. There does not seem to be any basis on which to argue that Aristotle, let us say, represents a worthier ideal of human excellence than Buddha.

Since education is the primary concern in the development of human potential, one ought not be surprised to encounter such ultimate conflicts in that sphere. How is one to judge such a conflict, though, if, like Mr. Palmer, one is called on to render a decision? Perhaps the best answer we can provide is that, if we recognize the value of a diversity of human ideals within a single nation, we ought to attempt to accommodate and acknowledge the legitimacy of each ideal. Thus, we may say, with an eminent contemporary philosopher,

> The region of the ethical, then, is a region of diverse, certainly incompatible and possibly practically conflicting ideal images or pictures of a human life, or of human life. . . . Any diminution in this variety would impoverish the human scene. The multiplicity of conflicting pictures is itself the essential element in one of one's pictures of man.[17]

This position does not of itself suggest which of the two teachers Mr. Palmer ought to hire. But it may provide some basis on which to restructure the dilemma in such a way that Mr. Palmer can appreciate more fully what ultimately is at stake in this decision.

I have tried to identify some of the underlying issues and principles that might be at stake in a personnel decision in an urban elementary school. I have touched on issues related to the maximization of beneficial consequences, rights and obligations, justice, and educational ideals. These issues and principles would, of course, be implicated in any school administrator's decision affecting others. A conscientious moral agent must consider each of these though they frequently point in different directions. The administrator's dilemma must be resolved in a decision, but there is not a single "correct solution" to be discovered. As Aristotle remarked long ago:

> For it is the mark of an educated man to look for precision in each class of things just so far as the nature of the subject admits; it is evidently equally foolish to accept probable reasoning from a mathematician and to demand from a rhetorician scientific proofs.[18]

The principal, like all of us, can never be sure that he has chosen the wisest or best course of action. If he aspires to being a conscientious moral agent he must consider the circumstances in all their complexity in the light of all the principles we have considered in all their complexity. And, having done so, he must decide to act. And, having acted, he must take responsibility for his actions. None of these things is easy to do. The anguish which sometimes accompanies the making of a decision bears witness to the profound importance as well as the arduousness of the moral life. A morally conscientious person takes responsibility for his own actions, but he acts, as we have said, on principle. He says, in effect: anyone at any time in these circumstances ought to act in the same way. He is therefore in a special sense a maker of universal laws. The philosopher Kant, more than any other writer, recognized and gave expression to the supreme value of such activity:

> Now morality is the only condition under which a rational being can be an end in himself; for only through this is it possible to be a law-making member in a kingdom of ends. Therefore morality, and humanity so far as it is capable of morality, is the only thing which has dignity.[19]

POSTSCRIPT: COMMUNITY CONTROL
AND ACCOUNTABILITY

Before concluding, I wish to relate the foregoing analysis to some recent discussions of community control and accountability. Although these topics are not directly implicated in Mr. Palmer's dilemma, they provide background for the contemporary controversy against which Mr. Palmer's deliberations take place. It has recently been contended that urban, local communities, like their suburban and rural counterparts, ought to control their own schools. There are at least two issues here: that of local as opposed to central control and that of lay as opposed to professional control. I have argued that those who are required to support schooling through taxes as well as those who stand to benefit or suffer from the results of schooling have a moral right to a voice in school governance. By the same token one could argue that the degree of control ought to be related to the extent of support for, and the extent to which one is affected by the results of, schooling. Where these principles conflict — where, for example, some persons contributing more are not as directly affected by the educational process as some persons contributing less — a rational way of giving one priority over the other needs to be found. In any case, an exclusively local control would be justified only if the school were to be supported entirely by local contributions and if the subsequent benefits and liabilities of schooling were confined to that local community. Our mobile, interdependent society makes it virtually certain that the impact of schooling in one community, whether good or bad, will be felt in other communities both near and far. On the other hand, it is reasonable to argue that the benefits and especially the costs of school failure will be borne primarily by those members of the local community whose own satisfaction is most closely related to the success or failure of the children; I mean, of course, the parents. This would suggest that, from the moral point of view, the parents in a community ought to have a substantial voice in the formation of the school policy. (I am assuming, of course, that children are as yet incapable of looking after their own best interests and therefore ought not to shoulder the responsibility of determining educational policy.)

This position should not, however, be accepted too hastily for it rests on two assumptions that should not be taken for granted. One is that parents are more vitally concerned for the welfare of their children than strangers. This seems to be a safe generalization, but it should not be considered more than that. Some parents in all communities (in all strata of society) may be indifferent to the needs and interests of their own children. And, as any experienced pediatrician will admit, some natural parents do not protect and nurture their children; some deliberately hurt and maim them. The belief in the inviolability of parental rights can be dangerous if it prevents one from acknowledging or dealing with those cases in which parents may be said to have forfeited their rights through their own deeds.

The second assumption is that parents are sufficiently knowledgeable about education to be entitled to a strong voice in the formation of school policy. Mere concern or liability for consequences is not sufficient, after all, for on that basis the children themselves could determine the educational policy of their schools. Here we confront the issue of local as opposed to professional control. The tradition in our country has been to say that the lay community formulates ultimate policy objectives and the professional staff selects the most effective means of realizing those objectives. This tradition has come under increasing attack, especially in urban areas, because the school's inability to teach that which the community considers crucial, (for example, reading mastery) has raised lay people's doubts about whether professional people actually possess the expertise to which they lay claim. Lay people have come to realize that school programs and policies of the most diverse sort having the most varied consequences can be accommodated under vague statements of ultimate objectives so that professional conduct is neither constrained nor guided by such statements. Closely related to the vague statement of objectives is an increasing skepticism on the part of lay people regarding the alleged separation of means and ends on which this tradition rests. A policy such as tracking, for example, which the professional staff may regard as mere neutral means to good ends, does in fact shape and control the nature and quality of the ends themselves. Finally, some community groups challenge the notion that all segments of the urban community share the same ultimate objectives or that the professional staff, regardless of its competence, is capable of wholeheartedly dedicating itself to the community's goals.

Space does not permit a thorough discussion of these complex issues. In the main, I believe these criticisms of the traditional stance to be well taken, but the undermining of the traditional myth does not provide those who advocate community control with the carte blanche that the more extreme among their number demand. As I pointed out earlier, the satisfactory fulfillment of the teacher's (and, by extension, the school's) responsibilities requires a degree of autonomy. It makes no sense to entrust the care of one's children to another person, whether teacher or not, for six hours a day and then to insist that that person not be permitted to make any decisions regarding the activities

of those in his charge. So the question will always be one of distributing control in some satisfactory way.

Those who deny that all segments of the community share the same
aspirations for their children frequently accuse the professional staff of
seeking to impose its ends, its values on a community that rejects those
values and ends. The notion of community tacitly invoked by such advocates of "community control" is that of a group sharing common
values and aspirations, what we might call a normative community.
But community control in this sense should not be confused with local,
neighborhood control. There is no guarantee that the residents of a
particular geographical school district will constitute such a normative
community. If the school district contains families who subscribe to
different normative communities, then transfer of control from the
professionals or from the central office to the local, lay community
will not solve the problem of imposition of alien norms. That problem
will simply reemerge in the local arena. Even if the school district does
constitute a normative community, it is not, as we saw above, entitled
to claim total control unless it is prepared to isolate itself completely
from other communities. If it is, then it is hard to see on what basis
outsiders, whether lay or professional, are entitled to interfere. At this
point, however, we should realize that we are confronting not a separate community which is part of a larger society, but one independent
society existing within the domains of another.

The question of who should govern the public schools cannot be ra-
tionally resolved with a slogan like "community control" or "professional control" for that matter. Various parties have a legitimate
claim to a voice in school governance. Yet no party is entitled to exclusive control over the lives of children. From time to time one or another interest group will contend that its legitimate voice in school
governance has not been sufficiently heeded. Whether the success of
these contentions will ever depend on their legitimacy rather than on
the raw power of those making them is doubtful so long as there is no
agreement on higher-level abstract principles by which to adjudicate
conflicts. The existence of many "normative communities" holding
dissimilar aspirations for children and divergent conceptions of the
mission of the school makes it difficult for such principles to win the
consent of all.

Space permits no more than a cursory examination of the question
of accountability, a question that is likely to be at the back of Mr.
Palmer's mind although it does not impinge directly on the dilemma

we have analyzed. Every institution in society is charged with some mission, however vaguely defined, and it follows from what we have already argued that those whom the institution is designed to serve, as well as those who contribute to its maintenance, are entitled to know how well the institution is functioning so that they may direct its course more wisely. Application of this general notion of accountability to schooling is fraught with difficulty, however. Part of the reason for this difficulty emerges when, in the light of our analysis, we confront the question: To whom should the school be accountable? Three points are salient. One is that the school, like the principal, has obligations to several parties, to children, to parents, and to the wider public, each with its own concerns and interests. Since there is likely to be lack of consensus both within and among these parties on precisely what the school ought to be held accountable for, it is hard to see how standards of success and failure can be formulated that are explicit enough to be operational yet broad enough to be acceptable to all interested parties. Another difficulty derives from the fact that those for whom the school is primarily responsible, the children, are clearly incapable of judging its success or failure. Their interests must be represented by others, but it is not so easy to determine who can best represent those interests: parents, teachers, or representatives of society at large. Finally, the fruits of schooling do not appear in a single season. Although the performance of the school must be judged in the present, its impact extends and is intended to extend into the near and distant future. The community to which the school ought to be accountable, then, does not yet exist, but is brought into existence in part by the process of schooling itself. If the question of whom the schools should be accountable to admits of no easy answer, there is another question that is equally problematic: What should the schools be accountable for? The reason for this is that, as we have seen, there is no agreement even within each interest group as to the scope and mission of the school. People holding diverse educational postures are not likely to agree either on what ought to be assessed or on how to assess it. I do not mean to deny the possibility or the desirability of assessing the extent to which a school meets specific objectives. The distinctive characteristics of schooling, however, raise formidable obstacles when models of accountability borrowed from other spheres of human endeavor such as business, engineering, or even medicine are applied to schools.

NOTES

1. For valuable criticisms of an earlier draft of this chapter, I wish to thank Robert Dreeben of the University of Chicago and Brian Crittenden of LaTrobe University in Australia. This chapter, written several years ago, reflects focuses of concern that are not so prominent today as they were at that time.

2. See Kurt Baier, *The Moral Point of View* (Ithaca, N.Y.: Cornell University Press, 1958), 187-213; Richard B. Brandt, *Ethical Theory* (Englewood Cliffs, N.J.: Prentice-Hall, 1959), 249f; R. M. Hare, *Freedom and Reason* (New York: Oxford University Press, 1963), pt. 1.; and John Rawls, *A Theory of Justice* (Cambridge, Mass.: Harvard University Press, 1971).

3. Baier, *Moral Point of View*, 216.

4. "Agreement between the Monroe City Board of Education and the Monroe City Education Association," in *Monroe City Public Schools: Professional Negotiations,* ed. Alan K. Gaynor (Columbus, Ohio: University Council for Educational Administration, 1971), 11.

5. Much of the preceding analysis depends on Joel Feinberg, *Doing and Deserving: Essays in the Theory of Responsibility* (Princeton, N.J.: Princeton University Press, 1970), 55-94.

6. See Richard Peters, *Authority, Responsibility and Education* (London: George Allen and Unwin, 1959), 83-95.

7. See Ian Westbury and William Steimer, "Curriculum: A Discipline in Search of Its Problems," *School Review,* 79 (No. 2, 1971), 263-265.

8. A. S. Neill, *Summerhill* (New York: Hart Publishing Company, 1960), 28.

9. George Dennison, *The Lives of Children* (New York: Vintage Books, 1969), 77.

10. *Ibid.,* 74.

11. *Ibid.*

12. Carl Bereiter, "A Time to Experiment with Alternatives to Education," in *Farewell to Schools???* ed. Daniel U. Levine and Robert J. Havighurst (Worthington, Ohio: Charles A. Jones Publishing Company, 1971), 21f.

13. Julian I. Taber, Robert Glaser, and Halmuth H. Schaefer, *Learning and Programmed Instruction* (Reading, Mass.: Addison-Wesley Publishing Company, 1965), 32f.

14. John E. Churchville, "On Correct Black Education," in *What Black Educators Are Saying,* ed. Nathan Wright, Jr. (New York: Hawthorn Books, 1970), 181.

15. *Ibid.,* 184.

16. *Ibid.,* 180f.

17. P. F. Strawson, "Social Morality and Individual Ideal," in *Readings in Contemporary Ethical Theory,* ed. Kenneth Pahel and Marvin Schiller (Englewood Cliffs, N.J.: Prentice-Hall, 1970), 347.

18. Aristotle, *Nicomachean Ethics* 1.3.1094b24-28.

19. Immanuel Kant, *Groundwork of the Metaphysics of Morals,* tr. H.J. Paton (New York: Harper Torchbooks, 1964), 102.

Chapter Eleven

Gertrude H. McPherson

What Principals Should Know about Teachers

Bring together a group of teachers, any group of teachers, and sooner or later they will start to talk about principals they have known. The principals are praised, or, more often, blamed; their "strange" behavior is examined with bewilderment, resentment, and sometimes admiration — the way one might discuss members of an unfamiliar tribe. The discussions tend to focus around how the principal acts, what he wants, what he demands, what he allows — all of which influence teachers' morale. Principals, it would seem, are significant role partners for teachers, and a principal is judged as good or bad depending upon how much he helps or hinders the individual teacher in doing her job.[1]

How the principal's role relates to that of his teachers is one of the facts about teachers that principals should know. But do not principals already know what they need to know about teachers? After all, they have been teachers; they work with them daily. Why should they bother to read this chapter? One reason is that the role orientation of a principal differs radically from that of a classroom teacher, and each perceives the same educational reality in a different way, often without recognizing that this is so. When a teacher becomes a principal, the expectations in the new role contradict and override those contained in the earlier one. Principals need to be told about teachers because they have inevitably forgotten.

This raises the question: Does one have to be one to know one?[2] No, but there are different kinds and degrees of knowing. Those outside

233

the school system learn *something* about teachers and "know" about them through listening, questioning, and watching.[3] Such investigators do not necessarily understand what it feels like to be a teacher; nor can they look at the world as a teacher does. This does not make their knowledge useless, nor mean that they should not attempt to learn more. What the principal is able to know about teachers may be even further removed from understanding them than what an outsider is able to know. The fact that the principal cannot see the world as his teachers do does not mean, however, that he can learn nothing. It simply means that what he learns will be selectively remembered to the degree that it fits his own perspective.

Even if the principal could learn more, how useful would it be to him? Many myths that principals hold about teachers are functional for them, and to avoid knowing the truth about teachers may be a form of protection. How can one justify one's own behavior and deny one's own failure if one knows too much about others' problems to transfer the blame to them when things go wrong?

Seymour Sarason, examining the different perspectives of teachers and principals, says that teachers believe that the principal demands that they cover the set curriculum. Teachers claim that this prevents them from teaching effectively. Principals, on the other hand, cannot understand why teachers are not flexible, innovative, and able to treat the curriculum as a guide rather than as a directive.[4] This contradiction in perspectives occurs despite the fact that there is helpful information available to both sides. It sometimes seems useful for both teachers and principals that they remain ignorant about each other. Knowledge that does not make a job easier to do, that does not change reality, is not knowledge one wants. Teachers, for their part, do not want to know that principals do not have much power. When teachers need a scapegoat, they invent a powerful principal whose interference prevents them from doing a good job. Principals who create similar myths about teachers for the same reasons likewise resist knowing what is real about teachers.

Nothing I have yet said leads me to suggest that the attempt to know be abandoned or that this chapter go unwritten. I personally believe that knowledge is better than ignorance; that principals do need to learn enough about teachers to be able, if only faintly, to see the world through their eyes; and that schools would do a better job if educators worked together rather than against one another. The books, articles, and studies that contain much information on teachers and teaching, by themselves, do little to bring about change. To be meaningful, knowledge must first change the orientations and then the actions of those who participate in the life of the school. With this limitation in mind, I would like to discuss *some*[5] of what principals should know if they are to work *with* rather than *against* teachers, if they are to complement the work of teachers and not undermine it.

PRIORITIES

Teachers and principals have different priorities. The differences can be clarified by examining the two positions as separate but overlapping role sets.[6] The role bargains made and the stances adopted by principals, as well as the orientations they have toward teachers, are molded by the pressures they face in their roles. These pressures often do not coincide with those that face teachers. The principal has to juggle teacher and parent, teacher and student; the teacher must juggle principal and parent, principal and student. The way each of these people deals with problems is different, and frequently one person's way remains a mystery to the other person.

The teacher, in filling her role, views the principal as a free agent, able to act in her interest, to protect her from parents, to support her against students, and to act as a partner in coalitions when asked — but to keep hands off when not asked. The teacher may be vaguely aware, but not fully realize, that the principal also has to juggle, that he is often more vulnerable than she to initial pressure from powerful citizens, parents, or the school board. Restrictions on the principal are not readily apparent to a teacher, but even when she senses them she often needs to believe that the principal is powerful in order to fix blame for her frustrations. I cannot speak from the vantage point of being a principal, but I suspect that he frequently sees teachers as being unfettered and uncontrollable, wanting him to exercise power he does not have and to do things he does not think he should do.

One way to deal with role conflict is to form coalitions in order to utilize the differing capabilities and interests of role partners to advantage. Why, then, do teachers and principals not assume that their interests coincide and thus stand together against their other role partners? In such a collegial model the principal acts as an educational and intellectual peer, first among equals, of teachers. Together, they form a "professional" team that works together for the best education. Sometimes this model is realized. Principals act to protect teachers from parents;[7] principals stand behind teachers in their control of unruly students; principals and teachers speak out together against parents, the community, or even the school board, for higher standards, more resources, new and innovative methods of teaching. But such things do not happen often, and, where collegiality is absent, there is lack of knowledge on all sides.

Schools may be, as some have suggested, domesticated and monopolistic organizations over which the public has little direct control. But schools are also organizations that are susceptible to infringement from outside groups, that lack clear lines of authority, that educate a clientele the schools do not choose and that frequently does not wish to be chosen, and that are held accountable to a public that holds the purse strings. Both principals and teachers confront these challenges to their autonomy and to their ability to make effective decisions. Since their priorities are different, principals and teachers often stand apart, against one another, rather than standing together against external and internal threats.

Their goal might seem to be the same—the best education for all students. But just what this goal involves is unclear. How to achieve it is even less clear, and principals and teachers approach it differently. A principal must structure the activities of the school so that students pass from one level to the next, from one school to another, without disruption or confusion; must coordinate the activities of isolated and segregated teachers and classes; must do all the paperwork involved in running a semibureaucratic institution; must pacify, mollify, cajole, and respond to parents who do not like what is happening to their children or to citizens who do not like what is happening in the school; and must try to find ways to satisfy his superiors without compromising his values. The principal believes he is accountable for the education in his school; research tells him that he is responsible for the organizational climate of the school.[8] In other words, he is the one on the firing line. When he accepts this responsibility he must also decide how to deal with teachers. If he assumes that teachers are trained experts who share his priorities and goals, he treats them quite differently than if he does not assume this. The techniques the principal uses to fit teachers to his priorities vary,[9] and some of those techniques are considered by teachers to be illegitimate interference.

The teacher's priorities are different. She must reach and teach all the students in her class, despite their individual differences; she must keep order and have control; she must protect herself from interference; she must preserve her dignity and self-respect; and she must produce learning. To do her job adequately, she may adopt techniques and orientations that seem to challenge the priorities of the principal.[10]

THE TEACHER ETHOS

Since Willard Waller's classic work, *The Sociology of Teaching*, appeared,[11] much research has focused on teachers.[12] As Olive Banks comments, one emerges from reviewing this literature struck by the "ambiguity of the teachers' position in modern society. This arises for several reasons, but mainly because [of] the size, complexity, and diversity to be found, not only amongst those who perform the teaching function, but also in the role itself."[13]

Without denying the wide diversity among teachers, some understanding of them as a group can be attained by looking at the "teacher ethos," brilliantly articulated by Dan Lortie.[14] He searches out its roots in the history of teaching in the United States and in the socialization of teachers. He probes its implications for teachers' satisfaction and achievement, as well as for the future of education.[15]

The teacher ethos is "the pattern of orientations and sentiments . . . peculiar to teachers" that "derives from both the structure of the occupation and the meanings teachers attach to their work."[16] It is composed of three elements: presentism, conservatism, and individualism. This ethos has been shaped in part by the characteristics of teacher socialization, which include eased entry and the lack of either a shared collegial culture or a legitimate claim to a distinctive body of arcane technical knowledge. It has been encouraged by the cellular structure of the school and the historic and contemporary status of teachers as employees. Not only do teachers not have a shared technical culture; they are not encouraged to build one. Expertise is experiential, not technical. Teachers teach as they were taught; they rely for direction on individual assessments and individual backgrounds. A teacher judges her success by her own standards, not those of superiors or colleagues. Nor do many teachers seek "professional" help from administrators. They turn more often to colleagues, but they do even that selectively, borrowing only when it fits what they already "feel comfortable with."[17]

The experience of an elementary supervisor in northern Saskatchewan clearly demonstrated the strength of the teacher ethos to me. It seems she had encouraged a somewhat inexperienced teacher to adopt a new teaching technique. When the supervisor visited the teacher a few weeks later, however, the teacher was using exactly the same techniques she had been using in the past because, as she said, she did not feel comfortable with the new one—although she recognized that the old one was not working.

Lortie suggests a characteristic of the occupation that encourages the dominance of the teacher ethos. The rewards of teaching are so structured that they go to those who are not fully committed to teaching.[18] The career system favors recruitment rather than retention, low rather than high involvement. True collegial identification among teachers does not, therefore, emerge. Without strong collegial relationships, teachers are rarely able to exercise collective power. Rather, they remain subordinate within the structure. In such a situation the capacity of the principal to influence the performance of teachers is concomitantly low. Although he might control many aspects of teachers' work, he is resented for doing this. What he lacks is power to direct them as teachers since rewards for adaptation are not in his hands.[19] In "The Balance of Control and Autonomy in Elementary School Teaching,"[20] Lortie points out that teachers have acquired a fair degree of autonomy in the classroom, an autonomy that principals hesitate to challenge directly.[21] This autonomy is not formally recognized within the authority structure of the school, however, so it is "fragile."[22] It can be and sometimes is taken away by administrators, if not through direct supervision, then through the imposition of numerous roles and regulations.[23] Because a teacher has a high degree of responsibility and little authority, her position in the school structure is not enviable. Her role partners make contradictory demands that must somehow be dealt with—by accommodation, manipulation, or management—whether she sees them as legitimate or illegitimate. Parents, students, specialists, community members, and administrators tell the teacher what to do and what to be, and there is little or no collegial support to protect her from these encroaching pressures. It is no wonder that teachers suffer from "endemic uncertainties."[24]

When a teacher is not sure how to accomplish the goals that others push on her, when she is not sure what goals she should be pursuing, when she sees herself and the school as being under attack from all sides, when her numerous jobs are rarely completed, when she has no adequate measures of success and a frightening sense of probable failure, when everyone thinks her business is his business and he knows how she should do what he thinks she should do, is it any wonder that she feels frustrated and seeks support?

The major bases for both teacher satisfaction and dissatisfaction lie in events that occur within the classroom.[25] This, then, is the center of a teacher's concern. The best can happen there, but also the worst, and it is hard to control the outcome. Psychic rewards are crucial, but they are in no way certain.[26] A teacher is never sure whether what she does will work, and afterward she is never sure whether it did work. Success is hard to define and even harder to measure.[27] As Lortie puts it: "Uncertainty is the lot of those who teach."[28]

Not knowing whether one's efforts are effective is difficult, but, in addition, a teacher has to do so many things that are hard to do and do them all at the same time.[29] The support that comes from working closely with peers is not to be found in teaching; nor does the assurance that one is doing a good job come from superiors. Superiors tend, instead, to emphasize ideal goals that the teacher knows she cannot achieve.[30]

Although they suffer these painful uncertainites, many teachers insist that they must be left alone and that they remain autonomous in the classroom if they are to have any control over outcomes or achieve any positive rewards.[31] Outside of the classroom, however, they want from the principal and other role partners whatever will make their job less frustrating.

This absence of collegial identification, combined with the process of socialization and the teacher ethos, helps to explain why teachers rarely ask that the control structure be changed or that they be given more power. They tend to accept the terms imposed upon them by the organization and the right of others to direct them. At the same time they would like more independence and greater resources. In keeping with their individualistic orientation, they try to strike individual bargains, rather than take collective action,[32] when they request support from the principal and autonomy in the classroom. Because they lack power, they know that they cannot demand either.

Teachers without Bosses

There are situations where there is no principal (or one in name only) that illustrate what teachers want from their principals. In an elementary school I studied, for instance, the principal refused to "play his role." He told the teachers, many of whom were older and more experienced than he, that they knew what they were doing and he would not interfere. Besides, he had no background in elementary education (he had been a high school science teacher). This refusal to take charge might seem to be ideal for independent teachers; instead,

the teachers complained loudly about the principal's laissez-faire attitude. Then, when he did act like a "boss," as he occasionally did, they
complained even louder. Ironically, they would pretend that he was
acting like a boss and then criticize him for doing so. Was the teachers'
behavior as irrational as it seems? The teachers did revel in their freedom — to teach as they wished, to plan their lessons, to make decisions — up to a point. When things were going well, they did like the
lack of interference. When there were problems, they resented the
principal's lack of interest, concern, or sympathy. And, in particular,
they resented his failure to protect or support them against other
members of their role set who pushed them around in ways they could
not resist. He did not, for example, protect them from parents; he did
not support their disciplinary measures, he made light of their problems; he never "came around"; he told them they were "professionals,"
but never treated them as such; and his major priority seemed to be
gaining acceptance from the high-status families in the community.

I also recently interviewed teachers in some isolated northern Saskatchewan communities. In some of the schools there was either no
principal or a teaching principal. The only "authority" figure was the
superintendent, who rarely visited classrooms. Many of the teachers
said they had no boss, which appears to have been both good (I like to
teach up here; I can do things my way; I'm not restricted the way I was
when I taught down south; I can plan my own curriculum; I am free)
and bad (Why doesn't he [the superintendent] visit? Why doesn't he
come around? It is hard to be so isolated, so alone; I don't know how
to teach these children; I don't know what works; I know the curriculum we have doesn't work). These teachers, like those described above,
want someone to listen, to care, to fight for more resources, to suggest
ways of dealing with difficult children and indifferent parents.

Blaming: Myths and Scapegoats

In those northern Saskatchewan schools where there was a "real"
principal, the reactions of the teachers seemed predictable (he identifies with the parents; he supports the children against me; he doesn't
see any problems; he doesn't give me backing for my discipline; he
never visits; he interferes in what is my business and then doesn't support me against others).

What these different situations reveal is that many, but not all,
teachers want to be autonomous in their classrooms. They want to be
able to teach in their way, to their rhythm, without interference. Some
of them want to have input into curriculum formation; others do not.

All, however, want protection from anyone outside who might inter-fere; they want "nonprofessional" routine jobs taken away from them; they want principals not to interrupt them and infringe on their valu-able teaching time. And they want support because not all children accept their authority; discipline in the classroom is not taken for granted.

At this point teachers themselves are unclear about what they want. They want support from the principal and backing for their own dis-cipline, and yet they believe that "successful teachers don't have to send their kids to the principal." They wonder how often they can call on the principal for help without losing his respect and encouraging him to interfere in other ways? There is one acceptable escape from this dilemma if the teacher can believe that certain children or certain types of children are not her responsibility. Then, if she cannot man-age them, she does not damage her reputation as an experienced teacher. Similarly, if all the teachers in a school are having discipline problems, then the children, their parents, or the community can be blamed, and the teacher can ask for support from the principal. If he does not give it, he becomes the villain.

If you listen to teachers, however, you realize that support means more than this to most of them. It means caring. Teachers are emo-tionally vulnerable, isolated from their peers, in constant contact with subordinates. They are under pressure to accomplish difficult, maybe impossible, tasks. Also, they are in competition with their peers, not for material rewards but for some elusive standard of success as teachers. Someone should care; someone should appreciate their ef-forts. Who is in a better position to do this than the principal? He should know how hard it is. What the teacher is saying to the princi-pal, then, is: "Leave me alone. Don't interfere in my classroom. Don't tell me how to teach. Protect me from all who challenge me. Support my decisions. *And* show you care about and appreciate me."

Lortie's data confirm this. His teachers want principals to be fair, not sticklers bound by rules. They want help with difficult students and parents. They want support and warmth. They feel that the prin-cipal's authority should be exerted over others in the schools, not over them, and his power should be used to lighten their burdens.[33] Be-cause teachers lack power to demand, they hope for these responses from principals, and they complain, but rarely act, when the re-sponses are not forthcoming. Frustrated by the excessive pressures and by not getting what they hope for, where do teachers turn? Some look inside, blame themselves, and may utimately give up teaching. Others look outside and blame someone else.[34] Blaming is not random; norms must first become established for legitimate blaming. So, teachers blame the children who do not try or who have the wrong attitudes. They blame the parents who interfere, who demand particularistic favors, who overidentify with their children, or who think they know more than the teacher. And, above all, teachers blame the principal. He is the authority figure; he is the one with the ability to make things work. If he does not, it is because he does not want to or does not care. Since he has the power, his failure to use it is deliberate. The principal, as scapegoat, becomes a bulwark against the teacher's own failure.

The Power of the Principal

How much actual power and authority does the principal have? Like the teacher, he seems to have greater responsibility than authority. Although he is the key official in the school, it is questionable how far he could go to satisfy teachers, even if he wished to.[35] Alternatively, Sarason suggests that a principal's actions reflect his perception of the limits on his authority more than the actual limits. Some principals have pushed more strongly against the seeming limits than others and have succeeded when they did so.[36]

Some researchers believe that a principal is powerless against teachers when they act as a group: "A principal who fails to meet the expectations of a majority of his teachers may find his authority severely undermined if not openly flouted."[37] P. C. Dodd attributes this powerlessness to the fact that it is difficult to fire tenured teachers. In addition, many teachers are specialists, and the teacher's role is a professional one. "The control over professionals in a formal organization is a delicate matter, even more so than the control over technical specialists. To the extent that the principal accepts the teacher as a professional person, he must also accept restrictions on his own authority."[38]

Other evidence supports Dodd's assertion that teachers can and do resist control by the principal when it does not "fit." A clear example appears in Harry Gracey's, *Curriculum or Craftsmanship*.[39] Gracey studied a school where most of the teachers verbally espoused the principal's dictum that "a teacher should start with each child where he is and take him as far as he can go," but only four of the twenty-three practiced what they preached.[40] The rest paid lip service to a creed, but either they did not know how to implement it or did not believe it

could or should be implemented. Their behavior seems more pragmatic than defiant, however. The messages from the principal were
double: "Teach my ideal way, but also complete the curriculum requirements." Coordination was important to the principal even in this
school, and somehow this coordination was supposed to be achieved
despite the use of completely individualized approaches by teachers.
How to do this was not made clear. Incidentally, but maybe importantly, the parents supported traditional teaching rather than the
more innovative stance of the principal. In practice, then, most of the
teachers did not conform to the principal's wishes.

Examples of such resistance to principals can be found. But
teachers generally see themselves, rather than the principal, as powerless. This perception reflects more than the principal's ability to manipulate rewards and punishments. It reflects the teacher ethos and the
teacher's status as an employee. Increased unionization and militancy
may change this, as may increased collegiality among teachers. At
present, teachers do not see themselves as a strong collegial group
challenging an interfering boss, but as individuals, albeit "experienced." They can ask, but not demand; they can want, but not be
guaranteed fulfillment. They are at the mercy of a figure who can and
does interfere. They can resent and complain about this, but they
cannot prevent it. If this perception is false, and sometimes it appears
blatantly so, teachers hold it because they need it.

Teachers' Dignity

We are looking here at mythmaking for the preservation of dignity
and self-esteem. Waller was probably the first,[41] but he will certainly
not be the last, to stress the importance of her "dignity" to the teacher,
even where it has obviously slipped away. She receives contradictory
messages in our society. She is supposed to achieve impossibly high
goals. Her work is important, and she, as a "professional," has a vital
service to perform. But she is an employee who should accept subordination and obey orders from above. There are few ways to handle
these contradictions and survive. One way, and it is a common one, is
to define the world in such a way that it hurts a little less by creating
myths: "If it weren't for . . . , then we could do our job. If it weren't for
parents, or children, or principals, or school boards, or janitors, we
could be good teachers."

Principals who want to succeed with teachers must recognize the
strength of these myths. What is even more important is that they, to-

gether with teachers, change the rules of the game so that playing it does not destroy them, the teachers, or, ultimately, the children they are trying to educate.

BEYOND THE TEACHER ETHOS

Lortie believes that the teacher ethos is going to limit teachers' claims to status in the future.[42] Unless they move beyond it, decision making, autonomy, and teaching itself may be taken out of their hands, either by a concerned public or by a centralized bureaucratic authority.

But, the reader might ask, what about professionalism? Does not the professionalism of teachers cloak them with authority? Why has this chapter emphasized only the teacher ethos, the teacher as individual craftsman, justifying classroom autonomy on the grounds of experience and the understanding of individual children? Why have I focused on teachers seeing principals as bosses who either try to control where they should not, or fail to control where they should? What about the supposed conflict between the bureaucracy of the school and the professionalism of teachers? Is it not professionalism that teachers claim as protection against control, that organizations such as the National Education Association have insisted on?

Much written about teachers deals with the employee-professional dichotomy,[43] and it cannot be ignored here. The distinction by itself, however, is too simple for the subject. The term "professional" has lost clear meaning both in the social science literature and in common parlance. It is positively valued and comes to mean what people want it to mean. Groups fight to be considered professional; individuals claim they are behaving in professional ways when they are disinterested, concerned, specialized, autonomous — anything considered generally good. What individuals mean by the term when they apply it to themselves or what sociologists mean when they apply it, refuse to apply it, or modify it to semiprofessional for any particular occupation merits further investigation. For teachers, at least, it is important to examine their orientations to authority and control without making easy assumptions that certain stances signify high or low professionalism.

For Lortie, professionalism among teachers would mean, at the least, collegiality, a shared technical culture, and some control over the occupation. Even when such a minimal definition is applied, the teacher ethos is not professional. Teachers holding the teacher ethos claim professional status because it seems to carry symbolic weight, but such a claim does not necessarily improve their position in the authority structure. Teachers cannot rely on collegial support; they are able to claim no arcane body of technical knowledge upon which to build group power; they have no specialized ranks within the occupation to allow career development; they do not control their own entry, licensing, or professional standards. Many want autonomy from vertical bureaucratic control, but the autonomy they request can be denied them. Chandler Washburne shows that, since the rewards for dedicated individual service are small (what he calls "professional role expectations"), teachers often abandon these goals and adopt a more readily rewarded bureaucratic role orientation.[44]

Lortie's teachers do not generally look to their superiors for educational guidance, and "they accord secondary position to officially designated sources of help."[45] Lortie also considers it risky "to think that supervisory arrangements constitute a potent repository of technical knowledge."[46] Priority, as has been noted, is placed on experience as the legitimation of learning how to teach. This, therefore, is a private, not a shared, legitimacy. "Teachers say that their principal teacher has been experience; they learned to teach through trial and error in the classroom."[47] These teachers turn for guidance neither to administrators nor to the shared expertise of colleagues.

Are teachers in any significant numbers abandoning the teacher ethos for a more collegial stance, claiming authority on the basis of specialized knowledge and colleagueship? If so, which teachers and under what conditions? Direct answers to these questions are not available. Some recent research on principal leadership styles[48] suggests how teachers would relate to principals if they were not dominated by the teacher ethos.

Neal Gross and Robert Herriott have investigated the usefulnes of a particular style of principal leadership: "executive professional leadership."[49] In their study they discovered not only principals who did not act like bosses in a vertical bureaucratic hierarchy, but also teachers who seemed to have moved beyond the teacher ethos. Gross and Herriott advocate greater use of this style by principals since it correlates highly with teacher morale and with teacher and student performance.

In this study teachers rated principals on an executive professional leadership (EPL) scale that showed the principal supporting the "professional" identity of his teachers, offering them constructive suggestions for dealing with problems, displaying high interest in improving the quality of the educational programs, and encouraging superior performance standards in the classroom.[50] The authors found that principals with high EPL scores also significantly involved the staff in their decisions, had egalitarian relationships with teachers, offered teachers their social and managerial support, and stood behind teachers in conflict with students.[51] Gross and Herriott then demonstrated that high EPL scores of principals were significantly correlated with high teacher morale.[52]

"That the principal's EPL was positively associated with indices of teachers' professional orientation to their work . . . indicates that a professional staff may perform more, not less, effectively when its administrators attempt to influence it."[53] If leadership is what the authors call professional, rather than administrative or bureaucratic, the principal tries to build a professional team, a collegial principal-teacher working group. The more professional the staff, the greater the interest they have in working with, rather than being bossed around by, the principal. The scale (except for one item) does not hint that a principal interferes through direct supervision inside the classroom. Instead, the principal works with a staff imbued with self-respect and professional identity to achieve mutual educational objectives. For such collaboration to work, teachers themselves must recognize the importance of collegiality and teacher competence. Such teachers must exist, or the correlation of EPL and teacher morale would not be as high. This study strongly suggests, then, that some teachers are moving beyond the individualistic, "I'll do it on my own" teacher ethos. Some, at least, value participation in decision making and working together.

Ambiguities

Some implicit assumptions of Gross and Herriott's study need to be questioned since they introduce ambiguity into the findings. The authors accept as self-evident that teachers are professionals. They include in their theoretical framework the possible conflict between "the authority structure of the school and the autonomy teachers may claim in their work,"[54] which contradicts nothing in the literature. Then, however, they ask: "How can an executive induce his professional subordinates to accept his influence?" The professional group, they claim, "can offer greater resistance to their formal superiors because of their superior technical training and technical competence."[55]

Gross and Herriott suggest that it is the professionalism of teachers that might prevent principals from exercising EPL. This seems strange. EPL is a leadership style that stresses collegiality and teachers' increased participation in decision making. Such a style seems eminently congruent with professionalism among teachers, if professionalism, at the very least, includes collegiality. For Gross and Herriott, however, teachers are professional if they want the principal to give them a free hand in the classroom. The teachers who participated in their study were asked how much direct control the principal should exercise over them, for example, through supervision of lesson plans, supervision of teaching, and the requirement that teachers discuss *all* major classroom problems with the principal.[56] Those who did not want him to have this kind of direct control were considered professional. The responses Gross and Herriott received have proved to be congruent with those of other studies: More than half of the teachers want the principal to have less control than he wants to exercise; the rest want him to have more.[57] Most teachers accept the legitimacy of the principal's office and his right to exercise general supervision.[58] They differ about whether to let him in[59] or keep him out of their territory—the classroom.

Teachers who want to keep the principal out are not, however, necessarily demonstrating a collegial stance. Lortie has shown that those teachers who do not want to be directly supervised hold strongly to the teacher ethos; in fact, the individualistic component of the teacher ethos is the basis for their wanting classroom autonomy. Gross and Herriott illustrate in their study the prevalent fuzziness in the definition of professionalism. If, for them, it is no more than an expression of the teacher ethos, an important basis for differentiating teacher stances becomes blurred.

Further, Gross and Herriott confuse their own concept of executive professional leadership. They describe two alternative stances a contemporary principal can take. He can devote himself completely to the performance of routine administrative chores, or he can be the intellectual and professional leader of his teachers.[60] The second stance is considered EPL, and it is favored by Gross and Herriott, who regret the ease with which principals seem to slip away from it. In their study they omit any consideration of the stance of the principal as line supervisor, or boss, the stance that they see as having been dominant in earlier times. Other research demonstrates that this stance has not, however, disappeared from the schools. It is usually taken by principals who define their teachers as incompetent, poorly prepared, or not oriented toward important norms.[61] Do Gross and Herriott believe that this stance has disappeared? Certainly not. In one provocative and disturbing sentence they subsume it within the concept of EPL. For, according to them, not only must the principal lead his teachers, but he also must command "the power to reward them for conformity to the standards he establishes and to punish those who deviate from them."[62] The image of the professional leader has become transformed from guidance and collaboration to control and direction. Is this a picture of the "acknowledged and appointed status leader," the "coordinator, consultant, and staff education leader"?[63] Is this the true *primus inter pares?* Or is it, instead, George Orwell's *Animal Farm,* where "All pigs are equal, but some pigs are more equal than others"?

I submit that here, as in the preceding example, Gross and Herriott have collapsed two stances into one. I believe, contrary to Gross and Herriott, that these stances are distinct and incompatible, rather than identical. In the first instance, a teacher can hold the individualistic teacher ethos *or* she can adopt collegial identification. In the second, a teacher can accept the principal as her boss *or* she can accept him as her professional colleague (high EPL). When teachers or principals mix the two stances, confusion and conflict result.

ALTERNATE STANCES AND POTENTIAL CONFLICTS

I shall describe stances that principals and teachers may adopt, as well as the effects of different combinations of these stances. A principal may adopt one of three common stances:

1. As an executive professional leader, he can be a senior colleague who works with and guides a group of "professional" teachers toward improved classroom outcomes.[64]
2. As a routine housekeeper, who has little time or inclination to be a professional leader, he may see himself providing coordination and administrative regulation for his teachers outside the classroom but leaving them strictly alone inside the classroom.
3. As "the boss," he may see himself as directly controlling the work of teachers *under* him, in part because he does not consider his teachers to be competent.

A principal might try to adopt more than one of these stances at the same time. One might try to hold the first and third simultaneously, presumably because, like Gross and Herriott, he sees no contradiction between them. Another principal might put the second and third together, in keeping with a picture of himself as a line supervisor within a vertical bureaucratic organization. Or a principal might carefully combine the first and second, distinguishing between being a line supervisor in administrative matters and a colleague of teachers in educational matters.

Teachers, in turn, may also adopt different stances.[65] Some, dominated by the teacher ethos, clearly distinguish between the territory of the teacher and that of the principal. The teacher is in charge of the classroom and should have autonomy there. The principal is in charge everywhere else, including curriculum planning and educational decision making. He should protect the teacher, not interrupt or bother her; he should help her with problems and perform administrative chores. These teachers want a principal who is a housekeeper, although they will also accept him as the "professional symbol" of the school. Teachers imbued with the teacher ethos find the principal important as a symbol of professional purpose and competence, who can potentially "reassure teachers about the quality of their teaching."[66] The teachers I studied never referred to themselves as professionals, but they expected the principal to represent them to the world as professional. He was supposed to ensure that the school presented a positive educational image; he was supposed to acquire resources and to run lively faculty meetings.[67] But to be a symbol is not necessarily to be a leader. Such teachers do not want a boss in the classroom nor a professional leader. Being a professional symbol is as far as they want the principal to go.

Other teachers, who also hold the teacher ethos, accept their employee status. Being an employee has always been a "fact" for teachers, whatever the rhetoric. Any control they have acquired over their work has come through informal acquiescence, not formal delegation. Research is needed to determine which teachers accept this reality unquestioningly and which challenge it. Among the factors that might influence this choice are sex, age, background, level of teaching experience, work with different principals or in different schools, type of training, and, possibly, personality. The employee-oriented teacher grants the principal the right, even the duty, to supervise, direct, and control her, in, as well as out of, the classroom. This teacher wants a boss, whatever else he may try to be. A line supervisor fills this need best, while a professional leader, professional symbol, or housekeeper is a disappointment.

As suggested above, not all teachers still clearly espouse the teacher ethos. Some are beginning to picture themselves as skilled colleagues, and they seek collegial control, autonomy, and hegemony over their classrooms and over educational decision making, the curriculum, and their conditions of work. For them, the professional leader is accepted (in fact, preferred) if, and only if, they see him as one of them, as the senior colleague. He must work *with* them, not over them, to achieve common educational objectives. Such a principal can work with teachers in or out of the classroom since, as a colleague, he is not going to interfere or make trouble. Should the principal also act as a boss, he invalidates his own claim to be a professional leader.

There are, however, some teachers who adopt a collegial stance without considering the principal as a colleague. He may be excluded by ideological fiat or because of the way he behaves toward them. For these teachers, he becomes "administration," good for doing the housekeeping and for protection whenever collegial control by the teachers themselves is not strong enough.

Relating the stances I have described to Gross and Herriott's study, I postulate that principals with high EPL, who involve teachers in decision making, give them social and managerial support, and stand with them against obstreperous pupils, help to raise the morale of teachers who have a joint collegial stance. These same principals may not work well with individualistic teachers who want a boss or a housekeeper, or with collegial teachers who deny that the principal is their colleague.

Turning what has been said earlier upside down, it is evident that teachers who define themselves as autonomous in the classroom are in trouble if their principal defines himself as the boss; teachers who want a boss are in trouble if their principal acts as a professional leader of professional colleagues; teachers who want a "professional symbol" or a professional leader are in trouble if their principal keeps his hands off and performs routine administrative tasks. Again, when styles and stances are not congruent, difficulties and conflicts arise, and, since principals have more clout than teachers, teachers are more likely to suffer from discrepancies.

It is important for a principal who wishes to be effective to learn his teachers' stances. Once these are known, it is up to him to decide if and how he can move the staff toward his style. Part of the job of making a school successful rests in his hands.

IMPLICATIONS

I have placed the onus on the principal to study his teachers and then to "educate" them to conform to the style he wishes to exemplify. I recognize that many factors restrict both a principal's ability to implement the style he considers most appropriate and his ability to influence teachers to accept it.

Some of the burden also falls on the teachers. If we are to reduce the conflict between teachers and principals, to focus their orientations together rather than against one another, teachers are going to have to contribute. Let us assume that some principals want to encourage the collegiality and "professionalism" of teachers and so give them more authority. Teachers must earn the right to be treated in this way. They have to become more competent and capable of handling the complex problems of teaching; they have to possess the skills necessary to do the job on their own. Only then can they expect (rather than merely hope for) the authority to make decisions and be held accountable for their performance. Once they become equals, they must work with the principal and accept his professional guidance as an asset rather than a liability or a threat to their efforts. For this to happen, changes in teacher socialization and possibly changes in the organizational structure of the school might be required.[68]

I find it difficult, however, to end on this positive note. Will attempts to prevent the principal from becoming the teacher's scapegoat and the teacher from becoming the principal's scapegoat further insulate public education from the public and the parents? Will what is taught and how it is taught become more of a "professional" decision made by experts, with even less input from the "clientele"? Will parents and children become the scapegoats? One can argue that this is exactly what should happen, that there is already too much interference from people who are not qualified to make educational decisions. Some educators, particularly when challenged about curriculum, textbooks, standards or absence of standards, take this position. As a former teacher, I am aware of the problem of boundary maintenance, the dangers inherent in lack of protection from parental interference and public encroachment. I do not believe, however, that any professional group, no matter how well trained or how superior in technical knowledge and skill, can any longer dogmatically claim freedom from accountability. Teachers and school officials are manning a public ship; their inputs are the children of the society. Teachers who attempt to place their own professional authority above the values, goals, and orientations of those whom they serve are on dangerous ground. This issue will have to be confronted in the future, and it will become increasingly important if teachers and principals come together as professional colleagues.

The problems that derive from a possible teacher-principal coalition against everyone else might, of course, not be those that confront us in the future. Growing organization and collegiality of teachers might result in even greater conflict with administrators and lead to attempts to limit the authority and power of the principal. He might be forced to become a routine administrator with no control over what his teachers do. New coalitions and alignments would then emerge. Or the teacher ethos might continue to dominate, and, if so, teachers would have less and less authority at a time when they are being asked to become more and more accountable. All that we can do, facing an unclear future, is remember Sarason's dominant theme: unless what we do (the ways we change) make things more meaningful for the children in classrooms, we have really changed nothing.[69]

AN ENEMY IN THE TENT

At the beginning of this chapter I suggested that principals will examine the information presented to them and select that which best fits their own perspectives and needs. I warned the reader not to make easy assumptions about how useful this endeavor would be for principals. Before I conclude, I feel I should, in fairness, raise another matter.

I was an elementary teacher in a small rural school from 1956 to 1966. Since then I have been a university professor, but time has not destroyed in me the feelings that surface in a teacher when she thinks about a principal: ambivalence and faint twinges of fear, of respect, of hostility. Because of my experience as a teacher, I immediately ask myself *why* principals want to know about teachers. Will what they learn be used against teachers? Teachers and principals are not equal partners in the educational enterprise. Power and authority, vulnerability, and autonomy — these are tricky matters. From a teacher's perspective, a principal has leverage and power that she does not have. Having defined herself and having been defined by others as subordinate in the school, the teacher well might wish to insulate herself against observation as a form of protection. She hopes that the principal is ignorant about some matters (anything he can use to manipulate or push her around), while he needs to know or to be told about others (whatever will help her).

A teacher asked to write about what principals should know about teachers is an enemy in the tent. And it was from within my perspective as a teacher that I decided what principals should be told. My biases have inevitably shaped this presentation. Besides the restrictions on the ability of a principal to learn certain things from me, a teacher, there are restrictions on my ability to tell him what he should know. It is to be hoped, despite the restrictions on both of us, that a little light has been shed on an important subject.

NOTES

1. In this chapter the teacher will be designated as female, and the principal as male. Such a designation mirrors reality, at least for the majority of elementary teachers.

2. Robert K. Merton, "Insiders and Outsiders: A Chapter in the Sociology of Knowledge," *American Journal of Sociology*, 78 (July 1972), 9-47.

3. An important theme in Seymour B. Sarason, *The Culture of the School and the Problem of Change* (Boston: Allyn and Bacon, 1971), chap. 4, is the failure of both inside and outside observers to "understand" the culture of the school. This leads them to many false assumptions that limit the effectiveness of the changes they propose.

4. *Ibid.*, 77-78.

5. Knowledge about teachers, based on research over the years in England, the United States, and Canada, is ever-expanding. The focus in this chapter is necessarily narrow and limited. For any comprehensive understanding of teachers, the reader must go far beyond the material presented here and the specific references cited.

6. Robert K. Merton, "The Role-Set: Problems in Sociological Theory," *British Journal of Sociology*, 8 (June 1957), 106-120; Gertrude H. McPherson, *Small Town Teacher* (Cambridge, Mass.: Harvard University Press, 1972).

7. Howard S. Becker, "The Teacher in the Authority System of the Public School," in *The Sociology of Education*, ed. Robert R. Bell and Holger R. Stub, rev. ed. (Homewood, Ill.: Dorsey Press, 1968), 298-309.

8. For summaries of relevant research, see Olive Banks, *The Sociology of Education*, 3d ed. (Toronto: Copp Clark Publishing Company, 1976) 197-198; and Sarane Boocock, *An Introduction to the Sociology of Learning* (Boston: Houghton Mifflin Company, 1972), 176-178. Even the local Saskatoon paper recently carried a story reporting on US research that demonstrated the importance of the principal as the key person in determining the quality of the educational program in the school.

9. James G. Anderson, in *Bureaucracy in Education* (Baltimore: Johns Hopkins Press, 1968), chap. 1, describes four possible patterns of control in formal organizations and the availability and use of each by school principals. He also specifies some of the criteria through which principals choose to use rules and regulations rather than rely on teachers' professional standards. These include sex, grade level and subject taught, and the environment and size of the school.

10. For fuller discussion of what has been described as "debureaucratization" by teachers, see Willard Waller, *The Sociology of Teaching* (New York: John Wiley and Sons, 1932); and Anderson, *Bureaucracy in Education*, 162-163.

11. Waller, *Sociology of Teaching.*

12. Two useful bibliographies of research on teachers and teaching are to be found in Dan Lortie, *Schoolteacher: A Sociological Study* (Chicago: University of Chicago Press, 1975); and in Boocock, *Introduction to the Sociology of Learning.*

13. Banks, *Sociology of Education,* 2d ed. (Toronto: Copp Clark Publishing Company, 1971), 157.

14. Lortie, *Schoolteacher.*

15. Lortie's findings are consistent with those of others; see McPherson, *Small Town Teacher.*

16. Lortie, *Schoolteacher,* viii.

17. *Ibid.,* esp. chap. 3.

18. *Ibid.,* 9.

19. *Ibid.,* 100.

20. Dan Lortie, "The Balance of Control and Autonomy in Elementary School Teaching," in *The Semi-Professions and Their Organizations,* ed. Amitai Etzioni (New York: Free Press, 1969), 1-53, esp. 13-15.

21. Lortie *(ibid.,* 9) relates this degree of autonomy to the ecological patterning of the school, the indivisibility of teacher tasks, and the definition of teaching as an art.

22. *Ibid.,* 15.

23. Anderson, *Bureaucracy in Education.*

24. Lortie, *Schoolteacher,* chap. 6.

25. *Ibid.,* 104.

26. *Ibid.,* 121.

27. A major problem for the teachers I studied was how to measure goal achievement. The result was that they became ritualistic and tried to assume that goal achievement would automatically follow (McPherson, *Small Town Teacher).*

28. Lortie, *Schoolteacher,* 133.

29. Philip Jackson, *Life in Classrooms* (New York: Holt, Rinehart and Winston, 1968).

30. Lortie, *Schoolteacher,* 150.

31. Francis S. Chase, in "Factors Productive of Satisfaction in Teaching," unpubl. diss., University of Chicago, 1961, 130, finds that freedom to operate on their own is the factor mentioned most frequently by teachers as contributing to teaching satisfaction. See also G. L. R. Grace, *Role Conflict and the Teacher* (London: Routledge and Kegan Paul, 1972), 64-70.

32. Lortie, *Schoolteacher,* 202-203.

33. *Ibid.,* 198, 119.

34. The need for research into "blaming" behavior has been pointed to by Ronald D. Lambert and James E. Curtis, "Education, Economic Dissatisfaction and Nonconfidence in Canadian Social Institutions," unpub. paper presented at the Canadian Sociology and Anthropology Association meetings, 1977, 21.

35. Some of the restrictions on the principal are described by Lortie in his *Schoolteacher,* 196-197. Other research on principals confirms his conclusions.

36. Sarason, *Culture of the School and the Problem of Change,* chap. 9.

37. P. C. Dodd quoted in Boocock, *Introduction to the Sociology of Learning,* 179.

38. *Ibid.,* 179-180.

39. Harry L. Gracey, *Curriculum or Craftsmanship: Elementary Teachers in a Bureaucratic System* (Chicago: University of Chicago Press, 1972).

40. *Ibid.*, 33, 34.

41. Waller, *Sociology of Teaching.*

42. Lortie, *Schoolteacher,* chap. 9.

43. One might suggest that everything written about teachers sooner or later grapples with this subject. Among other useful references here, see Ronald G. Corwin, *A Sociology of Education* (New York: Appleton-Century-Crofts, N.J.: Prentice-Hall, 1956); Bryan R. Wilson, "The Teacher's Role—A Sociological Analysis," *British Journal of Sociology,* 13 (March 1962), 15-32; and Gerald H. Moeller and W. W. Charters, "Relation of Bureaucratization to Sense of Power among Teachers," *Administrative Science Quarterly,* 10 (March 1966), 444-465.

44. Chandler Washburne, "The Teacher in the Authority System," *Journal of Educational Sociology,* 30 (May 1957), 390-394.

45. Lortie, *Schoolteacher,* 75.

46. *Ibid.*, 79.

47. *Ibid.*

48. See Banks, *Sociology of Education,* 3d ed., 197-200, for a clear summary of research in this area.

49. Neal Gross and Robert E. Herriott, *Staff Leadership in Public Schools: A Sociological Inquiry* (New York: John Wiley and Sons, 1965).

50. *Ibid.*, 27-29.

51. *Ibid.*, chap. 7. Unfortunately, they do not also investigate the relationship between the extent to which principals support teachers in conflicts with parents and their EPL.

52. *Ibid.*, chap. 3.

53. *Ibid.*, 162.

54. *Ibid.*, 94.

55. *Ibid.*

56. *Ibid.*, 103.

57. They note that, while the results are statistically significant, they do not signify an overwhelming desire for freedom from control. The authors do not relate these responses to the teacher's perceptions of a principal's EPL. It would be most interesting to probe the association here, as well as its relationship to teacher morale.

58. Lortie, *Schoolteacher,* 199.

59. More elementary than high school teachers are in this group. *(Ibid.,* 200.)

60. Gross and Herriott, *Staff Leadership in Public Schools,* 34.

61. See Lortie, "Balance of Control and Autonomy in Elementary School Teaching" and *Schoolteacher;* and Anderson, *Bureaucracy in Education.*

62. Gross and Herriott, *Staff Leadership in Public Schools,* 39.

63. *Ibid.*, 5.

64. For a discussion of the history of the development of this style and references to research done on such a leadership style, see *ibid.*, chap. 1.

65. Banks, in *Sociology of Education,* 3d ed., 193-197, summarizes some research relevant to the different stances that teachers adopt.

66. Lortie, *Schoolteacher,* 197.

67. McPherson, *Small Town Teacher,* 172.

68. Lortie, in *Schoolteacher,* chap. 9, makes some thoughtful suggestions for changes that might prove fruitful.

69. Sarason, *Culture of the School and the Problem of Change.*

Chapter Twelve

Frank W. Lutz

William E. Caldwell

Collective Bargaining and the Principal

From evolutionary beginnings in the 1930's and the 1940's, collective bargaining in education has come to maturity during the past fifteen years. The movement today is experiencing rapid growth, it commands high public visibility, and it has prompted the enactment of legislation by the state that is intended to help resolve conflict situations as they arise in education. The development and implementation of bargaining have required many adjustments in organizational roles to meet the demands of what has become a new area of administrative responsibility. One of the roles significantly affected is that of the building principal. When one proceeds beyond surface conflicts and concerns, it becomes evident that the forces providing a receptive climate for negotiations in the recent past have affected two aspects of the principal's role: role ambiguity and role autonomy.

Until recently the principal, like other educational leaders, has had a well-defined role that included not only experience as a former teacher, but recognition that the principal had been a head teacher or a master teacher. It was a combination of successful teaching experience and persistent efforts to acquire more knowledge that satisfied certification requirements for public school administration. Close physical proximity and a close working relationship convinced teachers that the principal was a respectable and enviable professional, a view supported by the isolation of the principal from the central office staff. Superintendents and school board members saw the principal as being the chief building administrator, "the captain of the ship." But this role is changing, and the direction is just now becoming discernible. It is dissatisfaction with those changes and the effect they are having that has caused principals to take more aggressive positions in relation to bargaining. One repeatedly hears the cry of the principal: "We never know what's going on in negotiations until we read it in the papers."

Why has the principal's traditional role been affected? A direct and significant explanation lies in the beliefs and practices that educational groups have adopted concerning collective bargaining during the last fifteen years. Principals have been excluded from participating in collective bargaining either by state law or by teacher choice. They represent "middle management," a characterization that tends to be viewed negatively at the present time. They cannot identify with the teaching staff, and they find it difficult to align themselves with the central office staff and the school board. Collective bargaining has often forced the superintendent and the school board to join into a negotiating bloc that does not include the principal, who has not been a close partner in the administrative team. The threat of a teacher strike may, for example, require central office staff and school boards to take immediate and effective action, thereby excluding the building principal from deliberations. The nature of these emergencies that arise as a result of collective bargaining with the teachers often precludes participation of principals in bargaining done at that level. Teacher organizations, on their part, exhibit a tendency to bypass the building principal by presenting their demands directly to either the school board or to the central office staff — the top echelons in the district's hierarchy. Because of such factors, building principals are not members of top management; thus they lack power to deal with the teacher organization's demands.

Apart from the ambiguities now appearing in the role of principal, there is also loss of autonomy. Teachers, superintendents, and school boards have, in an effort to cope with collective bargaining, concerned themselves with a number of demands, issues, organizational rules, and areas of expertise that were subject to the principal's discretion at an earlier time.

Teachers, through their powerful organizations, have demanded more involvement in making decisions. Agreements related to decision making are reached at the negotiating table and set down in explicit terms in the written contract. The growth of this trend is evidenced by the presence in over two thousand contracts of items requiring formal bilateral discretion, items that prevent the principal from acting unilaterally. Their presence, coupled with a degree of specificity, has limited the principal's sphere of activity and has resulted in a loss of professional discretion. In addition, the art of teaching has changed over the last few decades. Generalists have been supplemented with a growing number of specialists possessing far more specific knowledge. The principal, no longer recognized as a "teacher of teachers," has experienced further loss of discretion. As if this were not enough, teacher organizations are showing an increasing interest in management operations. They demand a rational and contractual voice in administrative operations and decisions. The building principal, like other administrative staff, can no longer claim the traditional luxury of operating on a "business as usual" basis — again at a loss of professional discretion.

The superintendent and the school board, in their efforts to deal effectively with collective bargaining, have exhibited more aggressive "boundary maintenance" behavior in attempting to keep certain issues within the sphere of managerial prerogative.[1] But in working to preserve their own autonomy, superintendents and school boards have often further restricted the administrative options available to building principals. They must carefully comply with all board policies and administrative procedures as well as with the teachers' negotiated contract in deciding on a course of action. Daniel Griffiths noted this "two master" notion as early as 1966.[2]

When collective bargaining was initially applied by educational groups, school administrators were caught with their guard down. In a frantic effort to acquaint themselves with the process, they examined closely its operation in the industrial sector and borrowed many of the techniques used by industry, including those aspects of the industrial model concerned with the composition of the negotiating team. Since the model stressed interaction between top management and leaders of the organized employees, the building principal tended to be overlooked from the inception of the negotiating process.

The move toward larger schools, for organizational or instructional purposes, encouraged more uniformity in administrative operations at the further expense of the principal's discretionary power.[3] In a large school system there is a tendency to bring about decentralization of the bureaucracy in order to remove some of the "depersonalization." This can be done by decentralizing the decision-making process or by restructuring the organization along supervisory lines. Unfortunately, the latter course is the one usually followed. An example of this is the practice of creating several smaller school districts within the larger New York City school system. Building principals find themselves reporting to a district superintendent located two miles away, whereas before they had reported to a district superintendent located twenty miles away. Under the old system, distance from the central office staff allowed a certain degree of autonomy; under the newer, smaller system, however, proximity requires more accountability. Larger systems and larger schools also need more extensive supervision of areas apart from the instructional one, areas such as pupil personnel and budgeting that might formerly have been part of the principal's responsibilities.

These, then, are the diverse forces and influences responsible for the creation of a far different climate. The loss of power experienced by the building principal is most readily apparent in day-to-day administrative operations. Principals find themselves the target for teacher-initiated grievances and feel the scrutiny of building representatives of teachers' organizations. To further complicate this already vexing position, the principal notices that vulnerability increases in conjunction with pressure from the general public as well as from the central office, the school board, and other professional groups in the face of new programs, demands for effective leadership, the need for accountability, and coverage by the news media.

The school principal has been and continues to be viewed by academicians as an individual occupying a key administrative position in the local district's hierarchy and, at the same time, possessing the opportunity to pursue change in an organizational unit small enough to be affected. These expectations create an ever-widening gap between what the principal sees as the need for strong administrative leadership at the building level and the simultaneous loss of power to both superiors and subordinates as a result of collective bargaining.

THE FORMAL ROLE OF THE PRINCIPAL

When analyzing the role of the principal in collective bargaining, one must view both formal and informal aspects of participation. The formal aspect relates to actual bargaining sessions and to grievances that arise either from the negotiated contract or from board policy. The prinicipal has a part in the actual bargaining process that culminates eventually in the written contract (contract negotiation), and he also has a part in resolving grievances that arise (contract administration). Both role functions are integral to the formal collective bargaining process.

Contract Negotiation

The principal's bargaining role has been unclear since the advent of educational bargaining. Specific and varying organizational postures are indicated here as each of the several techniques for accommodating administrative personnel in the bargaining process are presented.

One approach favored by many principals states that the principal should be a separate and full-fledged member of a distinct bargaining unit. In New York City principals and vice-principals have formed a bargaining unit that is affiliated with the International Teamsters Union. Similar administrative units have been established in many districts of varied sizes in states that permit such units. (This tendency is analyzed by Bruce S. Cooper in Chapter 13.) There are, however, some states where this practice is legislatively barred, so principals have joined teacher units or state-level teacher organization affiliates. This desire for a collective voice stems largely from perceived and real losses in principals' authority, increased demand for organized representation by national principals' associations, and role ambiguities at the local level. The presence of two or more units of educational professionals, however, can result in extensive in-house conflict. For example, principals and vice-principals, in attempting to improve their own wages and working conditions, may find themselves in potential conflict with teachers as they bargain for the same resources. Not only do conflict situations occasionally occur over personal welfare, but they emerge as well when building administrators try to influence work rules affecting the day-to-day operations of the school system. The school district's negotiating team can find itself faced with as many different demands on some common issue as there are bargaining units. The variation in demand can be significant, and the districts' negotiating units are placed in the untenable position of indicating support by agreeing to a stand on work rules for one professional organization and, at the same time, necessarily rejecting that same stand for another organization. The trend toward factionalism has a double-edged effect. It increases the number of bargaining positions, but selection of one position over another implies lack of interest in or support for other positions. This conflict can be seen occasionally in the industrial sector when a number of unions bargain for members within a single corporation.

The principal's role in distinct bargaining units is affected by a number of organizational and personal factors. The National Association of Secondary School Principals has endorsed the separate bargaining unit as the most appropriate vehicle for the development of a satisfactory role,[4] but building administrators do not possess sufficient power to control their own destinies. Larger, societal forces often restrict the number of professional alternatives available. In Rhode Island, state legislation prohibits principals from creating their own units for collective bargaining purposes. In California, Pennsylvania, and other states there are restraints on what building administrators may or may not do in collective organizations. Although participation in formal bargaining presents the greatest power option to the principal, both in effecting district and personal demands, the potential for conflict tends to be high. The gains achieved through organization can easily be lost in the further diminution of a principal's discretion in day-to-day building operation.

The second option open to the principal in formal bargaining is to hold a viable position on the management team. It is this team that assumes full responsibility for negotiating with a team representing the teachers' organization. Edward Shils and Taylor Whittier have stated that such a team should not exceed eight to ten members and should include one or more principals.[5] The duties of many of the individuals on the team are sufficiently flexible to allow the building principal to fit into a prescribed role that may or may not mirror the person's regular role as chief building administrator. For example, the principal may serve as the management team's recorder, special management representative, observer, spokesman, or in some other capacity.

Involvement in the actual negotiating process also varies. The principal may assist in the establishment of guidelines for negotiations or affect the demands at the table by presenting certain kinds of information or by adhering to a particular position. The building principal may propose counteroffers in such areas as work rules. The American Association of School Administrators and the National School Boards Association have endorsed this role for the building principal. Satisfaction with the management team strategy will depend on the effectiveness of those selected to represent principals, the reliability of feedback systems, and the ability of top management to maintain an open climate.

Lewis Coser has indicated that it is often difficult to deal with the real problems involved in negotiations. Prior personnel relationships tend to influence the ability to deal successfully with conflict. He has distinguished between realistic and unrealistic conflict as a means of examining this phenomenon.[6] Realistic conflict exists when the alternatives maintain the same identity and characteristics and negotiations are directly concerned with the solution. In unrealistic conflict the aggression generated in an effort to solve a problem shifts from one individual or group to another. If these distinctions are applied to collective bargaining, unrealistic conflict tends to close formal systems of authority; that is, the top management and the school board become defensive, close ranks, and view the problem and others involved in the bargaining process in an unfavorable light. The management team is, however, at least theoretically, an open system that makes it possible for the building principal to assume an integral and active part in the bargaining process. The question then remains: Can top management resist the defensive mechanisms and closed systems as the heat of negotiations rises and remain open enough for the proper functioning of a management team?

A fruitful modification of the role of building principal would be to make the principal a consultant to the negotiating team. This implies that there would be less power involved than there might be if principals had a separate negotiating unit of their own, but their role would be more clearly defined than would be possible with either alternative described earlier. There are fewer pitfalls. For instance, the principal is more likely to avoid loss of face in the eyes of teachers. The objectivity associated with the role of consultant also allows more opportunity to turn the bargaining process toward realistic conflict. Principals could be assigned specific roles related to their expertise or to one of the many different aspects of the bargaining process: setting policy guidelines, participation in management caucuses, drawing up counteroffers, framing agreement language, and so forth.

Still another alternative when considering the role of the principal in the formal bargaining process is simply no role at all. Some authorities have contended that proper attention to the needs and concerns of the building principals on the part of school boards and top management would eliminate the need to assign bargaining roles to principals. Regardless of the protection that districts have afforded principals, the principals have wisely rejected the inactive role.

Contract Administration

Principals must assume a formal role in the processing of grievances if they are to retain status in management. As representatives of the school board and top management to the staff in their buildings they are responsible for interpreting and carrying out the terms and conditions defined in the written contract. The building principal as the "first level of management" has direct interaction with the teaching staff, while holding accountability for managing the building. This position places the principal close to potential problems. Violations or disagreements concerning work rules are expected to be discussed, on an informal basis, between the involved parties and the building principal. According to Myron Lieberman, "as the teacher's immediate superior, he [the principal] is charged with meeting with the teacher for the purpose of resolving, in an informal way, the teacher's problem."[7] This initial stage for the processing of grievances is considered to be the most important one, for it is at this stage that the chances are greatest of finding solutions that satisfy all concerned.

The ability to interpret and apply the work rules in a uniform manner enhances the success of future attempts at mediating grievances. Successful mediation may do much to create positive attitudes toward the principal and to keep the solution of local problems where it belongs — at the local level.[8]

Experience in industry, where both professional and nonprofessional employees are involved, indicates that under normal conditions there are ten to twenty grievances per hundred employees per year. William Foote Whyte, noted industrial relations researcher, has examined grievance roles as they occur and fluctuate in industrial and business settings. Because he was concerned with the incidence of grievances, Whyte undertook an examination of organizations, some of which had an excessive number of grievances while others had only a few. He found that certain characteristics of organizations apparently affected attitudes and collective thought among workers, and he categorized the characteristics into a dichotomy of high and low resonance. Low resonance workers (a) were heterogeneous in background and experience, (b) faced different work problems, and (c) had little or no free time in work situations. In organizations where these three variables were present, the workers had relatively few grievances. Workers categorized as having high resonance were characterized as (a) being homogeneous in background and experience, (b) having similar work problems and working conditions, and (c) having a large amount of common free time during the workday. Such workers were involved in significantly more grievances.

In applying the resonance theory to teachers, one would expect grievances in school districts to be high as compared to other organizations. Teacher-training programs, past and present, coupled with similar socialization processes in school districts provide a high degree of homogeneity in the teaching force. This homogeneity is quite pronounced within the limits of a school building. Add to this characteristic the similarity of teacher problems within an educational organization and the many opportunities for communication and amplification of these problems during the working day, and teachers may be classified as having a high degree of resonance. This state of affairs accentuates the importance of the role of the principal in formal grievances.

The grievance system can be viewed in another way as it affects the building principal's role. The existence of such a system serves as a constant reminder to administrators that they can be held accountable for decisions. Administrators could enhance their management positions if the system were designed to assist in the maintenance of a "delicate balance between idiosyncratic needs and institutional demands"[9] by serving as a check on policy-making and policy-implementing machinery. The board and the superintendent are each included in the usual multistage grievance procedure since they are considered to be active agents in the appeals system. They are required to examine and judge alleged grievances. This type of exposure acts as a stimulant for a fresh reappraisal of district policies and implementation procedures. The identification of inequities associated with district policies through grievance procedures provides an excellent opportunity for administrators to change old policies so that they may better conform to the effectiveness of the school system's overall operations.

The identification process operating within the grievance system aids the administration in other ways as well. For example, prospective contract demands often take shape as the result of activities undertaken to alleviate grievances. This is a continuous and viable source of feedback for negotiations. The institution and effective implementation of a grievance system should be considered a valuable asset for the building administrator in the performance of duty and the clarification of an emerging role. The role will demand dual skill in effectively resolving work problems that surface as grievances and in managing grievance systems that increase the efficiency of management.

THE INFORMAL ROLE OF THE PRINCIPAL

There is a relationship between the principal and the staff within the school that is largely founded upon day-to-day decisions and involves the administration of informal rules. It is the administration of rules that, to a large extent, determines the leadership role of the principal, and the rules governing grievances are included. Alvin Gouldner has modeled rule administration as falling into three distinct categories, based on his research in industrial management. He contends that rules may be administered in a punishment-centered, representative, or mock fashion.[10] By using this model, Frank Lutz found relationships between teachers' perception of principals' leadership in New York City and the rule administration characteristics of principals.[11]

These relationships were such that principals with high representative rule administration (high joint principal-teacher decision making) were perceived to be the most professional by their staff and the most effective by their supervisors. Principals low in representative rule administration, with more punishment-centered or mock enforcement of rules were identified by the staff as having low leadership capability and by field observers as having more building-level problems. A more extensive testing of this model in education is required to give urban principals further insight into the administration of formal and informal rules.

Research that will provide considerable insight for principals in determining the framework of principal and principal-staff decision making is taking place in the behavioral sciences. Studies by behavioral scientists have significantly increased the knowledge available to those in leadership positions concerning the motivation of professional employees. Beginning with the work of Frederick Herzberg in 1959,[12] research has consistently shown that professional employees can be effectively motivated by factors within the control of first-level management. Factors largely outside the discretion of the building principal, such as salary, fringe benefits, and board policy, are now thought to have much less effect on the motivation of professionals and tend to create negative sentiment in their absence rather than increasing motivation by their presence. Responsibility, recognition, and the work itself appear to be crucial variables in professional motivation. These variables can be affected by the principal's rule in rule administration and joint principal-teacher discretion. The unanimity of this research is shown by Keith Davis[13] in reporting six studies representing supervisors in three countries and covering varied professional groups.

However valid and significant these findings are for the principalship, they must be interpreted in light of the evidence gathered by behavioral scientists in the area of leader-staff relationships. From the early writings of Follet to the research of the 1970's, needs of employees have been recognized as a key to high morale and productivity. Although viewed as the proponent of scientific and technical management, Mary Parker Follet believed that the real service of management was "to give an opportunity for individual development through the better organization of human relationships."[14] This mainstream of thought has surfaced consistently in past as well as in current educational management literature. Attention has been focused on the crucial problem of finding ways to integrate organizational objectives and individual goals. Chris Argyris discusses the possibility of developing an organization in which the individual may gain maximum expression and the organization gain optimization of its goals.[15] He stresses the importance of the relationship between motivational or psychological energy for organizational effectiveness. The prime factor relative to motivational or psychological energy is the individual's self-esteem or a good self-image. This sense of personal worth must be viewed by the organization as primary. The individual is not just an instrument to be manipulated for economic returns. The greater his feeling of worth, the more motivational energy the individual has to invest in activities that reward the organization. Conversely, as the feeling of worth is reduced, the individual's motivational energy is tied up in a search for rewarding experiences outside the work situation.[16]

Douglas McGregor agrees with Argyris that it is possible to satisfy both the needs of the organization and the needs of the individual. He sees "a genuine potential for a linkage of self-actualization with organizational goals."[17]

Turning from management theory to educational administration, the same concern for the individual's goals within an organizational framework is apparent. Jacob Getzels developed a model describing administration as a social process in which behavior is conceived of as a function of both the nomothetic and the idiographic dimensions of a social system. The idiographic dimension consists of the individual, his personality, and his need-disposition, while the nomothetic dimension includes the institution, its role, and its expectations.

Getzels, in a later publication, comments that the administrator is always confronted with the problem of knowing when to reinforce organizational goals and when to temper them.[18] He also notes that in a New York City teachers' strike it was quite apparent that the normative impersonal nature of the school system prevented teachers, as individuals or through their organization, from sharing in decision making.[19]

Egon Guba, an associate of Getzels, voiced a similar opinion when he wrote:

The unique task of the administrator can now be understood as that of mediating between these two sets of behavior-eliciting forces, that is, the nomothetic and the idiographic, so as to produce behavior which is at once organizationally useful as well as individually satisfying. Action which will lead to such behavior on the part of personnel is the highest expression of the administrator's art.[20]

The nomothetic and idiographic dimensions are reflected in Richard Lonsdale's reference to maintaining the organization in dynamic equilibrium. He states that this is a complex process that requires achieving the tasks of the organization and meeting the needs of the individuals within the organization.[21]

In summary, the urban principal must look to current and continuing research in behavioral science in order to select the correct role in the initiation, administration, and evaluation of work rules. His effectiveness in utilizing joint teacher-principal decision making will enhance his day-to-day effectiveness with the staff, reduce the number of grievances, and create positive sentiment toward the operation of the school district.

THE FUTURE OF THE URBAN PRINCIPAL
WITHIN EDUCATIONAL NEGOTIATIONS

Most of the trends noted above have implications for the future role performance and professional status of the urban principal. It seems clear that the principal cannot continue to exist in his old image and role. It has been noted that groups of individuals who hope for a messianic event that will overwhelm the forces of change and return them to the seat of power they occupied in "the old days" end up perishing rather than prospering. Of particular note is the experience of the Sioux Indians. In the latter 1800's, under the leadership of Crazy Horse, they began what was known as the Ghost Dance Cult. Wearing their Ghost Dance shirts, which they thought would ward off the white man's bullets, they believed that a great avalanche would envelop the white man and all good Indians would rise to live again, the buffalo would return, and they would rule their lands in the splendor that was once theirs. At Wounded Knee a major portion of their tribe was massacred by the United States Army in a shameful action.[22] In order to avoid a similar disaster in education, principals must recognize and adapt to their changing role, rather than inflexibly demanding return to the status quo.[23]

The merger of NEA and AFT and other union-affiliated teacher groups may become commonplace in the next decade. All teachers in the United States may once again be represented by a single organization, undoubtedly an organization strongly allied with organized labor. The merger of NEA-affiliated and AFT-affiliated local and state teacher organizations, and the joint efforts of NEA and AFT for a federal collective bargaining statute, is only the beginning, and no Ghost Dance shirt will be effective against such power.

As part of such an organization, principals will have an ineffective voice. The days when administrators dominated teacher organizations are, and should be, a thing of the past. The only effective recourse left to principals is to become a part of management or to develop an independent unit of their own, and a separate negotiating unit for principals will probably prove to be relatively ineffective. It would be too small to make effective demands without the support of a powerful teachers' unit, and it would become just a subunit of the teachers' organization. Principals would occupy a position similar to that of Third World countries in the political arena of the present world.

As a member of the administrative team, principals can and should function as an important part of the board-administrative bloc. This appears to be the only viable role for principals in the future. While principals must give up some independence in order to play such a role, they would gain power in doing so, much as a separate state in the Confederation lost some independence but gained power by becoming one of the United States.

A school board is a legal governmental body. It is responsible to the state for operating public education in a given geographic area. As such, it is entitled to representation at the building level. How else can they be assured that their policies are being carried out and that the public interest is being served in the classroom? If principals refuse to assume that role, school boards may be justified in eliminating their job.

As a member of the management team, principals should be asked and encouraged to play an important and effective role. They will benefit from the fact that they are needed on the management team. They will not suffer economically or professionally because school boards will have to recruit competent personnel and be forced to provide professional and economic rewards in order to fill the ranks of principals. The role is not an easy one, and the rewards must be sufficient, or the management team will suffer more than the principal. Such a role involves two responsibilities: creative management of the educational enterprise at the building level (administration of the contract and board regulations in order to produce a viable educational climate in the school), and participation in determining the direction of board policy (developing policy and negotiating contracts).

MANAGEMENT OF THE EDUCATIONAL ENTERPRISE

"Creativity" is the key word here. Principals will no longer be "captains of the ship" in the old sense. Both the contract and board policies will set the parameters for creative administration of the school, but they are not meant to specify every detail of work activity carried on daily. This is where the principal's responsibility lies in the future, and how well the principal copes with that responsibility will determine whether positive educational climates that can allow the educational process to operate effectively will continue to exist in the schools.

As teachers form state-wide associations, negotiations may be conducted at the state rather than the local level, and contracts may apply to the entire state educational system. Management and board teams at the local level should urge that such contracts be negotiated in much the same way that national contracts are now negotiated by the major labor unions. This would mean that major salary and fringe benefits are negotiated at the top level and other items related to working conditions are negotiated at the specific plant or local level. In education the major contract would be negotiated with the state, where the resources needed for salaries, retirement, insurance, and other forms of compensation are available. Local boards will become totally dependent on state and national resources to meet these demands in the next decade, which means that such issues are best negotiated at that level. Other bargaining areas such as teaching assignments, length of the working day, and local working conditions should be negotiated locally. If such a negotiation procedure were to develop, it would still probably be necessary to negotiate locally to adjust the salaries of those teaching in urban areas and other areas where the cost of living is high. Final negotiation in such a decentralized process would be accomplished at the individual building level, especially in urban centers where the teaching staff may number a hundred or more members. At that level the principal would become the management negotiator with the assistance of central office staff.

Ineffective principals will tend to be flooded with grievances related to technical violations of the established contract. Such grievances will "clog up the works," which is often the intention of the union. Ineffective principals respond with more punishment-centered rule administration that only acts to increase hostility on the part of the teaching staff. Such an arrangement is often described by top personnel in both the union and the central office as one where the parties involved "deserve each other."

Even without a negotiating procedure such as the one suggested, principals in urban schools will play a significant role in the bargaining process, for it is and will remain their province to administer any contract at the grass roots and to handle first-level grievances. Grievances handled by effective principals will tend to have considerable influence on the development of board policy and future negotiations since such grievances are often invited by the administration and pushed to third-level (school board) decision-making status by the union in order to establish written policy. Thus, the role of the principal in the future emerges as different also from the old model of teacher trainer or inspector. His new function as representative of the management team and organizational administrator at the building level will give the role of principal even more importance in the modern, complex educational organization.

NOTES

1. Frank W. Lutz, "Teacher Negotiations in Metropolitan Area Schools," in *Toward Improved Urban Education,* ed. *id.* (Worthington, Ohio: Charles A. Jones Publishing Company, 1970), 121.

2. Daniel E. Griffiths, "Viable Alternatives," in *The Struggle for Power in Education,* ed. Frank W. Lutz and Joseph Azzerelli (New York: Center for Applied Research in Education, 1966), 108.

3. David Lewin, "The Changing Role of the Urban Principal," *Elementary School Journal,* 68 (April 1968), 332.

4. Myron Lieberman and Michael H. Moskow, *Collective Negotiations for Teachers: An Approach to School Administration* (Chicago: Rand McNally and Company, 1966), 158.

5. Edward B. Shils and C. Taylor Whittier, *Teachers, Administrators and Collective Bargaining* (New York: Thomas Y. Crowell Company, 1968), 330-335.

6. Lewis A. Coser, *The Frontiers of Social Conflict* (New York: Free Press, 1956).

7. Lieberman and Moskow, *Collective Negotiations for Teachers.*

8. Keith Davis, *Human Relations at Work: The Dynamics of Organizational Behavior* (New York: McGraw-Hill Book Company, 1967), 259.

9. Frank W. Lutz, Lou Kleinman, and Sy Evans, *Grievances and Their Resolution: Problems in School Personnel Administration* (Danville, Ill.: Interstate Printers and Publishers, Inc., 1967), 72.

10. Alvin Gouldner, *Patterns of Industrial Bureaucracy* (New York: Free Press, 1954).

11. Frank W. Lutz, with Seymour Evans, *The Union Contract and Principal Leadership in New York Schools* (New York: Center for Urban Education, 1968).

12. Frederick Herzberg, Bernard Mauser, and Barbara Synderman, *The Motivation to Work* (New York: John Wiley and Sons, 1959).

13. Davis, *Human Relations at Work.*

14. Henry C. Metcalf and Lyndall Urwick, eds., *Dynamic Administration: The Collected Papers of Mary Parker Follett* (New York: Harper and Brothers, 1940), 141.

15. Chris Argyris, "The Individual and Organizations: Some Problems of Mutual Adjustment," *Administrative Science Quarterly,* II (June 1957), 24.

16. *Id., Integrating the Individual and the Organization* (New York: John Wiley and Sons, 1964).

17. Douglas McGregor, *The Professional Manager* (New York: McGraw-Hill Book Company, 1967), 77.

18. Jacob W. Getzels, James Lipham, and Roald F. Campbell, *Educational Administration as a Social Process* (New York: Harper and Row, 1968), 346.

19. *Ibid.,* 372.

20. Egon G. Guba, "Research in Internal Administration," in *Administrative Theory as a Guide to Action,* ed. Roald F. Campbell and James M. Lipham (Chicago: Midwest Administration Center, University of Chicago, 1960), 121.

21. Richard C. Lonsdale, "Maintaining the Organization in Dynamic Equilibrium," in *Behavioral Science and Educational Administration,* ed. Daniel E. Griffiths, Sixty-third Yearbook of the National Society for the Study of Education, Part II (Chicago: University of Chicago Press, 1964), 177.

22. Dee Brown, *Bury My Heart at Wounded Knee* (New York: Bantam, 1972).

23. Frank W. Lutz, "Ghost Dance of the Elementary Principal," *Pennsylvania Elementary School Journal,* 19 (December 1969).

Chapter Thirteen

Bruce S. Cooper

The Future of Middle Management in Education

In early descriptions of the role of school principal, the functions included the performance of minor administrative tasks, responsibility for discipline, and some teaching.[1] From these humble beginnings the position gained stature to the point where, by the early twentieth century, Ellwood Cubberley could compare it to "the priest in the parish."[2] Many of the responsibilities of school management came to rest on this administrator, including, in the words of Paul Revere Pierce, "the efficient operation of elementary and secondary schools," the direction, within limits, of "local administrative procedures" and of "classroom instruction," and the leadership of the "school community" and the "professional staff."[3] In effect, by the 1950's, school principals appeared to embody the very ideals of American education: individuality and efficiency.[4]

Recently, however, changes in the organizational environment of school systems have disturbed and alienated many principals. Cut off from top management's inner circle and distrusted by a unionized teaching staff, principals seemed to be in search of a new occupational identity. In a few short years, as school districts grew in size and complexity, principals no longer enjoyed ready and easy access to either the school board or the superintendent. Layers of bureaucracy, often thickened by administrative specialization, stood between building leaders and those who occupied the central office. Or, as one critic explained, "a part of the system could have stopped functioning and headquarters might not have known about it for several months, so slowly does information pass through the institution."[5] Top management often found its administrative staff simply too large and remote for easy consultation on matters of policy.

Furthermore, the relationship between principals and their teaching staff — always a primary locus of school operations — has suddenly been altered by unionization and contractual "work rules."[6] No longer does staff look solely to administration for direction. Instead, staff members enjoy union solidarity. And so, while the principal supposedly wields hierarchical authority over staff, the relationship is actually regulated by district-wide labor agreements and modulated by the power of the teachers' union. Skill at the bargaining table, moreover, greatly narrows the gap between teacher wages and benefits and those afforded supervisory personnel. In effect, no longer can the principal easily claim to be both school manager and instructional leader.

Emotionally, too, school administrators are in limbo. Once they felt like leaders; now they feel like "pawns."[7] Robbed of a clear identity, either as real managers or as part of the teaching process, they confront the dilemma of having vital supervisory duties but diminishing social status in many urban school systems. To make matters worse, the "community" and students, who had once revered — if not feared — the principal, now sometimes questioned the principal's right to control the lives of children. The intrinsic rewards of the office, the joy of authority, and the satisfaction of accomplishment are often dissipated as principals work to hold on to the "right" to lead.[8] Many of the problems besetting the modern school administrator are summed up in this description of principals in New York City:

If the union has emasculated him as boss, the bureaucracy has emasculated him as administrator. It gives the orders on teacher assignment, controls the flow of substitutes, shapes the curriculum, dispenses the budget, promulgates "circulars" by the thousands, and demands reports in volume . . . . Badgered by the union and the board, bludgeoned by the critics, buffeted by the community and its spokesperson, the principals' occupational psychology is to defend the status quo and their own expertise.[9]

Emerging in the last few decades, then, is a vital educational group — school principals — caught in a changed political setting, one where they are no longer treated as leaders or managers, are isolated by job and conditions, and are losing their sense of purpose. What's more, they are not alone in their quandary; hundreds of other school supervisory and administrative personnel experience the same difficulties. In fact, the problems seem common to "middle-management" groups outside the schools. All have limited access to authority, coupled with important leadership responsibilities.[10]

In a number of school systems, however, recent data indicate that school administrators are not just ignoring these problems. They have learned from the successes of teacher unions over the last fifteen years, and they now likewise seek new affiliations and collective action. It appears that unity among fellow sufferers not only relieves the feeling of personal isolation, but it also enhances power.

The *four* types of organizational affiliation open to mid-level administrators in the schools are each a unique group response to common problems. They include affiliation with community, wherein the administrator is selected and supported by members of the school's lay constituency; affiliation with top management, with mid-level administrators being an integral part of the so-called "management team"; affiliation with teachers, whereby the administrator is a "head teacher," a first among equals; and affiliation with administrators' unions, with middle-management bargaining collectively with the school board and the superintendent. Although each alternative will be treated in turn, greatest attention is paid here to the emergence of middle-management unionization, a new and unexplored phenomenon in American schools.[11]

AFFILIATION WITH SCHOOL COMMUNITIES

Community groups became involved in the governance of public schools in the 1960's. For many principals and supervisors, this trend toward "community control," or, at least, "community participation," threatened their careers.[12] For others, it offered a unique opportunity to rally community support for new programs and to pressure the central office for additional resources. Hence, a skilled building or program administrator was able to convert a clash between professionals and the public into collateral for educational improvement.

No data currently available show the number of principals who successfully work with community groups. The model of affiliation is, nonetheless, appealing from a number of viewpoints. It has a long and distinguished history among private schools. The heads of many non-public schools work "within an autonomous domain" created by a direct governing relationship between trustees and chief administrators.[13] It is perhaps unfair to compare public school principals with the heads of private institutions, for the administrators of voluntary corporations[14] work without many of the legal and political strictures that encumber public systems.[15] The complexities of operating within a "school system" are practically unknown to all private school heads except to those who work in Roman Catholic schools.

But when public school principals work closely with active community boards, that relationship approximates the conditions as they exist in private schools, and, in some ways, even the relationship between the school superintendent and the board of education. In a sense, principals with a strong community board become their own superintendent,[16] thereby eliminating much of the bureaucracy that binds the usual urban building administrator.

The Chicago school system is a case in point. In 1970 the creation of Local School Councils permitted "parents and school patrons to *share* in the process of arriving at decisions which affect local schools."[17] These councils are elected from each school attendance area and are "broadly representative of the community."[18] Of the membership, 60 percent are parents, but school personnel, public members, and even high school students are elected. The councils oversee the selection of principals (by nominating them from a list of eligible candidates), as well as matters related to "discipline, vandalism and public conduct, curriculum, safety of children, physical condition of buildings, community problems, school budgets, school policies and procedures, selection of textbooks, and lunchroom problems."[19] Since each cluster of schools in Chicago also has a district council made up of the leaders of the local councils, a mechanism is provided for publicizing problems to those at the top. From all accounts, an angry local school council is difficult to ignore at the district and school board offices. And during the brief history of these councils, no nomination from the community boards for principal has been overturned by the superintendent and board of education.

Though more information is needed on the activities of school councils and their principals, we recognize the potential for channeling public support for schools and for increasing the potency of school administrators. As a model for future middle-management affiliation, however, the principal-community board relationship has several serious weaknesses. It fragments the ranks of middle management. Each administrator is left to his or her own devices. Thus, rather than strengthening the supervisory corps (vis-a-vis the central office), the localist orientation atomizes it. The subjugation of professional administration to the will of the public can, also, in the absence of strong collegial support, undermine quality and lead to obsequious rather than stalwart leadership. Similarly, qualified principals can be forced out of their posts because of racial incompatibility with their community boards. Finally, a school system with hundreds of small, semiautonomous school boards returns us to the turn of the century when the nation had over a hundred thousand school systems. The same lack of coordination and quality among districts might occur if community boards were allowed to govern (note the problems with New York City's thirty-one school boards).

All things considered, the affiliation of school administrators with local community groups is an intriguing alternative for the future of school leadership. For principals and others, it overcomes a sense of anomie. It provides an increase in power for those running the schools. And it reinforces a much-heralded American value: local control over a public service.

AFFILIATION WITH TOP MANAGEMENT

Textbooks on administration often extoll the "management team" concept.[20] Its unity and rationality support what we know about efficient school operations. It has the ring of good common sense, as we note from this definition: "Teamwork is the manifestation of group effort, under the leadership of a chief school executive, engaged in planning, performing, motivating, and evaluating as a unit — not as independent categories of leadership specialists and generalists."[21] Further, it offers the school principal an opportunity to associate with those in control of the school system. Being a real team member, in effect, overcomes the sense of impotency and isolation that plagues middle management.

But the current structure of many urban school systems makes the administrative team more of a myth than a reality. With some 3,700 middle managers and some 200 top managers in the New York City school system, for example, it is hard to conceive of joint planning and implementation. With so much physical distance between staff at all levels, it appears difficult even to bring administrators together for cooperative management. And with so many levels within the massive school bureaucracy, individual leaders may become confused about who fellow "team" members are.

Even supporters of the "management team" notion confess that real cooperation is problematic. Paul Salmon of the American Association of School Administrators lays part of the blame at the feet of the superintendent whose time is overcommitted and who is often inaccessible to mid-level administrators. Further, he explains, "administrators and supervisory specialists on the superintendent's immediate staff often get bogged down with educational red tape and tend to become independent operators rather than interacting components in the management team."[22] Thus, while school leaders may desire to unify their command, as a team effort would require, the "pathological" nature of school systems (jumbled communications, overlapping jurisdictions, unclear role descriptions, and other indications of confusion) prevents even a semblance of a bureaucratic span of control or accountability.[23]

If, then, the future of middle management in education rests with building a true leadership team — not just a smoke screen for autocratic rule — something must be done to reorganize urban schools and to change the attitudes of boards of education and top management about management styles. Perhaps the best approach is decentralization, or breaking the system into smaller, more autonomous units. The cohesion found in many suburban and rural districts indicates that a dozen or so school administrators can work together as a team.

Ideally, the superintendent of a subdivision of a system could meet regularly with the entire administrative staff of the smaller unit. Policies affecting the schools could be hammered out in sessions if there is real give-and-take. Complaints could be aired and mechanisms for conflict resolution could be utilized. Only then could the urban school principal be considered part of a management cadre, and even then the going would be tough. Central office mandates could still override the decisions made by the subregional teams. Labor union activity might severely limit the prerogatives of the administrative group. And, since final authority in school systems rests with the board of education, management teams might be left handling the minutiae while the board and central superintendent retained control over major areas like budget, personnel, and facilities.

Still another approach to administrative team effort is through system-wide councils representing various middle-management and employee groups. These bodies would be granted certain powers to recommend and even to decide on issues relevant to their constituency. The central office and board of education would be bound to consider (veto or approve) these decisions, much the way Congress and the chief executive currently relate in national politics. This structure of checks and balances would, in some ways, guarantee that team *governance* (not just team "work") occurred. Whether elaborate mechanisms of cooperative management would be acceptable to decision makers in the schools remains to be seen. It might be noted that similar syndicalist measures have enjoyed success in the People's Republic of China and in modern Cuba. In West Germany, the coal and steel industries, for example, have established elaborate systems of "codetermination" whereby each level in the organization elects or appoints its own representative body (Figure 14-1): a general assembly for shareholders, a works council (*Betriebsrat)* for blue- and white-collar workers, and a management board (*Vorstand*) for directors. Each group sends members to the supervisory board (*Aufsichtsrat*), which oversees the operation of the firm.[24]

A similar structure could be established in American public schools. Members from employee and supervisory groups, the board of education, the superintendent's office, and even, perhaps, representatives of parent and consumer groups would meet as a policy-making council and would direct the "management" of the school system. Though such an arrangement is unlikely in American schools, it does give meaning to the notion of "management team"—parts of which might be useful. (For example, some school districts now schedule regular meetings of the presidents of the various unions, parent groups, and administrator groups to iron out problems before they reach the board of education.)

Whatever configuration of team management, participative management, or group decision making is employed, the future success of such devices rests with major restructuring of American school systems. The present school organization is simply too large and awkward to allow real integration of administrative levels into a team. And no matter what changes occur in the relationship among top, middle, and employee groups, school principals and other supervisors must ultimately work together in "teams" of some kind. The question is: How will they be structured and how effective will they be?

AFFILIATION WITH TEACHERS

In a number of experimental settings in the United States, school principals seek affiliation, not with other district administrators, but with their teaching staff. As "head" or "coordinating" teachers, they are often selected by their peers or serve on a rotating basis. They are first among equals. They forgo much of the legal-bureaucratic authority vested in them by boards of education and accept, instead, the mechanisms of consensus, or, in some cases, personal charisma.[25]

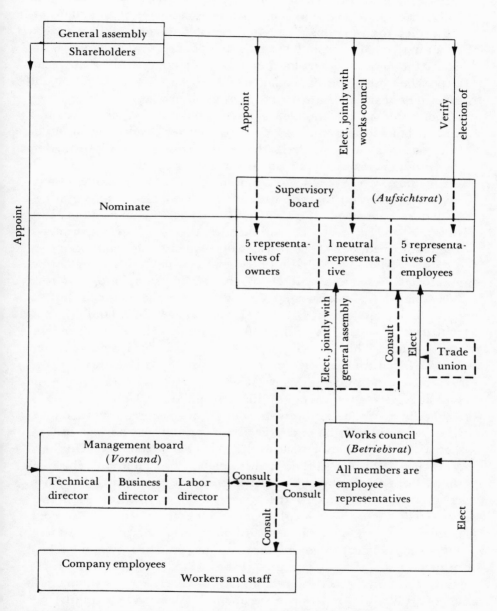

FIGURE 13-1. The system of codetermination in West German steel and coal industries (simplified)

They govern with the consent of the governed — at least as far as the rules of personnel selection and school district operation will allow.

Needless to say, mainstream public schools are not usually managed by an individual selected by the instructional staff (though university deans and departmental chairpeople are often elected by their faculties). The post is too important to the board of education and the superintendent to be entrusted to a group of teachers.[26] Furthermore, school codes and tradition leave major promotions to the board. In a limited but growing number of cases, however, leadership in public "alternative" schools and less-structured private schools is provided by the staff alone or by an individual selected by the teachers. After all, the ideology of the new schools movement is at heart antibureaucratic.[27] To the extent that top management recognizes that the success of these unique schools (for children who do not "fit" in traditional settings) depends on new leadership modes, the board and superintendent have turned to the teaching staff for suggestions on promotions.

Organizationally, affiliation between principal and staff takes several forms. In more radical school settings, for example, the two roles (teaching and administering) are fused — and the principalship, as such, disappears. Instead, the school is managed by a kind of "committee of the whole," comprised often of adults and children performing as equals. This form of operation is typical of private institutions like the Elizabeth Cleaners Street School, in New York City, where "*all* power is in the students' hands. They hire and fire staff, choose the buildings, set the schedule, formulate the philosophy, etc."[28]

In public schools, however, the state school code requires that a certified administrator be in charge. Thus, principals who wish to form close ties with staff must make an effort to change their use of authority, their self-concept, and even their image. One step toward change is simple: principals absent themselves from the school site altogether, creating, in the parlance of these new schools, an "off-site alternative" or "satellite school." Though these administrators are still "in command," they, by their physical distance, allow the staff (and sometimes the students) to govern the program.[29] They (the home-school principals) act, then, as lightning rods and facilitators for their off-site staff, thus gaining their support and the satisfaction of providing both a more traditional and more experimental program concurrently.

Another mode of alignment, principal to staff, is, in a sense, to join them — to attempt to reflect the leadership style and life-style of those whom they lead. A good example is Forest Adams, former principal of the Mantua-Powelton Minischool, a public community school in inner-city Philadelphia:

Conveying images—of himself, of the school—was, in fact, Adam's chief forte. His mind was as eclectic as his resume, forever jumping about from one idea to another, consistently inventive and witty. Usually outfitted in round, rimless glasses, jeans or slacks, and a dashiki, he had the look of a young black intellectual, yet he was outwardly friendly and tolerant. He had managed to get him*self* together, it seemed—to come to terms with being black in mid-century America.[30]

Further, these new-style administrators identify with teachers, receiving primary rewards and direction from them. Often they are less concerned about central office orders and are less attuned to other principals and supervisors in the school system. They realize that building a strong affiliation with staff requires undisputed loyalty to school as a small community, even if it means limiting their career aspirations and defying (within limits) the will of the central office. With these new programs, top management often seems willing to bend the rules or simply to ignore their pugnacity. Since some of these experimental schools have attracted outside funds from federal and foundation sources, the principal may be given wide latitude in relating to staff and setting school policies.

This mode of affiliation, principal with teachers, has a certain attraction. Teaching has long been an honored, if "shadowed," activity.[31] Administrators who function as part of the teacher group certainly gain a sense of tradition and worth. Since most school administrators have been classroom teachers, this emotional tie to staff is a comfortable one. Though little research has been done on the rewards of being a school principal, we can assume that a warm interaction with staff is a main source of job satisfaction. And for those principals who prize a close, personalized relationship with teachers, a formal affiliation as head teacher helps to ensure that they remain nonbureaucratic and involved. Thus, for them, it makes sense to ally both organizationally and emotionally with the teaching personnel.

As a pivot for power in the school district, however, an affiliation with teachers is of limited value. Even if principals remain teachers at heart, they may be prevented by law from joining the teachers' union. Hence, at bargaining time and in grievance cases, they may find themselves without representation and the protection of due process. Further, being neither simply teachers nor completely administrators could increase the strain on their defined role, particularly when they are held accountable to the board for conditions of buildings, the progress of students, and the actions of staff. Finally, principals who perceive of themselves primarily as teachers may be less willing to work for district-wide solidarity among school administrative personnel. While the relationship may be useful in ending their personal sense of isolation and impotency, it does little to increase the impact of middle management throughout the school system. Like the principal who relates mainly to the immediate community, the administrator who joins the teaching staff often maximizes personal interaction and avoids the problems of the occupational group.

As a future direction for the urban school principal, alignment with staff seems the least advantageous of the four affiliations. This relationship involves a single school and remains by design informal. The impact of one staff and one principal on school district policy remains minor. When we consider that alternative schools that encourage close administrator-teacher relations are themselves fairly tenuous (note the number of free schools that close), it would appear that the long-term effects of this form of affiliation on the practice of administration are limited. That is not to say that the model itself is illegitimate — not at all. For the children, staff, and leader of any given school, the arrangement pays dividends. As a means of influencing the system, however, it seems feeble.

AFFILIATION WITH MIDDLE MANAGEMENT UNIONS

Still another mode of affiliation is for administrators themselves to unionize.[32] As unlikely as it sounds, a number of school principals, vice-principals, central office supervisors, and other mid-level administrators bargain collectively with their boards of education for salaries, benefits, and employment and work conditions. Formerly antagonistic groups such as "field" and "central office" supervisors have overlooked earlier differences[33] to gain strength at the bargaining table. Unity is fostered by the sharing of union leadership positions, and in more than fifty-five instances administrators have sought to bolster their negotiating advantage by affiliating with the AFL-CIO through the American Federation of School Administrators (AFSA).[34]

Unionization seems to overcome a number of weaknesses perceived by principals and other administrators. It allows principals to formalize their relations with top management through negotiations, contracts, and, when necessary, grievance procedures. The administrators' union acts as a power base in dealing with teachers' unions. It provides an alternative avenue of appeal if and when the board, superintendent, or other groups overlook principals' needs. And union membership transcends the isolation of building leadership and offers a ready peer group, one that offers not only a forum for social support but also clout to deal with outside pressures.[35]

Even as part of a union, however, school administrators have limited power, and most of them know it. By law and common sense, they cannot strike. They are too few in number (a walkout of principals, for example, would hardly close down the schools) and their actions are unlikely to rally public support (the image of a school principal walking a picket line for an increase in a yearly salary of $25,000 has little public appeal). Instead, administrators' unions may seek to maximize their power by a national labor affiliation or by holding onto the coattails of the more influential teachers' associations. Using the reasoning that they, the supervisors, should, for the sake of "good administration," make proportionately more than those whom they direct, the middle manager can make a strong case for salary increments and other benefits and provisions similar to those awarded teachers. Further, in dealing with top managers with whom these new unions must bargain, administrators are in a position to embarrass the superintendent by publicly disagreeing on policy issues. Since most citizens consider the superintendent and mid-level administration part of the same district leadership, the administrators' union might gain concessions in bargaining by backing the central office and preserving the public sense of unitary management. Finally, and what is most important, school administrators are functionally vital to the board and superintendent. Since decisions made by those at the top are handed over to middle management anyway, school principals and other supervisors have enormous influence over what goes on in the school system. In other words, top managers need middle managers if the school organization is to operate on a daily basis.

This section covers the size, location, legal status, organization, and affiliation of supervisory unions in education. The data were gathered through a national survey and through selected visits to eight school systems with unions.

These new affiliations undoubtedly represent a change in personal attitudes for many school administrators, a reconciliation of "professional" and "unionist" viewpoints. They also signal a realignment of the relationship between top administrators and the middle ranks (for example, job titles may range from academic department heads, through principal and vice-principal, to central office directors, and even, in the city of Detroit, to the assistant regional superintendent). Quite unexpectedly, these unions seem to have become part of the national labor movement. Taken in the long view, however, this collectivization and unit bargaining does not seem a total break with the past. Instead, it is a logical extension of the consolidation and routinization long present in American education, manifest in devices like the single salary schedule, state certification, tenure, and so on. In a sense, the centurylong tendency to treat categories of personnel in similar ways has led to the collectivization of school middle managers.

Description of the Unions

Number, Location, Legal Status. Though no exact data are available on the total number of supervisory unions in the United States (for they are new and school boards often do not have to report to state agencies on local negotiations), my survey indicates a large and growing number of such unions in twenty-six states and the District of Columbia. In 1977 there were 1,277 public school administrators' unions, of which 95 percent (1,215) were located in the seventeen states, and the District of Columbia, that had laws permitting mid-level administrators to bargain. The remaining 63 unions were located in seven states with no bargaining legislation but where local school boards had voluntarily and extralegally recognized the administrators' associations as agents for collective negotiations. Table 13-1 shows the location, state control agency, and number of unions by state and in the District of Columbia.

It is apparent from Figure 13-2 that collective bargaining occurs most often in the industrialized states of the East, Great Lakes, and Far West, with obvious exceptions such as Florida, Kansas, and South Dakota. The best indicator of bargaining for administrators, according to Edwin Bridges and me, was the presence of teacher unionism, for in no case were there unions of administrators without the presence of teacher bargaining. Hence, we can say that "granting collective bargaining rights to teachers is a necessary, though insufficient, condition for granting similar rights to administrators."[36]

In each of these cases except Ohio, which will be discussed shortly, a state agency is designated to oversee labor relations in public schools: the state superintendent or commissioner of education (Washington and Connecticut); a single state labor relations agency for both public and private organizations (Massachusetts, Michigan, and Pennsylvania); and separate organizations for public employment relations alone (New York and New Jersey). Ohio, unusual among these states, has no employment relations legislation whatever, not even a "little Wagner Act" to regulate private sector labor activities.

State laws and local labor history provide keys to the emergence of

TABLE 13.1. Number of administrator unions and types of control agencies, 1975

State	Control agencies	Number of unions of school administrators
States with bargaining laws		
Alaska	Local School Boards	6
California	Education Employment Relations Board	2
Connecticut	State Board of Education	132
District of Columbia	Board of Labor Relations	1
Florida	No Commision	4
Hawaii	Public Employment Relations Board (PERB)	1
Kansas	PERB	4
Maine	Maine Labor Relations Board	14
Maryland	State Board of Education	12
Massachusetts	Massachusetts Labor Relations Board	100
Michigan	Michigan Labor Relations Board	75
Minnesota	PERB	215
New Hampshire	Public Employment Relations Commission (PERC)	3
New Jersey	PERC	310
New York	PERB	215
South Dakota	Department of Manpower Affairs	1
Vermont	Local School Boards	4
Washington	PERC	115
States without bargaining laws		
Illinois	No Commission	6
Missouri	No Commission	5
Ohio	No Commission	25
Pennsylvania	Pennsylvania Labor Relations Board	25
Rhode Island	No Commission	1
Virginia	No Commission	
Wisconsin	Wisconsin Employment Relations Commission	1
	Total	1,277

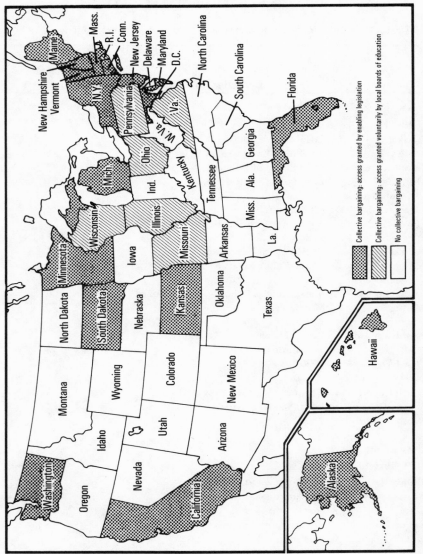

FIGURE 13-2. Map showing the presence of supervisory collective bargaining throughout the United States

school administrators' unions. Without supportive state legislation, it is doubtful that so many administrator groups would have gained bargaining rights. In Michigan and Massachusetts, for example, the laws simply extended to public employees the same basic rights long enjoyed by industrial employees. The Michigan Public Employment Relations Act, as amended in 1969, states that "it shall be lawful for public employees to organize together or to form, joint [*sic*] or assist in labor organizations, to engage in lawful concerted activities for the purpose of collective negotiations or bargaining or other mutual aid and protection . . . ."[37] In other states, laws specifically mention certified supervisory personnel: ("school principals and assistant principals shall be considered to be certificated employees unless a majority elect by secret ballot to be excluded. . . . ."), allowing them to bargain for wages and working conditions with their boards of education.[38]

Further, in many states the body of laws and rulings of labor relations agencies set supervisors clearly apart from teachers on the one hand and top school executives on the other. The Massachusetts Labor Relations Commission, to give just one example, ruled that teachers and supervisors should *not* be part of the same bargaining unit, so as "to minimize potential conflicts between the supervisor's loyalty to his fellow union members and his obligation to his employer."[39] Without these delineations from teachers and top managers, supervisory personnel might have little claim to separate negotiating status. They would instead remain members of the teachers' unions, as they have done in some districts, or would be considered part of management without any negotiating rights whatever.

The issue of whether supervisors are part of educational management has been resolved explicitly in many state labor laws. In New Jersey, for example, a law passed in 1968 indicated that "only the superintendent" was top management, denying the chief executive any confidential associates. A later law (1974) was less narrow, stating that executive management included "persons who formulated policies and practices" and those "involved in the collective bargaining process"[40] for the board of education. Data seem to indicate that, without legal support for public sector negotiations and the acknowledgement that middle managers are a distinct group of employees, widespread unionization of administrators would be unlikely.

The exception appears to be larger cities where, despite the lack of state labor statutes, local boards of education voluntarily and extralegally agree to recognize administrator groups and to negotiate with them. Perhaps superintendents simply find it easier to deal with one administrator organization rather than with ten or twelve smaller groups. Or perhaps school board members, concerned about the mounting power among teachers' unions, recognize the supervisors as a counterweight. Or, most likely, the presence of labor representatives on school boards in cities like Detroit, Milwaukee, Baltimore, and Cleveland might make it difficult for the board to refuse a plea for union recognition from principals and supervisors.

The best example of this last explanation is found in Ohio, which has more large cities than any other state, and which has approximately twenty-five voluntarily recognized administrator bargaining units (see Table 13-1). The Cleveland administrators' contract reads: "Until such time as collective negotiation legislation becomes effective in Ohio, . . . the Cleveland Council of Administrators and Supervisors is recognized as the sole representative of administrative and supervisory personnel with the exception of the Superintendent, the Deputy Superintendent . . . ."[41] In about seventeen other cities, including Chicago, Providence, Milwaukee, Arlington (Virginia), Kansas City (Missouri), and Baltimore, school supervisors have successfully argued for the right to bargain, in spite of the absence of supportive labor legislation. In the event of impasse or alleged unfair labor practices, however, these local associations have neither channels of appeal nor relevant state agencies to adjudicate the matter — unless they turn to the courts. Also, in the absence of public employment legislation, local school boards can flatly refuse to recognize *any* employee group.

It seems safe to say, then, that the growth of middle-management unionization in public education is tied to the political climate, both locally and state-wide. If, in the future, a federal law like the proposed H.R. 8677, the "National Public Employment Relations Act, 1973," or H.R. 777, an amendment to the private sector's Wagner Act, were to pass, of course, the machinery would be available for virtually all supervisory groups to organize.[42]

Organization. Data from eight sample school administrator unions show a wide diversity in internal structure, though a rough correspondence exists between the size of the association and its structural complexity. That is, large units like New York City's Council of Supervisors and Administrators (CSA) have full-time, paid staff and officers, a number of elected boards, and both geographic and interest-group representation on its governing board. Smaller unions often have no paid leadership and are governed by small boards elected at large.

Though the eight labor organizations studied are hardly a random sample of the nation's thousand or so administrators' bargaining units, they do serve as a useful starting point in the study of those organizations.

While all sample unions have elected officers, the large ones employ one or more of their leaders as full-time executives. For example, the presidents of the Philadelphia Association of School Administrators (PASA) and the Chicago Principals' Association are granted leaves without pay by their respective school boards while serving as union heads. Detroit's Organization of School Administrators and Supervisors (OSAS) and New York City's Council of Supervisors and Administrators (CSA), the nation's largest administrators' union, support not only their presidents but also the organizations' vice-presidents. From their operating budgets the unions pay their officials, in the language of the Philadelphia union's bylaws, "the equivalent to that to which he would be entitled had he remained in his previous assignment with the School District."

The Milwaukee Public School Administrators and Supervisors Council, Inc., hires an executive secretary to operate the organization while the union's officers remain at their school posts. The CSA (New York City) also employs an executive staff, in addition to the elected officers. They include an executive director, a legislative representative (lobbyist), a public relations director, a grievance director, and a field director. Overall, as Table 13-2 shows, unions appear able to afford one full-time staff member for every 500 members, though Cleveland has sufficient members but no paid staff and the Chicago Principals' Association has only 469 members and one staff member.

The absence of staff may be explained by the lack of money. The Cleveland union (with 500 members) charges annual dues of only $50.00 per member and has a budget of about $25,000, hardly enough to maintain an office and paid staff. Detroit, on the other hand, has many more members (1,300) and charges higher annual dues ($125.00 per member). Other unions, like New York City's, receive dues equal to a percentage (1.1 percent) of each member's salary and have much larger annual operating budgets (New York's is over $950,000 yearly).

Besides elected officers, most sample unions have one or more representative governing bodies (the exception being the union in Riverdale, Michigan, which, with only eight members, hardly requires an elected governing board). The choice of representatives to a union

TABLE 13-2. Characteristics of sample administrator unions grouped by staffing arrangements, 1975

Location, name, and union affiliation	Paid staff		Union size	Yearly budget	Governing board(s) (number of members)	Types of board representation	Groups included in union
	Number	Category					
New York City Council of Supervisors and Administrators	7	President Vice-president Five executive directors	3,497	$965,000	Advisory Committee (9 members) Executive Board (70 members)	Elected at large By school location and membership group	Principals, vice-principals, directors, supervisors, day-care directors, *et al.*
Detroit Organization of School Administrators and Supervisors (OSAS)	2	President Vice-President	1,200	1,200	Executive Board (17 members)	Membership categories	Assistant regional superintendents principals, vice-principals, directors, supervisors, building department heads
Chicago Chicago Principals' Association	1	President	469	143,000	Board of Directors (38 members)	School location and membership category	Officially, principals; Unofficially, vice-principals, and central office supervisors
Philadelphia Association of Supervisors Administrators (PASA)	1	President	730	115,000	House of Delegates (21 members)	School location and membership categories	Principals, vice-principals, directors, supervisors of central and 8 district offices
Milwaukee Public Schools Administrators Supervisors Council, Inc.	1	Executive secretary	560	60,000	Executive Committee (27 members)	Membership categories	Principals, vice-principals, central office staff, and recreation supervisors
Cleveland Council of Administrators Administrators and Supervisors (CAS)	None		500	25,000	Executive Committee (17 members)	Membership categories	Principals, vice-principals, and central office subject supervisors
Baltimore Public School Administrators Supervisors Association	None		341	21,000	Executive Committee (10 members)	Membership categories	Principals, vice-principals, central and area supervisors
Riverview, Mich. Riverview Administrators Cabinet (RAC)	None		8	288	None	-----	Principals and vice-principals

board usually reflects an attempt to involve all factions within the union ranks. For example, four unions elect members to their councils based on job category: The Milwaukee administrators group votes three representatives from nine professional groupings (such as the Milwaukee Elementary School Principals' Association, the Recreation Managers' Association, and the Central Office Professional Association) to serve on its Executive Committee. The Cleveland Council of Administrators and Supervisors, besides electing five officers and eight members at large, chooses vice-presidents to its Executive Committee from the ranks of the junior high, senior high, and elementary school principals, and from the central office curriculum supervisory group. The Detroit organization allots seats on its Executive Board according to the size of three constituent groups (building administrators, central office staff, and academic department heads). And the Baltimore union elects one board member from each member group: elementary, junior high, senior high, and regional-central office staff supervisors.

The unions in Philadelphia, Chicago, and New York City have a more complex system based on both membership job category and the geographic location of the member's school. For example, the House of Delegates, governing group of the Philadelphia association (PASA), has nine vice-presidents (representing job titles like elementary, secondary, and technical principals and also vice-principals, supervisors, assistant supervisors, and others) and one delegate from each of the school system's eight decentralized districts and the central office administrators.[43] The Chicago Principals' Association operates auxiliaries for its elementary school principals (ten such groups based on geographic clustering of schools), its high school principals, and, informally,[44] for its vice-principals and central office administrators. Each auxiliary sends two representatives to the union's board of directors.

Finally, the CSA in New York City has almost seventy members elected to the Executive Board. Delegates are elected from nineteen membership categories and from thirty-one decentralized districts based on a complicated formula. The outgoing president also serves on the board. Since the body may be somewhat large and cumbersome, a seven-person advisory committee of five officers and two members elected from the board meets regularly and handles minor administrative decisions for the membership.

These eight unions, large and small, staffed and unstaffed, function as the sole bargaining agents for middle management. They negotiate salaries, fringe benefits, and conditions of employment, transfer, and removal. These actions seem basic to any employee organization. In addition, the head of the union often speaks for all mid-level administrators. Through the informal structure of the union, the leaders can pass on the needs of the rank and file to top management and, conversely, can transmit to administrators the directives of the board and superintendent. The union can, then, potentially operate as a mechanism for communications and conflict resolution, making use of such accepted procedures as bargaining and grievance (due process).[45]

Affiliation. With the wildfire growth of these unions in the last four years, one might look for a strong national movement like the postwar efforts of the American Federation of Teachers[46] and the blue-collar unions of the 1930's, but this is not likely to happen. The thousand or so supervisory unions in education developed locally, with some help from public employment legislation in about seventeen states or some support from local labor in the remaining seven. One explanation for the localist nature of these new associations is that, until 1971, there were almost no national and state organizations to serve the local bargaining unit as a whole. Traditionally, groups like the National Association of Elementary School Principals, the National Association of Secondary School Principals, and the National Association of Supervisors and Curriculum Development have fragmented the middle-management ranks at the local school level, each group relating to its own particular members and lessening the solidarity so necessary for collective action. In Ohio and New York state leaders have moved to change this situation. Principals' and supervisors' associations in Ohio sponsor an umbrella organization, the Ohio Council of Administrative Personnel Associations (OCAPA), "designed to meet the unique service requirements of all inclusive local administrator associations."[47] Besides providing insurances, legal services, lobbying, and group advocacy, OCAPA membership also provides affiliation with the appropriate state association. Perhaps the efforts of OCAPA explain in some way the existence of some twenty-five local administrator unions in Ohio, in spite of the lack of a public employment (or private employment) law. Also, in response to AFL-CIO advances among school administrators in New York, the state elementary and secondary principals' associations formed a single organization, the School Administrators' Association of New York State (SAANYS) with offices in Albany and with nearly two hundred local affiliates.

Currently, about fifty-five union locals are affiliated with two new national associations, the American Federation of School Administrators of the AFL-CIO or the loose confederation of big-city associations, the National Council of Urban School Administrators and Supervisors (NCUSAS). The two organizations share a common origin. In 1970 several large-city middle-administrator groups inquired about an affiliation with the AFL-CIO. George Meany requested that local leaders like the late Walter Degnan (New York City) and Joseph DiLeonarde (Chicago) call a meeting of associates from other large-city systems. A meeting at Kennedy Airport, New York, brought leaders from major city administrator groups together, and NCUSAS was formed. It has no staff or office, per se, but it is operated by national officers. From the NCUSAS ranks came the first locals of AFSA. Degnan, head of Local #1, became the first national president, and DiLeonarde, the first national vice-president. Currently, it has over fifty-five locals, primarily in the Northeast, but also in places as diverse as Arlington (Virginia), and Scottsdale (Arizona), and a national office in New York City with three members on its executive staff.

Despite the efforts of Ohio's OCAPA, New York's SAANYS, AFSA, and NCUSAS to involve a thousand existing administrator bargaining units throughout the nation, the fact remains that most supervisory personnel groups are currently unaffiliated. Perhaps as AFSA opens regional offices and brings itself closer to local conditions more unions will join the movement. Or perhaps more professional associations will follow the lead of Ohio and New York and restructure their state organizations, thus becoming better able to serve local bargaining units. It seems likely that something will happen, as administrator unions call for outside assistance and lobbying potential in Washington, D.C., and their state capitals.

In summary, it is apparent that laws and practice in education will lead school administrators in increasing numbers to form coalitions of supervisory personnel and to negotiate contracts collectively. Though only a small portion of public school administrators enter into bargaining, signs point to an acceleration of these activities. First, as supervisors vie with teachers' unions for scarce resources and for authority in schools, the administrators' groups will continue to unionize. The more active the teachers, the more likely the administrators are to collectivize. Second, the mounting demand for "accountability" from boards and community will stimulate mid-level administrators to demand "input" into performance appraisal criteria and procedures. Without organizational strength, supervisors may find their traditional clubs and associations too weak and small to have an impact on those evaluating them. Third, as boards of education face the need to cut back on supervisory staff in the face of declining student enrollment and expanding costs, administrators will likely react collectively to protect their jobs. But perhaps the best clue to future collectivation in education is the continued expansion of centralized public bureaucracies. Should the state move to "full state funding," whereby the monies for education come completely from state government, then "full state negotiation"[48] is also a possibility. All public educators, even the superintendents, would be called upon to "bargain" with management (in this case, the state), and unionization at all levels would be likely.

IN CONCLUSION

There is a need for school administrators to affiliate. In the face of recent changes in school district size, complexity, and authority relationships, a number have already moved to become union members, to identify with teaching staff, to join closely with top management, and even to work directly with community groups.

These modes have much in common. They support the axiom: That a collective, structured response to an organizational problem is often superior to a personal, individualized one. For, though institutions have elaborate mechanisms for ignoring people, the organizations are not as well equipped to handle group pressures. Principals with allies cannot be overlooked. Each of the four alliances treated in this chapter involves principals and often supervisors in regularized relationships with other interested parties.

But the four modes of affiliation differ in at least two ways. First, the scope of affiliation varies between administrators who align themselves with essentially school-based groups and those involved with district-wide organizations. As shown in Figure 13-3, relations with teaching staff and community groups (cells *A* and *C*) are primarily local in orientation; alliances with central management and unions (cells *B* and *D*) involve others from throughout the school system. It is assumed that affiliations with broad-based groups may lead to greater influence, though this remains to be proved.

Second, affiliations vary in terms of level of formalization from relations based on rules, laws, and contracts (high formalization) to those resting on ad hoc arrangements, functional situations, and custom (low formalization). Again, it is assumed that a formalized situation offers the greater chance of receiving and maintaining an advantage

Scope of relations	Formalization of relations	
	Low (ad hoc)	High (contractual)
Low (school-based)	A Principal as "head teacher"	C Principal as executive of Community board
High (district-based)	B Principal as integral part of management	D Principal as mid-level administration union member

FIGURE 13-3. Dimensions of school administrator's affiliations

for administrators while ad hoc situations tend to change in unpredictable directions. For example, principals who are hired and governed by community boards often work within a formal set of procedures (recall Chicago, with its local school councils). Similarly, unions are backed in many states by labor rules and formal contracts. Conversely, affiliations between head teachers and staff in alternative schools and between "middle" and "top" management in school systems tend to be less regularized. In fact, the very notion of teamwork in alternative education and in management often rests on the obviation of formal status differences and the assertion that "we are all one happy family."

While it is too early to predict which of these four types of affiliation is most effective in improving the status of school administrators, it would seem that cell *A,* principal as "head teacher," being "low" on both breadth of involvement and level of formalization, holds the least promise. It involves few people and few procedural underpinnings. On the other hand, unionization ranks "high" on both variables and appears to put mid-level administrative personnel on a somewhat better footing with the top managers' and the teachers' unions in matters of wage negotiating, due process, and working conditions. The principal as executive of the community board and as an integral part of the management team falls somewhere between. Relations with local boards of community people are often routinized, but lack district-wide authority. As members of management, administrators gain access to power, but the precarious nature of the relationship weakens the impact.

Further, it is hard to know which type of relationship will gain favor with school administrators in the future. The rapid growth of unionization may continue as AFL-CIO's new Department of Public Employees gains momentum and state labor laws are passed. Other principals may opt to side with their staff, their communities, or their bosses, as local conditions dictate.

In fact, we can assume that, while administrators may be called upon to relate to *all* groups, they may choose to pursue one over the others, investing emotionally in a primary association. Whichever they select, there is sure to be conflict—as exists between an association with the superintendent and leadership in the union, or between a principal who backs the staff over a demand of the community and the local board.

What emerges from this analysis, then, is that the modern school principal is caught in a complex set of relationships and that there is great likelihood of considerable strain in filling the role. Perhaps social scientists have misled practitioners into believing that being a school leader is simply a matter of imitating "Great Men," becoming an "instructional leader," or being a "manager of change." The job is more complex. In the future principals may have to adjust their behavior to participate in union activities as they are concerned with wages and work conditions, to participate in staff cadres as they develop school curricula and programs, to participate in community councils as they set school-wide goals and policies, and to participate in management teams as they fulfill state and local requirements and are generally held accountable. If this sounds like a tall order, it is!

A key to success, it would seem, is a joining together, a sharing of problems, and a consolidating of social relationships. Life within a reference group may allow the leader to develop, to become, in the midst of tense situations, a whole and effective person. A sense of self, a set of allies, and an appropriate structure for making an impact on the rules of the game, if used together, may enable the administrator of the future to play a vital role in the nation's schools.

NOTES

1. For an early description, see *Ninth Annual Report of the Trustees and Visitors of the Common School of Cincinnati* (Cincinnati: the city, 1838), 5.

2. Ellwood P. Cubberley, *The Principal and His School* (Boston: Houghton Mifflin Company, 1923), 26-27.

3. Paul Revere Pierce, *The Origin and Development of the Public School Principalship* (Chicago: University of Chicago Press, 1935), 1.

4. See, for example, Roscoe V. Cramer and Otto E. Domian, *Administration and Supervision in the Elementary School* (New York: Harper and Row, 1960), 400-405; Paul B. Jacobson, William Reavis, and James D. Logsdon, *The Effective School Principal*, 2d ed. (Englewood Cliffs, N.J.: Prentice-Hall, 1963), 491-498; and on adminis-

trative efficiency, see Raymond Callahan, *Education and the Cult of Efficiency* (Chicago: University of Chicago Press, 1967).

5. David Rogers, *110 Livingston Street: Politics and Bureaucracy in the New York City School System* (New York: Vintage Books, 1968), 324.

6. See Edward S. Shils and C. Taylor Whittier, *Teachers, Administrators, and Collective Bargaining* (New York: Thomas Y. Crowell Company, 1968), 11-19.

7. Edwin M. Bridges, "Administrative Man: Origin or Pawn in Decision Making," *Educational Administration Quarterly*, 6 (Winter 1970), 7-25.

8. For a comparative description of public and private school principals and their problems, see Otto Kraushaar, *American Nonpublic Schools: Patterns in Diversity* (Baltimore: Johns Hopkins University Press, 1972), 175.

9. Bernard Bard, "New York City Principals: On the Razor's Edge," *Saturday Review*, January 24, 1970, 58, 71.

10. A more precise definition of "middle management" indicates that, as a group, they advise, but exercise "no real decision-making in the investment of major capital." William Gomberg, "Due Process Enters Management Theory," *Wharton Quarterly* 27 (Winter 1971), 8.

11. C. Wright Mills predicted widespread unionization among professional, white-collar employees over twenty-five years ago; see his *White Collar: The American Middle Classes* (New York: Oxford University Press, 1951), chap. 14, 301-323.

12. Mark M. Krug, "Chicago: The Principals' Predicament," *Phi Delta Kappan*, 56 (September 1974), 43-45.

13. Kraushaar, *American Nonpublic Schools*, 173.

14. The origin of the American high school can be traced to the private academy which was governed by a board of trustees, administered by a headmaster or headmistress, and partially financed by public funds. For a full description, see Michael B. Katz, *Class, Bureaucracy, and Schools* (New York: Praeger Publishers, 1971), 22-28.

15. For an analysis and description of the regulation of private education, see Donald A. Erickson, ed., *Public Controls for Nonpublic Schools* (Chicago: University of Chicago Press, 1968).

16. For an example in New York City, see Charles E. Wilson, "201 — First Steps toward Community Control," in *Schools against Children: The Case for Community Control*, ed. Annette T. Rubinstein (New York: Monthly Review Press, 1970), 211-227.

17. "Report on Local School Councils to the Board of Education," Recommendations (revised December 9, 1970), Office of the Superintendent, Chicago Public Schools, Document 70-1161, page 1 [emphasis in original].

18. *Ibid.*

19. *Ibid.*

20. Ernest Dale's textbook on management explains that cooperation is a core value in all organizations, a kind of social ethic. Certainly no social grouping would long exist without teamwork among managers and employees. See Ernest Dale, *Management: Theory and Practice* (New York: McGraw-Hill Book Company, 1965), 210-214; William H. Whyte, *The Organization Man* (New York: Simon and Schuster, 1956); and Edward C. Bursk, ed., *The Management Team* (Cambridge, Mass.: Harvard University Press, 1954). For a short discussion of the team effort in schools, see Thomas A. Shannon, *The Administrative Team: Resolving Management Conflict*

through Association (Arlington, Va.: National Association of Elementary School Principals, 1972), 5.

21. Paul B. Salmon, "Are the Administrative Team and Collective Bargaining Compatible?" *Compact,* 12 (June 1972), 3.

22. *Ibid.*

23. See chapter 9, "Administrative Controls," in Rogers, *110 Livingston Street,* 324-362, for a full discussion of the pathology of school bureaucracies.

24. See F. E. Emery and Einar Thorsrub, *Form and Content in Industrial Democracy* (London: Tavistock, 1969), 42-52. See also Ernie Roberts, *Workers' Control* (London: George Allen and Unwin, 1973), for a British example.

25. England's Summerhill School operated with high degrees of self-governance under the guidance of its late headmaster, A. S. Neill, who was highly revered. The all-school meeting provided a forum where a six-year-old had equal voting power with the school's head. Neill evidently exhibited great charismatic qualities. See A. S. Neill, *Summerhill: A Radical Approach to Child Rearing* (New York: Hart Publishing, 1950).

26. The status and self-perceptions of teachers are analyzed in Dan Lortie, *Schoolteacher: A Sociological Study* (Chicago: University of Chicago Press, 1975).

27. Cooper defines alternative schools in terms of their desires to replace structure with human interactions: *"New organizational structures:* other alternatives are attempts to be nonbureaucratic, communal/consensual social systems which seek to change education by avoiding the pitfalls of rule-bound organizations." See Bruce S. Cooper, "Alternative Schools and the Free School Movement," in *The Handbook of Contemporary Education* (New York: R. R. Bowker Company, 1977). For a description of what happens in private free schools, see also *id., Free School Survivial* (Minneapolis, Minn.: Burgess, 1976).

28. Allen Graubard, *Free the Children: Radical Reform and the Free School Movement* (New York: Pantheon Books, 1973), 112.

29. For an analysis of an off-site alternative, see Gerald Nesvold, "An Evaluation of an Off-Campus Alternative High School," unpub. diss., University of Pennsylvania, 1974.

30. Henry Resnik, *Turning on the System: War in the Philadelphia Public Schools* (New York: Pantheon Press, 1970), 167-168.

31. Lortie uses the notion of honored but shadowed in his *Schoolteacher,* chap. 2.

32. For a shorter treatment of this topic, see Bruce S. Cooper, "Middle Management Unionization in Education," *Administrator's Notebook,* 23 (Spring 1975).

33. Rogers describes the tension between supervisors in the schools and those at the central office in New York City. See his *110 Livingston Street,* 299ff.

34. In 1970, the AFL-CIO created an organizing committee to find out whether school administrators and supervisors would unionize in large numbers. The unit was called the School Administrators and Supervisors Organizing Committee (SASOC). In 1976, with about forty-five locals, SASOC became a regular part of the AFL-CIO, called the American Federation of School Administrators.

35. See Robert D. Helsby, "Just What Is the Role of School Management?" remarks by the chairperson, New York State Public Employment Relations Board (PERB), to the Pennsylvania School Boards Association, Philadelphia, October 24, 1974.

36. Edwin M. Bridges and Bruce S. Cooper, "Collective Bargaining for Adminis-

trators," *Theory Into Practice,* 15 (October 1976), 307; see also Bruce S. Cooper, "Collective Bargaining Comes to School Administrators," *Phi Delta Kappan,* 58 (November 1976), 202-204.

37. Michigan Public Employment Relations Act, Public Acts 336, amended, Section 17.445 (9).

38. See, for example, Washington Laws, 1973, Chapter 115, Section 1, page 792.

39. City of Chicopee School Committee and the Chicopee Federation of Teachers, Local 2416, AFT, AFL-CIO, Case No. MCR-1228, November 18, 1974, page 4.

40. The "New Jersey Employer-Employee Relations Act" (1968), Chapter 303, Section C.34: 13A-3(d), was amended in 1974 to give the assistant superintendents who were not eligible union membership. The amendment appears in the Laws of 1974, Chapter 123, Section C.34: 13A-S.3(f).

41. Agreement between the Cleveland Board of Education and the Cleveland Council of Administrators and Supervisors (1974), page 4. For a discussion of the problems of unionization in a state without public employment relations legislation, see an analysis of Illinois by Michael J. Bakalis, "Collective Negotiations in the Absence of Legislation," *Compact,* 12 (June 1972), 18ff.

42. I make an argument for a national law supporting administrative bargaining as part of a labor relations act for the public sector. The reasoning rests on current state-local practices, legislation, adjudication, and the likely disruption should federal law reverse the right to bargain enjoyed in 1,277 school systems in twenty-four states and the District of Columbia. See Bruce S. Cooper, "Federal Action and Bargaining for Public Supervisors: Basis for an Argument," *Public Personnel Management,* 6 (September-October 1977), 341-353.

43. Constitution of the Philadelphia Association of School Administrators, Article V, Section 2.B.

44. Since the Illinois school code does not recognize assistant principals and central office supervisors as separate job classifications, they technically are ineligible to be represented by the Chicago Principals' Association. But the Association has a set of auxiliaries for them and hopes to obtain full membership for them.

45. See John Rogers Commons, *Legal Foundations of Capitalism* (Madison: University of Wisconsin Press, 1957), for a discussion of how the union-management relationship not only resolves conflict but also provides a kind of "parliamentary government" for the organization. Bargaining resembles the legislative process, settling disputes through arbitration and appeal is like the judicial process, and carrying out the contract by both management and labor is the executive process (pp. 266ff.)

46. See Shils and Whittier, *Teachers, Administrators, and Collective Bargaining,* 22-23, for a description of teacher union history.

47. *OCAPA Gets It All Together* (Columbus: Ohio Association of Administrative Personnel Associations, n.d.), 2.

48. Hawaii has full-state funding since the entire state is a single school district. Recently the teachers negotiated a full-state contract. See Joan Lee Husted, "Winning a Statewide Contract," *Compact,* 15 (June 1972), 34. Also, Senator John F. Dunlap, chairman of California's Senate Committee on Education, believes that state-wide bargaining of teachers' and administrators' salaries is an excellent means for equalizing ependitures per pupil among California's 1,042 school districts. See John F. Dunlap, "California's Chicken-or-Egg Questions: Statewide Union of Statewide Bargaining First?" *Phi Delta Kappan,* 59 (March 1978), 458-461.

Chapter Fourteen

K. George Pedersen

Principalship in an Economic Context

Throughout this volume, one observation emerges consistently: important social and cultural changes have altered the role of educational administrator considerably in the past decade, whether at the university, college, school system, or individual school level.[1] Certainly the era when the authoritarian type of administrative head governed a particular organizational fiefdom without great concern for others has passed. Competent administrators of today must not only be concerned about the many publics that their institution serves; they must also increasingly consider the quality and quantity of resources available to their organization and how they can make maximum use of those resources.

Underlying the multiplicity of current demands by the clients of school systems is the plea for greater responsiveness on the part of educational institutions — or, to employ the jargon of the day, for greater "relevance." This call is subsumed under a variety of terms, but most often it appears today within the rhetoric of so-called "accountability,"[2] a term that has come to have a variety of meanings. What is implicit, however, regardless of the term used or its meaning, is a pronounced dissatisfaction with present educational policies and practices. Many people have expressed their unwillingness to leave the generation and implementation of educational policy in the hands of elected boards and school administrators. Demands for greater involvement in educational decision making grow from the belief that appropriate levels of productivity are not being realized in the public schools. Not only do schools appear ineffective in terms of the degree to which their goals are being attained, but they also seem unable to maintain a reasonable balance between resources allocated to education and the overall growth of the educational product. In blunter terms, it is the view of critics of the present educational system in the United States that resources, both human and other, are presently being inappropriately deployed and that better allocation of those resources would result in overall improvement.

That is the challenge for educational administrators, and they must be prepared to accept it for they have the responsibility for distributing scarce resources within the educational sector. They must respond to public concern over rising costs in education and competing demands for resources in other areas within the public sector. If they are to meet the challenge, they must face it with an understanding and confidence that require some familiarity with the economics of education. That awareness is, quite simply, the purpose of this chapter.

THE CASE FOR ECONOMICS

It is important at the outset to realize that schools are highly complex social systems that make extreme demands on administrative personnel.[3] Consider background preparation as a single example. An intense interest in the improvement of the qualitative dimension of life, combined with an associated decline in the recognition of material well-being as a major goal, demonstrates a need to appoint administrator-philosophers. Similarly, an increased concern for the values of people and the concomitant pressure for individualization argue for the appointment of administrator-psychologists. The need to understand the role of the school and its relationship to the broader society, along with skills in organizational analysis and social change, point toward the appointment of administrator-sociologists. The same argument can be made for the appointment of an administrator-behavioral scientist or an administrator-social scientist. It is in this same context that an awareness of the contribution of the economist is important.

Educational administrators, particularly those that function at the middle management level, are frequently loath to acknowledge inadequacy in what they consider to be the "dismal science." This attitude is somewhat surprising in view of what are frequently defined as the tasks of an administrator. While there is considerable disagreement about the definition of administrative functions, there appears to be a consensus that they include the mobilization of resources, the efficient use of scarce inputs, and maximum rationality in the making of decisions. And this is what the field of economics is all about. The reluctance of principals to accord economics its due stems from at least two sources. First of all, in many school systems there is limited decentralization of the fiscal decision-making process. Most important, budgetary and related planning decisions are made in the superintendent's office, and, as a consequence, principals have little opportunity to become involved in this dimension of administration. Then, there is a failure on the part of principals to recognize that they increasingly have opportunities to influence the allocation of resources.

For many years the responsibility for preparing, defending, and instituting a school system budget has rested almost exclusively within the superintendent's office. Until recently the nature of this process could best be described as incremental; a fixed percentage added for personnel salary increases, an additional sum for new faculty and staff, an allowance for increases in fixed costs, and so forth within each of the categories of the traditional line-item budget. Under this procedure, historical precedent was the basis for projecting future economic needs, and little or no thought was given to pursuing alternative means for achieving similar ends, let alone to searching for different ends. Such strategies as differentiated staffing, alternate instructional procedures, new types of facilities, and the employment of various technologies were most often ignored, and, consequently, the job of preparing a budget could be handled in a straightforward manner by a relatively small number of staff members in the central office.

It now appears that the modus operandi described above must be modified. Actually, some changes have already been made in more progressive school systems where program budgeting has been instituted.[4] In such systems professional personnel at all levels in the organizational hierarchy have become involved in fiscal planning because the individual school and its clients are considered unique and, therefore, important decisions concerning the allocation of resources must be made at that level within the organization. It is this fiscal view that is implicit in Alfred North Whitehead's statement when he emphasizes that "the first requisite for educational reform is the school as a unit, with its approved curriculum based on its own needs, and evolved by its own staff. If we fail to secure that, we simply fall from one formalism to another, from one dung-hill of inert ideas into another."[5]

Increasingly, senior administrative officials in local systems of education have concluded that greater fiscal and related authority will have to be delegated to school principals if the concept of accountability is to be at all meaningful.[6] The types of roles within the particular school, the incumbents in those roles, the substance of the program offering, and the equipment and supplies required — all constitute areas in which principals will need greater autonomy if fiscal decision making is to have any meaning at the level of the individual school. Much of the responsibility for budgetary decisions must also be shifted. After all, the budget is the operational definition of the aggregate values of a school system,[7] and, as such, it should genuinely reflect in fiscal terms the perceived needs of each of its member schools.

While a review of existing policies in some of the larger urban centers indicates a gradual movement toward more fiscal autonomy for building administrators, there are still important constraints. Teacher union agreements, parental interests and desires, and central office policies and directives are but a few of the factors that serve to limit a principal's discretion. Many principals, it must also be acknowledged, have failed to recognize or exercise their potential for influencing the allocation of resources within their respective schools; some even appear reluctant to exercise their authority in certain areas where they clearly have discretion.

The reasons for lack of initiative in the sphere of the principalship are probably many. A few possibilities are suggested here. In some cases there are principals who simply prefer that difficult decisions, such as those related to allocation, be made by someone else. Then there is a relatively common malaise in organizational behavior where individuals concerned have not been adequately prepared to make decisions of such importance. A related form of noninvolvement concerns those principals who find it difficult to overcome central office resistance to principal involvement in the budgetary process. Obviously budgetary authority carries considerable weight, and it requires a secure and confident superintendent to delegate such responsibility to principals. Then there is another group of administrators who, although aware of new approaches and techniques offered by the discipline of economics, are unable to move toward implementation because they lack sufficient time, appropriate support services, and adequate overall resources. Many of the approaches suggested by economists require a relatively sophisticated information system and strong institutional research competence. Finally, a relatively large group of principals remain unaware of possible planning alternatives proposed by economists. The remainder of this chapter is directed toward them.

SOME BACKGROUND

At no time in history has there been greater interest and concern about public education. One reason for this revival of attention is the dramatic rise in the cost of providing it, and another is an increased awareness of the benefits related to acquiring it. Since both concomitants are of direct concern to administrators, they are discussed further here.

The matter of rising costs requires limited elaboration, but it is this factor more than probably any other that is causing the public to question educational productivity. As an illustration of the cost growth factor, during the period from 1969-70 to 1970-71, the total amount expended for the operation of the American public elementary and secondary schools increased by $3.2 billion or 9.7 percent, to a record high of $35.9 billion. The increase in total expenditures, capital outlay, and interest in the same period was 8.4 percent, resulting in an overall figure of $42.4 billion.[8] Expenditures per pupil continued to increase, reaching $839 per pupil in average daily attendance in 1970-71, which was an increase of 113.5 percent over the decade and 9.5 percent beyond even the previous year. In addition to concern about increased expenditure, recent legal decisions have invalidated present systems of local-state financing. There is growing awareness that the state with the highest expenditure for education in the United States spends nearly three times more than the state with the lowest expenditure. Similar, but in many cases greater, discrepancies exist within states. This is particularly evident when rural-urban comparisons are made. Expenditures for education do affect the quality of education and the equality of educational opportunity available to each student.

So-called "equality of educational opportunity," which has been defined in a variety of ways,[9] is inherent in the cultural ethos of this country. Few people would argue that this is not a worthwhile objective of social policy, yet it is not the only goal that parents have for their children. This poses a dilemma that is articulated well by James Coleman:

The history of education since the industrial revolution shows a continual struggle between two forces; the desire of members of the society to have educational opportunity for all children, and the desire of each family to provide the best education it can afford for its children. Neither of these desires is to be despised; they both lead to invest-

ment by the older generation in the younger. But they can lead to quite different concrete actions.[10]

In essence, the American educational system attempts to respond to
both desires and many of its critics would argue that it fails to respond
adequately to either. Educational administrators, especially superintendents and principals, often find themselves in conflict with particular segments of their constituencies over conflicting purposes. Presumably the equity issue can be interpreted broadly to mean that the
public school system should provide the means whereby all children
can move into adult society as fully participating members, regardless
of such fortuitous factors as social origin and geographic location. Increasingly parents have become aware of the extensive benefits, both
private and social, that accrue as a result of better educational preparation. Despite concern for equity, however, several recent studies
have documented that important inequities continue to exist with
regard to the provision of educational services throughout this country. As David Kirp has dramatically emphasized:

Extensive sociological surveys of public schools reveal a disturbingly consistent pattern; poor children go to the most outmoded schools with the least motivated class-
mates; they use the shabbiest facilities and are taught by the least able teachers; they
do the worst and may be looked upon by the system as incapable of doing better.[11]

Having described two socioeconomic problems as they relate to public education, let us now consider the role that economists have
assumed to date. For more than a decade and a half, economists have
shown a marked interest in trying to establish the role of education in
relation to economic development. The very earliest of these studies
attempted to determine the relationship between educational attainment and income, and from these initial studies came the concept that
expenditures for education could be regarded, at least partially, as investment. This, in turn, led to the premise that more elaborate measures of investment, such as the "rate of return" provided for given
levels of schooling, could be used as the basis for important policy
decisions concerning further expenditures on education by local,
state, and federal governments.[12]

At the same time as this "investment in humans" approach was
gaining stature, another group of economists approached the problem
of economic growth by using the so-called "manpower requirements"
model. Under this approach it becomes necessary to predict the number of persons with differing levels of educational preparation that

would be required if particular economic goals were to be realized. This attempt at planning has been undertaken on a number of occasions at the national level, most frequently in developing countries. In recent years the models employed, which have become increasingly sophisticated and more highly quantitative, have enjoyed a certain modest success. As with the human capital approach, however, much more experience and analysis appears warranted before such economic models can satisfy the needs of government planners and policy makers as they attempt to predict needed flows of educational resources.

It is of interest to note that, while economists have had receptive audiences for their human-capital investment and manpower-planning theories, they have had limited influence on resource allocation in the field of public education. There is general agreement that, as a result of the evidence provided by economists to the effect that education is of importance to development, a greater flow of resources has been directed toward educational systems. But, as Charles Benson[13] rightfully points out, these additional funds continue to be distributed in the same traditional ways and with roughly the same evidence of productivity. Stated in another way, economists have made only a modest impact on the "production function"[14] of education. They have failed to convince educational decision makers that they should be more concerned with outputs than with inputs, that there are a number of quite legitimate quantitative measures of productivity that can be employed to measure educational growth, and that expenditures for education should always be considered in terms of alternatives, that is, in terms of what economists call "opportunity costs." Opportunity costs are those things that are given up as a result of making a particular choice,[15] a dimension of costing normally neglected by those responsible for educational budgeting and planning.

A BRIEF LOOK AT RESEARCH

Research evidence concerning the relationship of resource inputs to educational productivity is still in its initial stages. Until now, much of the effort has been directed toward levels and differences in fiscal support, a focus influenced largely by the argument that "more dollars buy more education."[16] Of late, this position has been challenged. More recent research suggests that, within some realistic ranges, variations in expenditure per pupil are at most only marginally related to differences in performance levels of students.

In one of the earliest studies dealing with the effects of resource input levels and allocation patterns, Alan Thomas provided the basis for much of his later scholarly endeavor.[17] By using differences in mean levels of achievement among a sample of high schools in the United States, he was able to conclude that the socioeconomic level of the community and the quality of teachers employed are important determinants of educational productivity. Another important finding of his suggests that the manner in which resources are allocated is more important than the level of expenditures. In Thomas' opinion, input-output studies can contribute in important ways to greater efficiency in the conduct of schools and school systems.

Jesse Burkhead and his associates,[18] in another important input-output study of high schools in Chicago and Atlanta, discerned a limited relationship between resources expended on education and student performance levels. A major finding of this research included the identification of family income as the major single determinant of high levels of educational performance. As has been pointed by innumerable social scientists, income actually serves as a proxy for a variety of familial and related characteristics. The high degree of correlation between income, educational level of parents, home environment, and educational aspiration for children makes it difficult to isolate the single important determinant.[19] Burkhead's research, later corroborated by Coleman[20] and others, shows the initial salary for teachers and the quality of teachers to be positive predictors of achievement.

Focusing now more on the fiscal aspect of the operation of schools, the work of both Burkhead and Coleman provides little support for the concept that differences in expenditure are closely correlated with student achievement levels. It is this finding that has been the focus of much academic debate and challenge.[21] Results derived do, however, raise serious doubts about the appropriateness of concentrating massive fiscal resources on programs for particular segments of the population. Rather, the research evidence points to the critical need to develop teaching talent of a high caliber, both in pre- and in-service programs.[22]

The issue of intradistrict differences in resources allocated to the various schools in a particular district has also received a certain amount of attention from researchers. The volume of research findings on this topic would undoubtedly be considerably greater were it not for the paucity of available data. Only recently, for example, have large-city systems made public such information as test results and expenditures per pupil. Previously administrators have argued that such data would be used only to make unfortunate school-by-school comparisons.

The first major study of this type was conducted by Patricia Sexton[23] in the city of Detroit well over a decade ago. Despite difficulties in obtaining data, she was able to demonstrate a positive correlation between level of expenditure and social status of the students attending a particular school. In many ways Sexton's study was the forerunner of similar studies conducted later in other settings. The results generally show that students from lower-class backgrounds attend schools where the facilities are below the district norm, where classes are larger and directed by less-qualified and more inexperienced teachers, and where support services of all kinds are less extensive. Her findings with respect to income and status have been confirmed on a number of occasions to establish both characteristics as important predictors of per-pupil expenditures by school.[24] Resources expended per student vary directly with median family income, with the assessed value of property, and with educational level in the adult population. In the case of race, it is no surprise to learn that it tends to be negatively related to expenditure level—the greater the proportion of nonwhite students, the lower expenditure per pupil.[25]

The extent to which resource disparity levels between districts are important has also been the subject of scholarly interest. As might be expected, the majority of these comparisons have been made between urban centers and their adjacent suburban rings.[26] Equally unsurprising, the differences identified tend to reflect the population shifts and related demographic and economic changes that began shortly after the Second World War.

With the movement of people to the suburbs occurring selectively according to middle- and upper-social-class status and with a similar exodus of many commercial and industrial enterprises, central cities of the United States are faced with two difficult problems. On the human side, disproportionate numbers of atypical and otherwise disadvantaged children remain in core areas, and, if their needs are to be met in meaningful ways, educational program costs will be higher.[27] From the fiscal perspective, with the exodus of many commercial interests the tax base for the support of educational services has eroded in recent years. In addition, central cities are plagued by so-called "municipal overburden," in that they must provide a greater number of governmental services, many of which are not needed in the suburbs but do benefit suburbanites who earn their livelihood in core areas. Redress in the form of state and federal intergovernmental transfers assists to some extent, but the economics of financing education in the larger cities in this country requires more attention.

Much research effort has been expended in attempting to explain district-to-district allocation disparities. Although there is nothing approaching consensus, certain tentative generalizations can be suggested. One of the more obvious causes of such differences in many states is the state-aid formula itself. Historically, many of these formulas were developed to equalize, at least in part, differences in fiscal ability between the wealthier cities and the poorer rural regions. In most states, fiscal capacities have changed quite markedly in recent years, but the method of state subvention has not. Consequently, rural areas tend to fare better than cities, and the same general pattern holds for suburban communities in relation to their urban neighbors.

The importance of median family income is also evident in attempting to explain interdistrict support levels. Both Jerry Miner and Thomas Dye,[28] in important studies, found that much of the variation in expenditure per pupil can be accounted for by income per capita. Somewhat surprisingly, the majority of the significant variables in accounting for differences between districts of expenditures for education are socioeconomic in nature. One might have suspected that political school system correlates would have assumed a much greater role in explaining such differences. As one example of this, Thomas James and his colleagues,[29] in their extensive national study of the determinants of expenditure, found such variables as level of educational achievement of adults, property values, median income, and race to be significant. Further studies have identified significant variables related to school district spending discrepancies to include the ratio of the population enrolled in the public school system and the extent of homeownership. To summarize, it appears that school systems characterized as serving an area where socioeconomic status is higher receive a larger allocation of resources, and that is what recent court decisions were meant to correct.

It must be evident by now that there is a scarcity of research into the financing and the economics of education. This lack of adequate information about the vast and complex fiscal arrangements that exist under the present federalist system makes reform difficult. It should be noted, however, that some important research has been completed and serves as the basis for continued and expanded inquiry. It is in the environment of the particular school that the research evidence is particularly meager. Little has been done to assist principals and their professional colleagues when they are making important decisions related to allocation of resources, perhaps because most have not had to make these decisions in the past. There are, however, some possible courses of action.

THE NEED FOR PLANNING

Until recent times there has, as was mentioned previously, been almost complete agreement among educators that greater fiscal resources would make it possible to respond to the majority of ills exhibited by public education. Recent research evidence, based in part on relatively dramatic infusion of funds into education as a result of the Elementary and Secondary Education Act and similar legislation, has severely challenged this long-held belief and, in the minds of many, relegated it to the status of educational mythology. This denial, coupled with increased competition for public dollars from other forms of social services, make it imperative that educational administrators seek and adopt more rational procedures for allocating scarce resources. Merely carrying on in the traditional manner is no longer adequate to the task. This would indicate that the planning function must receive more consideration than it has in the past.

Educational administrators have traditionally been required to plan for only a single-year period, even though many superintendents and principals are aware of the inadequacies of interim planning. For a variety of reasons, many of them beyond the immediate control of school administrators, they have been unable to extend the limited period of their planning function unless it was related to two activities: acquisition of school sites and the development of necessary facilities required to house students.

One of the major weaknesses of planning for such a limited time is that many decisions made by boards of education and administrators have serious long-term implications that continue to be ignored. For example, the decision to introduce a foreign-language program at the primary level, assuming that such an offering is to be extended progressively, has fiscal implications far beyond those related to the initial program. This is true of any program innovations that are incremental in nature. It is most important that educational decision makers recognize the critical need to extend the time frame of their planning activities.

The need for information is also critical if there is to be competent planning. In far too many cases, important decisions are made on the basis of affective considerations rather than upon sound analysis of the data. What is being demanded in school systems today is that the decision process become more formalized and provide for the acquisition and analysis of relevant information. A number of interested scholars have suggested that a systems approach to the administration of our schools be adopted.[30] Among other benefits to be gained from such an approach to problem solving would be a much more formal consideration of the planning function. Purposes and goals would have to be made more explicit, possible alternative strategies for solution would have to be identified and compared, programs responsive to the needs of the organization would have to be developed, required resources of all kinds would have to be acquired and allocated, and a sound program of evaluation would have to be employed following implementation. The results of the program would then be considered in light of the goals, and, if the program were considered satisfactory, the systems cycle would presumably be repeated with any appropriate modifications. Careful consideration of the various stages of this proposed planning process should make clear the need for a well-developed information system.[31] The satisfaction of each of these planning components is highly dependent on feedback from other elements within the systems cycle.

Such an approach appears to have much to commend it to practicing principals, but it should be noted that careful planning has important costs attached to it in terms of administrative and faculty time. Sound, worthwhile programs cannot be conceived in haste. In a complex operation such as education, even the definition of purpose and goals to be achieved is a most demanding assignment. Furthermore, the competent decision maker does not operate in isolation, but, rather, seeks expert opinions from a variety of sources. In the present-day urban school system there should be a division of institutional research and planning with a professional staff that assists principals in attempting to answer some of the difficult questions that confront them and their faculties. Electronic computers and related hardware should also be available to shorten laborious analysis. Identifying the important questions to be asked and deciding what information is needed to answer them remain the responsibility of the principal. Take as an example the issue of student follow-up (How successful is the "product" of education at the next stage of his or her career?). Careful conceptualization and consideration are required in order for such a problem to be resolved meaningfully, and questions of this magnitude must be posed if appropriate changes are to occur in the field of education.

Even if competent research support is not available within the school system, this need not provide the rationale for inaction. As a limited number of principals have already discovered, each school has within its files and its faculty information that can be profitably employed in the decision-making process. It is failure to formalize the planning function that frequently prevents the use of such data. Two of the more common problems in high schools, for example, are attrition and disruptive classroom behavior. Both problems are important, not only to the school but also to the broader community. Much of the data needed to understand these two problems is available within the school itself or within the attendance area. In order for the school to respond to the problems, a complete understanding of them is necessary, and this requires time and diligent analysis of the data collected.

Often principals need to be reminded that they already have access to much of the information they need in order to make sound decisions. Frequently such administrators are so pressured by day-to-day operational problems that the time needed to resolve more important problems is unavailable. Quite possibly some system of priorities needs to be determined, along with certain organizational changes within the school, so that the principal can direct attention toward gaining an adequate data base from which to make better-quality decisions. Characteristics of students, home backgrounds of students, student success, teacher characteristics, and important fiscal data are but a few examples of the kind of information needed.

One of the central tasks of management in any formal organization is planning, and it must be done with care and intelligence if it is to be successful. There is considerable evidence that educational planning has not been done carefully enough in the past and that important changes need to be made in this regard. In any particular school, planning and organization are the responsibility of the principal, and principals must treat these two dimensions of their work with utmost seriousness, for planning and organization are critical to the success of both the principal and the school. Intuitive procedures for planning must be replaced by more rational ones.

ECONOMIC APPROACHES TO DECISION MAKING

In considering economic decision-making models that apply to the field of education, two caveats need to be considered. The first concerns the appropriateness of the models. No reputable economist would attempt to argue that the findings and techniques of economics should be considered at the expense of other relevant fields of knowledge. What *is* being suggested is that economic thought has a contribution to make in the area of educational decision making and that this expertise should be part of the background of those responsible for making such decisions. In no sense can one argue, either, that economic criteria should become the sole basis upon which all educational planning should take place—quite the contrary, in fact. Coombs has appropriately described the situation:

> The world of education, as we see it, has become so complex and is in so serious a state that no one vocabulary—including that of pedagogy—can describe the whole of it. Hence we need languages and ideas from many intellectual disciplines and spheres of action to widen our view of the educational process to see the whole ever more clearly, and thus accomplish more and benefit more.[32]

The second caveat requiring emphasis is that the application of economic thought to the field of education has just begun. While the contribution of education has long been acknowledged,[33] only in the past two decades have economists become sufficiently interested in education to apply their techniques, and not until the last decade have the tools of economics been systematically and rigorously employed — and then predominantly at the national level. Relatively little effort has been expended to determine the relevance of the economist's tools in state and local systems of education. A review of the current literature suggests, however, that gradual but important changes are now occurring and that variants of the strategies of economics will continue to gain importance in educational decision making.

Reference was made earlier to input-output models and their application for the educational process. This type of analysis attempts to relate input data from an adequate sample of schools to some agreed upon measure of educational output for those institutions. In this way the relative importance of the various resources devoted to the educational process can be determined. Multivariate analysis, and predominantly the multiple regression technique, is utilized in order to derive the value of each of the various input coefficients, in concert with all other input variables being considered. The results may be derived for samples of schools of various types and sizes, for schools with student bodies of differing socioeconomic backgrounds, and for schools in differing regions of the country. [34]

This form of economic model helps the educational decision maker allocate his resources on a more rational basis. As Thomas[35] points out, a prime task of any administrator is to allocate resources over which he has control in such a way that maximum output will be derived. It should be particularly noted that, in the case of school principals, the most valuable input for which they are responsible is time — their own, their teachers', and their students'. By considering the results of input-output analyses derived for a variety of populations under differing conditions and from various regions, a principal can gain new insights into the most effective combination of inputs needed to achieve the goals appropriate to a specific institution. This should bring the institution closer to being a productive system.

Cost-benefit analysis is another measurement technique that allows comparisons between the total costs of a particular program and the total benefits derived as a result of its implementation through attempts to estimate returns on investment based on the quantification of total inputs and outputs in monetary terms. It has been used until now primarily to identify and evaluate national educational priorities and policies, but almost exclusively from the perspective of economic efficiency.

The two commonly derived objectives of the cost-benefit model are the current value of the benefits derived, less their present value costs, and the internal rate of return to investment. For example, using the latter as the desirable measure, Thomas Ribich[36] cites evidence to show that the return-on-investment from college or university graduation is in excess of 10 percent, including earnings foregone while in school as part of the investment. He goes on to suggest that returns may be as high as 50 percent for increments of education at lower levels. Economists, using this form of analysis, argue that such results should be considered in looking at alternatives in the allocation of resources. By using this method it is possible, for example, to make comparisons between education and other forms of investment within society; between various levels of education; and between vocational, general, and on-the-job forms of educational preparation.[37] The chances that it will be used at the local level appear brighter. For one thing, the use of cost-benefit analysis is valuable to teachers and administrators trying to make decisions concerning their own further education or the school system in which they might want to seek employment.[38] School systems could use the technique in trying to provide a more rational basis for salary differences and for the reward structure intended to improve teacher qualifications.[39]

Thomas[40] suggests that caution should be exercised when using the cost-benefit approach. He indicates, for example, that the benefits of education are not restricted totally to investment but that there is a consumptive dimension as well. In other words, individuals seek further education not only for what it will return in the way of future benefits, but also because they enjoy the education which they receive. In this sense, the benefits to education as investment are actually underestimated. Thomas states further, however, that if it can be assumed that the increased earnings associated with higher levels of education are really a reflection of greater innate ability, better motivation, or higher socioeconomic status, then the returns to education are overstated. Failure to recognize this aspect could lead to decisions that result in under- or overinvestment.

A variation of cost-benefit analysis, known as the cost-effectiveness approach, is somewhat modified in terms of economic orientation. While the cost-benefit model requires that both dimensions be in monetary terms, the cost-effectiveness model is more concerned with alternative fiscal allocations in the achievement of certain specific goals, and the latter need not be in monetary terms. For example, an educational administrator may wish to compare the instructional effectiveness of a teacher with a teaching machine in having students achieve a specific level of competence in a foreign language during a given time period. Assuming that both the teacher and the machine could do it equally well in the same period of time, the decision as to use presumably would be made on the basis of cost. It should be apparent that, for many educational purposes, the cost-effectiveness approach has a wider variety of applications than the cost-benefit model.

Essentially what is required in using the cost-effectiveness model is a clear specification of what is to be achieved, an understanding of what the alternatives are and what they cost, and a measure of how effective the alternatives are in attaining the goals sought. Once these data are available, a choice among alternatives can be made on the combined basis of cost and effectiveness. Of course, it is critical to have a variety of alternatives to consider under such an approach, and to continue to search for viable alternatives.

Let me briefly mention a special form of cost-effectiveness analysis known as linear programming. This is a mathematical technique that can be applied to a wide range of problems in an effort to arrive at optimal solutions. Essentially what is required is that the objective or objectives to be optimized be stated in terms of minimum levels of achievement and that all conditions or constraints under which the model must operate be set forth in proficiency terms, that is, the extent to which each condition can be expected to contribute to optimization. As an example, to return to the earlier problem of teaching a foreign language to children by means of a teacher or a teaching machine, it is quite possible that it is a combination of the two techniques that is optimal in terms of cost and effectiveness. A linear-programming model could provide an educational decision maker with this kind of information, while at the same time it identifies the most effective allocation of teacher and machine time for instructional purposes. Efforts to employ linear programming to date have been rather limited and restricted to larger studies with a national perspective.[41]

In addition to the models already described, there are other techniques that have been developed from what was originally termed operations analysis and that assist with the decision process. In general, these are designed to enhance the planning, control, and decision-making skills of administrators who find themselves responsible for organizations characterized by much in the way of change. Two of the better-known of these techniques are the Program Evaluation and Review Technique (PERT)[42] and Critical Path Management (CPM).[43] Both are network-modeling approaches designed to evaluate and review progress toward a particular stated goal. This is done by disaggregating a problem or project into a network of paths of sequential events that lead eventually to the culmination of a particular project.

Business and industry make considerably greater use of the development of systems theory than can be described here. To a considerable extent, advances have resulted from military and aerospace demands. Other planning strategies that have been developed are probability theory, decision theory, queuing theory, game theory, information theory, symbolic logic, and Monte Carlo techniques.[44] Undoubtedly educational decision makers will soon have a broader choice of techniques drawn from economics and related fields. Not all will be equally appropriate or helpful, but the work of economists will continue to have relevance for education, just as it does for business and industry.

THE BUDGET

As more authority is delegated to those at the local school level by central office administrators, greater fiscal responsibility must logically be assumed by the principal. The burden of responsibility falls naturally upon the building administrator and the members of the faculty to seek alternative means to satisfy local needs and carries with it the need for accountability. If decentralization in the allocation of resources is to succeed, it is imperative that principals understand the budgetary process and the value of the budget as a tool for planning, evaluation, and control. Better budgeting practices are needed. What normally transpires in this area of school operations fails to satisfy the three functions just described. A typical budget document for a school or school system usually satisfied only one of the functions, namely, that of control. Planning and evaluation are ignored or receive only minimal attention.

As Thomas[45] has astutely observed, the budget document can be reviewed from a variety of different perspectives, each of which contributes different but additional information to the decision-making process. The three dimensions that Thomas identifies are:

Economic — concerns the establishment of priorities and the allocation of resources in such a way as to maximize the attainment of organizational goals;

Technical — emphasizes the most appropriate procedures needed in order to optimize the teaching-learning process; and

Political — focuses on the need to mediate conflicting demands for resources and to generate adequate support for programs.

Thomas then goes on to suggest that most administrative decisions made in school systems involve more than one of these three dimensions. To use his example concerning the introduction of team teaching, such a decision has economic implications in that the costs would need to be compared with those in other forms of organization. The technical consideration requires that the educational efficacy of such an innovation be weighed. And the political aspect demands that adequate support from teachers, students, and the general public be mobilized in order to make such a change possible. All three perspectives, in the hands of a competent administrator, become operationalized in the budget document.

The educational budget is the means by which anticipated receipts and expenditures are categorized in a meaningful way in order to assist with control, evaluation, and planning. It represents the operational definition of the organization's values, for it explicates the pattern in which it is believed that the school's or school system's limited resources should be allocated. Unfortunately, in the typical educational organization, the extent to which rationality is the organizing principle behind the budgetary process is markedly limited.

Most school system budgets today are of the line-item type, and they are normally organized according to function, object, or organizational unit. For example, allocations may be made for instruction, administration, supplies and equipment, or transportation. Rarely, if ever, are these appropriations categories reconsidered at the time a new budget is prepared, and the budgeting process itself is normally an incremental one. That is to say, last year's budget is used as the basis for projecting the needs of the following year, with appropriate adjustments made to satisfy those areas that require additional funds.

Such a budget has extremely limited value when making decisions. Obviously, for example, by aggregating costs according to function across the various programs offered by a school system, there is no way to related input resources to program objectives. Other than to become aware that a particular category has increased or decreased over some previous period, little can be learned from the traditional form of budget document. Besides lacking any sort of performance measures, conventional budgets discourage the search for alternative means to achieve the organization's goals. In short, they conceal more information than they reveal. The alternative to consider is the program or performance budget, known better perhaps today as the Planning-Programming-Budgeting System (PPBS).[46]

The program budget is an outgrowth of the work of systems analysts. It is an approach to educational decision making that attempts to integrate all the various dimensions of planning and program implementation. In the briefest of terms, it is used to establish priorities among the various educational services that a school or school system may provide; to define the objectives of these various programs in operational terms; to provide for the consideration of alternative means to attain these objectives; to assess, through the use of cost-effectiveness or cost-benefit analyses, the appropriate implementation strategy; and to provide for evaluation according to program or performance. It is evident that this form of budgeting system is heavily dependent on strategies developed by systems analysis experts and on sound information systems. Both requirements fall well within the realm of possibility for modern urban school systems, and there appears to be increasing support among educators for this approach to resource allocation.

The environment within which principals of today find themselves is one of increasing demands. Not only are they faced with the usual expectations to provide educational leadership in their schools, but they increasingly find themselves in the position of having to defend to the public never-ending requests for additional resources to meet ever-growing needs of urban children. Education is also expected to deal with an expanded variety of society's ills. Unemployment and poverty, for example, have recently been redefined as educational problems.

The growing demands for increased productivity in urban school systems deserve an appropriate response. It is clear that traditional patterns of resource allocation have done little to improve the effectiveness of these educational units. In addition to improving their capacity as planners, principals need to become acquainted with at least the more elementary tools of the economist. The various strategies for analysis, the careful consideration of alternatives, and the need for better modes of evaluation — all offer sound potential returns to the principal and the school.

NOTES

1. Luvern L. Cunningham, *Governing Schools: New Approaches to Old Issues* (Columbus, Ohio: Charles E. Merrill Publishing Company, 1971).

2. In some ways this press is reminiscent of an earlier era in American education, as described by Raymond E. Callahan, *Education and the Cult of Efficiency* (Chicago: University of Chicago Press, 1962).

3. Jacob W. Getzels, James M. Lipham, and Roald F. Campbell, *Educational Administration as a Social Process* (New York: Harper and Row, 1968), 79-107.

4. For an enlightening discussion about the need for such reform, see David Rogers, *110 Livingston Street: Politics and Bureaucracy in the New York City School System* (New York: Vintage Books, 1968), 337-343.

5. Alfred North Whitehead, *The Aims of Education and Other Essays* (New York: Mentor Books, 1949), 25.

6. This notion of expanding the budgetary decision-making group, considered almost heretical ten years ago, has begun to appear peripherally in the literature on school administration. See, for example, Luvern L. Cunningham, "Our Accountability Problems," in his *Governing Schools*, 47-62; H. Thomas James, "Financing More Effective Schools," in *The Schools and the Challenge of Innovation*, Supplementary Paper No. 28 (New York: Committee for Economic Development, 1969), 12-27.

7. J. Alan Thomas, "Educational Decision-Making and the School Budget," *Administrator's Notebook,* 12 (December 1963).

8. K. George Pedersen, "Education," in *The Book of the States, 1972-73* (Lexington, Ky.: Council of State Governments, 1972), 302.

9. For a careful consideration of this topic, see C. A. Anderson, "Patterns and Variability in Distribution and Diffusion of Schooling," *Education and Economic Development,* ed. *id.* and Mary Jean Bowman (Chicago: Aldine Publishing Company, 1965), 341-342.

10. James S., Coleman, in the foreword to John E. Coons *et al., Private Wealth and Public Education* (Cambridge, Mass.: Harvard University Press, 1970), vii.

11. David L. Kirp, "The Poor, the Schools, and Equal Protection," *Harvard Educational Review,* 38 (Fall 1968), 644.

12. Much of the credit for the renaissance of this "human capital" approach to studies in the economics of education must be accorded Theodore W. Schultz, *The Economic Value of Education* (New York: Columbia University Press, 1963), and "Capital Formation by Education," *Journal of Political Economy,* 68 (December 1960), 571-583.

13. Charles S. Benson, "The Efficient Allocation of Educational Resources," in *Schools and the Challenge of Innovation,* 59-60.

14. A "production function" is an economic concept concerned with the mathematical relationship between inputs and outputs. It is important to the field of education because it emphasizes the idea of alternative approaches to achieve similar types of ends.

15. Mary Jean Bowman, "The Costing of Human Resource Development," in *The Economics of Education,* ed. E. A. G. Robinson and J. E. Vaizey (New York: St. Martin's Press, 1966), 422.

16. For an enlightening discussion of the effects of this perspective, see Stephen K. Bailey *et al., Schoolmen and Politics: A Study of State Aid to Education in the Northeast* (Syracuse, N.Y.: Syracuse University Press, 1962), 24-25.

17. J. Alan Thomas, "Efficiency in Education: An Empirical Study," *Administrator's Notebook,* 11 (October 1962), and *The Productive School: A Systems Analysis Approach to Educational Administration* (New York: John Wiley and Sons, 1971).

18. Jesse Burkhead, Thomas G. Fox, and John W. Holland, *Input and Output in Large-City High Schools* (Syracuse, N.Y.: Syracuse University Press, 1967).

19. Howard P. Tuckman, "High School Inputs and Their Contribution to School Performance," *Journal of Human Resources,* 6 (Fall 1971), 490-509.

20. James S. Coleman, *Equality of Educational Opportunity* (Washington, D.C.: U.S. Government Printing Office, 1966).

21. Samuel Bowles and Henry M. Levin, "The Determinants of Scholastic Achievement — An Appraisal of Some Recent Evidence, *Journal of Human Resources,* 3 (Winter 1968), 3-24.

22. This proposal is supported by numerous studies of educational productivity. See, for example, William E. Barron, "Measurement of Educational Productivity," in *The Theory and Practice of School Finance,* ed. Warren E. Gauerke and Jack R. Childress (Chicago: Rand McNally and Company, 1967); and Henry M. Levin, "A Cost-Effectiveness Analysis of Teacher Selection," *Journal of Human Resources,* 5 (Winter 1970), 24-33.

23. Patricia May Sexton, *Education and Income* (New York: Viking Press, 1961).

24. H. Thomas James, J. Alan Thomas, and Harold J. Dyck, *Wealth, Expenditures and Decision Making for Education* (Stanford, Calif.: School of Education, Stanford University, 1963); and H. Thomas James, James A. Kelly, and Walter I. Garms, *Determinants of Educational Expenditures in Large Cities of the United States* (Stanford, Calif.: School of Education, Stanford University, 1966).

25. Otto A. Davis, "Quality and Inequality: Some Economic Issues Related to the Choice of Educational Policy," in *The Quality of Inequality: Urban and Suburban Public Schools,* ed. Charles U. Daly (Chicago: University of Chicago Center for Policy Study, 1968), 89-110.

26. David C. Ranney, "The Determinants of Fiscal Support for Large City Educational Systems," *Administrator's Notebook,* 15 (December 1966).

27. For an interesting attempt to relate need and selected socioeconomic characteristics to financing, see Walter I. Garms and Mark C. Smith, "Educational Need and Its Application to State School Finance," *Journal of Human Resources,* 5 (Summer 1970), 304-317.

28. Jerry Miner, *Social and Economic Factors in Spending for Public Education* (Syracuse, N.Y.: Syracuse University Press, 1963); Thomas Dye, "Politics, Economics, and Educational Outcomes in the States," *Educational Administration Quarterly,* 3 (Winter 1967), 28-48.

29. James *et al., Determinants of Educational Expenditures,* 95-134.

30. Thomas, *Productive School.*

31. Benson, "Efficient Allocation of Educational Resources," 61-65.

32. Philip H. Coombs, *The World Educational Crisis: A Systems Analysis* (London: Oxford University Press, 1968), v.

33. In many respects, for example, the renaissance of interest in human capital formation is a rediscovery of ideas developed by Adam Smith, often regarded as the founding father of modern economics.

34. It should be carefully noted that the perceived functions of the public schools vary considerably by region. See, for example, Lawrence W. Downey, *The Task of Public Education* (Chicago: Midwest Administration Center, University of Chicago, 1959).

35. Thomas, *Productive School,* 80.

36. Thomas I. Ribich, *Education and Poverty* (Washington, D.C.: Brookings Institution, 1968), 9.

37. Two examples of this type of study are Walter I. Garms, "A Benefit-Cost Analysis of the Upward Bound Program," *Journal of Human Resources,* 6 (Spring 1971), 206-220; Ronald W. Conley, "A Benefit-Cost Analysis of the Vocational Rehabilitation Program," *ibid.,* 4 (Spring 1969), 226-252.

38. K. George Pedersen, *The Itinerant Schoolmaster: A Socioeconomic Analysis of Teacher Turnover* (Chicago: Midwest Administration Center, University of Chicago, 1973).

39. Valerien Harvey, "Economic Aspects of Teachers' Salaries," unpub. diss., University of Chicago, 1967.

40. Thomas, *Productive School,* 88.

41. Mary Jean Bowman, "The Human Investment Revolution in Economic Thought," *Sociology of Education,* 39 (Spring 1966), 134-136; Samuel Bowles, "A

Linear Programming Model of the Educational Sector," in *Economics of Education 2,* ed. Mark Blaug (Middlesex, Eng.: Penguin Books, 1969), 168-201.

42. Desmond L. Cook, *PERT: Applications in Education,* Cooperative Research Monograph No. 17 (Washington, D.C.: U.S. Government Printing Office, 1966).

43. Peter P. Schoderbek, ed., *Management Systems* (New York: John Wiley and Sons, 1967).

44. For details, see Claude McMillan and Richard D. Gonzalez, *Systems Analysis: A Computer Approach to Decision Models* (Homewood, Ill.: Richard D. Irwin, 1965).

45. Thomas, "Educational Decision Making."

46. A careful consideration of this form of fiscal planning has been prepared by Harry J. Hartley, *Educational Planning-Programming-Budgeting: A Systems Approach* (Englewood Cliffs, N.J.: Prentice-Hall, 1968).

Chapter Fifteen

Joan D. Meskin

Women as Principals:
Their Performance as Educational Administrators

THE STATISTICAL PICTURE

There is a notable underrepresentation of women in elementary and secondary educational administration, and it shows only minimal signs of abating.[1] According to the *25th Biennial Salary Survey of Public School Professional Personnel* undertaken by the National Education Association (NEA) in 1970-71, 67.2 percent of the teaching positions in the United States were filled by women, but only 15.3 percent of the principalships. Of these, women held 21 percent of the elementary, 3.5 percent of the junior high school, and 3 percent of the high school principals' positions. In addition, women comprised only 15 percent of the corps of assistant principals that year.[2] Data from the *26th Biennial Salary Survey* show us that, in 1972-73, the percentage of women in teaching had diminished slightly, to 66.4 percent, but that the percentage of women principals had shrunk to a greater extent — from 15.3 percent to 13.5 percent of the total group. Women, according to the later statistics, now represented 19.6 percent of the total group of elementary principals, 2.9 percent of the junior high school principals, and 1.4 percent of all high school principals. The percentage of women serving as assistant principals likewise decreased over the two-year period — from 15.0 percent to 12.5 percent of those holding the position.[3]

The NEA stopped publishing its salary surveys in 1972-73, and little nation-wide data on the representation of women in school administration is available for the following three years. In 1975-76, however, the National Center for Educational Statistics (NCES) began to break down the number of administrators in the fifty states by sex in its *Statistics of Public Elementary and Secondary Day Schools.* In the *Statistics* compiled for fall of 1975, this information is available for only 86 percent of the nation's school administrators. Six states (Alabama, Georgia, Maryland, Michigan, Nevada, and Virginia), whose 24,008 administrators represented approximately 14 percent of the nation-wide total (170,182) were unable to report separate counts of men and women in school administration at that time. Further, statistics were collected and presented in terms of aggregated groups — at the school level, elementary, junior high, and high school principals were grouped in a single unit that also included assistant principals from different types of schools; and, at the district level, general, deputy, associate, and assistant superintendents were considered as one group of "superintendents and assistants"[4] — making comparison with the more detailed NEA data somewhat difficult. Nonetheless, the percentage of the combined total of female principals and assistant principals from the forty-four states that were able to report numbers of administrators by sex in 1975-76 was 14.1, a figure much in line with earlier NEA findings.[5]

Several writers have commented on the steady decline in the percentage of women serving as elementary principals over the years. The Department of Elementary School Principals of the NEA documents this in their study of the *Elementary School Principalship in 1968.* They show that the woman "supervising principal" comprised 55 percent of the elementary principalship corps in 1928, 41 percent in 1948, 38 percent in 1958, and 22 percent in 1968.[6] The NEA's figures from the biennial salary surveys cited at the beginning of this chapter show this same trend. As noted, 21 percent of the group of elementary principals in 1970-71 were women, but, by 1972-73, the percentage was 19.6. Women have never been as strongly represented in the high school principalship as in the elementary one, but there, too, their numbers have dwindled over time. *The Study of the Secondary School Principalship,* published by the National Association of Secondary School Principals (NASSP) in 1965, indicates that, in 1963, 11 percent of all high school principals were women;[7] again, as has been mentioned, the later NEA salary surveys show that women represented only 3 percent of all high school principals in 1970-71, and 1.4 percent in 1972-73.

Women seem to fare slightly better in staff positions in central offices. NEA's data for 1970-71 show that 37.5 percent of central office administrators were female: 38.3 percent of the administrators in pupil personnel services, 46.3 percent of the administrators in instructional and supervisory areas, and 48.2 percent of those in "general administration." As for positions of higher "line" responsibility, however, women accounted for only 2.9 percent of all assistant superintendents, 7.5 percent of the deputy superintendents, and 0.6 percent of all general superintendents.[8] NEA's statistics for 1972-73 show women holding 35 percent of the administrative posts in central offices, a decrease from the earlier figure; the data also indicate that the proportion of women assistant superintendents increased over the two-year period, to 5.3 percent, but that the percentage of women deputy superintendents and general superintendents again declined, to 6.2 percent and 0.1 percent, respectively.[9] The figures for 1975-76 from the NCES indicate that, in the group of forty-four states able to report numbers of administrators by sex (representing 86 percent of the total number of school administrators working that year), 29.4 percent of "other" administrative officials — a group composed of central office administrators and specialists and administrative assistants — and 4.8 percent of the combined group of general, deputy, associate, and assistant superintendents were women.[10]

Because of such factors as special city-wide examinations for the principalship and the greater number and variety of administrative and subadministrative positions available in the urban school system, opportunity for women administrators in larger cities has traditionally been considered better than in other educational settings, at least on the principalship level. Data compiled for 1971-72 by the National Council of Administrative Women in Education (NCAWE) for fourteen large cities (Atlanta, Boston, Chicago, Cincinnati, Cleveland, Denver, Los Angeles, New Orleans, New York City, Omaha, Portland, San Diego, San Francisco, and Seattle) confirm this phenomenon.[11] Altogether women filled 29.8 percent of the principalship positions of these cities. Their strongest showing was at the level of the elementary principalship, where they accounted for 36.5 percent of the total corps. The variation of percentages of women holding this job in the fourteen cities was great, however. In four cities (Cleveland, New Orleans, Omaha, and San Francisco) women elementary principals outnumbered their male colleagues. In four others (Denver, New York City, San Diego, and Seattle) they comprised less than 25 percent of the total group of elementary principals. In "middle" schools (junior high schools or upper-grade centers) women accounted for only 13.9 percent of all principal positions. A still smaller proportion of high school principalships in the fourteen cities, 9.1 percent, were held by women.

The NCES's *Statistics of Public Elementary and Secondary Day Schools, Fall 1975* contains a special section on administrators in the twenty largest cities in the country.[12] Seventeen of these cities (Chicago, Cleveland, Dallas, Houston, Indianapolis, Los Angeles, Memphis, Milwaukee, New Orleans, New York City, Philadelphia, Phoenix, St. Louis, San Antonio, San Diego, San Francisco, and Washington) were able to report or estimate numbers of administrators by sex for 1975-76. As in the case of the state data, figures were collected and arranged in terms of composite groups: all principals and assistant principals were considered as one unit; all levels of superintendents as another. The percentage of combined numbers of principals and assistant principals from these seventeen cities was 26.4. The variation in the numbers of women holding in-school administrative positions in different cities was again great. In only two cities (Washington and Phoenix) did the number of women in these positions outnumber males; in five (Chicago, Dallas, Los Angeles, Memphis, and Milwaukee) women comprised less than 20 percent of the total combined group of principals and assistant principals.

A much smaller percentage of women hold superintendencies in large cities than principalships. The NCAWE survey for 1971-72 indicates that 12.5 percent of all superintendents — general, deputy, associate, assistant, area, and community (district) — in the fourteen large cities that they reported on were female.[13] The data from the NCES for 1975-76 on administrators in the nation's largest cities show that in the seventeen cities able to report or estimate numbers of administrators by sex, women accounted for 61 out of 347 "superintendents and assistants," or 17.6 percent of the total.[14] The category of "superintendents and assistants" supposedly covered only general, deputy, associate, and assistant superintendents,[15] but it is probable that those cities that had district superintendents included them as assistants in their counts; New York City reported a total of 83 persons in this category and Chicago, 38 — figures that could not have been arrived at without the inclusion of community (district) superintendents. Thus, although different cities are involved in the two sets of data, it is feasible to compare NCAWE and NCES figures and note that there seems to have been an increase of numbers of female superintendents in

large cities in the four year period between 1971-72 and 1975-76. Indeed, several major cities, including Washington, Boston, and Hart-
ford, did appoint women to the general superintendency during that
time period, and other large systems placed women in important, visible positions as well. Large cities have a long way to go, however, before women are adequately represented in the upper levels of the administrative hierarchies in education.

Attempts to explain the small number of women school administrators vary greatly. One view, based on the "traditional" image of a
woman's role, is that women have responsibilities as wives and
mothers. They must frequently stop work in order to have babies, and,
since their main function in life is to be homemakers, it is a waste of
time for a school district to offer them career advancement via administrative positions.[16] A closely related idea is that women simply do not
try hard enough to gain administrative posts. In the days before the
women's liberation movement gained momentum, women in education were seen as passive, nonprofessional types who shrank from major responsibilities and were apathetic about preparing themselves for
career advancement.[17] Although this viewpoint may still persist, particularly among those in charge of hiring potential administrators,[18]
today's observers are more likely to look beyond the lack of effort in
seeking administrative roles to point out the inner conflicts women experience when they consider becoming administrators. For one thing,
they are socialized to remain in a "woman's place." Women are conditioned to avoid success and feel threatened if they leave the socially approved "female" occupation of teaching and take on the more "mascu-
line" leadership role in administration.[19] Another factor that has
received much attention recently because of both the women's liberation movement and stress on equal job opportunities for women is that
outright discrimination against women exists in the promotion practices, if not in the official policies, of many school districts.[20] A related
idea is that women do not receive enough preparation for administrative positions, not because of their own inertia but because programs
in educational administration have not sought to recruit them or have
not offered them sufficient financial aid to support their studies in
graduate school.[21]

A REVIEW OF THE LITERATURE

In light of the statistics showing the paucity of women administrators in the schools and the spectrum of reasons used to explain why,
literature concerning women's performance in educational adminis-

tration is reviewed here in an effort to determine whether, in terms of educational ends and process goals, women as administrators are a resource worth developing. A case for equal opportunity will not be presented, pertinent as such an argument might be; rather, women are considered in terms of their actual performance in administrative roles.

The data used are embedded in a number of studies undertaken in the 1950's and the 1960's that were concerned with the attitudes of superiors and subordinates toward school administrators, as well as with job performances and styles of operation of administrators. The studies reviewed do not include all of the research efforts that have been undertaken on the administrative behaviors of men and women—a subject that seems to be one of enduring interest to scholars in the field of education.[22] The earlier research efforts reviewed here do, however, appear to represent the variety of approaches and findings of all of the "performance" studies; the majority of them also have the added advantage of being more comprehensive and extensive in scope than most of the later inquiries.[23]

The subjects of these studies were usually elementary school principals, primarily because the elementary principalship generally provided the only group of women in school administration large enough to compare with male colleagues in equivalent positions on something less than a regional basis. The choice of the subject pool does, however, indicate that caution is needed in applying the findings of the studies to be reviewed to all women administrators in education. Elementary schools are smaller than high schools, have different staff compositions, and may require another type of instructional leadership, and they are certainly different from central offices and other educational bureaucracies. Further, the studies performed were carried out with subjects from a variety of districts—both urban and rural—and thus may have only partial application to specific settings. In particular, the exigencies of the principalship in large cities, with their overcrowded schools, changing racial and ethnic composition of neighborhoods, formidable bureaucracies, and sometimes difficult demands from local groups having the power of "community control," are certainly different from those in other districts. The successful performance of the administrative role in such a milieu might well require additional characteristics besides those specified by the research to be examined. Despite these considerations, the results that will be reviewed from the following studies should be useful in indicating how women act as educational administrators.

Florida Leadership Project (begun in 1952)

One of the first important studies pertaining to the administrative performance of women in education, the Florida Leadership Project,[24] actually did involve high school as well as elementary school principals. A "Principal Behavior Check List" was administered to a group of eighty subjects; the principals were given eighty-six typical situations that they might face in their daily work routine ("How do you get teachers to participate in P.T.A.?" "What do you do if pupils make a decision that you believe is detrimental to the best interests of those concerned?") and asked to choose their probable course of action from one of approximately eight options. It was hoped that different patterns linking personality and behavior would emerge from the findings, but, when none did, the classification of leadership behavior as "democratic," "authoritarian," or "laissez-faire," developed originally by Kurt Lewin, Ronald Lippitt, and Ralph White,[25] was applied to the data. A jury of staff members at the University of Florida rated the checklist submitted by each principal for evidence of the three types of leadership behavior. Few instances of laissez-faire behavior appeared, and the principals were categorized according to the frequency with which they opted to act in a democratic or an authoritarian manner. Another jury, composed of professors with administrative experience, examined the checklist independently to see which behaviors they would consider "best practice" in a school setting. These correlated highly with practices considered to be democratic.

Variables culled from data on the schools and teacher-parent interviews were then related to the two evident leadership styles of principals. Although there seemed to be no relation between democratic or authoritarian style and pupil achievement, several links were found between leadership style and client attitude. For example, pupil attitudes were more favorable in the schools administered by the more democratic principals, teacher satisfaction with the "human relations" aspect of their job was likewise higher in these schools, and parental responses were more positive (except in the case of parents from the lower socioeconomic groups). On the whole, there seemed to be positive attitudinal effects when democratic principals were running the schools.

For our purposes, the most interesting findings of the study were that women tended to use both democratic practices and effective administrative practices more frequently than men. Women principals seemed to operate democratically 22 percent more often and in a more effective administrative fashion 18 percent more of the time than their male counterparts.[26] Elementary principals also tended toward the democratic leadership style more often than high school principals. The researchers of the Florida Leadership Project indicated that these findings might be partially confounded since practically all the women principals in the sample were located in elementary schools. The sex effect was, however, still regarded as a strong one.

Barter (1959)

A second pertinent study, performed by Alice S. Barter at the University of Michigan,[27] dealt with the administrative performance of women by examining district policy in hiring women for administrative positions and teachers' attitudes toward female principals. Barter's goals were to see how well women were represented as administrators in their school systems and how much the attitudes of teachers contributed to the status quo of women in the various districts. She sent questionnaires to all men and one-fourth of the women who taught in the elementary schools in eighteen school districts of a particular Michigan county and administered attitude scales, preference tests, and questions on their interest or lack of interest in the principalship as a career. She also sent a shorter questionnaire on promotional policies to the superintendent in each of the districts. The school districts in the sample were located in communities of various sizes (populations ranged from 2,000 to over 100,000); a large number of these, however, were suburbs and small cities in the size range of from 20,000 to 50,000.[28]

Barter discovered that, although women elementary school principals were "definitely in the minority,"[29] school districts did not discriminate against them, at least not in their official policies. Men and women teachers differed in their views concerning women principals, but they rated men and women principals as being equal in both abilities and personal qualities. Barter found that the majority of women teachers favored working under women principals, while only a small group (19 percent) of the men did. Men who had had experience teaching under women principals, however, had a more positive view toward women as principals than those who had not. (This finding at least calls into question the traditional view that men who work under women supervisors tend to dislike them intensely.[30]) Barter found, in addition, that men teaching at the elementary level were academically better prepared than women to assume principalship positions. Her findings led her to conclude that the principalship was effectively within the reach of those women who sought it. She felt that women were demonstrating apathy in preparing themselves for administrative leadership in the elementary school and needed to be stimulated to seek the principalship actively.

Hemphill, Griffiths, and Fredericksen (1962)

In 1962 John Hemphill, Daniel Griffiths, and Normal Fredericksen published the results of an elaborate study on *Administrative Performance and Personality*,[31] which produced, among other findings, some interesting information on the performance of men and women as elementary principals, as judged by their subordinates and superiors, and detailed the specific areas in which the different sexes excelled in terms of administration. The researchers sought to determine the dimensions of performance of the job of elementary school administrator, to provide information helpful in the process of selecting school administrators, and to provide materials and instruments for the instruction and study of school administration.[32]

The subjects who participated in the study were chosen from school districts on the basis of geographic location, size, and type of district. The authors stated that they had hoped the sample would be as varied as the population of elementary principals in the United States, though they would make no claim for its representativeness.[33] Thirty-two districts in sixteen different states were involved in the study, slightly under half of which were connected with communities that had populations of 40,000 or more, including several cities with populations above 100,000.[34] The final sample was composed of 232 elementary principals, 137 of them men and 95 of them women. The distribution of ages showed the women to be approximately ten years older on the average than the men. Men also tended to be married far more often than women; less than 10 percent of the men in the sample were single, whereas approximately 50 percent of the women were.[35] (The tendencies for women principals to be both older and unmarried reappear in the next two studies discussed).

Hemphill, Griffiths, and Frederiksen developed a complicated set of simulated materials and projective techniques dealing with a hypothetical school. Subjects were forced to place themselves in the role of the principal of the simulated school and deal with daily problems as if they actually held the position. The major research technique in the study was to give the principals "in-baskets" filled with a variety of memos and letters dealing with routine or crisis situations and to have them make actual responses to these in-basket items. Other instruments, such as tests of ability, interests, and personality, were given to the subjects. Opinions of teachers and superiors on the performance and ability of the subjects were also collected.

A scoring system was devised for the projective techniques used in the study. Forty categories were developed for the in-basket tests, including such areas as social sensitivity; whether the principal discussed problems with subordinates, colleagues, parents, or supervisors; whether he or she took action, delayed or postponed action, or temporized; and whether he or she followed a preestablished structure in dealing with new areas. Composite scores were calculated on dimensions such as "Exchanging Information" and "Maintaining Organizational Relationships." Factor analysis was used to probe the relationship of the different variables of the study.

Implications of the results were then explored. One of the first of these was the pertinence of findings for the selection and preparation of administrators. The first question the authors dealt with in this category was the perennial one: "Should men be selected for the principalship in preference to women?"[36] They inquired whether the practice of regularly appointing men rather than women to the elementary school principalship was justified by the administrative performances of the two sexes as demonstrated in their study. Their answer was "probably no."[37]

Several specific results of the study led the researchers to this indirect endorsement of the female administrator. In the first place, when elementary principal performance was evaluated by teachers and by superiors "both groups were somewhat negative toward men principals and generally positive toward the women principals."[38] The factor analysis, related to the composite scores developed from the in-basket task, showed specific categories in which women seemed to excel as opposed to men. Women were better in "Exchanging Information," "Maintaining Organizational Relationships," and "Responding to Outsiders." Men, on the other hand, showed more proficiency in "Complying with Suggestions Made by Others" (a general category that included the behavior of taking final action in solving problems) and "Analyzing the Situation." When teachers rated the different categories, they placed more value on those in which the performance of women happened to exceed that of men.

A closer look at some of the categories comprising the composite scores indicates certain stylistic differences in men's and women's administrative approaches and sheds further light on why both subordinates and superiors gave a more positive appraisal of the woman principal. Women seemed to be more thorough in their approach to in-basket items, used more information from the background materials, and discussed information more with both superiors and outsiders. Men, on the other hand, made concluding decisions more often, followed preestablished structures to a greater degree in problem solving, and took more terminal actions. According to the authors, generally "the difference between men and women in their performance on in-basket problems is that the women involved teachers, superiors, and outsiders in their work, while the men tended to make final decisions and take action without involving others."[39]

Aside from the obvious benefits of being more careful and thorough in gathering information and bringing it to bear on immediate problems, it is quite probable that women's administrative performances are greatly aided by this tendency to engage other people in their decision making. As professionals, or at least as semiprofessionals who are highly sensitive to issues of professional autonomy and status,[40] teachers may appreciate the principal who solicits their opinions on problems that arise in the school. Parents, community groups, and superiors may be flattered, too, although for different reasons, to have their viewpoints or expertise sought. In point of fact, in the last several years principals who have not spent time assessing community opinion before making decisions on many areas have frequently found themselves in serious trouble; this is particularly true in the large urban areas that have moved toward community control by making principals responsible in some respects to local community councils. The ability to involve others in work and to exchange information with them that women demonstrated in the Hemphill, Griffiths, and Frederiksen study may indeed be a vital characteristic for a successful principal.

Examination of other data from this study supplies us with yet more detail on why women might be superior to men as elementary school principals. Projective instructional situations showed women to be "more concerned with the objectives of teaching, pupil participation, and the evaluation of learning."[41] Superiors' ratings indicated that women were better in evaluating the performance of new teachers and more willing and able to provide instructional leadership in the school. In the important role of instructional leader, women principals seem to far outshine their male colleagues.

Gross and Trask (1964)

The most detailed study which compares the performance of men and women as educational administrators is Neal Gross and Anne

Trask's *Men and Women as Elementary School Principals,* later used
as the basis for their book, *The Sex Factor and the Management of
Schools,*[42] which was published in 1976. The study was a subinvestigation of the larger National Principalship Study begun at Harvard University in 1959 under Gross's direction. The National Principalship
Study surveyed over five hundred principals in forty-one cities with
populations of 50,000 or more. A stratified sample was used which
took into account geographic region, school level, per pupil expenditure of the system and size of city. Data from principals were collected
through a "Personal and Background Questionnaire," which each
principal filled out in his own community; a "Role Questionnaire,"
which was filled out at a special session held with other principals in
the community; and a personal interview. Teacher-informants in each
school also answered a questionnaire, as did the immediate supervisor
of each principal participating in the study.

The Gross and Trask substudy comparing men and women elementary principals attempted to answer questions on whether the sex of
principals affected their job histories and career decision making,
their orientation toward and reaction to their work, the way they carried out their roles, and the functioning and productivity of their
schools.[43] These questions, plus other more minor queries, were applied to the data collected from the 189 elementary principals who
participated in the National Principalship Study of which 91 were
women and 98 were men. The authors investigated a variety of variables on personal background, time of career decision, aspirations for
advancement, educational values, reactions to specific managerial responsibilities (for example, supervision of instruction and administrative duties), and general performance in producing both competent
students and a staff with good professional performance and high
morale.

Major findings of the study, based on both direct and indirect evidence, indicate that women's performance as elementary school principals is superior to that of men. Direct evidence was solicited by
teacher ratings on the professional performance of teachers in their
school, on students' academic performance, and on teacher morale.[44]
Each measure was a factor score derived from a number of questions
on the specific area covered by the teacher questionnaire.

Gross and Trask hypothesized that women principals would induce
more professional performances from the teachers in their schools
than men. This hypothesis was upheld, and further analysis showed

that the finding was not a function of the age of the principal nor the experience of the teaching staff. The finding was also basically replicated when the data were subdivided by region, size of city, socioeconomic composition of school, school size, and sex ratio of staff. Gross and Trask further hypothesized that, in those schools where the teachers performed in a more professional manner, the students would do better academically; they therefore predicted that schools run by women principals would produce more capable students. This prediction was upheld statistically, and the finding was sustained across socioeconomic levels and in all subclassifications of data by region, size of city, size of school, mean age of staff, and so forth. Finally, the researchers hypothesized that sex of the principals would *not* be related to the morale of their teachers; this hypothesis was also upheld.

In general, the direct measures of performance show that women elementary school administrators seem to do a better job when compared to men. Several indirect measures in the study corroborate this impression. For example, when educational values are considered, women principals showed a greater concern with individual differences and with the social and emotional development of the child than men principals. When evaluating teachers, women placed greater stress on teachers' technical skill and their responsibilities to the school organization than men. Women also tended to exert more supervisory control in their work and to worry less than male principals about their responsibilities. Several measures that could be interpreted as relating to good performance on the job — attempts to involve parents in school affairs or emphasis on teachers giving more service to pupils, to cite two examples — showed no difference between sexes in performance. By and large, however, analysis of many of the variables shows women to be more concerned with the individuality of their students and with their faculty and work responsibilities than men, and to be at least equally devoted to their administrative chores.

Many of the findings discussed above were predicted by Gross and Trask based on other discoveries about the background of the women principals in their study, their preparation and feelings about the job of principal, self-evaluations, and satisfactions.[45] The researchers established that the women principals on the average were much older than their male counterparts (about four-fifths of the sample of women were fifty years of age or older, but less than half the men were); 63 percent of the women were single as compared to 5 percent of the men. (These statistics on age and marital status strongly resemble those found in the Hemphill, Griffiths, and Frederiksen study reviewed earlier.) The women principals had decided on a teaching career much earlier than the men, and teaching was the first career choice of 80 percent of them (as opposed to 46 percent of the men in the sample). On the other hand, women first entertained the idea of becoming a principal at a far later age than men did, and, on the average, received their first principalship many years after; for example, over twice the percentage of women as men in the sample were forty-six years of age or more when they first assumed the role of principal. Many men in the group of principals studied actively decided to seek the principalship for reasons relating to occupational and social mobility and increase in income. Women, on the contrary, were frequently pushed into the principalship by "sponsors" who encouraged them professionally,[46] or else arrived there by a fortuitous accident (for example, by taking over the leadership role in a school during the illness of a regular principal). Once they became principals, women again showed less ambition to advance up the educational career ladder than men. They also seemed to find greater satisfaction in work related to instruction and to set a higher value on their ability to supervise instructional matters than male principals.

Gross and Trask often used the specific data they gathered on women's backgrounds and attitudes to formulate hypotheses on their performance, degree of comfort in their job situations, ability to relate to individual students and to parents, and so forth. Frequently their reasoning, especially when based on the factor of women's greater number of years in teaching, was upheld. The researchers consider this longer experience in the classroom as a crucial factor in accounting for the superior performance of women principals; in their later book they suggest that men are at a certain disadvantage in the elementary principalship because their relatively limited teaching experience does not supply them with the skills necessary to function as good instructional leaders.[47]

Though Gross and Trask do not specifically outline it as such, little by little a career portrait of the female principal emerges from their data. The woman principal begins her working years strongly committed to the occupation of teaching. Her eye is rarely on career advancement, and she concentrates instead on knowing the ins and outs of her profession. When, often by a fluke, she is promoted to a principalship in later life, her long years as a basic service professional in an organization stand her in good stead. She shows greater ability and self-confidence in directing the instructional program than men do simply because of her deeper understanding of the art of teaching, and she also demonstrates a high degree of ability in administering the school, the milieu in which she worked so long. Because again she is not seeking promotion from her present rank, she commits herself whole-heartedly to the role of principal and is able to master the job in a highly competent fashion.

Gross and Herriott (1965)

The last study to be reviewed, another subinvestigation of the National Principalship Study, is Neal Gross and Robert Herriott's *Staff Leadership in the Public Schools: A Sociological Inquiry*.[48] This study used the same basic research data from the National Principalship Study that Gross and Trask employed. It also concerned itself exclusively with elementary school principals, but, unlike the study prepared by Gross and Trask, only touched peripherally on performance differences between men and women.

Gross and Herriott's goals were simple: since they felt there was a growing controversy about what the role of the principal should be and whether or not the principal should attempt to provide staff leadership in the school, they sought to document whether leadership efforts of principals have an effect. They also wished to isolate specific determinants of leadership effort in the elementary principals they studied. To fulfill these goals, the researchers designed a special behavior called "Executive Professional Leadership" (EPL) and observed to what degree the principal-subjects of their study possessed it. EPL was specifically defined as "the efforts of an executive of a professionally staffed organization to conform to a definition of his role that stresses his obligation to improve the quality of staff performance."[49] It was measured through a form of Guttman scaling based on responses of teacher-informants to eighteen questions dealing with specific principal behavior. Teachers were asked to rank their principals on the frequency with which some of the following kinds of behaviors were exhibited: "Has constructive suggestions to offer teachers in dealing with their major problems"; "Gives teachers the feeling that their work is an 'important activity'"; "Makes teachers' meetings a valuable educational activity." Through the use of scaling techniques it was possible to divide the principals into the groups that possessed "highest," "moderately high," "moderately low," and "lowest" EPL.

Gross and Herriott related EPL to "organizational characteristics" of the elementary school. These characteristics, coincidentally, turned out to be the same as those used to measure principals' performance in the Gross and Trask study: teachers' morale, teachers' professional performance, and pupils' performance. Measures for teachers' morale and professional performance were based on the same list of questions for which special factor scores had been derived in Gross and Trask. In the Gross and Herriott study, however, factors were not used; instead, individual correlations were made between EPL and each separate question categorized under "teachers' morale" or "teachers' performance." In all cases, correlations were significant below the .001 level, showing a strong relationship between EPL and both these "organizational characteristics." When the researchers estimated the relation of pupils' performance to EPL, only one question was used: "Of the pupils you teach, what percent are one or more years behind grade level in reading ability?" At first, there was no apparent relationship between reading retardation scores and EPL, but, when the socioeconomic level of the family was held constant, a tendency toward a negative relationship between EPL and reading retardation score emerged. We can conclude from the data that schools which have principals with relatively high EPL produce teachers who give good professional performances and produce students who fare better academically.

Gross and Herriott proceeded to relate EPL to some traditional variables that are supposed to account for good administrators. They came up with some surprising and disturbing findings. The greater number of undergraduate courses in education that the principals in the sample had taken, the lower their EPL rating. "The highest EPL scores were obtained by principals who had taken the fewest graduate education courses and the lowest scores by those who had taken the most."[50] There was an inverse relationship between the number of courses taken in educational administration and EPL score, and there was no apparent relationship between previous administrative experience and EPL. Most interesting, in view of the findings of the Gross and Trask study, was the lack of a consistent relationship between length of teaching experience and EPL.

Other data in the Gross and Herriott study conflict with that in Gross and Trask. Most pertinent to our present investigation is the lack of any apparent relationship between EPL and sex. This finding, somewhat surprising after the Gross and Trask results, is modified when variables of marital status and age are considered. There seems to be a basically negative relationship between age and EPL, but, when the two variables are considered together, women principals

have higher EPL scores in two out of three age categories — the young-
est and the oldest. When the variable of marital status is added for a
three-way comparison, the relationship between sex and EPL becomes
yet more complicated:

For the young married principals, the men's scores on the average are greater than
those of the women, but for the young single principals the women are higher, a fact
clearly not apparent earlier. Among the married, middle in age, the trend is consistently for the married men to attain greater EPL scores than their female colleagues.
In the older married group, it is the women whose scores are the greater.

Of the four comparisons of sex which are possible, two favor the women and two
favor the men. Apparently, the relationship of sex to EPL is complex. Although the
number of cases in many of the cells is too limited to permit specific generalizations,
the findings show that commonsense predictions about the relationship of sex and
EPL — if they are to be made at all — should be made with great caution.[51]

It is possible to dismiss the Gross and Herriott findings with the
argument that the researchers are not measuring the performance of
the principals in the elementary school, but only their attempts to offer leadership to the staff. Donald Erickson, in a review article of the
Gross and Herriott study,[52] has questioned whether the researchers are
even measuring what they purport to; he points out, among other
things, that the EPL measure may be more a reflection of teacher affect and faculty attitude toward principals in general rather than an
indicator of an individual principal's leadership. Nonetheless, even
though EPL is not a direct performance measure and it has questionable face validity, it does correlate well with other measures previously
accepted as good indicators of principals' performance: teachers'
morale, teachers' professional performance, and pupils' performance.
The uneven and complicated findings of the relationship between sex
and EPL should at least be considered, if only to highlight the clearer
performance results favoring women administrators found in other
studies.

The studies reviewed here present a strong case for the effectiveness
of women, as represented by women elementary school principals, as
educational administrators. When we highlight some of the specific
findings concerning women administrators in these studies — their
propensity toward democratic leadership, thoroughness of approach
to problem solving, and talent in instructional leadership, as well as
the general effectiveness of their performance as rated by both
teachers and superiors — we puzzle over the small number of women

administrators employed by school districts and especially over the decline in the number of women in the principalship. It seems that, even
without the new emphasis on equal opportunity, school districts
should be eager to appoint such obviously competent professionals to
positions of administrative responsibility. Setting aside important considerations of fairness in appointment procedures, the effective job
performance of women administrators alone warrants a greater place
for them in the administrative hierarchy of school systems.

WHY WOMEN ARE SUCCESSFUL

What accounts for the generally positive feelings subordinates and
superiors have toward women administrators—at least toward those
on the elementary school level—that we have seen documented in
most of the studies that we have reviewed? What accounts for the special qualities these women principals seem to possess—the abilities to
work in a democratic manner, to exchange information, to maintain
good organizational relationships, and to be confident and effective
instructional leaders, among others? An answer often given to these
questions is that there are simply more women in the teaching force
than men; a larger pool to choose from means a better selection of
administrators. There is a certain ring of common sense in this reasoning, although it fails to account for any of the vital qualities identified
by the above studies that may be the key to female administrators' success. A related and somewhat more satisfactory explanation, at least
in regard to the elementary school, is that, while women principals are
rarely promoted from their positions, good men principals are frequently advanced to better jobs in the educational hierarchy. Those
men who are left as elementary principals may comprise a less talented
cohort, lacking the best from among their number. Studies of elementary school principals may well be comparing a representative, well-
balanced group of women with a less competent group of men.

Another reason for female administrators' good performances,
which is more pertinent to the specific work styles studies have identified as characteristic of them, has to do with women's special personality attributes. A mass of psychological literature has been written
about the personality differences between men and women, particularly about women's greater dependency needs and men's stronger aggression drives.[53] Many people today, particularly those involved in
the women's liberation movement, pass off these differences as arti-
facts of cultural discrimination in child-rearing practices. One psy-

chological characteristic of women that has not yet been isolated for particular attack is their supposedly greater field-dependence. On the surface this quality looks like a weakness; in actuality it may be one of women's greatest strengths.

Field-dependence is the quality of orienting one's self to the context of a problem rather than to the problem's object. It has been measured in several technical ways; the best known of these is the rod-and-frame task in which the subject, sitting in a darkened room, must "adjust a luminous rod to the true upright when both it and a surrounding luminous frame are tilted."[54] If he adjusts the rod to the "true upright," he is classified as more field-independent; if he adjusts it perpendicular to the tilted frame he is more field-dependent. The quality is a perceptual one, but it is related to many other attributes, for example, cognition, personality, and social behavior.[55] It is generally considered better to be field-independent; it is an attribute children seem to acquire as they mature, and the principal researcher of field-independence and field-dependence, H. A. Witkin, considers field-independence as representing a higher level of psychological development.[56] In several dozen studies women and girls have performed in a more field-dependent fashion than men and boys.[57]

It is quite possible, however, that field-dependence, supposedly a negative characteristic, may be one of the qualities that accounts for the special approaches that women administrators take to problems, which, in turn, brings them greater success in their jobs. The thoroughness and greater use of background information employed by women on the in-basket tasks in the Hemphill, Griffiths, and Frederiksen study may be owing to their strong need to explore the context of a problem. Similarly, women's habits of talking more to superiors and subordinates than men, exchanging information more often, and working harder to maintain organizational relationships (noted in the same study) may be related to their field-dependence. Their distinctive approaches to problem solving and decision making may well result in the more "democratic" leadership style documented in the reports of the Florida Leadership Project. What the psychologists see as a deficit may actually be an important key to the success of female educational administrators.

Other personality traits attributed to women which have frequently been perceived of as detrimental—such as passivity, emotional sensitivity, and compliance—may also be turned to their advantage in school administration. Jean Grambs has suggested that women's ability to tolerate attack and not respond with immediate counterattack may stand her in good stead in dealing with aggression in general and student rudeness in particular.[58] She also feels that women's adaptability and willingness to compromise may help them survive in the midst of the many diverse influential groups making often conflicting demands on the way schools should be run.[59]

A final explanation for women's generally positive performance as educational leaders, particularly in the elementary school, is related to the sex-typing of occupations and to the general career pattern of the female teacher-principal. As noted earlier, Gross and Trask believe that women are more effective as elementary school leaders because of their many years experience in the classroom. Going beyond this explanation and taking into account the career portrait of the woman principal that can be constructed from the Gross and Trask data, we would suggest that it is not only the lengthy time spent in the process of teaching, but the whole commitment to the classroom and the world of school during the teaching years that helps make women superior administrators.

The commitment is by no means accidental. Teaching has traditionally been a "woman's" profession. We have noted how the dearth of female educational administrators across the nation contrasts with the large majority of women teachers. Girls are generally socialized to regard teaching as an appropriate occupation from the books they read, the models they see before them in school, and the opinions of their families; men are less frequently influenced to regard teaching as a suitable career. Gross and Trask reported that 65 percent of the women principals in their sample first considered the idea of teaching when they were grammar school students, but only 11 percent of the men had thought of it at such a young age.[60] Furthermore, teaching, for women, has been essentially a dead-end occupation. There has always been little chance for vertical movement up a career ladder, and the gradual displacement of the female elementary school principal, however it has come about, has only accentuated this problem. Women who have entered the teaching profession have, for many years, done so with the strong expectation that they would remain teachers all during their working lives. It is because of this expectation that so many commit themselves to learning their trade, to sensitizing themselves to individual differences among students, to perfecting their skills in instructing children and to learning the important aspects of the way schools operate — in short, to acquiring all the knowledge needed to function well as a classroom teacher. This strong immersion in the teaching role provides knowledge and resources that prove invaluable once the woman teacher steps into a position of school leadership and may indeed be an important factor in accounting for her fine performance as a principal. The fact that she generally does not desire or expect to take on a higher position and approaches the principalship with the same deep commitment that she has brought to the role of teacher may be another element in her administrative success.

TRENDS IN THE FUTURE

Times change. The influence of the women's liberation and equal opportunity movements are more pervasive than meets the eye. Articles written in the 1950's and 1960's on female administrators seem almost laughable today when their authors begin eulogizing about woman's fundamental roles as mother, wife, and hearthside companion.[61] The women's liberation movement is trying to change child-rearing patterns so that personality differences among boys and girls in such areas as aggression and dependency will cease to be inculcated by the culture. It has also taken a hard look at sexist biases in the school curriculum and extracurricular activities and at the sex-role stereotyping that permeates the textbooks children read[62] and has influenced change in these areas. It is quite possible that, if this movement continues to be influential and if it does produce some lasting effects in the elimination of sexist stereotyping of roles and in occupations, proportionately fewer women and more men will eventually consider teaching in public schools as an appropriate career. If so, numbers of men and women in the teaching field could well be equalized in the future. At that point one could truly test out the frequently alleged idea that women school principals' performance seems superior to that of men only because these principals are selected from a larger group of potential candidates.

Another possible consequence of the equal rights and women's liberation movements, as well as of the comparatively recent raft of federal legislation and regulations aimed at providing equal job opportunities for women (for example, Title VII of the Civil Rights Act of 1964 as amended by the Equal Employment Opportunity Act of 1972, Executive Order 11246 as amended by Executive Order 11375, Title IX of the Education Amendments of 1972, or the Higher Education Act),[63] is that women teachers will probably become increasingly more interested in obtaining promotions and more militant about demanding their equal rights if their districts discriminate against their appointment to administrative positions. Litigation in this area has, up to the present, been initiated on a small scale only,[64] but women administrators and their supporters have been compiling evidence of discrimination in various school systems, and there is every reason to believe that their cause will soon receive the same national attention as that of women in academia in recent years.

With more ambition to move upward in the education field and more legal ammunition behind her, the female teacher of tomorrow may be highly career oriented. Unlike her counterparts today, if we may generalize from the analysis of the woman elementary teacher given in this chapter to all teachers, she may well be less devoted to the teaching role and more interested in teaching as a stepping-stone toward higher-level positions. She may thus spend less time and energy immersing herself in her profession and seek a principalship only a few years after she commences teaching, possibly with a view toward still further promotion. An ironic result of this process might well be that she ends up as a less effective principal.

NOTES

1. An earlier, less comprehensive analysis of this topic appeared as "The Performance of Women School Administrators — A Review of the Literature," *Administrator's Notebook,* 23 (No. 1, 1974).

2. *25th Biennial Salary Survey of Public School Professional Personnel,* Research Report 1971-R5 (Washington, D.C.: Research Division, National Education Association, 1971), 10.

3. *26th Biennial Salary Survey of Public School Professional Personnel,* Research Report 1973-R5 (Washington, D.C.: Research Division, National Education Association, 1973), 9.

4. National Center for Educational Statistics (NCES), *Statistics of Public Elementary and Secondary Day Schools, Fall 1975,* NCES 76-145 (Washington, D.C.: U.S. Government Printing Office, 1976), 41 and 43.

5. *Ibid.,* 16.

6. Department of Elementary School Principals, *The Elementary Principal in 1968* (Washington, D.C.: Department of Elementary School Principals, National Education Association, 1968), 11.

7. John K. Hemphill, James M. Richards, and Richard E. Peterson, *Report of the Senior High-School Principalship.* I, *The Study of the Secondary School Principalship* (Washington, D.C.: National Association of Secondary School Principals, 1965), 4.

8. *25th Biennial Salary Survey,* 10.

9. *26th Biennial Salary Survey,* 9.

10. NCES, *Statistics of Public Elementary and Secondary Day Schools,* 16. The explanation is on pages 41 and 43.

11. *Wanted: More Women—Where Are the Women Superintendents?* (Arlington, Va.: National Council of Administrative Women in Education, 1973), 9.

12. NCES, *Statistics of Public Elementary and Secondary Day Schools,* 17. The explanation is on page 8.

13. *Wanted: More Women,* 9.

14. NCES, *Statistics of Public Elementary and Secondary Day Schools,* 17.

15. *Ibid.,* 41, 43.

16. *Wanted: More Women,* 1. Also, see comments of panelists in Clare Broadhead *et al.,* "The Woman Principal, Going the Way of the Buffalo?" *National Elementary Principal,* 45 (April 1966), 6-11. A tongue-in-cheek exposition of this and other frequently proposed reasons for the general paucity of women administrators can be found in Edith Cavendar, "Women in Administration? You've Got to Be Kidding!" *NASSP Bulletin,* 50 (December 1974), 90-94.

17. Alice S. Barter, "The Status of Women in School Administration," *Education Digest,* 25 (October 1959), 41.

18. Cathleen V. Cairns, "Women and School Administration," *Journal of Educational Thought,* 9 (December 1975), 171.

19. *Ibid.,* 165, 172-175; Suzanne E. Estler, "Women as Leaders in Public Education," *Signs,* 1 (Winter 1975), 366, 368.

20. Suzanne S. Taylor, "Educational Leadership: A Male Domain?" *Phi Delta Kappan,* 55 (October 1973), 125; Thelma Barnes, "America's Forgotten Minority: Women School Administrators," *NASSP Bulletin,* 60 (April 1976), 87-93; Andrew Fishel and Janice Pottker, "Women Teachers and Teacher Power," *Urban Review,* 6 (November-December 1972), 41.

21. Catherine Dillon Lyon and Terry N. Saario, "Women in Public Education: Sexual Discrimination in Promotions," *Phi Delta Kappan,* 55 (October 1973), 121.

22. Some other interesting studies on the leadership and administrative performance of men and women in education not reviewed in this chapter include Helen M. Morsink, "Leader Behavior of Men and Women Secondary School Principals," *Educational Horizons,* 17 (Winter 1968-69), 69-74; John Hoyle, "Who Should be Principal—a Man or a Woman?" *National Elementary Principal,* 48 (January 1969), 23-24; Edward J. Van Meir, Jr., "Leadership Behavior of Male and Female Elementary Principals: A Comparison by Sex," *Marquette University Education Review,* 4 (Spring 1973), 8-11; Catherine A. Longstreth, "Analysis of the Perceptions of the Leadership Behavior of Male and Female Secondary School Principals in Florida," unpub. diss., University of Florida, 1973; Betty A. Spence, "Sex of Teachers as a Factor in Their Perception of Selected Leadership Characteristics of Male and Female Elementary School Principals," unpub. diss., Purdue University, 1971; and K. Jessie Kobayashi, "A Comparison of Organizational Climate of Schools Administered by Female and Male Elementary School Principals," unpub. diss., University of the Pacific, 1974.

23. An overview of the findings of most of the existing research on the comparative leadership ability of men and women school administrators can be found in Andrew Fishel and Janice Pottker, "Performance of Women Principals: A Review of Behavioral and Attitudinal Studies," *Journal of the National Association of Women Deans, Administrators, and Counselors,* 38 (Spring 1975), 110-117.

24. Reported in Hulda G. Grobman and Vynce A. Hines, "What Makes a Good Principal?" *NASSP Bulletin,* 40 (November 1956), 5-16; and in Kimball Wiles and

Hulda G. Grobman, "Principals as Leaders," *Nation's Schools*, 56 (October 1955), 75-77.

25. Kurt Lewin, Ronald O. Lippitt, and Ralph K. White, "Patterns of Aggressive Behavior in Experimentally Created 'Social Climates,'" *Journal of Social Psychology*, 10 (May 1939), 271-299.

26. Grobman and Hines, "What Makes a Good Principal?" 14.

27. Barter, "Status of Women in School Administration," 40-41; and *id.*, "The Status of Women in School Administration — Where Will They Go from Here?" *Educational Horizons*, 38 (Spring 1959), 72-75.

28. Population estimates from Rand, McNally, and Company, *Commercial Atlas and Marketing Guide — 1959* (Chicago: Rand, McNally, and Company, 1959), applied to communities listed in Barter, "Status of Women in School Administration — Where Will They Go from Here?" 73.

29. *Ibid.*, 74.

30. Burleigh B. Gardner, *Human Relations in Industry* (Chicago: Richard D. Irwin, 1945), 270.

31. John K. Hemphill, Daniel E. Griffiths, and Norman Frederiksen, *Administrative Performance and Personality* (New York: Bureau of Publications, Teachers College, Columbia University, 1962).

32. *Ibid.*, 330.

33. *Ibid.*, 12.

34. Population estimates from Rand, McNally, and Company, *Commercial Atlas and Marketing Guide — 1959*, applied to districts listed in Hemphill, Griffiths, and Frederiksen, *Administrative Performance and Personality*, 13. Figures for 1959 were used because data for the study were collected between May 1958 and June 1959.

35. Hemphill, Griffiths, and Frederiksen, *Administrative Performance and Personality*, 66.

36. *Ibid.*, 332.

37. *Ibid.*, 334.

38. *Ibid.*, 333.

39. *Ibid.*

40. Amitai Etzioni, *Modern Organizations* (Englewood Cliffs, N.J.: Prentice-Hall, 1964), 89.

41. Hemphill, Griffiths, and Frederiksen, *Administrative Performance and Personality*, 334.

42. Neal Gross and Anne E. Trask, *Men and Women as Elementary School Principals*, Final Report No. 2, Cooperative Research Project No. 853 (Cambridge, Mass.: Graduate School of Education, Harvard University, 1964); *id.*, *The Sex Factor and the Management of Schools* (New York: John Wiley and Sons, 1976).

43. *Id.*, *Men and Women as Elementary School Principals*, 1-1, and *Sex Factor and the Management of Schools*, 1-2.

44. *Id.*, *Men and Women as Elementary School Principals*, chap. 12, and *Sex Factor and the Management of Schools*, chap. 12.

45. *Id.*, *Men and Women as Elementary School Principals*, chaps. 2 to 4 and 6, and *Sex Factor and the Management of Schools*, chaps. 2 to 5 and 7.

46. See Margaret Cussler, *The Woman Executive* (New York: Harcourt, Brace,

and Company, 1958), chap. 2, and Margaret Hennig and Anne Jardim, *The Managerial Woman* (New York: Anchor Press/Doubleday, 1977), chap. 9, for discussions of how women often attain managerial positions in industry through the sponsorship of an influential superior.

47. Gross and Trask, *Sex Factor and the Management of Schools*, 221.

48. Neal Gross and Robert E. Herriott, *Staff Leadership in Public Schools: A Sociological Inquiry* (New York: John Wiley and Sons, 1965).

49. *Ibid.*, 22.

50. *Ibid.*, 66.

51. *Ibid.*, 82.

52. Donald A. Erickson, "Essay Review: Some Misgivings Concerning a Study of Leadership," *Educational Administration Quarterly*, 1 (Autumn 1965), 52-59.

53. Walter Mischel, "Sex-Typing and Socialization," in *Carmichael's Manual of Child Psychology*, 3d ed., ed. Paul H. Mussen (New York: John Wiley and Sons, 1970), I, 6.

54. Herbert J. Pick, Jr., and Anne D. Pick, "Sensory and Perceptual Development," *ibid.*, 807.

55. Jerome Kagan and Nathan Kogan, "Individual Variation in Cognitive Processes," *ibid.*, 1340.

56. Pick and Pick, "Sensory and Perceptual Development," 808.

57. *Ibid.*; and Kagan and Kogan, "Individual Variation in Cognitive Processes," 1334.

58. Jean Dresden Grambs, "Women and Administration: Confrontation or Accommodation?" *Theory Into Practice*, 15 (October 1976), 298.

59. *Ibid.*, 299.

60. Gross and Trask, *Men and Women as Elementary School Principals*, 3-3, and *Sex Factor and the Management of Schools*, 57.

61. See esp. Broadhead *et al.*, "Woman Principal," 11.

62. See Terry N. Saario, Carol Nagy Jacklin, and Carol Kehr Tittle, "Sex Role Stereotyping in the Public Schools," *Harvard Educational Review*, 43 (August 1973), 386-416.

63. For a description of the development of these and other laws and regulations, see Jacqueline P. Clement, *Sex Bias in School Leadership* (Evanston, Ill.: Integrated Education Associates, 1975), 12-26, 44-45.

64. Georgia Dullea, "Women in Classrooms, Not the Principal's Office," *New York Times*, July 13, 1975, Section 4, E7; "Chronicle of Race, Sex and Schools," *Integrated Education*, 14 (March-April 1976), 40.